Cloud IoT

The Internet of Things (IoT) is one of the most disruptive technologies, enabling ubiquitous and pervasive computing scenarios. IoT is based on intelligent self-configuring nodes (also known as things) interconnected in a dynamic and global collaborative network infrastructure. In contrast, cloud computing has virtually unlimited capabilities in terms of storage and processing power, speed, and is a more mature technology. Due to intrinsic nature of cloud computing and IoT, they both complement each other. Currently, we are witnessing a trend in exploiting the use of both the cloud and IoT together.

Key Features

- Presents the latest developments in cloud computing
- Presents the latest developments in the Internet of Things
- Establishes links between interdisciplinary areas where IoT and the cloud both can play a role in improvement of process
- Intends to provide an insight into non-IT related models for the improvement of lives
- Bridges the gap between obsolete literature and current literature

This book is aimed primarily at advanced undergraduates and graduates working with IoT and cloud computing, researchers, academicians, policymakers, government officials, NGOs, and industry research professionals.

Cloud IoT
Concepts, Paradigms, and Applications

Edited by
Jitendra Kumar Verma
Deepak Kumar Saxena
Vicente González-Prida Díaz
Vira Shendryk

CRC Press
Taylor & Francis Group
Boca Raton London New York

CRC Press is an imprint of the
Taylor & Francis Group, an **informa** business
A CHAPMAN & HALL BOOK

Cover image: ZinetroN/Shutterstock

First edition published 2023
by CRC Press
6000 Broken Sound Parkway NW, Suite 300, Boca Raton, FL 33487-2742

and by CRC Press
4 Park Square, Milton Park, Abingdon, Oxon, OX14 4RN

CRC Press is an imprint of Taylor & Francis Group, LLC

Library of Congress Cataloging-in-Publication Data
Names: Verma, Jitendra Kumar, editor. | Saxena, Deepak (Deepak Kumar), editor. | Gonzalez-Prida, Vicente, 1975- editor. | Shendryk, Vira, editor.
Title: Cloud IoT : concepts, paradigms, and applications / edited by Jitendra Kumar Verma, Deepak Saxena, Vicente González-Prida Díaz, Vira Shendryk.
Description: First edition. | Boca Raton : Chapman & Hall/CRC Press, 2023. | Includes bibliographical references and index. |
Identifiers: LCCN 2022011771 (print) | LCCN 2022011772 (ebook) | ISBN 9780367726171 (hardback) | ISBN 9780367726188 (paperback) | ISBN 9781003155577 (ebook)
Subjects: LCSH: Internet of things. | Cloud computing.
Classification: LCC TK5105.8857 .C64 2023 (print) | LCC TK5105.8857 (ebook) | DDC 004.67/8--dc23/eng/20220622
LC record available at https://lccn.loc.gov/2022011771
LC ebook record available at https://lccn.loc.gov/2022011772

ISBN: 978-0-367-72617-1 (hbk)
ISBN: 978-0-367-72618-8 (pbk)
ISBN: 978-1-003-15557-7 (ebk)

DOI: 10.1201/9781003155577

Typeset in Times
by SPi Technologies India Pvt Ltd (Straive)

Contents

Preface

The Internet of Things (IoT) is one of the most disruptive technologies, enabling ubiquitous and pervasive computing scenarios. IoT is based on intelligent self-configuring nodes (also known as things) interconnected in a dynamic and global collaborative network infrastructure. The essential idea behind IoT is the pervasive presence of things able to understand, measure, infer, and even modify the collaborative environment. IoT is made of real-world small things, widely distributed, with limited storage and processing capacity, which involve concerns regarding reliability, performance, security, and privacy.

Another key technology, cloud computing, has virtually unlimited capabilities in terms of storage and processing power, speed, and is a more mature technology. Due to the intrinsic nature of cloud computing and IoT, they both complement each other. Recently, we are witnessing an increasing trend of exploiting the use of both cloud and IoT together; a new paradigm known as cloud IoT has emerged. It has many noteworthy consequences of exploiting collaboration, standardization, and instilling intelligence in the social network, home, and work-life scenarios. The goal of this book is to present the state of the art in the application of IoT, cloud, and cloud IoT. In this endeavor, the book is divided into four parts.

Part I focuses on the infrastructural issues when integrating IoT and cloud. Chapter 1 discusses the challenges generated by the integration of cloud and IoT and offers some possible solutions. Chapter 2 discusses the practical implementation of an asset management system according to ISO 55001, offering some implications for cloud and IoT. Chapter 3 discusses cloud enterprise systems and their evolution to Industrial Internet of Things (IIoT). Chapter 4 discusses decision making of the optimum inspection interval of a motor-fan assembly gaining advantage from cloud IoT for inspection, monitoring, testing, and preventive measures.

Part II focuses on some cloud and IoT solutions addressing the crucial issue of climate change. Chapter 5 discusses a cloud-based solution that can be used to identify threats to marine ecosystems and to issue an early warning. Chapter 6 directs its focus on smart poultry farms that can generate their own power using solar devices. Chapter 7 discusses the use of cloud IoT for pollution monitoring, a key step in addressing climate change. Chapter 8 discusses software solutions for energy balance calculations in energy management systems for smart buildings.

Part III discusses smart living in different contexts. Chapter 9 focuses on an application of current relevance, by providing a comparison of cloud-IoT-based frameworks for identification and monitoring of COVID-19 cases. Continuing in the domain of digital health, Chapter 10 discusses telemedicine, telehealth, and e-health, outlining a digital transfiguration of standard healthcare systems using cloud and IoT. The next two chapters move to the domain of smart cities. Chapter 11 offers the design of a smart accident prediction system, and Chapter 12 discusses an efficient lightweight location privacy scheme for the Internet of Vehicles (IoV). Chapter 13 discusses energy-efficient vehicle registration protocol in VANET environment preserving privacy at the same time.

Part IV focuses on the security aspect in IoT and cloud. Chapter 14 outlines an emotion-independent face recognition-based security protocol in IoT-enabled devices. The next two chapters bring blockchain into the focus by Chapter 15 discussing blockchain-based web 4.0 and Chapter 16 highlighting the significance of elliptic curve cryptography in blockchain IoT. Chapter 17 discusses the application of a bio-inspired metaheuristic approach for lightweight trust evaluation in IoT networks. Finally, Chapter 18 discusses an authentication protocol for e-payment systems using smart cards.

Editors' Biographies

Dr. Jitendra Kumar Verma is an assistant professor at the Indian Institute of Foreign Trade (IIFT), New Delhi (Kakinada Campus Cell), in IT discipline. Prior to joining IIFT, he served at Amity University Haryana, Galgotias University, and Deen Dayal Upadhyaya College (University of Delhi). He received his degrees of MTech and PhD in Computer Science from Jawaharlal Nehru University, New Delhi, in 2013 and 2017, respectively. He obtained his degree of BTech in Computer Science & Engineering from Kamla Nehru Institute of Technology (KNIT), Sultanpur, in 2008. Over his short career, he has published numerous papers in peer-reviewed international journals, books with renowned publishers, conference proceedings papers, and book chapters. He has organized several international conferences, seminars, and workshops. He delivered numerous invited talks and seminars at several platforms of national and international repute. Dr. Verma authored one book, *Green Cloud Computing* (Lambert Academic Publishing, 2016), and edited four books, *Applications of Machine Learning* (Springer Verlag, 2020), *Computational Intelligence and Its Applications in Healthcare* (Elsevier Academic Press, 2020), *IoT and Cloud Computing for Societal Good* (Springer International Publisher, 2021), and *Advances in Augmented Reality and Virtual Reality* (Springer Verlag, 2022).

He is an awardee of the prestigious DAAD "A New Passage to India" Fellowship (2015–2016) funded by the Federal Ministry of Education and Research – BMBF, Germany, and German Academic Exchange Service. He worked at Julius-Maximilian University of Würzburg, Germany (mother of 14 Nobel Laureates including the Discovery of X-Rays), as a visiting research scholar.

His core research interests include software engineering, Internet of Things, social computing, image processing, artificial intelligence, and soft computing techniques. Dr. Verma has organized several international conferences, seminars, and workshops. He has delivered several invited talks. He is associate editor and guest editor of many international journals. Dr. Verma is a member of several national and international societies/professional bodies, including ACM (USA), IEEE Industrial Applications Society (USA), IEEE Young Professional (USA), IEEE (USA), Institut De Diplomatie Publique (United Kingdom), Hyderabad Deccan ACM Chapter, Computer Society of India (New Delhi), and Soft Computing Research Society (New Delhi). He serves as a reviewer for various high-impact international journals, conferences, and workshops.

Dr. Deepak Saxena is an assistant professor at the School of Management and Entrepreneurship, Indian Institute of Technology Jodhpur. He holds a PhD in Business from Trinity Business School, Trinity College Dublin (Ireland), and MTech (Industrial and Management Engineering) from Indian Institute of Technology Kanpur.

Before moving to Ireland for his PhD, he worked with the Indian Space Research Organisation, the Council for Scientific and Industrial Research, and the Defence Research and Development Organisation. He is interested in the area of digital transformation, with a special focus on public service organizations.

He has previously taught at Birla Institute of Technology and Science Pilani, Trinity College Dublin, Dublin Institute of Technology, and American College Dublin. His research is published in *Australasian Journal of Information Systems, International Journal of Project Management, Journal of Information Science, Electronic Journal of Information Systems Evaluation, and Electronic Journal of e-Government.* He has presented his papers at the British Academy of Management, European Conference of Information Systems, European Academy of Management Conference, the UK Academy for Information Systems Conference, and the Midwest Association for Information Systems Conference.

Dr. Vicente González-Prida Díaz currently works for a private company as Project Manager sharing his professional performance with teaching activities for degree programs in Spain and LATAM, as well as the development of research projects for the university.

In the academia, he has been honored with the following recognitions:

Extraordinary Prize of Doctorate by the University of Seville

National Award for PhD Thesis on Dependability-RAMS by the Spanish Association for Quality

National Award for PhD Thesis on Maintenance by the Spanish Association for Maintenance

Best Nomination from Spain for the Excellence Master Thesis Award bestowed by the European Federation of National Maintenance Societies

First Class Honours in the Executive Master in Business Administration, by the Chamber of Commerce

Dr. González-Prida has edited four books (IGI-Global 2015, 2017, and 2019; Springer Verlag 2018), regarding Maintenance Modeling, RAMS, Asset Management, and Decision Making, and has authored two books (Confemetal 2018; Springer Verlag 2014) about ISO-55000 and After Sales Management.

His research works have been presented at conferences like WCEAM, ESREL, IEEE, and ESREDA and published in journals such as *Reliability Engineering and System Safety, Production Planning and Control, IMA Journal of Management Mathematics, Computers in Industry*, among others.

His main interest is related to ILS, RAMS, Life Cycle Optimization, as well as the Industry 4.0 and Disrupted Technologies.

Finally, Dr. González-Prida is member of the Technical Committee of the Engineering Institute of Spain, fellow of the Club of Rome (Spanish Chapter), member of the Technical Advisory Board for the Observatory of Intelligence, Security and Defence, among other institutions.

Dr. Vira Shendryk started her academic career in September 2002 at the Sumy State University, Ukraine. Her current position is Deputy Head of Computer Science Department, Head of the Information Technology Section, Associate Professor at Sumy State University.

She was a visiting scholar at McMaster University, Canada, in 2012; visiting professor at Malmo University, Sweden, in 2013; and Riga Technical University, Latvia, in 2014. Her research interest is focused on the field of Information Systems and Decision Science, particularly in decision making under uncertainty. She has written over 200 journal articles and conference papers and presentations. She has also been a Member of the Editorial Board of the International Journal of Green Computing (IJGC), Manchester Journal of Artificial Intelligence and Applied Sciences (MJAIAS), and a Member of Programme Committees for the International scientific conferences in Ukraine, Lithuania, Austria, and Poland.

Contributors

S. Aarthi
Computer Science & Engineering Department, School of Computing
SASTRA deemed to be university
Thanjavur, Tamil Nadu, India

Farooq Ahmad
Department of Computer Application
Integral University
Lucknow, India

Intyaz Alam
School of Computer and Systems Sciences
Jawaharlal Nehru University
New Delhi, India

Suresh Attri
Department of Environment, Science, and Technology
Government of Himachal Pradesh
Shimla, India

Bannishikha Banerjee
Assistant Professor, School of Engineering
PP Savani University
Surat

Vishal Bhatnagar
Netaji Subhas University of Technology (East Campus)
Geeta Colony, Delhi, India

Pratik Chaturvedi
Defence Terrain Research Laboratory
Defence Research and Development Organization
New Delhi, India

Adolfo Crespo
University of Seville, Spain

Indu Dohare
School of Computer and Systems Sciences
Jawaharlal Nehru University
New Delhi, India

Varun Dutt
Indian Institute of Technology Mandi
Mandi, India

Mohammad Faisal
Department of Computer Application
Integral University
Lucknow, India

Edgar Fuenmayor
University of Zulia
Venezuela

K. Geetha
Computer Science & Engineering Department, School of Computing
SASTRA deemed to be university
Thanjavur, Tamil Nadu, India

Olga Gerasimenko
Kremenchuk Mykhailo Ostrohradskyi National University
Ukraine

Vicente González-Prida
University of Sevilla & UNED
Spain

Foram M Joshi
Department of Applied Science & Humanities
G H Patel College of Engineering and Technology
Gujarat

Abhishek Kaushik
Adapt Centre
Dublin City University

Ganesh Khekare
Department of Computer Science & Engineering
Parul University
Vadodara, Gujarat

Fredy Kristjanpoller
University Federico Santa María
Chile

Manoj Kumar
School of Computer and Systems Sciences
Jawaharlal Nehru University
New Delhi, India

Pankaj Kumar
Department of Chemistry, College of Energy Studies
UPES
Dehradun, India

Sushil Kumar
School of Computer and Systems Sciences
Jawaharlal Nehru University
New Delhi, India

Mykhailo Kushch-Zhyrko
Kremenchuk Mykhailo Ostrohradskyi National University
Ukraine

C. Mala
Computer Science & Engineering Department
NIT
Trichy, Tamil Nadu, India

Carmen Martín
University of Toulouse
France

S.M. Masum Ahmed
Heriot-Watt University
Edinburgh, Scotland

Vita Ogar
Ostrohradskyi National University
Kremenchuk, Ukraine

Arvind Panwar
Universal School of Information Communication and Technology, Guru Gobind Singh Indraprastha University
Delhi, India

Carlos Parra
University of Seville
Spain

Andrii Perekrest
Kremenchuk Mykhailo Ostrohradskyi National University
Ukraine

François Pérès
University of Toulouse
France

Duni Chand Rana
Department of Environment, Science, and Technology
Government of Himachal Pradesh
Shimla, India

Seema Raut
G H Raisoni Institute of Engineering & Technology
Nagpur, India

Faisal Rehman
Faculty of Pharmacy
DIT University
Dehradun, India

Geetali Saha
Dept of Electronics and Communication
G H Patel College of Engineering and Technology
Anand, Gujarat

Tushar Saini
Indian Institute of Technology
Mandi

N. Sasikaladevi
Computer Science & Engineering Department, School of Computing
SASTRA deemed to be university
Thanjavur, Tamil Nadu, India

Deepak Saxena
School of Management and Entrepreneurship
Indian Institute of Technology
Jodhpur, India

Mahak Sharma
Maharajah Sayajirao University of Baroda
Baroda, India

Md. Shehzad
Southern University
Bangladesh

Shyla
Guru Gobind Singh Indraprastha University
Delhi, India

Karan Singh
School of Computer and Systems Sciences
Jawaharlal Nehru University
New Delhi, India

Siddharth Singh
Faculty of Pharmaceutical Sciences
PDM University
Bahadurgarh, India

Antonio Sola
Ingeman
Spain

Gagandeep Tomar
Indian Institute of Technology
Mandi

Poonam Vashishta
Faculty of Pharmaceutical Sciences
PDM University
Haryana, India

and

Indian Institute of Technology
Mandi

Jitendra Kumar Verma
Indian Institute of Foreign Trade, New Delhi
(Kakinada Campus Cell), India

Pushpneel Verma
Bhagwant University Ajmer

Pablos Viveros
University Federico Santa María
Chile

Ashok Kumar Yadav
School of Computer and Systems Sciences
Jawaharlal Nehru University
New Delhi, India

Sargam Yadav
Dublin Business School
Ireland

Mohammad Zeyad
Universidad del País Vasco/Euskal Herriko Unibertsitatea

Part I

Integrating IoT and Cloud

1 Challenges Generated by the Integration of Cloud and IoT

Farooq Ahmad and Mohammad Faisal
Integral University Lucknow, India

CONTENTS

1.1 INTRODUCTION

Cloud and IoT are the two innovations that are boundlessly embraced by the web. These technologies are blended to allow use in large applications. Cloud computing gives a craving to IoT to cause an upset in the frontline time frame. A large number of smart applications can be built by the IoT method and can make more noteworthy opportunities for the clients with the measurements created. Because of the large amount of information, this age may incite the necessities that have a bit of leeway of the utilization of virtual sources and putting away limits. For this situation, IoT turns out to be increasingly normal as its far-advancing, additional fundamental to consolidate with distributed computing.

The Internet of Things (IoT) worldview depends on savvy and self-configuring hubs (things) interconnected in a dynamic system. It speaks surely of one of the most extreme technology, empowering standard, and inescapable processing situations. IoT is for the most part described by genuine worldwide small things/nodes, comprehensively circulated, with restricted storage and preparation limit, which include concerns in regards to unwavering quality, execution, security, and protection. On the contrary, cloud computing has positively boundless capabilities in expressions of storing and handling power, is an undeniably increasingly full-grown technology, and has limit of the IoT issues as a base halfway settled. Subsequently, a novel IT worldview wherein cloud and IoT are two corresponding technologies combined by and large is anticipated to enhance both present-day and future Internet [1, 2]. We call cloud IoT to this new worldview.

DOI: 10.1201/9781003155577-2

The blend of distributed computing and IoT needs heaps of devices which produces voluminous data and that can be processed with a faster pace using capacity of distributed computing. This mix offers some significant characteristics as follows:

On-Demand Self-Service: A consumer can unilaterally provision computing capabilities, such as server time and network storage, as needed automatically without requiring human interaction with each service provider.

Expansive Network Access: This offers differing availability options. The resources of cloud computing might be gathered over a wide scope of network-associated devices like mobiles, PCs, and tablets. At this level, clients would be able to even form network of old devices to those sources in a stand-out way.

Resource Pooling: This portrays around the realities that can be imparted to the clients all over the locations and each time with the necessary authorizations for getting to. With regards to IoT, an IP adapt to be given to each issue and offers the put away realities with different clients.

Quick Elasticity: This capacity empowers IoT with the guide of managing the storage space, versatile computing power depicts about becoming the storage space, including or putting off the clients, upgrading the product arrangement quick, and, as a general rule, networking and so forth.

Estimated Service: This capacity ascertains the use of data like stockpiling, transfer speed, and vivacious bills of clients inside the cloud space. It is completely characterized as pay steady with use.

1.2 BACKGROUND AND BASIC CONCEPTS

Here, we go through the fundamentals of IoT and cloud and outline the qualities essential for their integration.

1.2.1 Internet of Things

The resulting wave inside the time of computing is anticipated to be outside the universe of customary work area [3]. In accordance with this perception, a special worldview known as Internet of Things immediately got ground over the most recent couple of years. IoT indicates towards "an overall system of interconnected things that are exceptionally addressable" [4, 5] which are combined on the Internet. The essential thought behind it is the inescapable nearness around individuals of things, ready to measure, surmise, comprehend, and even manage close environment. IoT is powered with mobile devices; that is, not just complex devices including cell phones but also ordinary devices, for example, food, dress, furnishings, paper, tourist spots, landmarks, gems, and so on [6, 7]. These things, act as sensors or actuators that can collaborate with each other for user's objective.

The key component in IoT is, without question, its effect on consistent presence of forthcoming clients [4]. IoT has extraordinary effects both in artworks and residential situations, where it can assume a fundamental job in the resulting in helped living, domestics, e-wellbeing, smart transportation, etc. Major significances are additionally anticipated for business (e.g., calculated, business computerization, transportation of merchandise, and security). These are portrayed in Figure 1.1. As per these contemplations, in 2008 IoT has been accounted for by methods for US National Intelligence Council as one of the six technologies with potential impact on US intrigues more like 2025 [7]. In fact, in 2011 the assortment of interconnected gadgets surpassed the assortment of individuals [3]. In 2012, the quantity of interconnected devices was required to be 9 billion, and it was anticipated to arrive at the cost of 26 billion through 2022. Such numbers advocate that IoT will be one of the principal assets of huge information [8].

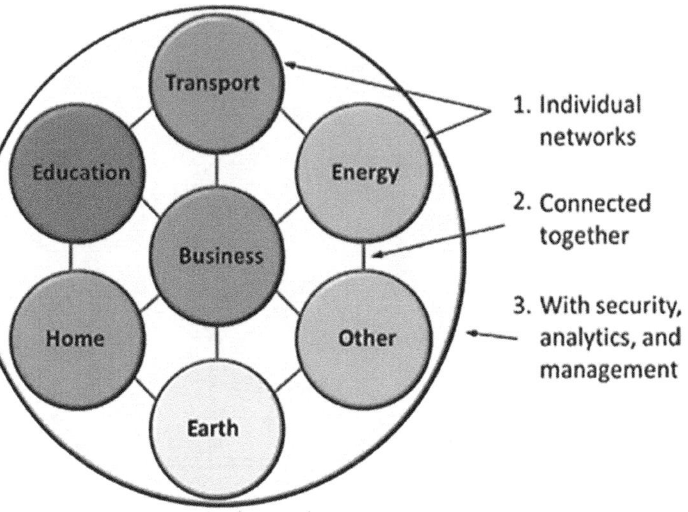

FIGURE 1.1 IoT as a network of networks.

Source: Cisco IBSG, April 2011.

In the following, we define a few vital aspects associated with IoT.

RFID: In IoT situation, a key capacity is played through radio-frequency identification (RFID) frameworks, composed of one or more readers and numerous tags. These technologies assist in automated identification of anything they're appended to and permit things to be relegated to specific virtual environment to be incorporated into a network, and to be identified with virtual records and administrations [6]. In an ordinary utilization situation, readers trigger the label transmission by means of producing an appropriate signal on unauthorized movement of item from local network. RFID tags are typically passive (they don't require on-board power supply), anyway there are likewise labels fueled from batteries [4, 9].

(Wireless) Sensor Networks: Another key angle in IoT environments is spoken to through sensor networks. For instance, they can coordinate with RFID structures of things, accepting data about position, movement, temperature, and so forth. Sensor networks are typically made out of a conceivably high number of detecting hubs, conveying in a wi-fi multi-bounce style. Wireless sensor networks (WSNs) may also give different helpful records and are being benefited from in a few areas like healthcare, government, and environmental services (natural disaster relief); defense (military target tracking and surveillance); perilous condition investigation; seismic detecting; and so on [7]. Be that as it may, sensor systems should confront numerous issues concerning their interchanges (short communication range, protection and security, reliability, mobility, etc.) and resources (vitality contemplations, storage capacity, processing capacities, bandwidth availability, etc.). Additionally, WSN has its own resource and plan imperatives (which are application-and environmental factors specific) and that intensely rely upon the size of the checking environmental factors [7]. The scientific network profoundly tended to various difficulties identified with sensor networks at different layers (e.g., energy efficiency, reliability, strength, and adaptability.) [4].

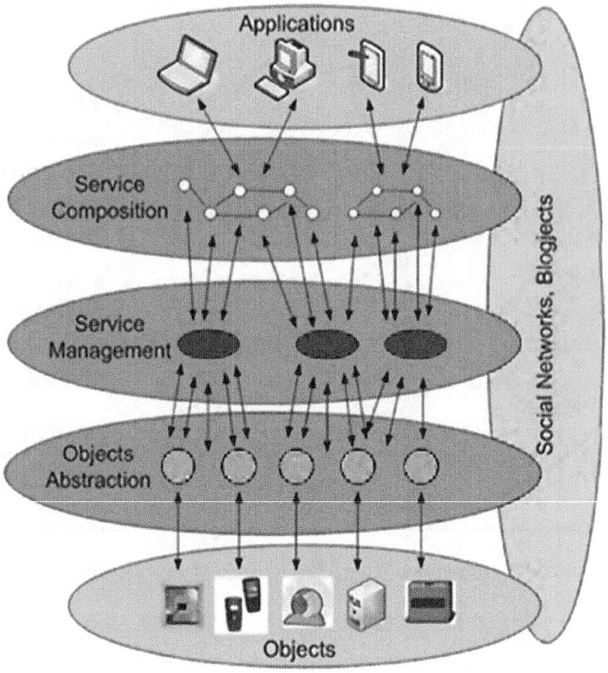

FIGURE 1.2 IoT paradigm: an overall view.

Source: [6].

Addressing: A wireless technology, for example, RFID and Wi-Fi, IoT paradigm is adjusting the Internet into a completely included future Internet [9]. While Internet advancement prompted an unmatched interconnection of people, current pattern is fundamental to the interconnection of objects, to make a smart environment [3]. In this specific circumstance, the potential to uniquely pick out matters is essential for the achievement of IoT when you consider that this lets in to uniquely cope with a large wide variety of devices and manage them through the Internet. Uniqueness, dependability, persistence, and scalability represent essential features related to the creation of a unique addressing schema [3]. One-of-a-kind identification issues might be tended to through IPv4 to a degree (for the most part an assortment of living together sensor gadgets might be identified geologically, anyway no longer separately). IPv6, with its Internet mobility attributes, can moderate a number of tool identification troubles and is expected to play a crucial role in this field.

Middleware: Due to the heterogeneity of the participating objects, their limited storage and processing abilities and the massive style of packages involved, a key function is played by the middleware among the matters and the utility layer, whose significant point is the reflection of the functionalities and report aptitudes of the devices. The middleware can be partitioned into a fixed number of layers such as (see Figure 1.2): object abstraction, service management, service composition, and application [6].

1.2.2 Cloud

The word "cloud" alludes to a huge network or Internet. In other words, we can say that a cloud is a technology-empowered complex infrastructure, remotely accessible, with smooth or user-friendly customer support facilities. It is depicted in Figure 1.3. Clouds can offer streaming services over public and personal networks, that is, WANs, LANs, or VPNs.

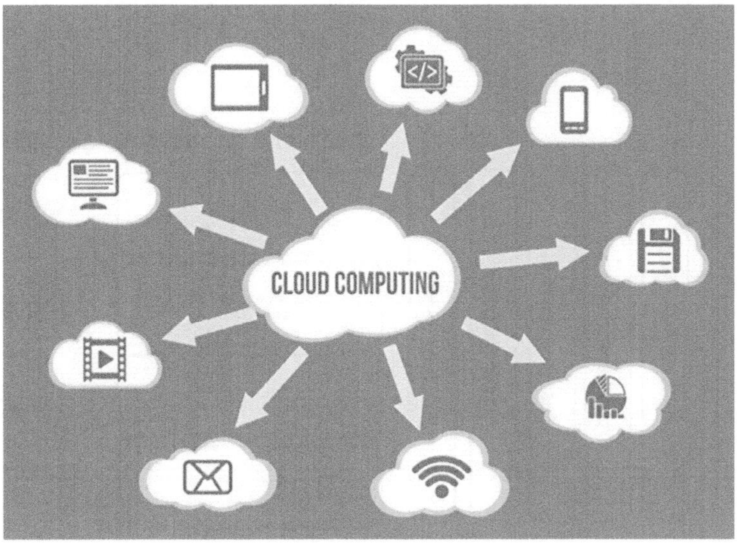

FIGURE 1.3 Network of cloud computing [10].

Cloud computing empowers in manipulating, configuring, and accessing hardware and software sources remotely. It gives online records storage, infrastructure, applications, reduced costs, increased sales, more security, more reliability, and multi-tenancies (which means entire projects are put away inside one application); moreover, there is no need to buy any software, it's far fast to get started, there aren't any servers or bulk storage, no technical teams, and no upgrades. All you need is a login ID and password. To be capable of customizing settings and working on your own application is the energy of cloud computing.

Cloud computing gives platform independency, because the software is not compulsory to be installed internally on the PC. Cloud computing therefore empowers extra mobility and collaboration for our enterprise applications.

Cloud computing may be defined as turning in computing power (CPU, RAM, network speed, storage, OS software) for a provider over a network (typically on the Internet) in inclination to physically having the computing resources in the customer's location.

"Cloud computing method on demand delivery of IT resources thru the net with pay-as-you-go pricing. It affords an answer of IT infrastructure at low cost." [10]

The essential components of cloud computing have been accounted inside the definition furnished via National Institute of Standard and Technologies (NIST) [11]:

> Cloud computing is a model for enabling ubiquitous, convenient, on-demand network access to a shared pool of configurable computing resources (e.g., networks, servers, storage, applications, and services) that can be rapidly provisioned and released with minimal management effort or service provider interaction. This cloud model is composed of five essential characteristics, three service models, and four deployment models.

Even though the main concept of cloud computing was no longer new, the term headed out to advantage reputation after Google's CEO Eric Schmidt utilized it in 2006 [12], and in the course of the most recent couple of years the presence of cloud computing has exceptionally affected IT industry. Cloud computing offers the accessibility to limitless storage [13] and at low charges, wherein virtualized resources can be rented on the basis of avalbility to required services. Big businesses (Amazon, Google, Facebook, etc.) extensively accepted this paradigm for supplying resources over the Internet, gaining both financially savvy and specialized benefits.

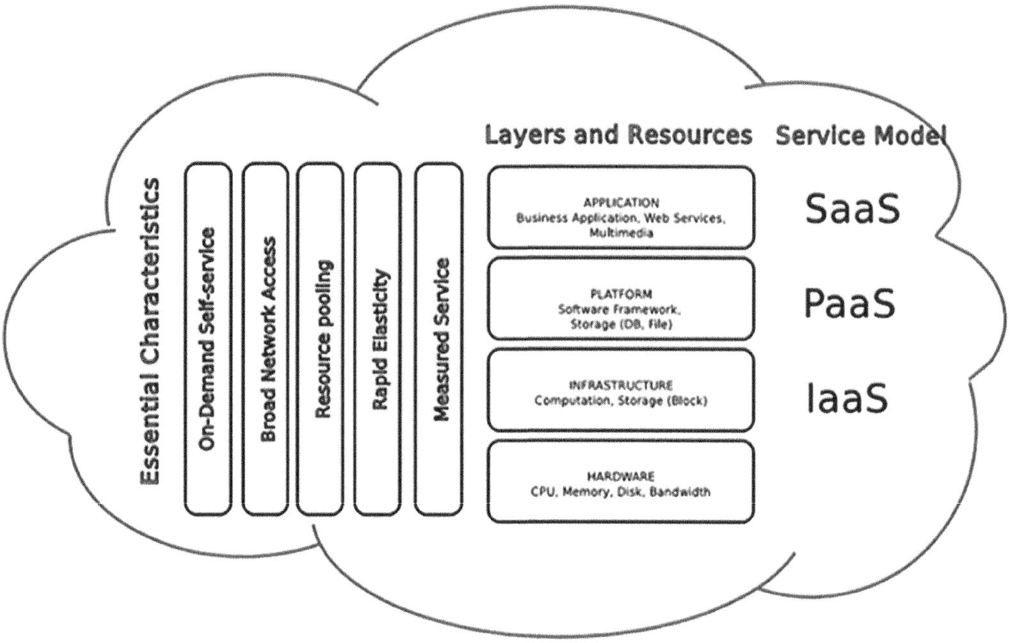

FIGURE 1.4 Cloud paradigm: an overall view [15].

Cloud computing is an unruly technology with significant ramifications for the shipping of Internet benefits in addition to for the IT sector overall.

However, numerous technical-and business-related troubles are nevertheless unresolved. Particular issues have been observed for each network models, which might be especially related to safety (e.g., records protection and integrity, network protection), secrecy (e.g., data confidentiality), and provider-stage contracts, which could frighten off potential clients [14]. Figure 1.4 summarizes the primary components of cloud: the principal traits which make it an effective model, its layered architecture, and the usual provider models.

1.2.2.1 Why Cloud Computing?

Small and some large IT agencies observe traditional strategies to provide their corporation with its much-wanted IT infrastructure. That implies, for IT companies, we want a server room, which is a simple requirement for IT businesses.

In that server room, we will have a database server, mail server, firewalls, routers, networking, modems, switches, QPS (Query Per Second) software (determining what number of queries or how a great deal load the server will be capable of handle), configurable systems, excessive Internet speeds, and a team of protection engineers.

To set up such IT infrastructure, we need to devote a lot of money. To overcome these troubles and to lessen IT infrastructure costs, cloud computing is a worthwhile alternative.

With the increase in the variety of laptop and cellular users, data storage has converted a concern in all fields. Big-and small-scale agencies nowadays flourish with records and spend a large sum of money to hold this information. It requires sturdy IT assists and garage hubs. Not every organization can give the high fee of domestic IT infrastructure and backup aid services. Cloud computing is taken into consideration as a cheap solution. Perhaps its effectiveness in data storage, computation, and lower preservation fees has flourished in attracting even bigger industries as well.

Cloud computing reduces the hardware and software at the client's end. The best component that the user is capable to run is the cloud computing system's interface software, which may be as easy as a web browser, the cloud community taking care of the rest. We as a whole have skilled cloud computing at certain point in time; a number of the most standard cloud offerings we've used, or keep to use, are mail services like Gmail, Hotmail, or Yahoo, which are cloud computing systems dependent on the Internet. When one updates their Facebook status, then it may be the usage of a cloud computing system.

While accessing an email service, our information is put away on the cloud server and no longer on our PC. The generation and infrastructure in the back of the cloud are imperceptible. It is less significant whether cloud contributions are principally founded on HTTP, XML, Ruby, PHP, or other particular technology than whether it's miles easy to use and functional. An individual client must be able to connect with the cloud system from his own devices like a desktop, computer, or mobile.

1.2.2.2 Classifications of Cloud Computing

Private cloud: At this time, computing resources are organized for one specific agency. This technique is relevant for intra-enterprise interfaces, where the computing sources are governed, claimed, and worked with the aid of similar business enterprises. A private cloud denotes cloud computing sources utilized only by method of a sole business or business enterprise depicted in Figure 1.5. A private cloud is positioned physically at the business's on-site data center. Some businesses additionally pay third-party service vendors to host their private cloud. A personal cloud is one wherein the facilities and infrastructure are preserved on a non-public network. [16]

Community cloud: Nowadays, computing resources are furnished for a community and organizations. The community clouds are a hybrid form of personal clouds built and functioned mainly for some centered group.

Community clouds are regularly designed for groups and groups operating on combined projects, applications, or research, which needs an imperative cloud computing facility for building, dealing with, and implementing such projects, irrespective of the answer hired [17]. Community clouds are designed to satisfy the requirements of a network depicted in Figure 1.6.

Such groups involve human beings or agencies that have shared benefits. Community clouds are designed to fulfill the wishes of a community.

Public cloud: It is normally used for B2C (business to consumer) kind exchanges. The mentioned computing resources are owned, administered, and functioned via the government, or an academic, or professional corporation depicted in Figure 1.7.

The public clouds are owned and functioned by a third-party cloud facility suppliers, who promises their computing resources like servers and storage over the Internet. Microsoft Azure is an instance of a public cloud. With a public cloud, entire hardware, software, and other serving infrastructure are owned and accomplished by means of the cloud supplier. We can get entry to these services and control one's account using an Internet browser. [16]

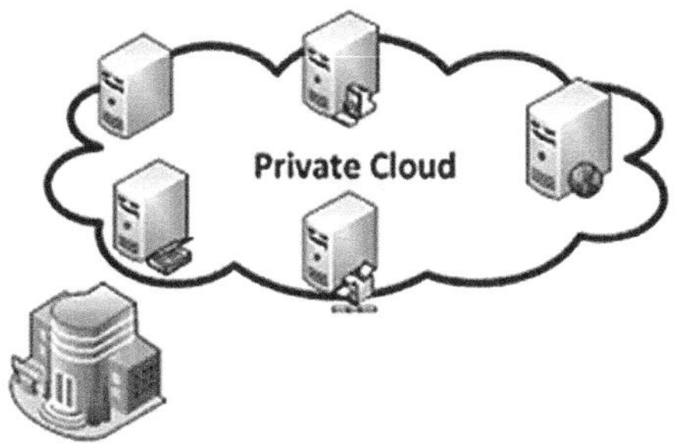

FIGURE 1.5 Private Cloud [16].

FIGURE 1.6 Community Cloud [17].

FIGURE 1.7 Public Cloud [16].

Virtual private cloud: Virtualization offers various benefits together with saving time and energy, reducing costs, and minimizing universal threats:

- Offers the capability to manage resources efficiently
- Surges productivity, as it offers safe faraway access
- Offers for data loss avoidance

A virtual private cloud applies the usage of a mutual data center infrastructure of hardware and software. The data center is most likely off-premises and mutual with several organizations. If the data center is not public, it'd be private cloud.

The higher layers of the cloud computing stack (PaaS and SaaS) in a virtual private cloud are devoted to an organization. The lower IaaS is mutual in a virtual private cloud. A virtual personal cloud may contribute in a hybrid cloud.

Hybrid cloud: It is used for both forms of exchanges – B2B (business to business) and B2C (business to consumer). This deployment approach is referred to as hybrid cloud as the computing resources are certain collectively by unique clouds, depicted in Figure 1.8.

Hybrid clouds integrate public and personal clouds, destined together by a generation that sanctions statistics and programs shared among them. By allowing facts and applications to move

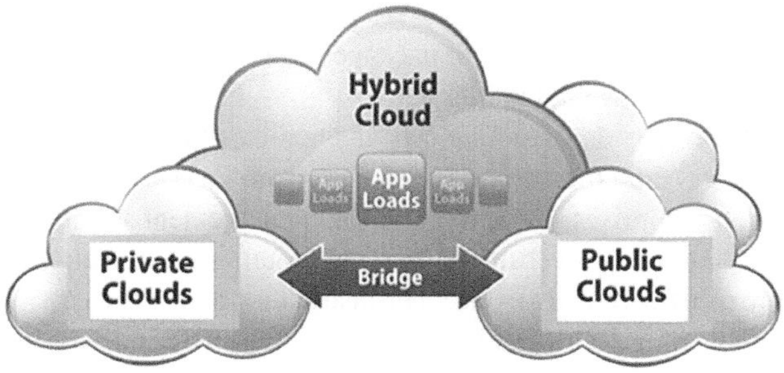

FIGURE 1.8 Hybrid Cloud [16].

between personal and public clouds, hybrid cloud provides organizations with more elasticity and extra deployment choices.

1.2.2.3 Cloud Computing Services

SaaS (Software as a Service): SaaS is a software delivery version wherein packages are hosted by means of a supplier or carrier company and made for clients over a network (the Internet).

SaaS is turning into a progressively standard distribution model as underlying technologies assist service-oriented architecture (SOA) or web services. Over and done with the Internet, this provider is accessible to customers everywhere in the world.

Usually, software applications need to be bought in advance and then installed onto the computer. SaaS users on their end, instead of buying the software program, enroll in it, generally on a monthly basis through the Internet.

Any person who desires to get the right of entry to a specific quantity of software can subscribe as a user, whether a few human beings or a large number of employees in a company. SaaS is well suited to all Internet-empowered devices such as MS Office 365.

Numerous essential jobs like accounting, sales, invoicing, and planning are achieved using SaaS.

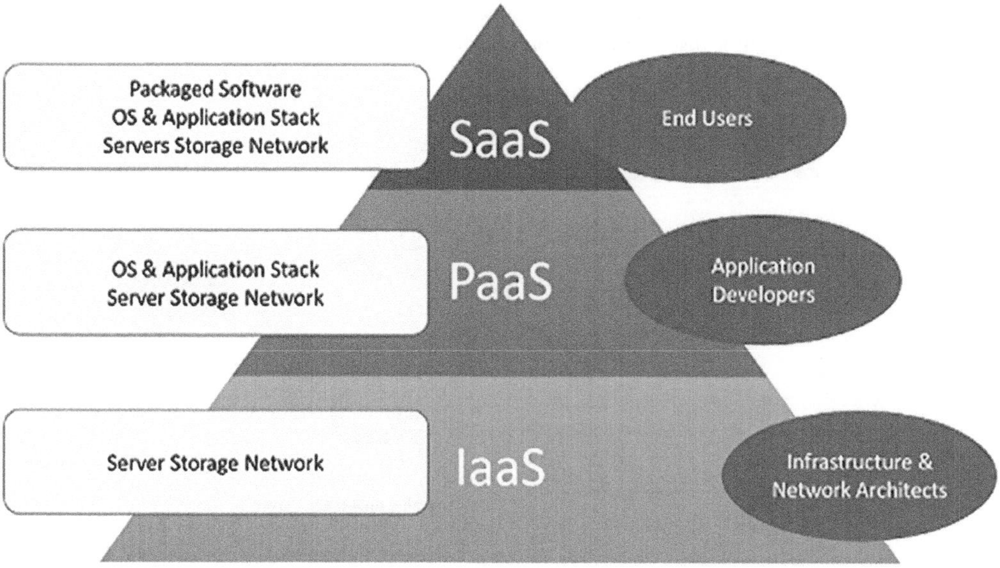

FIGURE 1.9 Cloud Service Models.

Source: https://medium.com/@IDMdatasecurity/types-of-cloud-services-b54e5b574f6.

PaaS (Platform as a Service): Platform as a Service is called PaaS; it offers a platform and environment to permit developers in constructing packages and services. The provider is hosted within the cloud, which users can access via the Internet.

PaaS services need to be up to date continuously and new capabilities must be additional. Software developers, web developers, and the corporate can gain from PaaS. It presents the platform to help software development. It comprises software guide and management services, storage, networking, deployment, testing, collaborating, website hosting, and retaining applications.

IaaS (Infrastructure as a Service): IaaS (Infrastructure as a Service) is an essential service model of cloud computing along with PaaS (Platform as a Service). It offers an access to computing resources in a virtualized environment "the cloud" on the Internet. It presents computing infrastructure like virtual server space, network connections, bandwidth, load balancers, and IP addresses. The pool of hardware resource gathered from a couple of servers and networks is typically disbursed throughout the numerous data centers. It gives redundancy and reliability to IaaS.

It's a complete package deal for computing. For limited agencies seeking to reduced fees on IT infrastructure, IaaS is one of the acceptable solutions. Consequnetly, less money is invested on renovation and shopping for new components like hard disc drives, community connections, and outside storage device, which a corporate proprietor spend could have saved for additional fees by the use of IaaS.

1.2.2.4 Cloud Computing Architecture

Cloud computing includes components: the front quit and the back cease. The front-end includes the client part of the cloud computing system. It consists of interfaces and applications that might be essential to access cloud computing platforms, for example, web browsers. These are depicted in Figure 1.10.

Cloud computing dispenses the file system that is unfolded above multiple hard disks and machines. Data is certainly not saved in one location only, and just in case one unit fails, some others will take over automatically. The user's disk area is owed on the distributed system, even as any other vital thing is the algorithm for resource distribution. Cloud computing is a robust dispensed atmosphere, and it deeply relies upon robust algorithms. [18]

Peer-to-Peer (P2P) Architectures versus Cloud: In P2P computing networks, each computer either acts as a patron or a server for the alternative computers within the network, with the intention to permit shared right to use diverse resources, for example, files and peripherals, without the

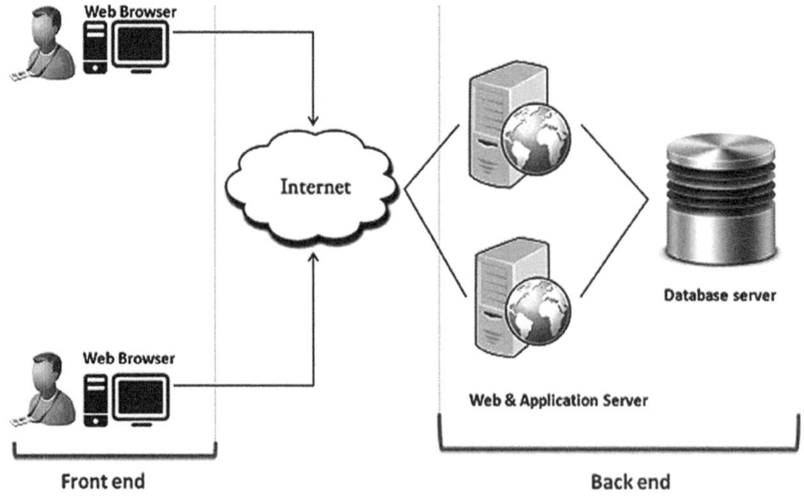

FIGURE 1.10 Cloud Computing Architecture [18].

necessity of a central server. P2P computing is described as the sharing of computer offerings and sources via nonstop exchange. Various benefits of the P2P technique comprise progressed scalability, and it's going likewise to dispose of the requirement for expensive infrastructure. [19]

In a P2P network of hosts, resource sharing, processing, and communication manipulation are absolutely decentralized. Every host acts as a server (provider) of selected services. However, it relies upon the alternative nodes within the community for different services. The entire customers are identical on the network.

Cloud computing is flexible and scalable regarding resource distribution. However, P2P architectures are inexpensive and easier to manage.

Cloud computing desires great preliminary economic funding and decent technology experts while P2P deployments have restricted extensibility stuff.

Client-Server Architecture versus Cloud: In a client-server model, every computer can behave like both a server and a client. [19]

Client-server architecture is a form of scattered computing wherein the consumers rely on the quantity of servers that will supply them with the services. Thus, its scalability includes more expenses (processing electricity costs, management prices, and administrative costs). On the other hand, the cloud protects costs, time, and employees. The entire resources are shared through the client. There is no extra cost incurred as it is in the client-server architectures. Note that in the client-server deployments, a minimum of one server is compulsory. Therefore, greater prices are involved. The cloud is, as a result, cheaper.

Client-server architecture ensures that there is certain logical separation of components, services, and resources. Normally, we realize user interfaces in a neighborhood implementation (also known as "client") and corporate records and other sources in a remote accomplishment (also known as "server"). Several examples:

- MSN Messenger – incorporates a service run on the local machine, whereas a back-end service helps communication at a remote location.
- Facebook – carries a tiny application (the web browser) and a remote service (their servers). [20]

1.2.2.5 Cloud Security Concerns

Security is becoming more and more important. Unluckily, IT infrastructure are turning out a bigger and common issue, making protection a priority for cloud companies to consist of with their service contributions. Individuals are scared of putting their data in the cloud, so obviously, anticipated that cloud suppliers take extra effort to safeguard customers. The greater the safety the suppliers offer their customers, the more invulnerable their customers will be in their selection to save their data to the cloud. As greater and extra clients share their practices with others, cloud suppliers have the chance to show their honesty and attain flat wider spectators. When it arises to cloud computing, it appears that anything is possible. As more gates proceed to open up and the connection between these in the house reinforces, it is a thrilling time for cloud authorities and customers involved; all at once the concern for cloud security will increase also. As per the rate of cloud acceptance surges, we seem to be advancing to seeing what arises next.

1.3 NEED FOR AND THE BENEFITS OF CLOUD-IOT INTEGRATION [21, 22]

The current tendency is shifting toward the familiar web, and connected devices nowadays have been overlapped by the range of persons on the earth. These devices have now touched billions and are predicted to develop more in the near future. These linked units extend hastily as they encompass large quantity of information. Thus, there is no risk to keep the statistics locally and concisely. In this situation, a rental storage area is wanted, and this fact is used in such a way that it is earned. The processed facts are an attention to the person for greater processing, which is now not viable

TABLE 1.1
Interdependent Characteristics of IoT and Cloud

IoT	Cloud
Common things are organized everywhere	Universal resources are utilized from all the places
Real-world things	Basic resources
Computational competencies are limited	Computational competencies are unlimited
Limited storage capability	Unlimited storage capability
Big data Source	Manages Big data

at the IoT end. Frequently, this computation and processing would possibly use on a rental basis. This is feasible solely with cloud computing with the integration of IoT and produces new patterns. Actually, cloud acts as an intermediate layer in between functions and belongings where all the vital functionalities are concealed before the implementation and suggests the effect on the growth of future applications. Cloud and IoT together arise with some of the mutually supporting characteristics that encourage the cloud and IoT patterns. These are described in Table 1.1.

Following are benefits of merging cloud with IoT [22]:

Affordable: Customers do not have to make any investments in their infrastructure or equipment, so cloud proves very good value in the long run. In addition, the payment of cloud is through the "pay as you go" approach, relying on the demand of the needed resources, to the service provider. In this way, the patron avoids useless or more payments and solely gives the same quantity as the resources are used with the aid of the commercial enterprise – fewer resources and much affordable extra money.

Secure: If your laptop computer or business phone is lost, then the vital business information goes along with it, and it does no longer lessen any terrible tragedy. But if the information is saved in the cloud like OneDrive, then patron does no longer have to fear it, because it can be accessed by means of using any device or computer and remotely can wipe all quintessential information from the misplaced device.

Efficient growth: The top-of-the-line potential of resources in the cloud is used, so the cloud solutions show to be very beneficial. Cloud no longer only enhances the efficiency of the enterprise however additionally increases the efficiency of the employees, because the use of cloud applications can be used by means of personnel now, not simply in the workplace but anywhere – all of their mails, documents, everything – so with the help of the cloud proper in effect, "office on the go" is realized.

Elastic and scalable: Whether it is bandwidth, storage, or any different resource, the whole thing can be superior and reduced according to the enterprise demand in the cloud. It is much higher than the old ways of Internet hosting where the prescribed resources are given and whether you use them or not, you have to pay the full amount.

Avoiding downtime or delay: Cloud is a network of related servers. Therefore, if any node fails, then all of its load is taken away by way of the second cloud node, so the business site is on the cloud server, or cloud services are never down.

Disaster recovery: Big commercial enterprises can come up with the money for extra IT resources for disaster management; however, this is an additional cost for SMBs because IT resources used for disaster management are left empty, as they will be used only at the time of that disaster. Cloud SMBs furnish a low price and secure disaster healing mechanism.

Environmental compatibility: Cloud conserves power and offers efficient technical solutions to the enterprise by emitting less carbon percentage than efficient use of resources ensuing in green computing.

Incentives for new experiments: For a developer, or a tester or IT engineer, it offers scope to test experiments without problems with the cloud – harmless stay environment – and this cloud check infrastructure, which will be modified frequently in accordance to testing. It can be very low-priced in contrast to the trade in the real environment.

1.4 CLOUD AND IOT: DRIVERS FOR INTEGRATION [15]

In general, IoT can benefit from the virtually limitless abilities and sources of cloud to compensate for its technological constraints (e.g., storage, processing, and communication). To quote a few examples, cloud can offer a wonderful solution for IoT service administration and composition as nicely as for imposing functions and offerings that take advantage of the matters or the data produced with the aid of them [23]. On the other hand, cloud can benefit from IoT by way of extending its scope to deal with real-world issues in a greater dispensed and dynamic manner, and for handing over new services in a variety of real life's scenarios. In many cases, cloud at the middle layer between the things and the applications, hiding all the difficulties and functionalities. This will impact future utility development; processing, and transmission will generate new challenges, especially in a multi-cloud environment [24].

Most of the integration drivers fall into three classes, which are communication, storage, and computation, while a few others are extra simple and have implications in all such categories, that is, they are cutting edge.

IoT being characterized via a very high heterogeneity of devices, technologies, and protocols, it lacks different important properties such as scalability, interoperability, flexibility, reliability, efficiency, availability, and security. Since cloud has proved to supply them [25–27], we become aware of them as some of the major cutting edge cloud-IoT drivers. Two different cutting edge drivers are the ease of use and the reduced value received with the aid of each customer and vendor of applications and services [26]. Indeed, cloud facilitates the flow between IoT data collection and data processing and permits rapid setup and integration of new things, while preserving low charges for deployment and for complex facts processing [28]. As a consequence, analyses of unprecedented complexity [26, 29] are possible, and data-driven choice making and prediction algorithms can be employed at low cost, imparting capability for increasing revenues and reduced risks [30].

Communication: Data and application sharing are two necessary cloud-IoT drivers falling in the conversation category. Cloud-IoT model personalized ubiquitous purposes can be conveyed through the IoT, while automation can be applied to both statistics series and distribution at low cost. Cloud offers an effective and low-cost solution to connect, track, and control anything from somewhere at any time by using customized portals and built-in apps [28]. The availability of high-speed networks permits effective monitoring and management of remote issues [28, 29, 31], their coordination [25, 27, 29], their communications [25], and real-time [28].

It is well worth bringing up that even though cloud can significantly enhance and simplify IoT communication, it can still represent a bottleneck in some scenarios: indeed, over the ultimate 20 years data storage density and processor electricity improved of a factor of 10^{18} and 10^{15}, respectively, while broadband capability multiplied solely of 10^4 [32]. As a consequence, practical obstacles can arise when attempting to switch large amounts of information from the aspect of the Internet onto cloud.

Storage: IoT involves by way of definition a massive quantity of information sources (i.e., the things), which produce a large quantity of non-structured or semi-structured data [24], which also have the three characteristics typical of big data [33]: extent (i.e., facts size), range (i.e., statistics types), and velocity (i.e., data generation frequency). Large-scale and long-lived storage, possible thanks to the truly unlimited, low-cost, and on-demand storage ability supplied by cloud, represents an important cloud-IoT driver. Cloud is the handiest and cost-effective answer to deal with data produced by IoT [28] and, in this respect, it generates new possibilities for records aggregation [25], integration [30], and sharing with third parties [30]. Once into cloud, data can be handled as homogeneous via well-defined APIs [25], can be covered by applying top-layer safety [26], and can be at once accessed and visualized from any region [28].

Computation: IoT devices have restricted processing and power sources that to get rid of on-site data processing. Collected data are usually transmitted to extra powerful nodes where aggregation and processing are possible, but scalability is a challenging issue to attain without a suitable infrastructure. Cloud offers really unlimited processing skills and an on-demand utilization model. This represents some other vital cloud-IoT drivers: IoT processing expectations can be properly satisfied for performing real-time information evaluation (on-the-fly) [26, 28], for implementing scalable, real-time, collaborative, sensor-centric functions [25], for managing complicated events [28], and for assisting challenge offloading for power saving [25].

Scope: As the matters add capabilities, and more people and new sorts of statistics are connected, users unfold throughout the world shortly enter the Internet of Everything (IoE) [34, 35], a community of networks where billions of connections create unprecedented possibilities as well as new risks. The adoption of the cloud-IoT model permits new clever offerings and purposes primarily based on the extension of cloud through the things [27, 28], which allow the cloud to deal with a quantity of new, real-life scenarios, giving delivery to the Things as a Service paradigm [36–38].

1.5 INTEGRATION CHALLENGES [15]

We have discussed how integrating cloud and IoT gives various benefits and fosters the start or improvement of a variety of fascinating applications. These are depicted in Figure 1.12. At the same time, we have viewed that the complex cloud-IoT scenario imposes quite a few challenges for most of the purposes that need to be handled to experience its benefits. Following are some of the challenges of this integration.

Security and Privacy: When vital IoT applications go toward the cloud, concerns occur due to the lack of, for example, belief in the service provider, information about provider level agreements (SLAs), and information about the physical area of data. Hence, new challenges require specific interest [39–41]. Such a disbursed machine is exposed to countless feasible attacks (e.g., session riding, SQL injection, go website scripting, and side-channel) and necessary vulnerabilities (e.g., session hijacking and virtual computing device escape) (Figure 1.11).

Multi-tenancy can also compromise protection and lead to sensitive data leakage. Moreover, public-key cryptography can't be utilized at all layers due to the computing energy constraints imposed by using the things. These are examples of topics that are presently under investigation in order to tackle the massive challenge of protection and privacy in cloud IoT.

Heterogeneity: A huge challenge in cloud IoT is related to the broad heterogeneity of devices, operating systems, platforms, and services reachable and may be used for new or elevated applications.

Cloud platforms heterogeneity is also a non-negligible concern. Cloud services generally come with proprietary interfaces, causing useful resource integration and mash-up to be right personalized based on the specific providers. This trouble can be exacerbated when users undertake multi-cloud approaches, that is, when offerings depend on a couple of carriers in order to enhance application overall performance and resilience or dealer lock-in [42]. These components are only partially solved with the aid of cloud brokering, voluntarily applied through cloud vendors (in shape of federation) or through third parties.

IoT services and applications have usually been conceived as isolated vertical solutions, in which all device components are tightly coupled to the specific software context. For every feasible application/service, companies have to survey goal scenarios, analyze requirements, pick hardware and software environments, combine heterogeneous subsystems, develop, supply computing infrastructure, and supply carrier maintenance. On the other hand, cloud IoT should ease IoT service delivery [43]. However, although PaaS-like fashions would symbolize a regular solution for facilitating the

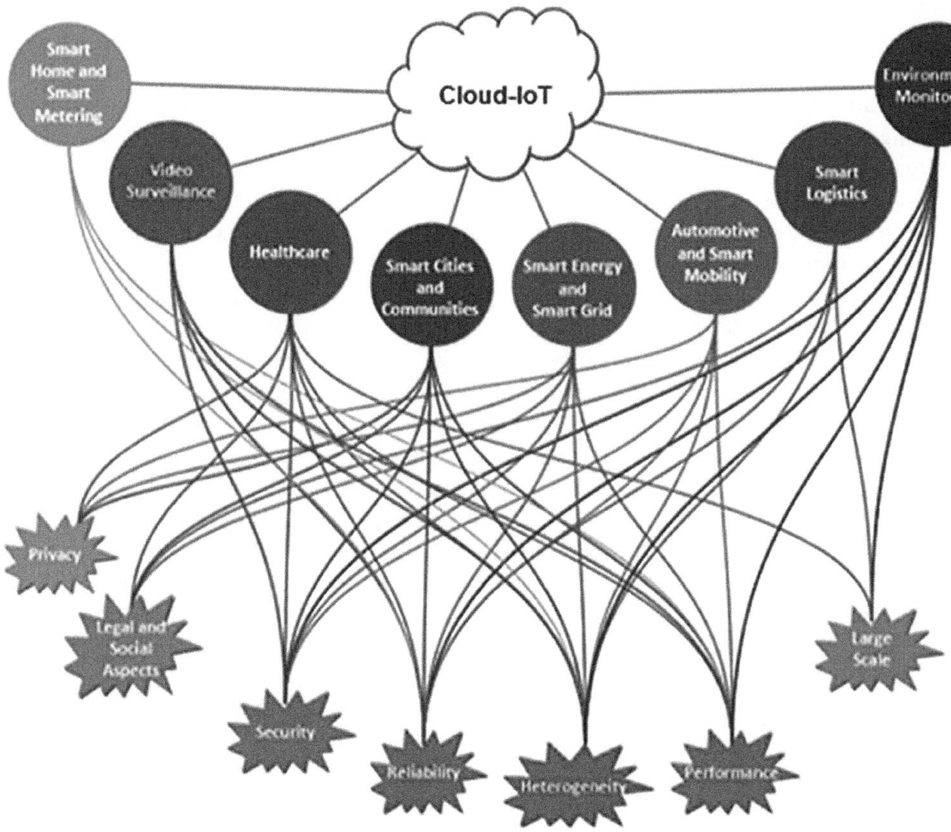

FIGURE 1.11 Application scenarios driven by the cloud-IoT model and related challenges [15].

deployment of IoT applications, their implementation requires tackling the large venture of heterogeneity. For instance, the interaction with (management of) large amounts of particularly heterogeneous things (and the associated facts produced) has to be top addressed in the cloud at different levels.

Performance: Often cloud-IoT applications introduce specific overall performance and QoS necessities at countless ranges (i.e. for communication, computation, and storage aspects), and in some specific situations meeting necessities can also not be effortlessly achievable. In particular, acquiring steady desirable community overall performance to reach the cloud is a fundamental challenge, considering that broadband extend did no longer follow storage and computation evolution [28, 32]. In fact, in numerous eventualities (e.g., when mobility is required) provisioning of information and offerings needs to be performed with excessive reactivity [38, 44]. Since timeliness might also be closely impacted by means of unpredictability problems, real-time functions are mostly prone to overall performance challenges [27, 28]. Usability and user trip can also be affected via poor QoS (e.g., when multimedia streaming is needed) [45].

Reliability: When cloud IoT is adopted for mission-critical applications, reliability issues typically arise, for example, in the context of intelligent mobility, vehicles are regularly on the cross and the vehicular networking and conversation are often intermittent or unreliable. When applications are deployed in resource-constrained environments, a number of challenges associated with system failure or no longer usually reachable devices exist [44].

On the one hand, cloud competencies assist to overcome some of these challenges (e.g., cloud enhances the reliability of the devices by means of allowing to offload heavy tasks and for that reason to increase devices' battery duration or offering the opportunity of constructing a modularized architecture) [46, 47]; on the other hand, it introduces uncertainties associated to information middle virtualization or aid exhaustion [36, 45]. The lack of reliability analyses and of the development of specific case research exacerbates the challenge.

Large Scale: Cloud IoT approves to plan novel functions aimed at integrating and examining data coming from real-world (embedded) devices [28, 38, 48–51]. Some of the depicted situations implicitly require the interplay with a very massive wide variety of these devices, generally distributed throughout wide-area environments. The massive scale of the resulting systems makes usual challenges tougher to overcome (e.g., requirements about storage potential and computational capability for in addition processing is difficult to be satisfied when dealing with long-lived information collected at high rate). Moreover, the distribution of the IoT units makes monitoring duties harder, considering they have to face latency dynamics and connectivity issues.

Legal and Social Aspects: These are two important challenges, partly related. Legal aspects are extremely important. For example, a cloud-IoT service is based totally on user-provided data. In this case, on the one hand, the service provider has to conform to different global laws. And, on the other hand, users have to be provided with incentives in order to contribute to data collection. In more normal terms, social factors are of hobby for lookup and are currently viewed as a fascinating project because, often, the investment into omnipresent Internet-capable units is now not reasonable in each and every scenario. It is extra convenient to provide the probability to users to take part in submitting records that signify an issue [52]. The authors of [53] have identified a set of troubles to be addressed by using any gadget that incorporates human beings as a supply of sensor data, in order to continue to be relied on by way of its users (such as integrating the qualitative observations generated via human beings with the machine-generated quantitative observations, or the need to symbolize and control records quality, reliability, reputation, and trustworthiness). Users may want to also be empowered with new building blocks and tools: accelerators, frameworks, and toolkits that allow the participation of users in IoT as carried out on the Internet through Wikis and Blogs [54]. Such equipment and techniques have to allow researchers and professionals to learn about consumer work, giving users an active position in technological know-how design. To gain this, these equipment should enable users to easily scan more than a few graph possibilities in a cost-effective way. Related to this challenge, researchers are making an attempt to grant sufficient equipment for enforcing a cooperative prototyping approach, place customers and designers explore together applications and their relations.

Big Data: With an estimated wide variety of 55 billion devices that will be networked through 2022, specific attention ought to be paid for data transportation, storage, access, and processing of the big quantity of records they will produce. IoT will be one of the fundamental sources of large data, and cloud will enable to shop it for lengthy time and to perform complex analyses on it. The ubiquity of cellular units and sensor pervasiveness certainly call for scalable computing platforms (every day 2.5 quintillion bytes of records are created) [8]. Handling this data easily is an indispensable challenge, as the ordinary utility performance is fairly structured on the data management provider [8]. For instance, cloud-based methods for big data summarization based totally on the extraction of semantic function are really beneath investigation [55]. Hence, following the NoSQL movement, each proprietary and open source options adopt alternative database technologies for big statistics [56]: time-series, key-value, report store, vast column stores, and layout databases. Unfortunately, no perfect data management solution exists for the cloud to manage big data [30]. Moreover, data integrity is an essential factor, now not solely for its influence on the qualities of service, however, also for protection and privacy-related elements in particular on outsourced data [57].

Sensor Networks: Sensor networks have been defined as the primary enabler of IoT [30] and as one of the five technologies that will form the world, offering the ability to measure, infer, and recognize environmental indicators, from refined ecologies and natural resources to urban environments [3]. Recent technological advances have made efficient, low-cost, and low-power miniaturized devices reachable for use in large-scale, far-flung sensing applications [58]. Moreover, smartphones, even though confined with the aid of energy consumption and reliability, come with a variety of sensors (GPS, accelerometer, digital compass, microphone, and camera), enabling a broad range of cellular functions in different domains of IoT. In this context, the timely processing of large and streaming sensor data, problem to power, and community constraints and uncertainties have been identified as the most important assignment [59]. Cloud presents new possibilities in aggregating sensor statistics and exploiting the aggregates for larger insurance and relevancy, however, at the same time affects privacy and safety [59]. Furthermore, lack of mobility being a common element of common IoT devices, the mobility of sensors introduced via smartphones as nicely as wearable electronics represents a new task [19].

Monitoring: Monitoring is a vital exercise in cloud environments for potential planning, managing resources, SLAs, overall performance and security, and troubleshooting [60]. As a consequence, cloud IoT inherits the same monitoring necessities from cloud; however, the related challenges are similarly affected with the aid of volume, variety, and velocity characteristics of IoT.

Fog Computing: Fog computing is an extension of basic cloud computing to the part of the network (as fog is a cloud close to the ground). It has been designed to help IoT applications get characterized by latency constraints and requirements for mobility and geo-distribution [61–63]. Even though computing, storage, and networking are resources of each of the cloud and the Fog, the latter has specific characteristics: side location and location awareness implying low latency; geographical distribution, and a very giant wide variety of nodes in contrast to centralized cloud; aid for mobility (through wi-fi access) and real-time interaction (instead of batch processes); assist for interplay with the cloud. Authors of [64] proposed an evaluation showing how building Fog computing initiatives is challenging. Indeed, the adoption of fog-based techniques requires various specific algorithms and methodologies dealing with reliability of the networks of smart devices and running underneath specific conditions that ask for fault-tolerant techniques.

1.6 HEALTHCARE APPLICATION THROUGH CLOUD IOT [15]

The adoption of the cloud-IoT model in the healthcare field can deliver numerous opportunities to medical IT, and specialists consider that it can significantly improve healthcare offerings and make contributions to its nonstop and systematic innovation [45]. Certainly, cloud IoT employed in this scenario is able to simplify healthcare techniques and permits to enhance the medical offerings by way of enabling the cooperation among the different entities involved. Ambient assisted living (AAL), in particular, pursuits at easing the daily lives of humans with disabilities and chronic scientific conditions.

Through the utility of cloud IoT in this field, it is possible to supply many progressive services, such as collecting patients' vital data by using a network of sensors linked to clinical devices, delivering the records to a medical center's cloud for storage and processing, good managing facts provided with the aid of sensors, or guaranteeing ubiquitous get right of entry to, or sharing of, medical data as electronic healthcare records (EHR) [45, 65, 66], depicted in Figure 1.12.

Cloud IoT allows cost-effective and high-quality, familiar medical services [45, 65]. Pervasive healthcare applications generate a giant quantity of sensor statistics that have to be managed right for in addition to evaluation and processing [67]. The adoption of cloud represents a promising solution for managing healthcare sensor statistics efficiently [67] and allows to summarize technical details, eliminating the want for expertise in, or control over, the technology infrastructure [66, 68]. Moreover, it leads to the easy automation of the technique of collecting and handing over facts at a decreased value [45]. It in addition makes cellular devices suitable for health statistics delivery, access, and communication, also on the go [69]. Cloud approves to face frequent challenges of this utility scenario such as security, privacy, and reliability, via improving medical records protection and service availability and redundancy [45, 68]. Using the efficient administration of sensor data, it is viable to supply assisted-living offerings in real-time [70]. Moreover, cloud adoption allows the execution (in the cloud) of secure multimedia-based health services, overcoming the issue of moving with heavy multimedia and safety algorithms on devices with constrained computational

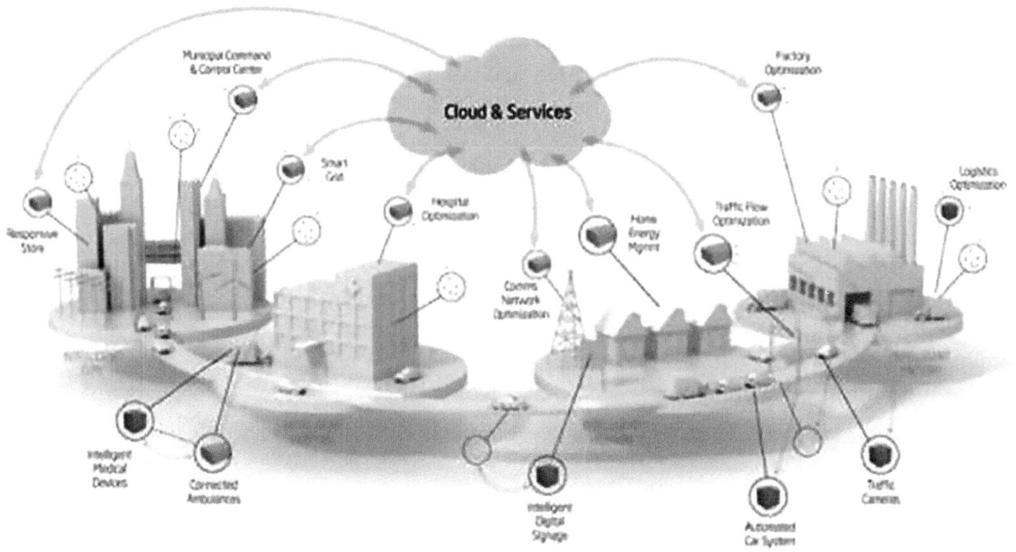

FIGURE 1.12 Services made possible through cloud-IoT model.

Source: http://siliconangle.com/.

capacity and small batteries [69], and it gives a flexible storage and processing infrastructure to function both online and offline analyses of information streams generated in healthcare body sensor networks.

In the healthcare domain, common challenges are associated with the lack of trust in information safety and privacy by users (exposure to hacker attacks, violation of medical information confidentiality, data lock-in and loss of governance, privilege abuse), overall performance unpredictability (resource exhaustion, statistics switch bottlenecks, have an impact on real-time services, streaming QoS), legal problems (contract law, intellectual property rights, information jurisdiction), and nevertheless object of investigation [45, 69, 71].

REFERENCES

[1] Zhou, J., Leppanen, T., Harjula, E., Ylianttila, M., Ojala, T., Yu, C., Jin, H., 2013. Cloudthings: A common architecture for integrating the internet of things with cloud computing. In: *CSCWD*, 2013. IEEE.

[2] Chao, H.-C., 2011. Internet of things and cloud computing for future internet. In: *Ubiquitous Intelligence and Computing*. Lecture Notes in Computer Science.

[3] Gubbi, J., Buyya, R., Marusic, S., Palaniswami, M., 2013. Internet of Things (IoT): A vision, architectural elements, and future directions. *Future Generation Computer Systems* 29 (7), 1645–1660.

[4] Atzori, L., Iera, A., Morabito, G., 2010. The internet of things: A survey. *Computer Networks* 54 (15), 2787–2805.

[5] Bassi, A., Horn, G., 2008. *Internet of Things in 2020: A roadmap for the future*. European Commission: Information Society and Media.

[6] Evangelos, A. K., Nikolaos, D. T., Anthony, C. B., 2011. Integrating RFIDs and smart objects into a unified Internet of Things Architecture. *Advances in Internet of Things* 2011.

[7] Intelligence, S. C. B., 2008. Disruptive civil technologies. Six technologies with potential impacts on US interests out to 2025.

[8] Dobre, C., Xhafa, F., 2014. Intelligent services for big data science. *Future Generation Computer Systems* 37, 267–281.

[9] Yan, L., Zhang, Y., Yang, L. T., Ning, H., 2008. *The Internet of Things: From RFID to the next-generation pervasive networked systems*. CRC Press.

[10] https://www.javatpoint.com/cloud-computing-tutorial
[11] Mell, P., Grance, T., 2009. The NIST definition of cloud computing. *National Institute of Standards and Technology* 53 (6), 50.
[12] Zhang, Q., Cheng, L., Boutaba, R., 2010. Cloud computing: State-of-the-art and research challenges. *Journal of Internet Services and Applications* 1 (1), 7–18.
[13] Spillner, J., Müller, J., Schill, A., Jun. 2013. Creating optimal cloud storage systems. *Future Generation Computer Systems* 29 (4), 1062–1072. http://dx.doi.org/10.1016/j.future.2012.06.004
[14] Subashini, S., Kavitha, V., 2011. A survey on security issues in service delivery models of cloud computing. *Journal of Network and Computer Applications* 34 (1), 1–11.
[15] Botta, Alessio, de Donato, Walter, Persico, Valerio, Pescap´e, Antonio, 2016. Integration of Cloud Computing and Internet of Things: A survey. *Future Generation Computer Systems* 56, 684–700.
[16] https://azure.microsoft.com/en-gb/overview/what-is-cloud-computing/
[17] https://www.techopedia.com/definition/26559/community-cloud
[18] http://sritsense.weebly.com/uploads/5/7/2/7/57272303/unit_iv1.pdf
[19] https://pdfs.semanticscholar.org/5f40/86a14e68192850d16436efa743329581d459.pdf
[20] https://stackoverflow.com/questions/2600454/cloud-computing-overclient-server-differences-cons-and-pros
[21] E. Deepak Chowdary, D. Yakobu, Cloud of Things (CoT) integration challenges. In: *2016 IEEE International Conference on Computational Intelligence and Computing Research.*
[22] Mohammad Riyaz Belgaum, Safeeullah Soomro, Zainab Alansari, Muhammad Alam, Shahrulniza Musa, Mazliham MohdSu'ud, Challenges: Bridge between Cloud and IoT.
[23] Lee, K., Murray, D., Hughes, D., Joosen, W., Nov 2010. Extending sensor networks into the cloud using amazon web services. In: *Networked Embedded Systems for Enterprise Applications (NESEA), 2010 IEEE International Conference on.* pp. 1–7.
[24] European Commission, 2013. Definition of a research and innovation policy leveraging Cloud Computing and IoT combination. Tender specifications, SMART 2013/0037.
[25] Fox, G. C., Kamburugamuve, S., Hartman, R. D., 2012. Architecture and measured characteristics of a cloud based internet of things. In: *Collaboration Technologies and Systems (CTS), 2012 International Conference on.* IEEE, pp. 6–12.
[26] Dash, S. K., Mohapatra, S., Pattnaik, P. K., 2010. A survey on application of wireless sensor network using cloud computing. *International Journal of Computer science & Engineering Technologies* 1 (4), 50–55.
[27] Suciu, G., Vulpe, A., Halunga, S., Fratu, O., Todoran, G., Suciu, V., 2013. Smart cities built on resilient cloud computing and secure Internet of Things. In: *Control Systems and Computer Science (CSCS), 2013 19th International Conference on.* IEEE, pp. 513–518.
[28] Rao, B. P., Saluia, P., Sharma, N., Mittal, A., Sharma, S. V., 2012. Cloud computing for Internet of Things & sensing based applications. In: *Sensing Technology (ICST), 2012 Sixth International Conference on.* IEEE, pp. 374–380.
[29] Parwekar, P., 2011. From Internet of Things towards cloud of things. In: *Computer and Communication Technology (ICCCT), 2011 2nd International Conference on.* IEEE, pp. 329–333.
[30] Zaslavsky, A., Perera, C., Georgakopoulos, D., 2013. Sensing as a service and big data. arXiv preprint arXiv:1301.0159.
[31] Fox, G. C., Kamburugamuve, S., Hartman, R. D., 2012. Architecture and measured characteristics of a cloud based internet of things. In: *Collaboration Technologies and Systems (CTS), 2012 International Conference on.* IEEE, pp. 6–12.
[32] Jeffery, K., 2014. Keynote: CLOUDs: A large virtualisation of small things. In: *The 2nd International Conference on Future Internet of Things and Cloud (FiCloud-2014).*
[33] Zikopoulos, P., Eaton, C., et al., 2011. *Understanding big data: Analytics for enterprise class Hadoop and streaming data.* McGraw-Hill Osborne Media.
[34] Abdelwahab, S., Hamdaoui, B., Guizani, M., Rayes, A., 2014. Enabling smart cloud services through remote sensing: An internet of everything enabler. *Internet of Things Journal, IEEE* 1 (3), 276–288.
[35] Evans, D., 2012. The internet of everything: How more relevant and valuable connections will change the world. *Cisco IBSG*, 1–9.
[36] Christophe, B., Boussard, M., Lu, M., Pastor, A., Toubiana, V., 2011. The web of things vision: Things as a service and interaction patterns. *Bell Labs Technical Journal* 16 (1), 55–61.

[37] Distefano, S., Merlino, G., Puliafito, A., 2012. Enabling the cloud of things. In: *Innovative Mobile and Internet Services in Ubiquitous Computing (IMIS), 2012 Sixth International Conference on*. IEEE, pp. 858–863.
[38] Mitton, N., Papavassiliou, S., Puliafito, A., Trivedi, K. S., 2012. Combining Cloud and sensors in a smart city environment. *EURASIP Journal on Wireless Communications and Networking* 2012 (1), 1–10.
[39] Bhattasali, T., Chaki, R., Chaki, N., 2013. Secure and trusted cloud of things. In: *India Conference (INDICON), 2013 Annual IEEE*. IEEE, pp. 1–6.
[40] Simmhan, Y., Kumbhare, A. G., Cao, B., Prasanna, V., 2011. An analysis of security and privacy issues in smart grid software architectures on clouds. In: *Cloud Computing (CLOUD), 2011 IEEE International Conference on*. IEEE, pp. 582–589.
[41] Subashini, S., Kavitha, V., 2011. A survey on security issues in service delivery models of cloud computing. *Journal of Network and Computer Applications* 34 (1), 1–11.
[42] Grozev, N., Buyya, R., 2014. Inter-cloud architectures and application brokering: Taxonomy and survey. *Software: Practice and Experience* 44 (3), 369–390.
[43] Li, F., Vögler, M., Claeßens, M., Dustdar, S., 2013. Efficient and scalable IoT service delivery on Cloud. In: *Cloud Computing (CLOUD), 2013 IEEE Sixth International Conference on*. IEEE, pp. 740–747.
[44] He, W., Yan, G., Xu, L. D., May 2014. Developing vehicular data cloud services in the IoT environment. *Industrial Informatics, IEEE Transactions on* 10 (2), 1587–1595.
[45] Kuo, A. M.-H., 2011. Opportunities and challenges of cloud computing to improve health care services. *Journal of medical Internet Research* 13 (3).
[46] Yun, M., Yuxin, B., 2010. Research on the architecture and key technology of Internet of Things (IoT) applied on smart grid. In: *Advances in Energy Engineering (ICAEE), 2010 International Conference on*. IEEE, pp. 69–72.
[47] Wang, C., Bi, Z., Xu, L. D., May 2014. IoT and cloud computing in automation of assembly modeling systems. *Industrial Informatics, IEEE Transactions on* 10 (2), 1426–1434.
[48] Petrolo, R., Loscri, V., Mitton, N., 2014. Towards a smart city based on cloud of things. In: *Proceedings of the 2014 ACM International Workshop on Wireless and Mobile Technologies for Smart Cities*. ACM, pp. 61–66.
[49] Lazarescu, M., 2013. Design of a WSN platform for long-term environmental monitoring for IoT applications. *Emerging and Selected Topics in Circuits and Systems, IEEE Journal on* 3 (1), 45–54.
[50] Bo, Y., Wang, H., 2011. The application of cloud computing and the internet of things in agriculture and forestry. In: *Service Sciences (IJCSS), 2011 International Joint Conference on*. IEEE, pp. 168–172.
[51] Xiao, Y., Simoens, P., Pillai, P., Ha, K., Satyanarayanan, M., 2013. Lowering the barriers to large-scale mobile crowdsensing. In: *Proceedings of the 14th Workshop on Mobile Computing Systems and Applications. HotMobile'13*. ACM, New York, NY, USA, pp. 9:1–9:6. http://doi.acm.org/10.1145/2444776.2444789
[52] Atkins, C., et al., 2013. A cloud service for end-user participation concerning the Internet of Things. In: *Signal-Image Technology & Internet-Based Systems (SITIS), 2013 International Conference on*. IEEE, pp. 273–278.
[53] Corsar, D., Edwards, P., Velaga, N., Nelson, J., Pan, J., 2011. Short paper: Addressing the challenges of semantic citizen-sensing. In: *4th International Workshop on Semantic Sensor Networks, CEUR-WS*. pp. 90–95.
[54] Cvijikj, I. P., Michahelles, F., 2011. The toolkit approach for end-user participation in the Internet of Things. In: *Architecting the Internet of Things*. Springer, pp. 65–96.
[55] Ji, Y.-K., Kim, Y.-I., Park, S., 2014. Big data summarization using semantic feature for IoT on cloud.
[56] Copie, A., Fortis, T.-F., Munteanu, V. I., 2013. Benchmarking cloud databases for the requirements of the Internet of Things. In: *34th International Conference on Information Technology Interfaces*, ITI 2013. pp. 77–82.
[57] Liu, C., Yang, C., Zhang, X., Chen, J., 2014. External integrity verification for outsourced big data in cloud and iot: A big picture. *Future Generation Computer Systems*.
[58] Akyildiz, I. F., Su, W., Sankarasubramaniam, Y., Cayirci, E., 2002. Wireless sensor networks: A survey. *Computer Networks* 38 (4), 393– 422.
[59] Zhao, F., 2010. Sensors meet the cloud: Planetary-scale distributed sensing and decision making. In: *Cognitive Informatics (ICCI), 2010 9th IEEE International Conference on*. IEEE, pp. 998–998.

[60] Aceto, G., Botta, A., de Donato, W., Pescap`e, A., 2013. Cloud monitoring: A survey. *Computer Networks* 57 (9), 2093–2115.
[61] Bonomi, F., Milito, R., Zhu, J., Addepalli, S., 2012. Fog computing and its role in the internet of things. In: *Proceedings of the First Edition of the MCC Workshop on Mobile Cloud Computing. MCC'12*. ACM, New York, NY, USA, pp. 13–16. http://doi.acm.org/10.1145/2342509.2342513
[62] Zhu, J., Chan, D., Prabhu, M., Natarajan, P., Hu, H., Bonomi, F., March 2013. Improving web sites performance using edge servers in fog computing architecture. In: *Service Oriented System Engineering (SOSE), 2013 IEEE 7th International Symposium on*. pp. 320–323.
[63] Aazam, M., Huh, E.-N., Aug 2014. Fog computing and smart gateway based communication for cloud of things. In: *Future Internet of Things and Cloud (FiCloud), 2014 International Conference on*. pp. 464–470.
[64] Madsen, H., Albeanu, G., Burtschy, B., Popentiu-Vladicescu, F., July 2013. Reliability in the utility computing era: Towards reliable fog computing. In: *Systems, Signals and Image Processing (IWSSIP), 2013 20th International Conference on*. pp. 43–46.
[65] Gachet, D., de Buenaga, M., Aparicio, F., Padr´on, V., 2012. Integrating internet of things and cloud computing for health services provisioning: The virtual cloud carer project. In: *Innovative Mobile and Internet Services in Ubiquitous Computing (IMIS), 2012 Sixth International Conference on*. IEEE, pp. 918–921.
[66] Löhr, H., Sadeghi, A.-R., Winandy, M., 2010. Securing the e-health cloud. In: *Proceedings of the 1st ACM International Health Informatics Symposium. ACM*, pp. 220–229.
[67] Doukas, C., Maglogiannis, I., 2012. Bringing IoT and cloud computing towards pervasive healthcare. In: *Innovative Mobile and Internet Services in Ubiquitous Computing (IMIS), 2012 Sixth International Conference on*. IEEE, pp. 922–926.
[68] Alagoz, F. et al., 2010. From cloud computing to mobile Internet, from user focus to culture and hedonism: The crucible of mobile health care and wellness applications. In: *ICPCA 2010*. IEEE, pp. 38–45.
[69] Nkosi, M., Mekuria, F., 2010. Cloud computing for enhanced mobile health applications. In: *Cloud Computing Technology and Science (CloudCom), 2010 IEEE Second International Conference on*. IEEE.
[70] Forkan, A., Khalil, I., Tari, Z., 2014. Cocamaal: A cloud-oriented context-aware middleware in ambient assisted living. *Future Generation Comp. Syst.* 35, 114–127.
[71] Doukas, C., Maglogiannis, I., 2011. Managing wearable sensor data through cloud computing. In: *Cloud Computing Technology and Science (CloudCom), 2011 IEEE Third International Conference on*. IEEE, pp. 440–445.

2 Practical Implementation of an Asset Management System According to ISO 55001

A Future Direction in the Cloud and IoT Paradigm

Vicente González-Prida
University of Sevilla & UNED, Sevilla, Spain

Carlos Parra and Adolfo Crespo
University of Seville, Sevilla, Spain

François Pérès and Carmen Martín
University of Toulouse, Toulouse, France

CONTENTS

2.1 INTRODUCTION

Standardization can be considered a process to implement generic best practices in organizations. Together with other benefits, the different standards are generally intended to improve business policies, reducing risks and uncertainties in work procedures (Crespo et al. 2018). Among the standards, ISO 55001 provides a series of requirements that seek the improvement of decision-making on assets management, reducing costs, enhancing operations quality, as well as increasing business profitability and users' satisfaction among other advantages. Standards are typically generic since they must be useful for a wide range of organizations. Therefore, this contribution is intended to

DOI: 10.1201/9781003155577-3

summarize specific tools and methods, providing solutions for the reliability and risk management of complex systems (Zio & Coit, 2019).

Usually, the implementation of a management system based on ISO 55000 refers to industrial physical assets, that is, machines, test equipment, and laboratory devices, all those items necessary for the production process. Obviously, the value realized by the asset will depend on the organization and may change throughout its useful life. The concept of value does not only refer to value from an economic point of view. Today, responsible companies extend this concept to the field of social, environmental, etc.

Besides effective and well-known maintenance management models (Crespo 2006), this document starts responding to some preliminary questions that any organization wonders about at the beginning of an implementation process (Crespo et al. 2019): what must be considered a physical asset? How is the asset accountability value included in a financial balance linked with the TOTEX? (The total expenditure related to an asset), why should the company invest in implementing an Asset Management System? After providing some first answers, this contribution is focused on explaining tools that are useful to implement in a practical way. Finally, connections to risk standards and uncertainty references (Aven 2012) are commented together with some conclusions. In that final section, some remarks are also commented about the possibility to apply the ISO 55001 principles to an intangible asset management system.

2.2 PRELIMINARY QUESTIONS AND ANSWERS

When an organization initiates the implementation of an Asset Management process, usually appears some hesitations about what an asset really is. Since this word is widely used in accountability area, there are sometimes some misunderstandings about what should be assumed as "asset." According to the international accounting standards, a balance sheet includes a column related to "assets," which refers to company goods and rights, and a column related to "liabilities," which refers to debts and obligations. Liability is organized in terms of enforceability, and asset column is organized in terms of liquidity. This asset column includes current assets (cash, inventories, loans to clients, etc.) and non-current or fixed assets which consider intangible assets (like copyrights), properties (like buildings, terrains, etc.), as well as plants and equipment (machines, systems, etc.). Hence, it is possible to ask what a physical asset is then. Those machines or equipment included in the fixed asset part of a financial balance sheet is, in other words, the physical assets of the company.

2.2.1 How Is the Physical Asset Linked with the Accountability Concept?

The accountability value included for such line of the balance refers to the monetary value invested in such machines. It is basically linked with the acquisition cost, which is reduced every year by the corresponding depreciated cost. There is no monetary disbursement connected to such depreciated costs. Apart from that, there is the concept of total cost of the asset ownership, which refers to all those costs that the asset may incur during its completely useful life cycle, once the item has been acquired. Complementary to this concept, there is also the term "total value of the asset ownership," which refers in this case to the profits that can be earned by the asset during its whole lifecycle. The key point with all this clarification is that once the machine is totally depreciated (from the accountability viewpoint), the asset on the contrary is usually able of course to keep on providing value and it may incur naturally at different costs (for operation, maintenance, etc.). These costs do imply a monetary disbursement. Hence, it is possible to ask what the total life cycle cost of an asset is then. It will be the sum of the CAPEX, represented by the acquisition cost (and linked with the value included in the balance sheet), plus the OPEX, represented by the sum of installation and commissioning costs, O&M costs, and plus disposal cost (or minus the asset remaining value). This life cycle cost is also known as TOTEX.

2.2.2 Why Should a Company Invest in Implementing an AM System?

Besides these first questions, an organization intended to implement an Asset Management Process usually wonders why to invest resources in that task. Usually, there is a list of theoretical benefits that can be summarized in aspects like better investment decision, increased efficiency to deliver, achievement of intended outcome, increased quality, better risk/opportunities management, enhanced reputation/social responsibility, etc. All these aspects are certainly profiting items gathered from the implementation of an Asset Management Systems, but they are not sufficiently tangible as desired by a board of directors. In order to make more practical and convincible the arguments, here below are some examples in order to justify the implementation effort:

- In reference to investments, an appropriate Asset Management System helps to compare assets and, consequently, is a good tool that supports the decision on what to buy, what to renew, or what to keep on maintaining.
- In reference to assurance policies, an exhaustive Asset Management System helps to control the assets, mainly those considered critical, to increase knowledge on the assets and, consequently, to receive bonuses or discounts from the assurance companies, reducing the corresponding expenses or increasing the corresponding allowance.
- In reference to the supply chain management, and connected to the first bullet, data compiled can be considered as an additional factor (besides purchasing cost, quality, and delivery time) to decide the purchase of an item or service to one provider in front of other bidders.

2.3 PRACTICAL CLARIFICATION ON ASSET MANAGEMENT CONCEPT

Asset management is usually understood as "those coordinated activities of an organization to realize value from its assets." Sometimes, this definition is not enough to convince the different levels of an organization about the implementation of such a management system. Therefore, it is useful to set questions in order to understand how the organization is managing its asset. For instance:

- What is the Asset Inventory?
- Who is responsible for the Assets?
- How important are these Assets for the Company?
- How will these Assets behave?
- Are the resources assigned efficiently for each asset?
- What is the performance of the Assets?
- How much will the assets cost during their whole life cycle?
- How are the Assets linked to the business goals?

In general, Asset Management responds to these questions and takes decisions according to data. Among the previous questions, one of the most important and strategic questions is the last one related to the link to the business goals. In order to create value, organizations can establish different types of strategies. Economically, strategies of companies are basically focused on obtaining a benefit, whether short or long term. Understanding that the benefit follows this formula profit = revenues – expenses, strategies can be materialized in objectives that will be aimed at, for example:

- In order to increase revenue or increase customer value (they would be growth strategies) or
- In order to improve cost structure and increase asset utilization (they would be productivity strategies)

From the perspective of physical assets, what should a machine do for the organization to increase revenue? It will be interesting that when the machine is necessary, it fails little, which means it has high reliability. Likewise, what should a machine do for the organization to reduce costs? It will be interesting that the operation and maintenance costs are low. In order to do this, downtimes must be reduced. That means in this sense, it is interesting that the asset has a high maintainability. In short, the above concepts are encompassed by the term "availability," which considers a high average operating time (linked to reliability) and a low repair time (linked to maintainability). In other words, the creation of value implies business general objectives to which, there are objectives in the management of assets that must be aligned. For that purpose, it is needed to follow those processes established in the company for such asset management. Aligned with the objectives of the company, the objectives of asset management should be, for example, to:

- Improve quality, reliability, and availability;
- Be more cost efficient;
- Extend the service life, etc.

An important aspect in asset management is the concept of maintenance, since it has a very important function throughout the life cycle of machines. According to ISO 13306, maintenance is considered as those activities focused on reducing failures. For this purpose, two types of maintenance can be distinguished, one applied before a failure (event in which the asset loses the conditions to fulfill its function) and prevent it from taking place (preventive) or after it (corrective) for restoring the equipment to conditions in which it fulfills its required function. The rest of the subdivisions comply with different criteria. For example, the corrective can be done immediately or deferred and even programmed. Preventive maintenance has been subdivided into condition or systematic, depending on whether it is carried out based on the conditions observed in the equipment or based on a series of predetermined measures of its use respectively. Taking ISO 13306 on maintenance terminology as a reference, the predictive maintenance would be a type of condition-based maintenance. Condition-based maintenance includes the detection, diagnosis, and prognosis of failures using, generally, data-mining techniques. Therefore, detecting or diagnosing are equally relevant to predicting.

Maintenance and asset management are related, but they must be distinguished. Generally, maintenance is understood as those activities aimed at reducing faults and keeping the operation of a machine. This is therefore an operative activity with a short/medium-term vision. Asset management adds a more strategic and long-term vision, since it considers activities that will be carried out throughout the asset life cycle. This includes, therefore, economic aspects such as the possibility of new investments, extensions of useful life, and replacements, as well as operational aspects. That means, decision-making may change, if the operational context varies, as well as logistics aspects of spare parts management, training, subcontracting, etc. In other words, asset management has a greater scope than maintenance, both in time horizons and in organization areas.

2.4 PRACTICAL VIEW ON ISO 55000 FAMILY OF STANDARDS

The family of standards ISO 55000 is constituted by three norms:

- ISO 55000: which refers to terminology and principles
- ISO 55001: which refers to the requirements
- ISO 55002: which includes guidelines for the implementation

This family of standards is structured on a "Plan-Do-Check-Act cycle" basis. It is basically a Deming cycle, similar to the one applied for the ISO 9000. According to this cycle, value is added by creating alignment from the "context" element through to the "improvement" element. However, this system cannot work isolated – it must be integrated with other management systems within the business. How must this standard be focused on a company? All these aspects shall be translated into a series of processes and procedures of the company. For sure, many procedures already exist in every company, although they must be updated, considering now this new vision on asset management. Other procedures will need probably to be new. In any case, it is important to review the whole body of documents in order to assure that Asset Management is incorporated into the business policies, strategies, plans, and processes – that means, in other words, to apply a gap analysis to the company procedures system.

Once the company has decided to implement an Asset Management System according to the ISO 55000, it will require, as inputs, the knowledge of the business context and interest parties, the identified risk and opportunities, as well as other aspects like the business management policies, legal requirements, and the asset inventory. With these inputs, the proposed asset management process will be a cyclical management framework, where the main tools are:

- Criticality analysis (applied to the asset inventory at a specific taxonomy level)
- Reliability Centered Maintenance (as part of the asset operation and maintenance)
- RAM analysis (useful as indicator for the asset performance)
- Root cause analysis of failures (applied to improve knowledge on incidents and non-conformities)
- Life cycle cost analysis (needed for CAPEX/OPEX decisions)

As outputs, the company shall obtain a management plan for each asset that will be more exhaustive for those assets considered as critical. These outputs must be linked to those company procedures related to continuous improvement, management review, investments procedure, etc. Possible collaborative projects in this field are of course all those related to find support from the application of new technologies, in particular IoT in order to automatize as much as possible the data compilation and cloud tools in order to facilitate the remote connectivity and the data transmission and storage.

2.5 REVIEW OF TOOLS FOR THE ASSET MANAGEMENT SYSTEM

2.5.1 Asset Inventory and Criticality Analysis

This methodology shall enable a prioritization in the assets inventory:

- To reduce resources where they are less needed (non-critical assets)
- For improvements in routine maintenance plans
- To assign resources where they should be more targeted, even with a contingency plan (critical assets)

First, the company must have an asset inventory for each manufacturing center, which is a list of all the assets used by such factory (owned or leased). In order to make the list, it will be needed to define previously the intervention level. This level will depend on each manufacturing center, where such center should define the list referred to the level in which the maintenance plans are applied. There is a standard (ISO 14224), which is generally used for its clarity when defining taxonomy and levels, although it is for the petrochemical field. The taxonomy may range assets from the most general classification (the industry or the business line) to the most concrete (as the components or parts). It is usually structured in the form of a tree, in a parent–child relationship between levels. Systems or equipment unit (level 6 or 5 of the ISO 14224 classification) commonly makes the assets inventory.

Once the asset inventory is known, the criticality analysis is performed. The criticality of an asset is an indication of how important it is for the business in terms of realizing value. Since the criticality in terms of value is difficult to measure, what is applied is the calculation of the dual problem:

that is to say, criticality will be a measure of the worst-case impact that the failure of the asset could have on the business. This methodology would consist, for instance, the product of the frequency of a failure (or a factor that refers to the greater or lesser occurrence of a failure event), multiplied by the consequence of this failure (which may refer to the costs generated by the failure or a factor of the greater or lesser effect that this failure event has). The different factors require a consensus among experts, constituted by the Asset Management Team. Among the factors, usually safety is enhanced in front of the other ones (operational impact, maintenance cost). Once applied to this analysis, the list of assets can be ranked (as a Pareto's graphic), where there will be non-critical, medium, and critical assets.

2.5.2 Process for Non-Critical Assets

In non-critical assets, an increment in the frequency of failures does not lead to drastic changes in their criticality. The frequency of its revisions in the maintenance plan can be modified, without affecting the operational availability of the plant. What to do with these non-critical assets? They must be studied by a cost-risk-benefit analysis considering that, sometimes, the necessity of such non-critical assets may be due to legal reasons. In any case, these actions allow the company to get early savings (early quick wins):

- Removal of unnecessary maintenance activities for the asset
- Cost savings on preventive maintenance activities for the asset
- Assessment of criticality status change, resulting from modifications to preventive maintenance activities

On the other extreme of the Pareto's graphic, the critical assets appear. With these items, it is recommended to perform an RCM analysis (Reliability Centered Maintenance). It allows us to know the root cause of the problems, possible weaknesses of the assets, and thus to allocate the necessary resources. Therefore, these assets will follow the following sections.

2.5.3 Process for Critical Assets

Those elements with high criticality deserve a deeper and exhaustive treatment. The methodologies suggested for these assets are (among other possible ones):

- RCM (Reliability Centered Maintenance): This tool is a kind of FMEA versioned to physical assets. With this methodology, failure modes and their effects are analyzed, and current maintenance policies are improved. In order to apply properly this analysis, a multidisciplinary team is needed where the areas of Operations, Maintenance and Occupational, Health and Safety (OHS) are at least represented.
- RAM (Reliability, Availability, and Maintainability): These parameters or metrics are calculated in order to get information about the asset performance. They are useful, for example, on work progress, labor rate assessment, etc. In order to obtain these results, it is necessary to gather data such as Operating and Repair Times
- LCC (Life cycle cost): The total cost of the asset is estimated during its useful life. It is similar to an EAC (estimation at completion analysis), where possible deviations can be observed or decisions if the useful life should be extended, if the asset should be replaced, etc. can be taken.

The fact of estimating the cost throughout the life cycle allows comparing, for example, different options to know which machine can be more or less convenient when deciding on an investment. In the case of an asset in function, calculating the incurred cost (similar to an ITD, incurred to date), and estimating the cost until its completion (similar to the ETC, estimation to completion), can provide a useful knowledge as to:

- cost deviations (if the asset is incurring more or less costs than planned),
- if extending the asset's useful life (considering the extra cost) may be interesting,
- if the replacement of an already amortized asset may be a good choice.

After the application of this practical process, a management plan is obtained for each asset. It usually includes a summary that compiles the main results of all the above-mentioned analyses as well as a decision sheet that the asset management team proposes. These possible actions shall be reported to the senior managing board in order to decide for instance:

- Discard the asset
- Reduce maintenance
- Maintain the current level of maintenance
- Reduce Repair Time
- Increase maintenance
- Replace the asset

2.6 INTELLIGENT ASSET MANAGEMENT FOCUSED ON CLOUDIOT

Intelligent asset monitoring enabled by CloudIoT comprises aware and integrated units that may run as a "single strategic system." That enables entities and companies to transform digitally their operations. Now with CloudIoT, they have become a single smart solution. Therefore, it offers many advantages in comparison to traditional solutions. This transformational technology may change the way of doing things and disrupts consequently business processes. Intelligent asset monitoring (enabled by CloudIoT) achieves to perform everything that traditional solutions can do, allowing additionally to know where the asset is located, what the asset condition is, the asset lifecycle management, control of processes, etc., including also intelligence to automated workflows, alert timing, data insights, dynamic asset monitoring, predictive maintenance, cross-domain analytics, and real-time visibility. Intelligent asset management generally comprises the following aspects:

- Tracking of remote asset
- Asset condition monitoring
- Asset life cycle management
- Automation of asset workflow
- Predictive asset maintenance

There can be many derivative solutions or variations of these in order to make CloudIoT specific to an industry or a business process (Saraubon et al. 2019). Intelligent asset management applications in various industries can be found, for example, in logistics (Agalianos et al. 2020), healthcare industry (Lee et al. 2015), or railway sector (Sarkar et al. 2020).

Most companies that have high-cap assets on their facilities or spread across different locations have many issues to solve, such as assets with poor health, excessive maintenance costs, high mean time to repair, and ineffective performance. CloudIoT focused on intelligent asset management may offer a more holistic approach to asset control rather than a module-based approach. CloudIoT provides asset management the right visibility for organizations to overcome these challenges. The main advantage of CloudIoT is the capability to access domain data and seamlessly integrate it with a unified solution so that management has the knowledge to make the right decision. CloudIoT solutions may bring the inherent value of automation, innovation, and digital transformation.

Traditional alternatives provided a lot of data but lacked information. There was a great deal of human involvement, offline data, iterations, etc. The time delay made many reactive activities or excessive of preventive tasks.

CloudIoT solutions may connect however machines with people, with processes and systems in ways never seen before. This makes automation easier. Human intervention is required only for decision-making in the place of performing routinely tasks. The main advantage of intelligent asset monitoring is the automation of all this. Thus, one increases accuracy, reduces costs, improves process efficiency, and eliminates non-compliance. Physical checks, routine tasks, and regular monitoring can be drastically reduced and can now be performed based on the condition and actual use of the asset.

The possibilities of providing innovative added value with intelligent asset management are endless. Data analytics aids in real-time or near-real-time decision-making with the help of machine learning techniques and other advanced intelligent tools. Data from multiple machines embedded with information on product usage can reveal new insights that have never been seen before. This enabled management to find innovative decisions and solutions to meet the common challenges that their company has faced for many years.

2.7 CONCLUSIONS AND FUTURE RESEARCH LINES

At the beginning of this document, the physical assets and the asset management concept were linked to the business goals through the introduction of accountability concepts and the definition of profits as the results of the difference between revenues and expenses. Another way to see the effect of asset management on the business goals is by using economic ratios such as ROIC (Return on Invested Capital). This is the percentage obtained by dividing the result of the net operation profit after taxes (NOPAT), by the invested capital.

Among the elements that would be part of the Net Operating Profit can be found:

- Improvements in OHS, Operations and Maintenance, as well as in processes
- Reductions in labor and storage rates for spare parts and tools
- Applications of Lean techniques, continuous improvement, good practices
- Among the elements that would be part of Invested Capital can be found
- Disposal of obsolete or unused equipment, optimizing inventory
- Improvements in investments and resource allocation
- Meeting performance requirements, reduction of downtimes

Together with this, new challenges appear for the integration of Cloud and IoT tools in order to simplify the handling of the big data generated by all this set of methodologies. The new industrial scenarios require the application of concurrent engineering concepts where IoT presents useful advantages as, for instance, when it is intended to implement such a management system as the one depicted in this chapter. In a few words, this document contributes to justifying the advantages of implementing an asset management system and describes in a practical way a general process according to the main topics of the ISO 55001 requirements. Nevertheless, future lines may deal with intangible asset management system, according to ISO 55001. In particular, knowledge management refers to those activities needed to realize value from the know-how and the human resources of a company. For this case, it will be needed for the application as well of the standard ISO 30401, which refers to the requirements for implementing a knowledge management system.

To conclude, companies in the digital age are transforming to combine products and services in unique ways to offer their products as a service. A CloudIoT solution focused on intelligent asset management is the key to incorporating new lines of service or new business models in organizations and companies. Traditionally, a company's physical assets, once seen as a cost or burden on the balance sheet, can now be managed effectively to generate additional revenue. With more data, control, and vision, a company can observe trends in which it can identify new market opportunities. Capitalizing on those opportunities can generate more revenue for the business.

REFERENCES

Agalianos, K., Ponis, S. T., Aretoulaki, E., Plakas, G., & Efthymiou, O. (2020). Discrete event simulation and digital twins: review and challenges for logistics. *Procedia Manufacturing*, *51*, 1636–1641.

Aven, T. (2012). The risk concept-historical and recent development trends. *Reliability Engineering & System Safety*, 99, 33–44. ISSN 0951-8320. DOI: 10.1016/j.ress.2011.11.006.

Crespo, A., González-Prida, V., Gómez, J. (Eds.). (2018). *Advanced Maintenance Modelling for Asset Management. Techniques and Methods for Complex Industrial Systems*. Springer International Publishing. ISBN 978-3-319-58045-6.

Crespo, Márquez A. (2006). *The Maintenance Management Framework. Models and Methods for Complex Systems Maintenance*. London. Springer Verlag.

ISO/EN 13306, Maintenance terminology. (2017)

ISO 14224:2016, Petroleum, petrochemical and natural gas industries - Collection and exchange of reliability and maintenance data for equipment.

ISO-30401-2018, Knowledge management systems. Requirements.

ISO 55001: 2014, Asset Management-Management systems-Requirements.

Lee, C.K.M., Cheng, M.N., & Ng, C.K. (2015). IoT-based asset management system for healthcare-related industries. *International Journal of Engineering Business Management*, 7(Godište 2015), 7–19.

Saraubon, K., Chinakul, P., & Chanpen, R. (2019, December). Asset Management System using NFC and IoT Technologies. In *Proceedings of the 2019 3rd International Conference on Software and e-Business* (pp. 124–128).

Sarkar, D., Patel, H., & Dave, B. (2020). Development of integrated cloud-based Internet of Things (IoT) platform for asset management of elevated metro rail projects. *International Journal of Construction Management*, 1–10.

Zio, E., & Coit, D. (2019). Preface for SI: RAMS optimization. *Reliability Engineering & System Safety*, 106620.

3 ERP on the Cloud
Evolution, Benefits, and Critical Success Factors

Deepak Saxena
School of Management and Entrepreneurship, Indian Institute of Technology Jodhpur, Jodhpur, India

Jitendra Kumar Verma
IT Discipline, Indian Institute of Foreign Trade, New Delhi (Kakinada Campus Cell), India

CONTENTS

3.1 INTRODUCTION

Enterprise Resource Planning (ERP) systems are considered the lifeblood of modern business. An ERP may be defined as *configurable information systems package that provides seamless integration of information and information-based business processes within and across functional areas in an organization* (Kumar and van Hillegersberg, 2000, p.23). The importance of ERP systems may be understood from the fact that virtually all Fortune 500 companies run on ERP systems. Moreover, many are now moving to cloud-based ERP, which is the key focus of this chapter. The chapter is organized as follows. The next section puts the development of cloud ERP in context by discussing the evolution of ERP systems since the late 1960s. This is followed by outlining distinct benefits of cloud-based ERP systems. Thereafter, critical success factors for cloud ERP are discussed. It covers the factors that are drawn from traditional ERP research that are still applicable to cloud ERP, as well as the factors that are unique to the cloud-based environment. Finally, the chapter concludes by noting the development of enterprise of things – formed by the integration of Internet of Things with the ERP system.

DOI: 10.1201/9781003155577-4

3.2 EVOLUTION OF ERP SYSTEMS

This section provides a quick overview of the evolution of ERP systems and their use in organizations from its genesis in the 1960s to the present (Figure 3.1). Rather than focusing on a package or a company, the discussion is oriented towards the evolution of the ERP artefact in general since the 1960s.

3.2.1 MRP: Predicting Material Requirement (1960–1970s)

Material Requirement Planning (MRP) systems were developed in the late 1960s to assist organizations in determining the number of parts, components, and materials needed to manufacture the final product. MRP systems calculated the product or parts requirements based on the bill of materials, inventory data, and the master production schedule and determined when to release the material

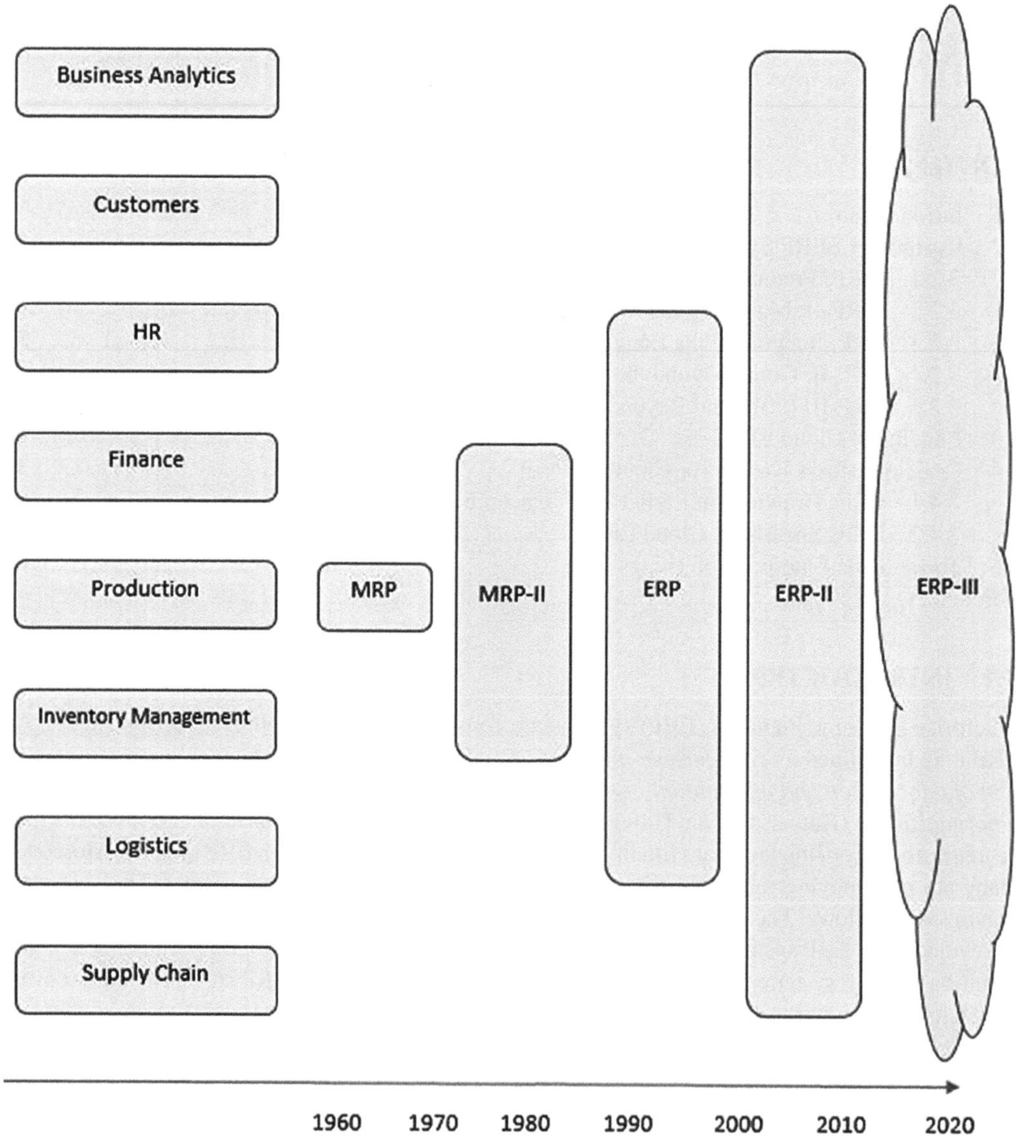

FIGURE 3.1 Evolution of ERP systems.

replenishment order (Alwabel et al., 2006). These systems were particularly useful for the bigger production plants engaged in producing a variety of products using several components. MRP systems were adopted by the manufacturing industry to reduce the inventory cost and to maintain the safety stock. However, one limitation of MRP systems was that they worked only when the demand was predictable and when the master production schedule was available. Therefore, a need arose for additional functionality to support the planning process. This resulted in the advent of MRP-II systems.

3.2.2 MRP-II: Managing the Manufacturing Resources (the 1980s)

Manufacturing Resource Planning (MRP-II) systems were introduced in the 1980s with a focus on optimizing manufacturing processes. This was done by synchronizing the material handling with the production requirements. It integrated the financial and production system and included activities such as purchasing, production planning, production scheduling, shop floor management, and distribution management. MRP-II systems provided long-range, intermediate, and short-term plans, which could be adjusted depending on the changing requirements of the plant. Some MRP-II systems also had simulation capability to enable predictions. However, MRP-II systems were difficult to integrate seamlessly and were prone to errors (Alwabel et al., 2006). Therefore, organizations looked for a seamless system which could be integrated with the other areas of the enterprise. This resulted in the advent of ERP systems in the next decade.

3.2.3 ERP: Integrating the Enterprise (the 1990s)

ERP systems were developed at the beginning of the 1990s with the promise of providing enterprise-wide cross-functional integration and coordination. ERP systems were based on the technological foundations of MRP and MRP-II and provided tighter and real-time integration beyond merely integrating the manufacturing process. ERP systems integrated business processes like accounting, financial management, human resource management, project management, maintenance scheduling (Davenport, 1998) along with the standard functions provided by the MRP-II system, such as inventory management, manufacturing, distribution, and transportation, thereby providing accessibility, visibility, and consistency across the enterprise (Rashid et al., 2002). The ERP systems could also support a variety of production approaches such as Just-in-Time or lean production methods.

ERP systems were different from their predecessors in three significant ways. First, a distinctive feature of the ERP system was the seamless integration of various functions within the organization (Davenport, 1998). This was made possible by the development of relational database systems that could support complex database operations. In contrast to different files, ERP systems used a single relational database to store the data. Therefore, changes made by one function were visible to other functions in real time. Second, ERP systems were also architecturally different from the earlier systems, in the sense that they offered modular implementation. This meant that different functionalities of the software were available to users as different modules of a single ERP package and companies could choose to include or exclude certain modules depending on their needs. Third, ERP vendors claimed to include industry 'best practices' (Davenport, 1998) in the workflow of the software, which purported to provide a competitive advantage to the implementing organization. As the decade progressed, vendors started offering new packages to cover additional functions of the organization (Rashid et al., 2002).

3.2.4 ERP-II: Going beyond the Enterprise (the 2000s)

After recovering from the burst of the dot-com bubble in early 2000s and subsequent consolidation of the vendors (Jacobs and Weston, 2007), ERP designers focused their attention on providing extended functionality to their ERP systems, often termed as Extended ERP or ERP-II. This phase was primarily marked by the inclusion of modules which linked external stakeholders (e.g. customers and suppliers) of the organization into the ES package (Alwabel et al., 2006; Rashid et al., 2002) to facilitate e-commerce. This resulted in the development and inclusion of modules such as Customer Relationship Management and Supply Chain Management in ERP packages. The second set of extensions was introduced to make better use of data stored in the ERP system by using advanced mathematical and decision-making techniques to optimize business operations. This resulted in the development of modules such as Business Intelligence as an add-on to the core ERP package.

3.2.5 ERP-III (2010 and Beyond)

ERP is now being offered using cloud-computing technology, sometimes termed 'ERP-III' (Saeed et al., 2012; Wan and Clegg, 2010). Cloud-based ERP provides service to its users by connecting with the computing 'cloud,' which is usually hosted on vendor's site. This does not require expensive hardware and software installation at client's site, thereby significantly reducing the clients' infrastructure costs. The global cloud-ERP market was valued (AMR, 2018) at $13 million in 2016 and is expected to reach $32 million by 2023, growing annually at the rate of 13.6% from 2017 to 2023, thus making it a more promising opportunity for ERP vendors. It is no surprise then all major on-premise ERP vendors are also offering cloud-based versions, for example, SAP HANA S/4, Microsoft Dynamics 365, or Oracle NetSuite. The next section discusses the benefits of cloud ERP.

3.3 BENEFITS OF CLOUD ERP

Cloud ERP offers the same set of benefits as standard ERPs do – operational efficiency, data standardization, business process integration, real-time data processing, implementation of best practices, cost savings, standardized reporting, etc. These benefits are not explored here in detail since such benefits are widely documented elsewhere (e.g. Davenport, 1998). This section focuses on the benefits that are gained primarily due to cloud-based implementation of ERP.

1. *Lower setup costs*: Since the hosting environment and infrastructure is often shared among clients, setup cost for cloud ERP is much lower (Bharathi and Mandal, 2015; Johansson et al., 2015) than that for on-premise ERP. Cost for cloud ERP mostly consists of the subscription costs, provided basic computing and network infrastructure are already established. While the exact pricing may vary depending on many factors(hosting location, number of users, number of applications required, and level of customization required), setup costs are significantly lower for cloud ERP than those for the on-premise ERP (requiring in-house infrastructure, in-house ERP team, and licensing costs).
2. *Lower IT management costs*: In case of a cloud-based ERP, the organization can manage with limited IT infrastructure and with a smaller IT team since most work is conducted by the vendor, thus reducing the IT management cost (Bharathi and Mandal, 2015; Johansson et al., 2015). In contrast, on-premise implementation usually requires a large IT infrastructure and ERP team even after the implementation to ensure smooth functioning and to resolve operational issues.
3. *Higher reliability*: Since ERP vendors use the same cloud infrastructure for their clients (unless the client has specifically requested a private cloud), they implement higher redundancy and reliability measures (Elmonem et al., 2016; Saeed et al., 2012) than what individual client may be able to implement. As part of their cloud infrastructure, cloud ERP vendors maintain high-capacity data centres and employ specialists to reliably manage and optimize the cloud. Moreover, they employ stronger security mechanisms to protect their business interest.

4. *Version control and upgrades*: In case of on-premise ERP, different clients may be running diverse versions of ERP with different levels of customization. Thus, it becomes a complicated and costly exercise to maintain diverse ERP implementations. In contrast, since the vendor uses the same instance of ERP software to provide cloud services to its clients, it becomes easier to perform ERP maintenance (Elmonem et al., 2016; Saeed et al., 2012) in terms of version control and upgrades.
5. *Scalability*: On-premise ERP requires careful planning and project management to scale up the operations (implementing new modules or including new locations for instance) so much so that it becomes an independent project. In contrast, cloud ERPs are designed to be scalable (Bharathi and Mandal, 2015; Saeed et al., 2012) in a way that the implementing organization may start small and add more business processes as and when they are ready. Moreover, cloud-ERP vendors provide standard application programming interfaces (APIs) to connect the ERP with other cloud applications such as electronic document management systems or knowledge management systems.
6. *Mobility*: On-premise ERP is mostly designed to provide access from the work systems connected to the Local Area Network (LAN) and occasionally via Virtual Private Network (VPN), cloud ERP gives a huge boost to employee mobility (Peng and Gala, 2014) as they can access cloud ERP via a web browser as long as they have a working device and an active internet connection. Moreover, cloud ERP vendors are now increasingly providing mobile apps to access ERP on the go. Mobility of the cloud ERP is a crucial tool in ensuring seamless business connectivity beyond functional and geographical boundaries.

3.4 CRITICAL SUCCESS FACTORS FOR CLOUD ERP

The concept of 'success factors' was first introduced by Daniel (1961) in his seminal HBR article *Management Information Crisis*. He differentiated among three types of useful data for companies – environmental, competitive, and internal. He argued that in reporting internal data, a company's information system must be discriminating and selective. An information system should focus on success factors, which according to him usually are three to six for most of the companies within an industry. He defined success factors as those key jobs which must be done exceedingly well for a company to be successful. Rockart (1979) refined the concept further and introduced the notion of Critical Success Factors (CSF) defining it as those few critical areas where things must go right for the business to flourish. If the results in these critical areas are found to be inadequate, organization's efforts for the period are bound to be less than desired. He notes that the CSF areas should receive constant and careful attention from the managers. Over the years, the CSF approach has been extensively used in diverse areas of information systems and business, including in the area of ERP implementation.

3.4.1 CSFs Drawn from Earlier ERP Research

ERP research in the past has identified a list of CSFs for on-premise implementation (see Finney and Corbett, 2007; Saxena and McDonagh, 2017; Shaul and Tauber, 2013). Most CSFs identified for the in-house implementation are also applicable in the cloud ERP context with minor adjustments as discussed below:

1. *Business Process Reengineering*: The design of the ERP package is based on the best practices in an industry, whereas organizational business processes are often a product of its history and evolution. Consequently, there is often a mismatch between the business processes inscribed within the ERP and the business process followed in the organization (Davenport, 1998). While in-premise ERP provides the option of software customization, cloud-based ERP vendors usually share the same instance of the software for their

subscribers, thus limiting the scope for customization. Hence, the issue of business process reengineering assumes greater significance in the cloud ERP context.

2. *Change Management*: Due to significant changes introduced by the business process reengineering, organizational roles and responsibilities may also change (Davenport, 1998; Saxena and McDonagh, 2014), resulting in limiting or increasing the influence of certain user groups. This often results in employee dissatisfaction, or even resistance. To address these issues, user engagement, training, and communication (Huq et al., 2006) are often recommended as a strategy for successful change management during ERP implementation.
3. *Project Management*: Since an ERP project requires huge mobilization of organizational resources, dedicated project teams with a balance of IT and business knowledge are recommended (Rothenberger et al., 2010; Saxena and McDonagh, 2017) for successful ERP implementation. Other recommendations include the appointment of experienced project manager, constitution of steering committee, and most importantly a formalized project approach and methodology. While the same level of project management effort may not be required in the cloud-based ERP project, it still requires significantly more effort than traditional IT projects.
4. *Top Management Vision and Support*: ERP implementation is a resource-intensive and often a long-term exercise. For this reason, continuous top management support is considered crucial (Dong et al., 2009) in terms of visioning and planning, leadership, and resource allocation. Top management support is considered equally crucial for cloud ERP projects (Gupta and Misra, 2016; Peng and Gala, 2014), especially in negotiating the subscription cost of the ERP.
5. *Inter-departmental Coordination*: An ERP implementation may also result in the change in power structure, for instance, reduced power of purchasing department since vendor information is directly available to the line managers via ERP. Hence, it often results in inter-departmental rivalry. Moreover, since the business processes often cut across departments (Davenport, 1998; Saxena and McDonagh, 2014), inter-departmental coordination becomes crucial. Since there are limited (most popular) modules on offer via cloud ERP (Gupta et al., 2017), the issue may become tricky due to some departments being on cloud ERP and others working with legacy systems.
6. *Vendor Management*: ERP vendor, while acting as a partner in the implementation process, also acts towards maximizing its profit. Moreover, once the ERP package is implemented, the organization is often locked-in with the product and the vendor. This issue is equally applicable to in-house (Markus and Tanis, 2000) as well as for cloud-based (Peng and Gala, 2014; Demi and Haddara, 2018) ERP. Therefore, careful contracting and effective vendor management remain a critical factor during ERP implementation.
7. *Consultants*: ERP consultants often act as a bridge between the organization and the vendor. These consultants have the required domain knowledge as well as an understanding of the system architecture. Hence, experienced consultants or external advisory support is recommended (Ko, 2014) for successful ERP implementation. Considering that cloud-based model is relatively new, its understating in the client organizations is even less. Hence, the involvement of consultants becomes more critical for cloud ERP.
8. *Implementation Strategy*: Depending on the complexity of the project, an organization may choose between a big bang approach versus an incremental approach (Davenport, 1998; Saxena and McDonagh, 2017) for implementing traditional ERP. The big bang approach involves implementing all modules all at once and helps in maintaining an efficient interface between the modules. In contrast, an incremental approach involves implementing modules one by one and has the benefit of cumulative learning. Since it offers many modules, same considerations are also applicable to cloud ERP (Panorama Consulting, 2019).
9. *Knowledge Management*: The issue of knowledge management in an ERP project needs to be considered at three levels – knowledge transfer from the consultants to the client,

knowledge management within the implementation team, and knowledge transfer from the implementation team to the end users. This often requires new knowledge management framework and a new knowledge structure in the organization (Lee and Lee, 2000). The issue of knowledge management acquires special salience in the context of cloud ERP, since it is often feared that it may result in the loss of IT competency (Duan et al., 2013; Elmonem et al., 2016; Gupta et al., 2017) in the client organization.

10. *Contextual Factors*: Many external factors such as national or industry context have key influence on ERP implementation. Since most ERP packages are developed in Western countries, they need to be localized for the needs of developing countries. In recent years, in many Asian countries (especially in China and South Korea), local vendors are providing solutions to satisfy local needs at a lesser cost (Liang and Xue, 2004). Cloud computing has, in fact, resulted in the proliferation of small cloud-based ERP vendors, thereby breaking the monopoly of industry leaders.

3.4.2 CSFs Specific to Cloud ERP

However, cloud architecture has also introduced some CSFs specific to cloud ERP. These factors are discussed below.

1. *Public vs Private Cloud*: By definition, cloud services are hosted by an external vendor that could be the ERP vendor or a third-party service provider. Within the cloud service, a client may opt for exclusive space (private cloud) or shared space (public cloud), as shown in Figure 3.2. Private cloud is more costly but provides more flexibility and bandwidth (Panorama Consulting, 2019). This option is more suitable for bigger organizations with

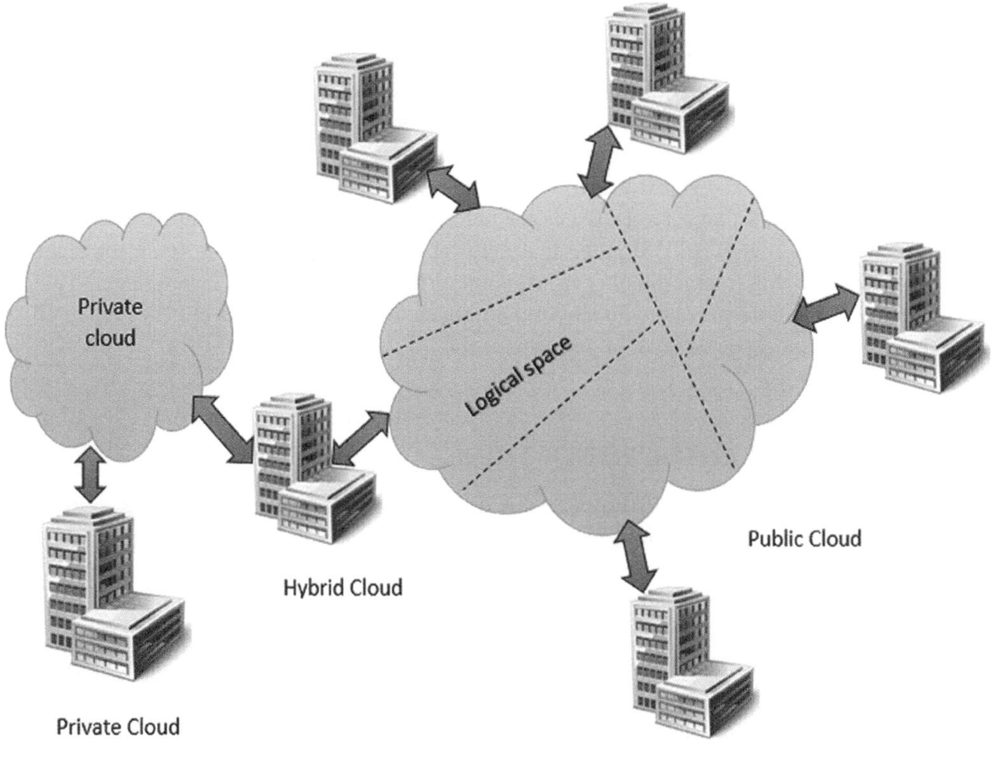

FIGURE 3.2 Cloud architecture for ERP implementation.

complex requirements. In contrast, public cloud is shared by several clients, though operating in separate logical space. This option is cheaper and more suitable for small and midsize organizations (Johansson et al., 2015) with relatively straightforward requirements. Depending on the situation, a client may also opt for a hybrid solution, hosting sensitive processes on a private cloud (or even in-house) and the rest on the public cloud.

2. *Total Cost of Ownership*: Cloud-based ERPs are designed in a way that they allow for regular maintenance and upgrades from the vendor. This results in a longer ERP lifecycle for cloud-based implementation (Demi and Haddara, 2018; Saxena and McDonagh, 2019). While it results in relative stability for the client, it also results in higher total cost of ownership due to recurring subscription cost, usually on a per user basis. In other words, while the upfront cost is significantly lower for cloud ERP (in comparison to in-house ERP), the long-term cost may be higher due to hidden costs in the contract (Elmonem et al., 2016; Gupta et al., 2017). This would especially be a case if the organization expands considerably to include more business processes or more number of users. In contrast, total cost of ownership may be lower for in-house ERP if the organization is a large complex organization that already owns critical IT infrastructure. Thus, organization size, growth potential, and existing IT infrastructure influence the total cost of ERP ownership.
3. *Data Security*: Data security seems to be the biggest concern (Elmonem et al., 2016; Gupta et al., 2017; Verma and Katti, 2015a) for organizations contemplating cloud-based ERP. Especially larger enterprises are more apprehensive in moving their critical applications to the cloud since potential loss due to security and privacy breach is higher for them (Johansson et al., 2015). However, the concerns regarding security seem to be misplaced since no severe breaches are reported by major cloud ERP vendor. Moreover, since cloud vendors are aware that they are the most visible targets, they invest heavily in ensuring the security of their offerings (Panorama Consulting, 2019) lest they lose multiple customers. All major cloud-service providers employ much tighter security controls often enabled by machine learning and artificial intelligence tools.
4. *ERP Performance*: Another concern raised for cloud ERP is the expected level of performance – both in terms of network performance and cloud performance. Usually performance of the cloud is not a big concern since not only do the cloud-service providers ensure redundancy and excess capacity on the cloud, they also use different load-balancing techniques (Verma and Katti, 2015b) to optimize the cloud performance. While Gupta and Misra (2016) show that network issues are not significant for small and midsize organizations, Johansson et al. (2015) argue that network bandwidth may be an issue for bigger organizations with a large number of users requiring high amount of data transfer. Thus, larger organizations may go with a hybrid approach to ensure that their critical ERP applications provide expected level of performance.

3.5 TOWARDS THE ENTERPRISE OF THINGS

Throughout its evolution history, ERPs have been designed to allow for greater integration from the shop floor to other business functions (such as finance, human resource management) to strategic decision-making (via business analytics) in order to boost efficiency. After cloud-based services, the next phase of ERP is most likely to be enabled by the Internet of Things (IoT). IoT is basically a network of smart connected devices with some data processing capabilities. IoT arguably forms the bedrock of next industrial revolution, often named Industry 4.0 (Chand et al., 2018; Majeed and Rupasinghe, 2017), allowing for an automated and intelligent manufacturing process. Integrating IoT network with the enterprise would arguably mark the next phase of ERP evolution. This would allow for real-time data availability to ERP and improved business intelligence. Moreover, by introducing some automated processing at the edge nodes, it may also support the cloud ERP by sharing workloads with the core ERP application server (Chand et al., 2018), ensuring a high-performance level at the cloud.

While the potential benefits of IoT integration with cloud ERP are immense, certain developments await. For instance, based on a survey of around 200 executives involved in IoT projects, Rathmann (2017) reports that while the use of IoT devices is increasing, direct use of IoT data by the enterprise systems remains very limited. Majority of the organizations are using IoT data for the shop floor management with only 16% of respondents reporting IoT data being linked to the ERP system. Especially large firms seem to have a high level of sensor data without its subsequent use in enterprise decision-making. This leaves a huge gap with significant data being lost due to a lack of appropriate interfacing between IoT devices and ERP systems. Protocols and standards need to be developed for IoT integration with ERP. While there are some recent solutions from the industry (e.g. SIMATIC IOT2000 or SAP Leonardo IoT Bridge), the interface needs to be perfected and consistent across vendors to promote widespread integration of IoT with ERP. Technology continues to evolve and cloudIoT seems to be the next stage of ERP evolution, that is, towards an *Enterprise of Things*.

REFERENCES

Alwabel, S. A., Zairi, M., and Gunasekaran, A. (2006). The evolution of ERP and its relationship with E-business. *International Journal of Enterprise Information Systems (IJEIS)*, *2*(4), pp. 58–76.

AMR (2018). *Cloud-based ERP Market by Component, Function, End User, and Industry Vertical: Global Opportunity Analysis and Industry Forecast, 2017–2023*. Allied Market Research.

Bharathi, V., and Mandal, T. (2015). Prioritising and ranking critical factors for sustainable cloud ERP adoption in SMEs. *International Journal of Automation and Logistics*, *1*(3), pp. 294–316.

Chand, S., Lal, S., Chen, S., and Devi, A. (2018, December). Cloud ERP implementation using edge computing. In *2018 5th Asia-Pacific World Congress on Computer Science and Engineering (APWC on CSE)*, Nadi, Fiji, pp. 235–240. IEEE.

Daniel, D. R. (1961). Management information crisis. *Harvard Business Review*, *39*(5), pp. 111–121.

Davenport, T. H. (1998). Putting the enterprise into the enterprise system. *Harvard Business Review*, *76*(4), pp. 121–132.

Demi, S., and Haddara, M. (2018). Do cloud ERP systems retire? An ERP lifecycle perspective. *Procedia Computer Science*, *138*, pp. 587–594.

Dong, L., Neufeld, D., and Higgins, C. (2009). Top management support of enterprise systems implementations. *Journal of Information Technology*, *24*(1), pp. 55–80.

Duan, J., Faker, P., Fesak, A., and Stuart, T. (2013). Benefits and drawbacks of cloud-based versus traditional ERP systems. In *Proceedings of the 2012–13 course on Advanced Resource Planning*, Nadi, Fiji.

Elmonem, M. A. A., Nasr, E. S., and Geith, M. H. (2016). Benefits and challenges of cloud ERP systems–A systematic literature review. *Future Computing and Informatics Journal*, *1*(1–2), pp. 1–9.

Finney, S., and Corbett, M. (2007). ERP implementation: A compilation and analysis of critical success factors. *Business Process Management Journal*, *13*(3), pp. 329–347.

Gupta, S., and Misra, S. C. (2016). Compliance, network, security and the people related factors in cloud ERP implementation. *International Journal of Communication Systems*, *29*(8), pp. 1395–1419.

Gupta, S., Misra, S. C., Singh, A., Kumar, V., and Kumar, U. (2017). Identification of challenges and their ranking in the implementation of cloud ERP. *International Journal of Quality & Reliability Management*, *34*(7), pp. 1056–1072.

Huq, Z., Huq, F., and Cutright, K. (2006). BPR through ERP: Avoiding change management pitfalls. *Journal of Change Management*, *6*(1), pp. 67–85.

Jacobs, F. R., and Weston, F. C. (2007). Enterprise resource planning (ERP)-A brief history. *Journal of Operations Management*, *25*(2), pp. 357–363.

Johansson, B., Alajbegovic, A., Alexopoulo, V., and Desalermos, A. (2015, January). Cloud ERP adoption opportunities and concerns: The role of organizational size. In *2015 48th Hawaii International Conference On System Sciences*, pp. 4211–4219. IEEE.

Ko, D. G. (2014). The mediating role of knowledge transfer and the effects of client-consultant mutual trust on the performance of enterprise implementation projects. *Information & Management*, *51*(5), pp. 541–550.

Kumar, K., and van Hillegersberg, J. (2000). Enterprise resource planning: Introduction. *Communications of the ACM*, *43*(4), 22–26.

Lee, Z., and Lee, J. (2000). An ERP implementation case study from a knowledge transfer perspective. *Journal of Information Technology*, *15*(4), pp. 281–288.

Liang, H., and Xue, Y. (2004). Coping with ERP-related contextual issues in SMEs: A vendor's perspective. *Journal of Strategic Information Systems*, 13(4), pp. 399–415.

Majeed, A. A., and Rupasinghe, T. D. (2017). Internet of things (IoT) embedded future supply chains for industry 4.0: An assessment from an ERP-based fashion apparel and footwear industry. *International Journal of Supply Chain Management*, *6*(1), pp. 25–40.

Markus, M. L., and Tanis, C. (2000). The enterprise systems experience-from adoption to success. *Framing the Domains of IT Research: Glimpsing the Future through the Past*, 173, pp. 207–173.

Panorama Consulting (2019). *2019 ERP Report: People, Process, Technology*. Panorama Consulting Solution.

Peng, G. C. A., and Gala, C. (2014). Cloud ERP: A new dilemma to modern organisations? *Journal of Computer Information Systems*, *54*(4), pp. 22–30.

Rashid, M. A., Hossain, L., and Patrick, J. D. (2002). The evolution of ERP systems: A historical perspective. In *Enterprise Resource Planning: Solutions and Management* (pp. 35–50). IGI Global.

Rathmann, C. (2017). *Industrial Internet of Things (IoT) and Digital Transformation*. IFS white paper.

Rockart, J. F. (1979). Chief executives define their own data needs. *Harvard Business Review*, 57(2), pp. 81–94.

Rothenberger, M. A., Srite, M., and Jones-Graham, K. (2010). The impact of project team attributes on ERP system implementations: A positivist field investigation. *Information Technology & People*, *23*(1), pp. 80–109.

Saeed, I., Juell-Skielse, G., and Uppström, E. (2012). Cloud enterprise resource planning adoption: Motives and barriers. *Advances in Enterprise Information Systems II, 429.*

Saxena, D., and McDonagh, J. (2014). Towards a more holistic approach to the study of enterprise systems: The case for integrating process inquiry and sociomateriality. In *British Academy of Management Conference 2014*, Belfast, UK.

Saxena, D., and McDonagh, J. (2017). Yet another 'list' of critical success 'factors' for enterprise systems: Review of empirical evidence and suggested research directions. In *UK Academy of Information Systems Conference 2017*, Oxford, UK.

Saxena, D., and McDonagh, J. (2019). Evaluating ERP implementations: The case for a lifecycle-based interpretive approach. *Electronic Journal of Information Systems Evaluation*, *22*(1), pp. 29–37.

Shaul, L., and Tauber, D. (2013). Critical success factors in enterprise resource planning systems: Review of the last decade. *ACM Computing Surveys (CSUR)*, *45*(4), pp. 1–39.

Verma J.K., and Katti, C.P. (2015a). View on security, privacy and trust issues in cloud computing environment. *International Journal of Latest Trends in Engineering and Technology (IJLTET)*, *5*(3), pp. 490–494.

Verma J.K., and Katti, C.P. (2015b). A survey on load balancing techniques in cloud computing environment. *International Journal of Latest Trends in Engineering and Technology (IJLTET)*, *5*(2), pp. 469–478.

Wan, Y., and Clegg, B. (2010, October). Enterprise management and ERP development: Case study of Zoomlion using the dynamic enterprise reference grid. In *International Conference on ENTERprise Information Systems*, pp. 191–198. Springer, Berlin, Heidelberg.

4 Case Study Based on Optimal Inspection Timing for a Motor-Fan Assembly

A View on Performance and Reliability in Cloud IoT

Edgar Fuenmayor
University of Zulia, Maracaibo, Venezuela

Carlos Parra
University of Seville, Seville, Spain

Vicente González-Prida
University of Sevilla & UNED, Seville, Spain

Adolfo Crespo
University of Seville, Seville, Spain

Antonio Sola
INGEMAN, Seville, Spain

Fredy Kristjanpoller and Pablos Viveros
University Federico Santa María, Valparaíso, Chile

CONTENTS

4.1 INTRODUCTION

Companies develop maintenance plans to guarantee the continuous service of their systems and equipment, in such a way as to increase reliability and availability. In recent decades, maintenance has been a protagonist of success, to the extent that companies have become more solid and reliable,

DOI: 10.1201/9781003155577-5

when understanding that poorly planned maintenance is responsible and limits the volumes of production, affects the product or service quality, deteriorates customer service, conditions accidents, damages the environment, and originates indirect costs that long exceed the traditional planned maintenance costs. The general idea of maintenance is changing each day; these changes are due to the increase in automation (robotics, Internet of Things, for example), which makes the machinery complex; new maintenance techniques; and new approaches to how maintenance departments and whole companies are organized. The maintenance is also reacting to new expectations; this includes more importance to aspects of safety and environment, knowledge of the existing connection between maintenance and quality of the service or product; and an increase in pressure exerted to get a high availability of equipment.

These changes facilitates the test of attitudes and knowledge of the staff and maintenance staff that goes from the mechanic to the manager, must adopt new ways of thinking and acting, looking for a new way to avoid inefficiencies in maintenance, trying to find a strategic framework that synthesize the new advances so that they can evaluate rationally and apply those who are of greater validity for them and their business. Due to the need to increase the reliability and availability of physical assets, the development or design of maintenance plans made decisive the use of methodologies such as RCM, FMECA, FMEA, RBI, from the early stage of asset life cycle for this way to adapt the asset care plan to the current context. On the other hand, it is critical to define the optimal time interval for asset inspections based on monitoring their condition for deterioration, and thus it is necessary to know the optimal inspection frequency that must be timely in order to avoid equipment functional failure (Fuenmayor, 2017).

4.2 COST-RISK ANALYSIS MODEL

To estimate the optimum inspection frequency, the construction of two curves is required. One that represents the cost associated with the different inspection policies modeled to different frequencies. The other curve indicates the risk costs associated with the asset failure or loss of its primary or secondary function, being risk = Likelihood of Failure × Consequence. These two curves are combined in a decision model known as cost-risk model (Woodhouse, 1993; Parra and Crespo, 2015). In recent years, large industrial corporations, especially the oil, gas and petrochemical, and manufacturing industries, have turned their attention to the "cost-risk" decision model, because it allows to compare the costs associated with a maintenance action against the level of risk reduction or improvement in performance because of this action; in other words, the model allows to know "how much is obtained by what is spent."

The "cost-risk" analysis is particularly useful to decide on scenarios where there are different interests in conflict, such as the "operation-maintenance" scenario. The operations department requires that the equipment or process operate for a long time to achieve production goals while, on the other hand, the maintenance department requires that process or physical asset be stopped with some frequency for inspection and repairs and be able to get reliability in them. The cost-risk model is indicated to solve the previously mentioned conflict, since it allows estimating the optimal level of risk and the appropriate frequency of inspection to obtain maximum benefit or minimal impact on the business. In the cost-risk model, three curves that vary in time highlight the following:

- The risk level curve (Risk = Likelihood of Failure × Consequences). The increase in the failure rate, which leads to the increase in failure probability and reliability reduction; the increase in operating costs and the loss of performance are among other variables to be considered for the estimation of risk. This curve is ascendant on time.
- The curve of the inspection costs (direct plus indirect costs), in which are simulated the costs of different inspection frequencies. This curve is descendant in time.

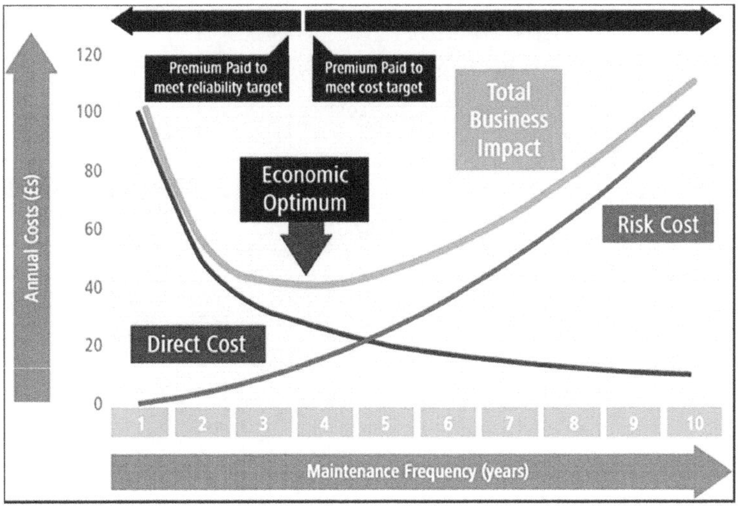

FIGURE 4.1 Inspection frequency optimization.

Source: Asset management an anatomy. IAM. 2015.

The total impact on the business curve results from adding point-to-point risk and inspection costs curves. The minimum or inflection point of this curve represents the minimum possible impact on the business and is located on the value that can be translated as the period or optimal frequency to carry out the maintenance action. To do inspection to the left of this point would lead to incurring a very high cost. Carrying out the inspection to the right of this point would be to take too much risk. For this reason, the recommendation is to perform the inspection at the optimal point of the total impact on the business curve (Figure 4.1).

The difficulty of the use of the model focuses on the estimate or modeling of the risk curve, since it requires the estimation of the probability of failure (and its variation over the time) and the consequences. The risk, fundamental base of the decision model described above, is probabilistic nature term, which is defined as the "probability of having a loss" and is commonly expressed in currency units. Mathematically, the risk is calculated with the following equation:

- R(t) = Probability of Failure × Consequences
- Total Business Impact = Inspection Costs + "Not to Do Inspection" Risk

The analysis of risk equation allows understanding of this indicator power for diagnosis and decision-making, because it combines probabilities or failure frequencies with consequences, allowing the comparison of assets such as dynamic equipment, which normally show high failure frequencies with low consequences, with static equipment, which normally have low failure frequencies and high consequences. The risk behaves like a balance, which allows weighing the influence of these magnitudes, probability, and consequence of failure, in a decision. Modern maintenance supported in reliability engineering requires a careful process of equipment and systems diagnostic. The diagnosis based on risk can then be understood as a process that seeks to characterize equipment and systems' current state and predict future behavior.

For the achievement of an integrated diagnosis, the risk should be estimated using all available information, that is, it must include the failure history analysis, condition, and technical data. In this way, they can be identified as preventive and corrective actions that may effectively optimize costs and minimize their impact on the business. Understanding that "risk" is the indicator for an integrated diagnosis, the process to estimate it is then analyzed in detail. Figure 4.2 shows graphically the decomposition of the risk indicator.

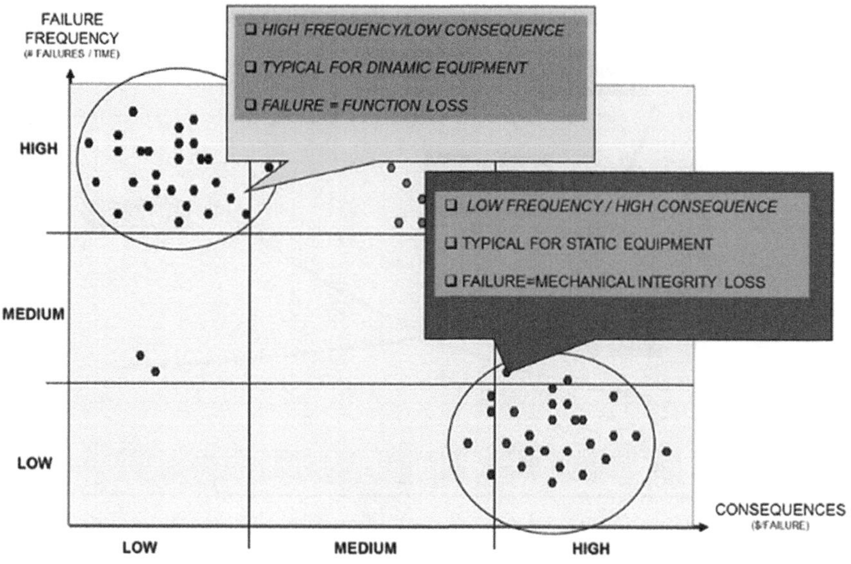

FIGURE 4.2 Diagnosis process. Risk indicator decomposition.

Source: Reliability Engineering and Risk Probabilistic Analysis. R2M. 2004.

4.3 INSPECTION PURPOSE AND ON-CONDITION TECHNIQUES

The purpose of the inspection could be early detection of any undesirable event that may affect human safety, impact the environment, and decrease the profitability of the business, since the functional failure can be anticipated. When functional failures of the physical assets do not impact considerably to organizations from the economic point of view, it may not be necessary to invest money and time in an inspection routine, since it generates a cost (direct or indirect) that is not profitable for the business. The main purposes of an inspection are as follows:

- Detect or monitor the risk of a failure in such a way as to avoid a catastrophe or event with serious consequences through the monitoring of the asset condition.
- Detect the failure of a function that has already occurred and is not evident to operations personnel.

4.3.1 Condition Based Tasks

Any selected task based on condition (predictive or conditioning monitoring) must meet the following additional criteria:

- There must be a well-defined possibility of failure.
- There must be an easily discernible P-F range (or failure development period).
- The task interval must be less than the most likely shorter P-F interval.
- Physically, it must be possible to perform the task at a time interval less than the P-F interval.

It is important to figure out what to do to avoid, eliminate, or minimize the negative effects of a potential failure as quickly as possible. This is called the P-F interval minus the task interval. Most of the time, failure modes don't happen right away in every case. It is very likely that you can tell that the parts in question are in the last stages of deterioration before they break down completely in these kinds of situations. A "potential failure" is a condition that can be seen that indicates that a functional failure is about to happen or is in the process of happening. This is what people call the

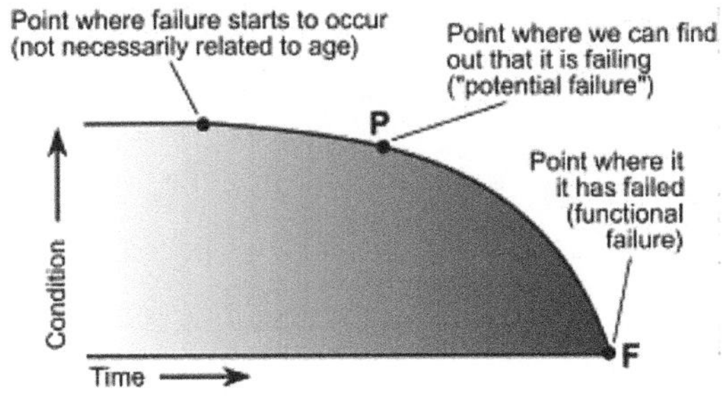

FIGURE 4.3 P-F curve.

Source: A Guide to the Reliability-Centered Maintenance (RCM) Standard SAE JA1012, 2002.

evidence of imminent failure. People can take action if this condition is found. They can try to keep the element from completely failing and/or to avoid the consequences of a failure mode.

The final phases of the failure process are depicted in Figure 4.3. This is referred to as the P-F curve because it illustrates how a failure begins, deteriorates to the point at which it can be detected ("P"), and then continues to deteriorate at an accelerated rate until it reaches the functional failure point ("F").

The points between P and F in Figure 4.3 indicates if there is a functional failure. This is where you can take action to prevent the functional failure and/or its consequences (if possible or not to have a significant action will depend on how fast the functional failure occurs). Condition-based tasks are those that are meant to look for problems before they happen. Condition-based tasks are named this way because the parts are checked and then put back into use with the understanding that they will keep working in the way they were supposed to. They will keep going on the assumption that the failure mode in question will not happen before the next inspection.

This is also called predictive maintenance because it tries to figure out whether and when an item will break down based on its current behavior. Condition-based maintenance, on the other hand, is when the need for corrective action or to avoid consequences is based on an evaluation of the item's condition. It's also important to think about how long it took for the potential failure to happen, or how many stress cycles it went through, before it turned into a real failure. As shown in Figure 4.4, the P-F range is shown, and the gradual deterioration to failure can be seen in the figure.

The P-F interval tells how often condition-based tasks should be done. Between reviews, the P-F interval must be shorter than the interval between reviews. This way, we can find out about a possible failure before it turns into a functional failure. It's also important that the condition of the potential failure is clear enough that the person who is trained to do the inspection will be able to find it if and when it happens (or that the chance of the potential failure not being found is low enough to keep the risk of an unanticipated failure mode from being too high for the asset owner or user) (A Guide to the Reliability-Centered Maintenance Standard). There are many different ways to describe the P-F interval. It can be the warning period, the period when a problem starts to happen, or the time when something goes wrong. It can be measured in any way that shows how much stress someone has had (running time, units of output, stop-start cycles, etc). It ranges from a few hundredths of a second to a few hundred years for different types of failure.

If an on-condition task is done more often than the P-F interval, there is a chance that the potential failure will be completely missed. On the other hand, if the task is done at a fraction of the P-F interval, resources will be wasted. Whenever possible, task intervals should be shorter than the shortest P-F interval that can be used in real life. Most of the time, choosing a task interval that is half of this P-F interval is enough. There are times when you should choose task intervals that are not the same as the P-F interval. This could be because of the net P-F interval, which we'll talk about later. Or, it could be because the asset's user has relevant historical data that shows that a different fraction is appropriate.

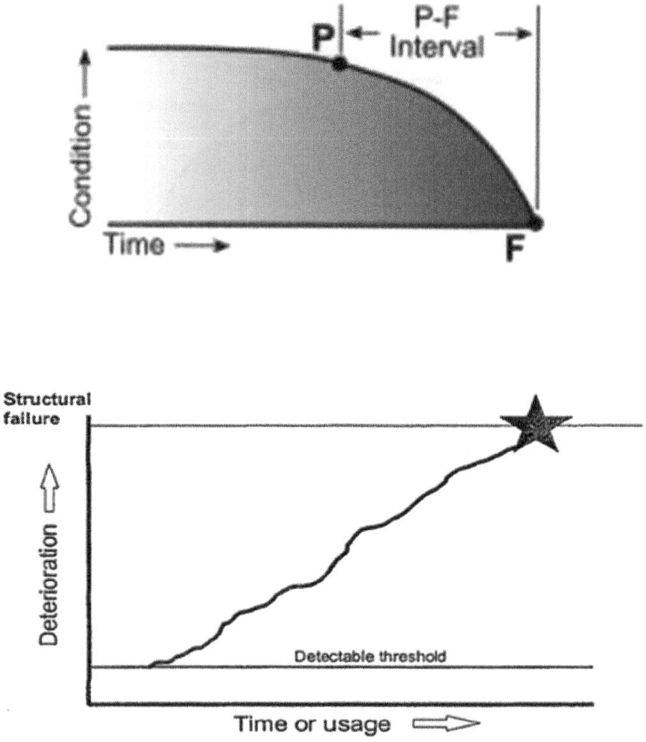

FIGURE 4.4 P-F range and the progressive development of the deterioration to failure.

4.3.2 The Net P-F Interval

The net P-F interval tells you how long you have to take action to avoid or lessen the effects of a failure mode. On-condition tasks must have a net P-F interval that is longer than the time needed to avoid or mitigate the effects of failure mode. Technically, it's not possible to do the on-condition task if the net P-F interval is too long. In practice, the amount of time it takes varies a lot. In some cases, it may only be a matter of hours or even minutes (to shut down a machine or evacuate a building). There may be times when weeks or even months have gone by (say until a major shutdown). Longer P-F intervals are usually a good thing for two reasons:

- This means that it's possible to plan the corrective action more carefully and thus more carefully so that you can avoid the failure mode's consequences.
- There are fewer required on-condition inspections.

As a result, considerable effort is being expended on identifying potential failure conditions and on-condition techniques that result in the longest possible P-F intervals. However, in some instances, very short P-F intervals may be used.

4.3.3 Categories of On-Condition Techniques

The following are the four major categories of on-condition techniques:

a) Techniques that consider changes in the quality of the product. Often, when a machine makes something that has a flaw, that flaw is caused by a machine-failure mode. Many of these defects start to show up over time, giving us a good idea of what could go wrong before it happens.

b) Techniques for keeping an eye on the main effects. Speed, flow rate, pressure, temperature, power, and current, for example, are some of the primary effects that give more information about the condition of the equipment. Gauges, computers, and chart recorders can all be used to keep an eye on the results.
c) Techniques that are based on how people think (look, listen, feel, and smell).
d) Techniques for monitoring the state of things. These are ways to find out if something might go wrong that requires special equipment (which is sometimes built into the asset that is being monitored). To separate these techniques from other types of on-condition maintenance, they are called condition monitoring.

Following a lot of different possible failures, there may be more than one type of on-condition task that is right for the situation. A unique set of skills and abilities will be needed for each of these. If this is the case, it means that no single task category will always be more cost-effective than any other. Thus, in order to avoid bias when choosing tasks, it is important to do the following:

a) Consider all of the things that could happen before each failure mode, as well as all of the on-condition tasks that could be used to look for these signs.
b) It's important to follow the RCM task selection criteria very closely in order to figure out which of the tasks is likely to be the most cost-effective way to predict a failure mode in question.

Notably, any built-in devices designed to determine whether a failure mode is occurring or is about to occur should meet the same technical feasibility and cost-benefit criteria as any on-condition maintenance. Additionally, when such devices are integrated into a system, they add a new function or functions, along with new failure modes, and should be analyzed accordingly.

4.4 OPTIMAL INSPECTION TIMING ASSESSMENT MODEL

In Figure 4.5, the most important parameters in the estimation of the optimum inspection frequency are shown, such as deterioration of start point, wear rate, failure point, and measurement accuracy. It should be noted that the model considers asset deterioration, allowing to determine the date for the next inspection. This model has limitations with regard to the variables associated with the

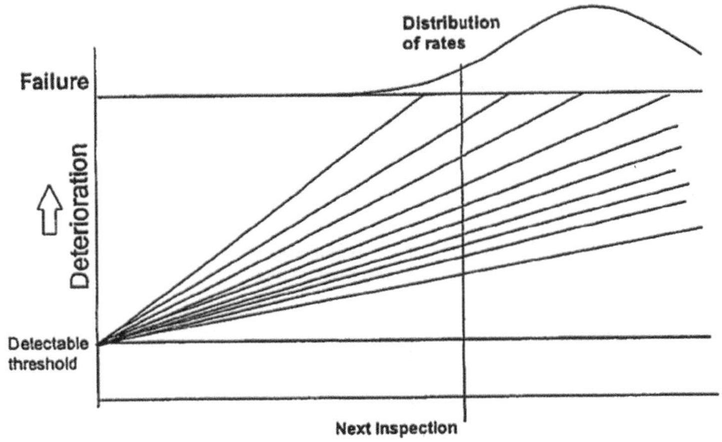

FIGURE 4.5 Combining the uncertainties.

Source: Inspection and Maintenance Optimal Frequency Course. TWPL. 1999.

consequences of the loss of primary or secondary functions. It must establish an inspection program in the organization in order to be able to build the condition monitoring or deterioration trend curve, from asset start of operation or after a major repair, is to say data management. To forecast deterioration, lognormal probabilistic distribution was used in this model, since it is the distribution that shows the longest "tail" for predicting deterioration (see Figure 4.7) compared to Weibull and Gamma distributions, allowing a shorter date for the next inspection and thus decreasing the probability of prematurely achieving a functional failure or function loss.

Generally, the rate at which the deterioration will occur is not known. Figure 4.6 shows the variation of time to failure probabilistic distribution that could be expected as a result of the variation in deterioration rate.

In many cases, even if the purpose of the inspection may be preventing the catastrophic consequences in failure mode (for example, a pressure vessel break), there may be another level of failure before critical failure mode. There may be multiple levels of failure, as shown in Figure 4.7.

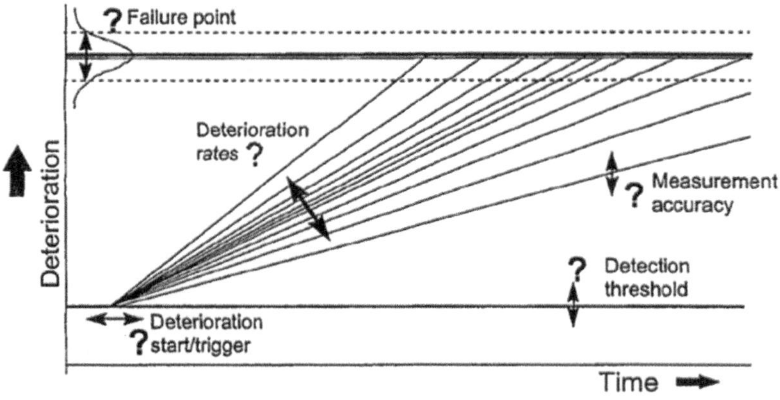

FIGURE 4.6 Time to failure distribution.

Source: Inspection and Maintenance Optimal Frequency Course. TWPL. 1999.

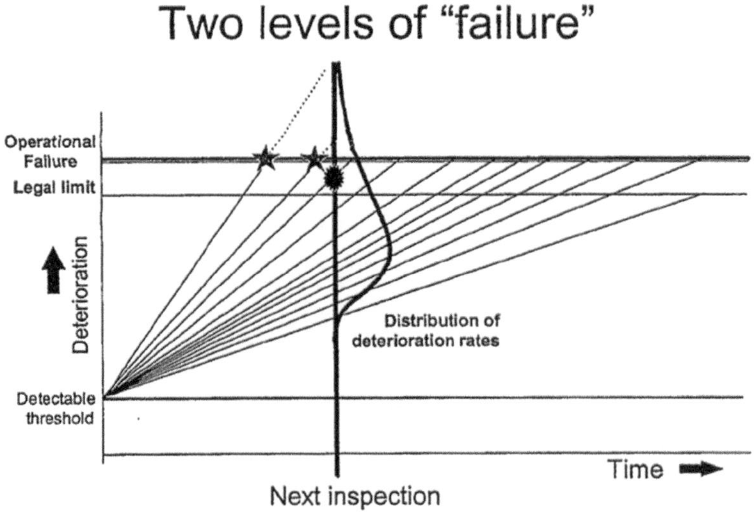

FIGURE 4.7 Multiple failure levels.

Source: Inspection and Maintenance Optimal Frequency Course. TWPL. 1999.

4.5 CASE STUDY

In this case study, the analysis was made with the help of a spreadsheet, considering all the variables described previously. Additionally, to validate the results obtained with the spreadsheet they were compared with the numerical values thrown by well-known worldwide asset management software, which demonstrates the certainty of the data. Data shown herein is altered to meet confidentiality requirements. A motor-fan arrangement is installed in a petrochemical plant for 20 years of continuous operation, in which the recommendations of the licenser and technical department have been met in terms of preventive maintenance actions.

The plant reliability engineers already settled a reliability-based maintenance plan using RCM methodology, and he is arranged to optimize the inspection frequency according to condition monitoring for mechanical vibrations in the different measurement locations as shown by Dynamic

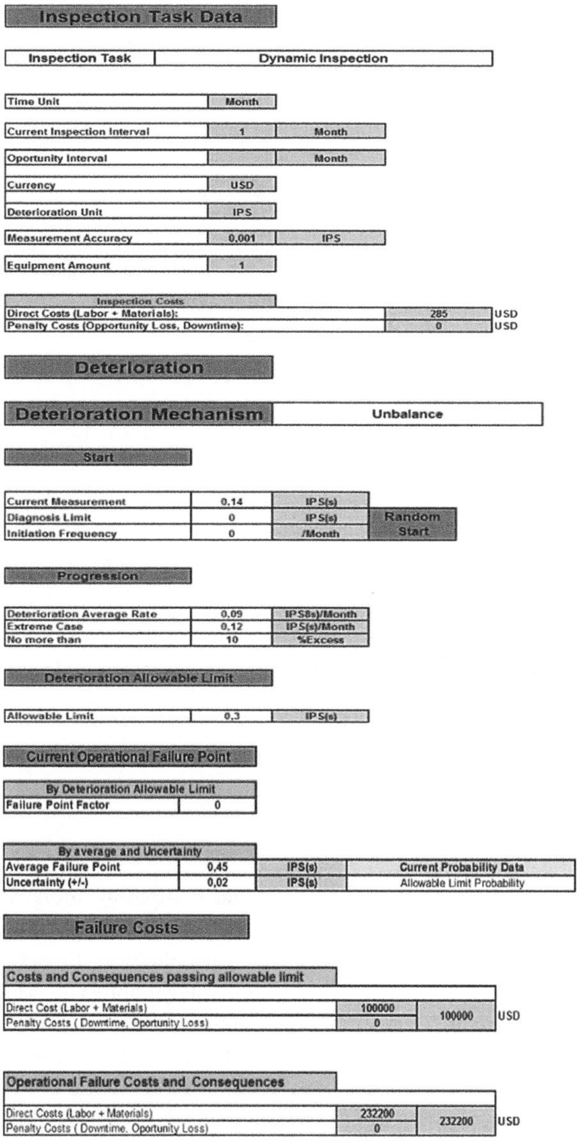

FIGURE 4.8 Input data for optimal inspection timing assessment model.

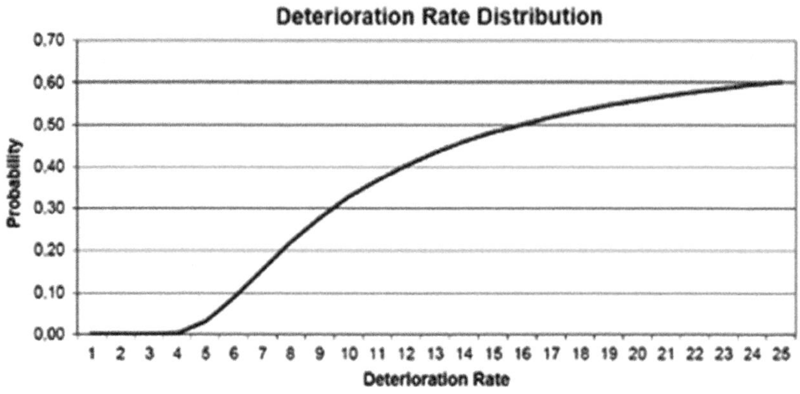

FIGURE 4.9 Deterioration rate distribution.

Source: Fuenmayor 2019.

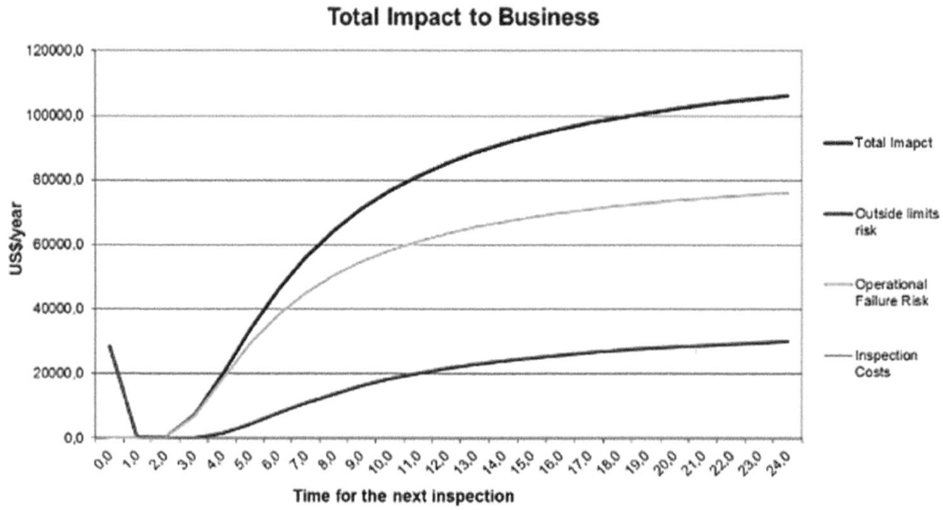

FIGURE 4.10 Mathematical model results graph.

Source: Fuenmayor 2019.

Equipment Inspection Department Reports using cloud computing tools. If inspection activities are not carried out, the reliability of the productive process would be affected due to the loss of primary function, and the consequences would be serious since the operating costs would increase and would reduce the asset performance with the time due to unavailability of backup equipment. Large amount of inputs and big data can be leveraged by using tools in the cloud and IoT technologies. The input data for the mathematical model is shown in Figures 4.8 and 4.9).

Below is the results Table 4.1 indicating the optimal interval for the next inspection. These results are obtained through the application of a mathematical model (using cloud computing tools) that includes the deterioration at different frequencies considering costs, risks, and performance (Figure 4.10, Table 4.1).

TABLE 4.1
Results of the Optimal Interval for the Next Inspection Assessment

Costs Expressed as (USD/Month)

		Predictive Inspection		
Time to Next Inspection (Months)	Inspection Costs	Outside Limits Risk Costs	Operational Failure Risk Costs	Total Impact Costs
0,0	28500	0,00	0,00	28500,00
1,0	**282**	**0,00**	**0,00**	**282,18**
2,0	142	0,29	426,82	568,90
3,0	95	172,94	6805,37	7073,00
4,0	71	1581,94	18224,46	19877,47
5,0	57	4421,87	29174,07	33652,83
6,0	47	7784,94	38067,38	45899,75
7,0	41	11023,26	45021,68	56085,60
8,0	36	13891,59	50464,51	64391,68
9,0	32	16349,92	54779,66	71161,21
10,0	28	18434,48	58255,85	76718,81
11,0	26	20201,25	61101,09	81 328,22
12,0	24	21705,04	63464,49	85193,27
13,0	22	22993,11	65454,01	88469,02
14,0	20	241 04,26	67148,82	91273,43
15,0	19	25069,74	68607,97	93696,70
16,0	18	25914,55	69876,14	95808,50
17,0	17	26658,72	70987,67	97663,14
18,0	16	27318,34	71969,28	99303,45
19,0	15	27906,42	72842,08	100763,49
20,0	14	28433,56	73622,90	102070,70
21,0	14	28908,43	74325,32	103247,31
22,0	13	29338,19	74960,43	104311,57
23,0	12	29728,79	75537,33	105278,51
24,0	12	30085,22	76063,57	106160,66

4.6 RESULTS AND CONCLUSIONS

The next inspection, according to this model, must occur within one month. However, monitoring operational variables is recommended to ensure that the physical asset operates in the operational environment for which it was selected. The cost of performing the inspection task at various frequencies was used to resolve this calculation, as was the risk of not performing the inspection task. It should be noted that the results obtained using a spreadsheet have been validated and are very similar to those generated by a well-known global asset management software that is used in a variety of industrial sectors. The small difference is due to the accuracy of the commercial software's model, which cannot be determined for confidentiality reasons. The spreadsheet's mathematics incorporates the necessary parameters and adjustments defined in the standards and references consulted.

Calculating the optimal inspection frequency or interval between inspections is a critical parameter for monitoring asset deterioration, as failures are predictable. It is possible to facilitate this by utilizing intelligent cloud and IoT systems. After identifying the potential failure point, the maximum time allowed for asset operation can be determined. When it comes to assets whose primary function is containment, such as static equipment, establishing an appropriate inspection schedule is critical due to the consequences of losing the primary function.

In summary, it is not sufficient to design a "perfect" maintenance plan that considers all possible failure modes via the various tools or methodologies that assist in determining not only WHAT to do but also WHEN to perform the maintenance and/or inspection action to aid in asset management decision-making.

The optimal inspection frequency must be calibrated or revised if the operational environment in which the asset is installed changes over time, as well as the rate of deterioration, as this may affect reliability and performance, among other variables, as a result of the effect on the asset's ability to perform its function (s). As demonstrated in the first pages of this document, as an asset ages, its reliability decreases as its failure rate increases. As a result, it is recommended that inspection plans be tailored to the equipment's age and condition, taking into account the equipment's life cycle costs in order to select tasks that are not only technically feasible but also economically profitable and budget friendly.

REFERENCES

Campbell, J.D., Jardine, A.K.S., and McGlynn, J. (2011). *Asset Management Excellence: Optimizing Equipment Life-Cycle Decisions*, CRC Press.

Campbell, J.D., and Reyes– Picknell, J.V. (2016). *Uptime, Strategies for Excellence in Maintenance Management*. Canada, CRC Press.

Crespo, A. (2006). *The Maintenance Management Framework. Models and Methods for Complex Systems Maintenance*. London. Springer Verlag.

Fuenmayor, E. (2017). Calculando la Frecuencia Optima de Mantenimiento o Reemplazo Preventivo. Revista Predictiva 21 N° 23. https://www.predictiva21.com

Fuenmayor, E. (2019). Calculando la Frecuencia Optima de Inspección. Considerando Costos, Riesgo y Desempeño. Revista Predictiva 21 N° 27. https://www.predictiva21.com

Gulati, R. (2021). *Maintenance and Reliability Best Practices. 2021*. Third Edition, Industrial Press, Inc.

Jardine A.K.S., and Tsang A.H.C. (2014). *Maintenance, Replacement, and Reliability (Theory and Applications)*, Second Edition, CRC Press.

Macro Project EU 1488, 2008, https://www.macroproject.org

Moubray, J. (1997). *Reliability Centered Maintenance, RCM II*, Second Edition, Industrial Press, Inc.

Parra, C., Crespo, A. (2015). *Ingeniería de Mantenimiento y Fiabilidad Aplicada en la Gestión de Activos. Desarrollo y aplicación práctica de un Modelo de Gestión del Mantenimiento (MGM). Segunda Edición.* Editado por INGEMAN, Sevilla, España, Escuela Superior de Ingenieros Industriales.

SAE JA1012. 2002. *Una guía para la Norma de Mantenimiento Centrado en Confiabilidad (MCC).*

Woodhouse, J. (1993). *Managing Industrial Risk, Getting Value for Money in Your Business*, London, Chapman & Hall.

Woodhouse, J. (2014). *Asset Management Decision-Making: The SALVO Process, Strategic Assets: Life Cycle Value Optimization*, United Kingdom, TWPL.

Part II

Addressing Climate Change

5 Predictive Edge Computing of SST Time-Series-Based Marine Warning System using Cloud Computing Infrastructure

Geetali Saha
G H Patel College of Engineering and Technology, Vallabh Vidyanagar, India

Bannishikha Banerjee
P.P. Savani University, Surat, India

Foram M Joshi
G H Patel College of Engineering and Technology, Vallabh Vidyanagar, India

CONTENTS

5.1 INTRODUCTION: BACKGROUND AND DRIVING FORCES

Advances in the domain of IoT devices and cloud have led to a revolutionary ascension in data analytics in a multidimensional manner. There is hardly any domain existing today which is untouched by the influence of such development. Many popular frameworks that are gaining market reach include ThingSpeak, ThingWorx, Zetta, IBM Watson, The Thing System, Pentaho, SkySpark, SensorCloud, realTime.io, OpenRemote, Platform.io, Statistica (Dell), AllJoyn, Brillo Carriots, Ericsson IoT-Framework, AirVantage, IoTivity, ThingSquare, Tellient, EvryThng, Intel IoT Platforms, OpenIoT, Devicehub.net and LinkSmart [51]. Climate disruptions and monitoring the same continue to be a challenge as more and more people start inhabiting its different locations and interfering with its intrinsic characteristics, thereby causing chaos and inconsistencies. This is further affected by innumerable natural processes. Many researchers have devised various Integrated Systems that can capture variations happening on the ground level and link it to the application layer and beyond working in three dimensions of sightedness – Insight – it essentially involves understanding of the hidden characteristics, outsight – correlates the happenings to surrounding influences and Foresight – perceives possible outcomes due to present and past conditions.

DOI: 10.1201/9781003155577-7

Further, we can map various Earth parameters to cloud Infrastructure through IoT devices.

The name 'Blue Planet' has been coined for the Earth because of the existence of its oceans. They tend to provide almost 60 percent Earth coverage with variable depths at different locations from a few meters to as deep as hundreds of kilometres. And hence an in-depth knowledge of the oceans is required in order to understand the Earth's climate system. Hence, we can conclude that the Earth's climate is largely driven by water coverage [1]. A column of ocean water only 3 m thick contains as much heat capacity as the entire atmospheric column above it [2]. This and other key properties of the Earth's oceans make it a huge reservoir of heat, water, and carbon dioxide. The oceans are huge buffers and follow dynamics which is slowly varying. These features make them key regulators of the Earth's climate system. However, for any drastic climatic change, it is the Marine Ecosystem that is hit with the first and hardest blow and based upon study conducted by various groups over time, it is found that sea surface temperature (SST) is one parameter that has maximum correlation to such occurrences.

Time series exist everywhere from financial data, weather data, demand of electricity load, costing of essential goods, businesses, statistics, astronomy, pattern recognition, medical data, earthquake prediction, etc. Linear time series are comparatively simpler to model. However, most of the real-life data belong to the nonlinear class of time series. Its dynamism is challenging and may leave certain details unexplained if incorrectly modelled.

It is this study of various hydro time series at different locations across the world that has revealed interesting facts and details about surprisingly linked influences on the marine world and the aquatic population with various ocean parameters, most prominently the SST. Consider a study undertaken by a group of researchers in the Mauna Loa Observatory located at Hawaii, where they targeted to detect the concentration of atmospheric Mercury element (Hg0) during 2002 and 2009 [4]. They correlated it to the SST time series using empirical mode of decomposition technique to detect identical periodic patterns of occurrence. Further, they also succeeded in establishing a correlation with relative humidity (RH) and cross correlation with ozone concentrations. Advanced very high resolution radiometer (AVHRR) [5, 6, 10] data is also a very active source of data that provides reliable time series. Such data basically comprising of images taken during day and night passes of the satellite, clearly indicate the formation of temperature fronts that in turn contribute significantly towards the food chain of aquatic flora and fauna. At the coasts of the Beaufort Sea, such significant temperature front formations were detected when single image edge detection (SIED) based analysis was executed during a span of 11 years from 1998 to 2008 specifically at the Mackenzie Shelf and at the Amundsen Gulf Region at the onset of summer season [5]. There have been instances observed at various locations that are not directly linked to the sea, yet under the effect of stratification and mixing of layers at various depths the oceanic heat gets redistributed. Historical estimates recorded at seven well-observed large marine ecosystems (LMEs) across the United States have revealed the existence of astonishing relationship between the variation in the SST Anomaly and the environment of the marine ecosystem over a period of observation ranging from 1981 to 2015 [6]. A study spanning 130 years from 1880 to 2010 undertaken by scientists from the Council of Scientific and Industrial Research (CSIR), National Institute of Oceanography (NIO), revealed year-wise co-occurrences of positive Indian Ocean Dipole (IOD) and El Niño events, negative IOD and La Niña events, only negative IOD, only positive IOD, pure El Niño, pure La Niña, and no events to the changes in SST values at the Arabian Sea and the Bay of Bengal. Their research article [7] further reveals that when the Anomalies exceed 0.4 °C, it is linked to El Niño events and to La Niña events for lower SST Anomalies. Common dolphins [8] were found to exhibit an inversely proportional projection of population with respect to the SST increment at the Alboran Sea using approximately 20 years of data. In the coastal areas of the Italian Seas [9] using approximately a decade long span of data, limited comparisons are possible whereas in the basin region, the SST values tend to exhibit good agreement although the data is collected from variable sources like International Comprehensive Ocean Atmosphere Data Set (ICOADS), Italian Institute for the Environmental Protection and Research (ISPRA), Rete Ondametrica Nazionale – (RON) and a combination of

AVHRR and NOAA satellite data. A variable SST change level was detected in the shallow and the deep areas of the Yellow Sea when measurements were conducted for a period of almost three decades from 1981 to 2009 [10] using Empirical Orthogonal Function (EOF). A strange huge green tide had disrupted the 2008 Olympics sailing competition in the Qingdao coast. Later, a study spanning five years from 2008 to 2013 linked the astronomical growth of green algae to SST Anomalies in this part of the Yellow Sea [11]. A review of various remote sensing methodologies like Optical, Synthetic Aperture Radar (SAR), Microwave, and Thermal by Rajesh and Dwarakish [12] links the concentration of Chlorophyll, which is one of the most significant physical contributors to the Marine biome. R. Salles [13] had considered time series SST data from the Atlantic Ocean contributed by Prediction and Research Moored Array in the Tropical Atlantic (PIRATA) buoys and tried to predict future values in variable horizons.

Tropical cyclones are found to be linked to the SST over the North Pacific Ocean as well as to the Indian Ocean [14, 15] as per the studies undertaken by two independent groups of researchers almost in the same time frame of 2012. Tropical cyclone heat potential (TCHP) is a major contributor towards the building up of a cyclone and is highly correlated to the SST values. A. Wada et al [14] opted for linear regression techniques using daily dataset of 2002–2005. M.M. Ali et al. have used 25,000 temperature profiles in 1997–2007 [15] and further estimated the ocean subsurface thermal structure [16] using SST data from a buoy location at the Arabian Sea 15.5°N, 61.5°E, both using artificial neural network (ANN). This inclination towards ANN is attributed to various inherent characteristics of the NN right from its inception, to modelling, to ADALINE (ADAptive LINear Elements). In 1986, David E Rumelhart, Geoffrey E. Hinton, and Ronald J Williams [17] proposed back propagation of errors.

5.2 LITERATURE REVIEW

W.W Hsieh and B. Tang [18] have presented the use of neural network for the Nino belts, including P4 and P5. Later, F. Tangang [19] also contributed by finding SST anomalies.

In 1998, all three used sea level pressure (SLP) also for prediction [20]. In 2000, A.H. Mohanan [21] again extended the lead time ahead. All of them used Reynold's SST Dataset [22] and its improved version [23]. Changes near the Indian Ocean are linked to the Pacific Ocean [24] and Asian Australian Rainfall frequency [25]. El Niño and La Niña events can be forecasted to near precision, and its peculiar relationship with the Indian Ocean SST (IO SST) is realized [24–28]. K.C. Tripathi et al [29] in 2006 identified such a region in the Indian Ocean and with 52 years data, he performed time series prediction. Later, in 2008, K.C. Tripathi [30] et al mapped the Indian summer monsoon too with data from four worldwide locations. S.B. Mohongo [31], in 2013, identified two more locations with HadISST. In 2013, Patil et al. [32] identified six such locations and performed prediction. In 2016 Patil et al. [33] clubbed numerical techniques and neural methods. Many researchers undertook the task to identify such key locations that link the oceans worldwide. Most of them have indicated that the tropical Pacific, the equatorial Pacific and the Indian Ocean are prime locations for investigation [18–21, 34].

Apart from that, various IoT-based techniques are getting attention using combinational NN techniques for predicting climate characteristics/parameters. An IoT-based predictive model is used to estimate the rainfall based on decision tree, k-nearest neighbourhood, multiple linear regression and random forest techniques where the random forest reveals minimum RMSE [45]. An IoT-based setup projects variation in temperature that can lead to changes in soil composition by altering the concentrations of micro- and macro-nutrients, thereby affecting the productivity and sustainability of the crops [47]. Various such IoT cloud-based setups exist in various domains. A few of them are tabulated in Table 5.1.

Consider the existing systems round the world, a few are in the inception stage, and a few more in the advanced implementation stage. Trento [36] happens to lead the rank among Italian cities as far as living standards and job-seeking chances are concerned. It uses FI-WARE technology.

TABLE 5.1
Existing Cloud IoT-Based Systems and Their Details

No	Author Names	Technology	Application	Remarks
36	Yunchuan. Sun, H. Song, A.J. Jara, R. Bie	SCC-smart and Connected communities	Culture preservation Community sustainability	Case Study-Smart Tourism & Sustainable Cultural Heritage at TreSight, Trento, Italy
37	Yan Huang, P. Gao, Y. Zhang, J.Zhang	ArcGIS Enterprise 10.6.1	Platform to sense remotely, images, image database, maintenance, transforming and use with ArcGIS	Comparative of 1] UAV Dataset Sony Nex-5T 2] Aerial Dataset-Zeiss RMK 3] Satellite dataset – zy3-l.
38	Shifeng. Fang, L. D. Xu, Y. Zhu, J. Ahati, H. Pei, J. Yan, Z. Liu	IIS – Integrated Information System combining Internet of Things (IoT), e-Science, Geoinformatics [RS, GIS and GPS] and Cloud Computing	Climate change, Monitoring the environment Environmental Managing the details	Case Study – Xinjiang, northwest China and Central Eurasia, 50 years data from 1962 to 2011 Air temperature hourly data Rainfall hourly data
39	S. Liu, H. Webb, L. Guo, X. Yao, X. Chang	Integration of R-Pi, IoT, ZigBee module-WSN NoSQL database DynamoDB, Relational database Oracle	EC2 service AWS based Modern agricultural IoT Monitoring system J2EE platform	—
40	B.N. Lawrence, J. Churchill, V.L. Bennett, M. Juckes, P. Kershaw, S. Pascoe, S. Pepler, M. Pritchard A. Stephens	Report of the first-year usage and short-term planning for JASMIN architecture and JASMIN super data cluster	Data analysis UK community Earth observation, Climate monitoring	100 Numerical experiments by 29 Modelling centres 61 Climate Models.
41	Aras.C. Onal, O. B. Sezer, M. Ozbayoglu, E. Dogdu	LinkedSensorData – RDF US dataset – Location-based dataset recorded with weather sensor	Air temperature, Visibility Wind speed, Pressure, Relative humidity – clustering and sensor anomaly detection	Continental USA, The Rocky Mountains; 2 clusters – one – 3687 data points, the other with 3319
42	E. Oyekanlu	SQLite	To transmit prediction alerts about machine health to IIoT cloud	Edge analytical database for fault identification, prediction and recommendation.
43	A.Truskinger, M. C. Fields, P. Eichinski, M. Towsey, P. Roe	QCIF Cloud Infrastructure	Acoustic sensors to monitor and register various ecological changes	The QUT Ecoacoustics Research Group
44	E. Solaiman R. Ranjan, P.P. Jayaraman, K. Mitra	Synchronized edge device, network and the cloud	The IoT application Ecosystem	—

CrowdSensing, a bracelet that can be worn also has data collected on weather and surrounding, can be integrated to provide better infrastructure facilities. Tourism cards that promote various added advantages and features like discounted access to various outlets and rides, keeping a tab on crowd concentration, emphasizing on interconnecting food, location, facilities and tourism, all under one big umbrella. An enormous amount of data gets generated due to various Earth missions per minute, say if we consider the case of Earth Observing System Data and Information System (EOSDIS), which alone generates about 3.0 TB/day that can be channelized in a proper manner using ArcGIS based cloud computing solution as shared by [37]. Integrated systems are found to monitor Air Temperature and rainfall using remote sensing techniques with IoT by Fang et al. [38]. Using Amazon AWS and Amazon EC2, [39] have achieved hybrid storage of Eco agricultural data. JASMIN [40] provides storing and processing options to Centre for Environmental Data Archival (CEDA) data. IBM BlueMix framework [41] is used to record sensor readings for Environmental parameters. Critical parameters can be transmitted to reduce the burden over cloud Gateways by phase-wise transmission as achieved by E. Oyekanlu [42]. A highly innovative application to track fauna using acoustic sensors is devised by Truskinger et al. [43] using a hybridization of cloud and local data.

5.3 PROPOSED SET UP

In Figure 5.1, the prediction modules sit at the vicinity of the sensors. Gateway is an intermediate between cloud and the prediction model. The predicted results are shown by the warning system. A schematic diagram of the prediction and warning system is as shown in Figure 5.1. A further flow of events is presented in Figure 5.2, which shows how such prediction modules can be embedded in the cloud infrastructure.

We have considered the reconstructed Hadley Centre Sea Ice and Sea Surface Temperature data set (HadISST) obtained from National Center for Atmospheric Research (NCAR) across the Niño 1+2, Niño3, Niño3.4 and Niño 4. These are calculated from the Kaplan SST and area averaged for monthly data from the year 1870 to the present. The data [3, 35] is made available by Earth System Research Laboratory (ESRL)-National Oceanic and Atmospheric Administration (NOAA). A total of 1805 readings are available till May 2020. The first 1700 readings are given for training the data, and the remaining 105 are predicted using the proposed algorithms.

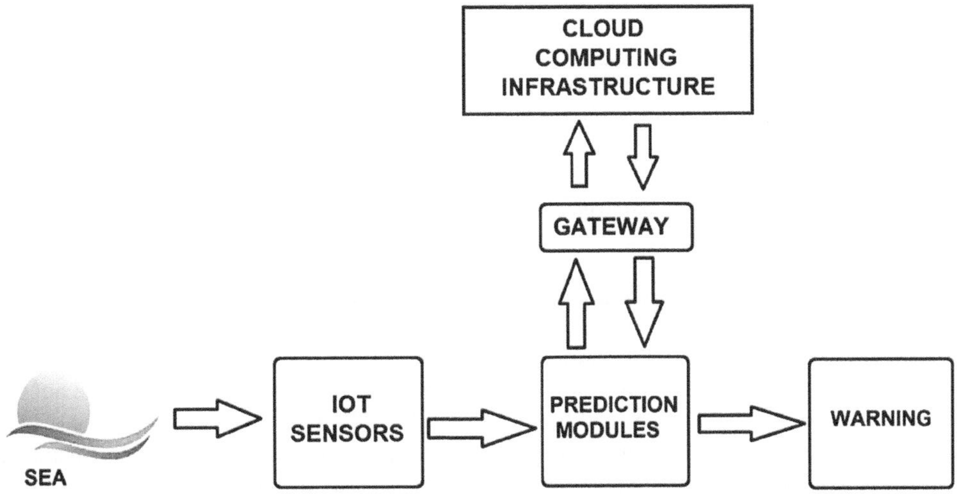

FIGURE 5.1 Schematic diagram of the prediction and warning system.

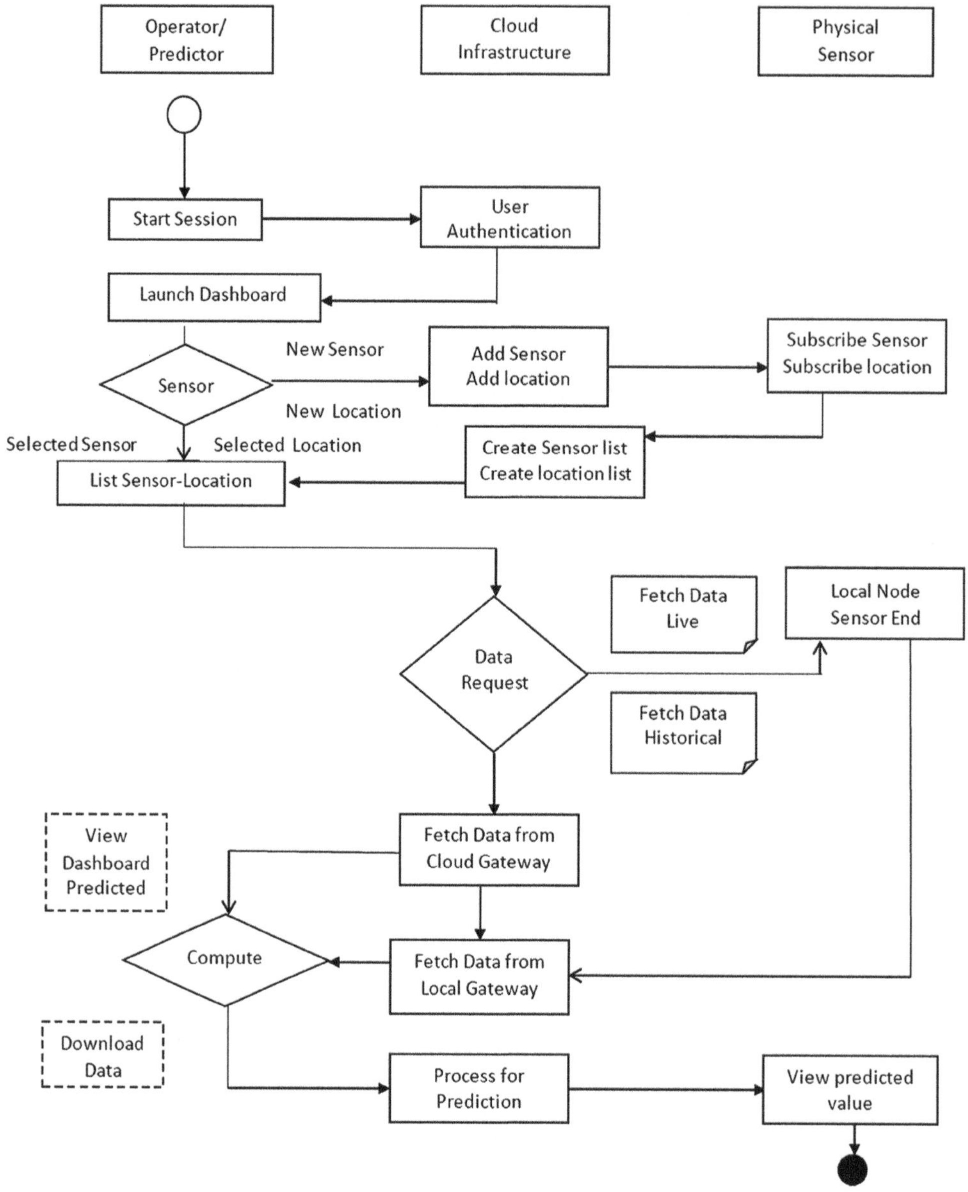

FIGURE 5.2 Proposed flowchart for the prediction and warning system.

5.4 NONLINEAR AUTO REGRESSION (NAR) USING MATLAB TOOL

Nonlinear auto regression (NAR) techniques are known to be very popular in predicting outcomes based on temporal data. Various researchers have found various applications based on the nonlinear auto regression techniques. G. Saha and N.C. Chauhan [48–50] have used NAR Network, which is basically a feed-forward multilayer perceptron to evaluate various parameters like weather parameters like max temperature, relative humidity, pressure and winds. Also, they have established dependency relationship between SST and sea surface salinity, sea bottom temperature and sea bottom salinity. Also, correlation of SST with air temperature, meridional/and zonal winds. A basic block diagram representation of the same is shown in Figure 5.3. And its neural structure is shown in Figure 5.4.

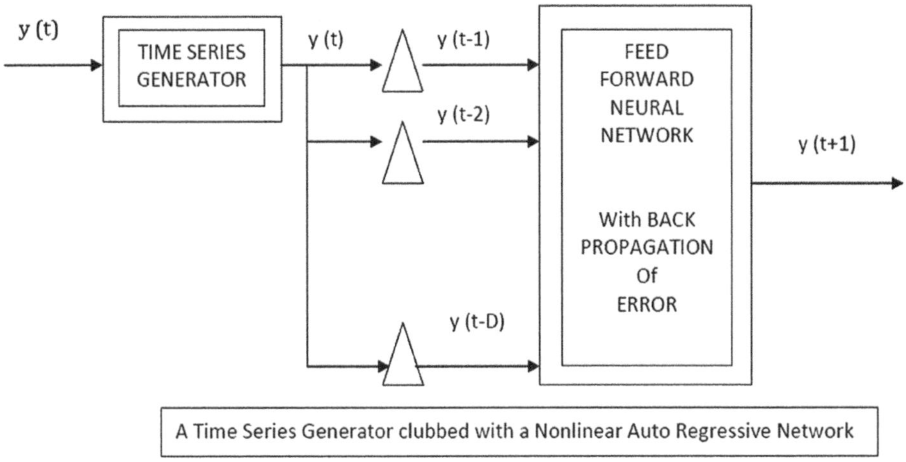

FIGURE 5.3 Block diagram representation of a NAR network for a time series [50].

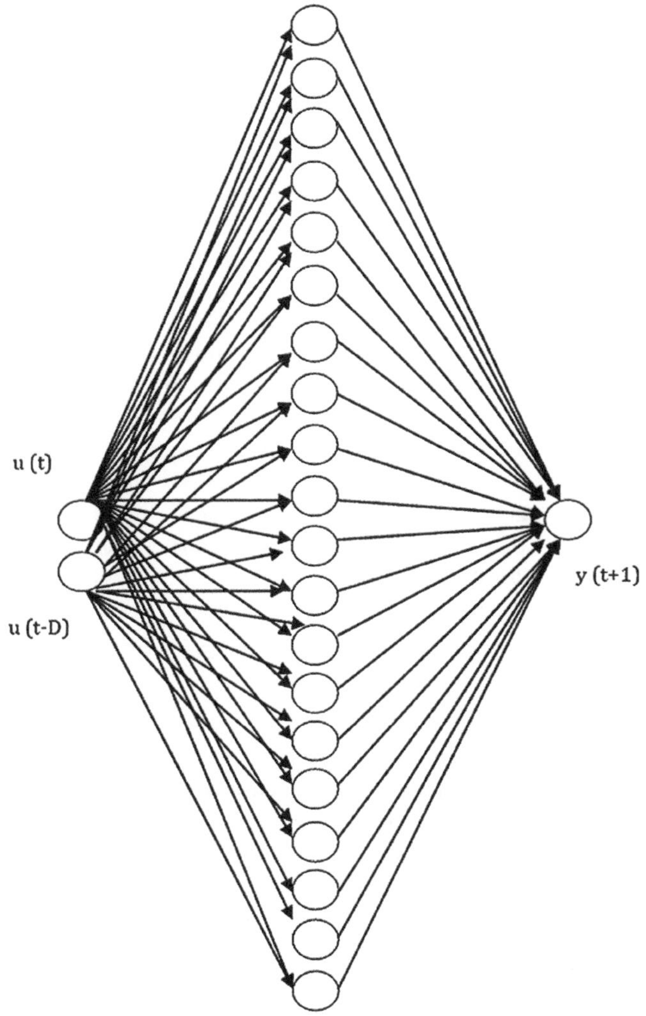

FIGURE 5.4 Neuron level visualization of D time delay in nonlinear auto regressive network [50].

TABLE 5.2
Optimized Algorithm for Various Values of Hidden H and Delay D Neurons

Nino(1+2)				Nino3				Nino3.4				Nino4			
D	H	MSE	RMSE	D	H	MSE	RMSE	D	H	MSE	RMSE	D	H	MSE	RMSE
12	1	0.35	0.5928	12	1	0.2968	0.5448	12	1	0.0374	0.1933	12	1	0.0095	0.0975
12	2	0.2871	0.4951	12	2	0.4027	0.6346	12	2	0.0054	0.0738	12	2	0.014	0.1184
12	3	0.2542	0.5042	12	3	0.4273	0.6537	12	3	0.0021	0.0457	12	3	0.008	0.0897
12	4	0.4214	0.6491	12	4	0.284	0.5329	12	4	0.0022	0.0469	12	4	0.0011	0.0325
12	5	0.6081	0.7798	12	5	0.2352	0.4849	12	5	0.0013	0.0366	12	5	0.0024	0.0491
12	6	0.5827	0.7634	12	6	0.2571	0.507	12	6	0.0281	0.1676	12	6	9.9*10-5	0.01
12	7	0.3971	0.6302	12	7	0.1761	0.4197	12	7	0.0144	0.12	12	7	0.0099	0.0993
12	8	0.367	0.6058	12	8	0.2894	0.538	12	8	0.0052	0.0718	12	8	0.0065	0.0809
12	9	0.3461	0.5883	12	9	0.4011	0.6333	12	9	0.0147	0.1213	12	9	0.0121	0.11
12	10	0.3213	0.5668	12	10	0.1946	0.4411	12	10	0.019	0.1378	12	10	0.021	0.1448
12	11	0.3414	0.5843	12	11	0.2898	0.5383	12	11	0.0031	0.0554	12	11	0.003	0.0545
12	12	0.4239	0.6511	12	12	0.2392	0.4891	12	12	0.0019	0.0439	12	12	0.0061	0.0781
12	13	0.4098	0.6402	12	13	0.195	0.4416	12	13	0.0224	0.1495	12	13	0.0228	0.1509
12	14	0.5135	0.7166	12	14	0.3185	0.5644	12	14	0.0068	0.0827	12	14	0.0053	0.073
12	15	0.3565	0.5969	12	15	0.1399	0.374	12	15	8.7*10-4	0.0297	12	15	0.004	0.0635
12	16	0.4443	0.6665	12	16	0.2128	0.4613	12	16	1.7*10-4	0.013	12	16	0.0213	0.1461
12	17	0.3178	0.5637	12	17	0.1865	0.4319	12	17	3.9*10-4	0.0199	12	17	0.0142	0.1192
12	18	0.3406	0.5836	12	18	0.8237	0.9076	12	18	0.0274	0.1654	12	18	0.0021	0.0453
12	19	0.379	0.6156	12	19	0.4608	0.6788	12	19	0.019	0.1379	12	19	0.0129	0.1136
12	20	0.2428	0.4928	12	20	0.3475	0.5895	12	20	0.0011	0.0335	12	20	0.0056	0.0747
12	21	0.3065	0.5537	12	21	0.3171	0.5631	12	21	0.0017	0.0417	**12**	**21**	**7.2*10-5**	**0.0085**
12	22	0.4684	0.6844	12	22	0.2232	0.4724	**12**	**22**	**2.2*10-6**	**0.0015**	12	22	0.0086	0.0928
12	**23**	**0.2241**	**0.4734**	12	23	0.1682	0.4101	12	23	0.0179	0.1339	12	23	0.0137	0.1171
12	24	0.2532	0.5032	12	24	0.1236	0.3516	12	24	0.0088	0.0941	12	24	0.0106	0.1029
12	25	0.2698	0.5194	12	25	0.4976	0.7054	12	25	0.0209	0.1447	12	25	0.0098	0.0988
12	26	0.2391	0.489	12	26	0.304	0.5513	12	26	0.013	0.1141	12	26	0.0347	0.1864
12	27	0.3071	0.5542	12	27	0.252	0.502	12	27	0.0385	0.1961	12	27	0.0113	0.1064
12	28	0.3122	0.5588	12	28	0.2772	0.5265	12	28	0.0154	0.1241	12	28	0.0133	0.1154
12	29	0.3435	0.586	12	29	0.1787	0.4227	12	29	0.0104	0.1019	12	29	0.0033	0.0574
12	30	0.2447	0.4946	**12**	**30**	**0.048**	**0.2191**	12	30	0.0024	0.0491	12	30	0.0318	0.1785
12	31	0.4235	0.6508	12	31	0.1932	0.4396	12	31	0.0045	0.0668	12	31	5.2*10-4	0.0228

The proposed setup has used a delay D of 12 neurons corresponding to every monthly data, and the value of hidden neurons H is calculated based on error computations. Table 5.2 uses the major error parameters to compute the optimized values of hidden neurons that would lead to minimum error. Table 5.3 contains the predicted values of the last five months using optimized values of the hidden neuron (H).

TABLE 5.3
Actual and Forecasted Values of Last Five Months using Optimum NAR Algorithm

Niño (1+2) site for D = 12 and H = 23						
Month	**Actual**	**Forecasted**	**CC**	**MAE**	**MSE**	**NSE**
01/2020	24.6	24.33019	0.96	0.2698	0.0728	0.9608
02/2020	26.29	25.98955	0.98	0.3004	0.0903	0.9903
03/2020	26.29	26.6209	1	0.3309	0.1095	0.9883
04/2020	25.69	25.2166	1	0.4734	0.2241	0.9628
05/2020	24.22	24.4678	1	0.2478	0.0614	0.9365
Niño 3 site for D = 12 and H = 30						
Month	Actual	Forecasted	CC	MAE	MSE	NSE
01/2020	25.95	25.92224	0.99	0.0278	0	0.9816
02/2020	26.55	26.61081	0.99	0.0608	0.0037	0.9943
03/2020	27.09	27.07376	1	0.0162	0	0.9999
04/2020	27.82	27.6009	1	0.2191	0.048	0.9888
05/2020	26.83	27.54956	1	0.7196	0.5178	0.7599
Niño 3.4 site for D = 12 and H = 22						
Month	Actual	Forecasted	CC	MAE	MSE	NSE
01/2020	27.22	27.14357	1	0.0764	0.0058	0.9103
02/2020	27.25	27.01607	1	0.2339	0.0547	0.327
03/2020	27.25	27.60887	0.991	0.3589	0.1288	0.58
04/2020	27.62	27.68684	1	0.0668	0.0045	0.9896
05/2020	28.26	27.90545	1	0.3546	0.1257	0.9251
Niño 4 site for D = 12 and H = 21						
Month	Actual	Forecasted	CC	MAE	MSE	NSE
01/2020	29.14	29.05548	1	0.0845	0.0071	0.9876
02/2020	28.92	29.0009	1	0.0809	0.0065	0.9774
03/2020	28.98	28.82204	1	0.158	0.025	0.9303
04/2020	29.11	29.1015	1	0.0085	7.2*10-5	0.9999
05/2020	28.99	29.2408	1	0.2508	0.0629	0.8299

5.5 LONG SHORT-TERM MEMORY (LSTM) USING PYTHON PROGRAMMING

LSTM networks are a class of deep neural network that comprises of a sequence input layer and an LSTM layer. A *sequence input layer* inputs sequence or time series data into the network. An *LSTM layer* learns long-term dependencies between time steps of sequence data and finds wide application in forecasting time series. Figure 5.5 shows the block diagram of an LSTM cell. And the LSTM layer structure has two layers of 10 neurons each. Figure 5.6 are the legends used in a reference LSTM cell (Table 5.4).

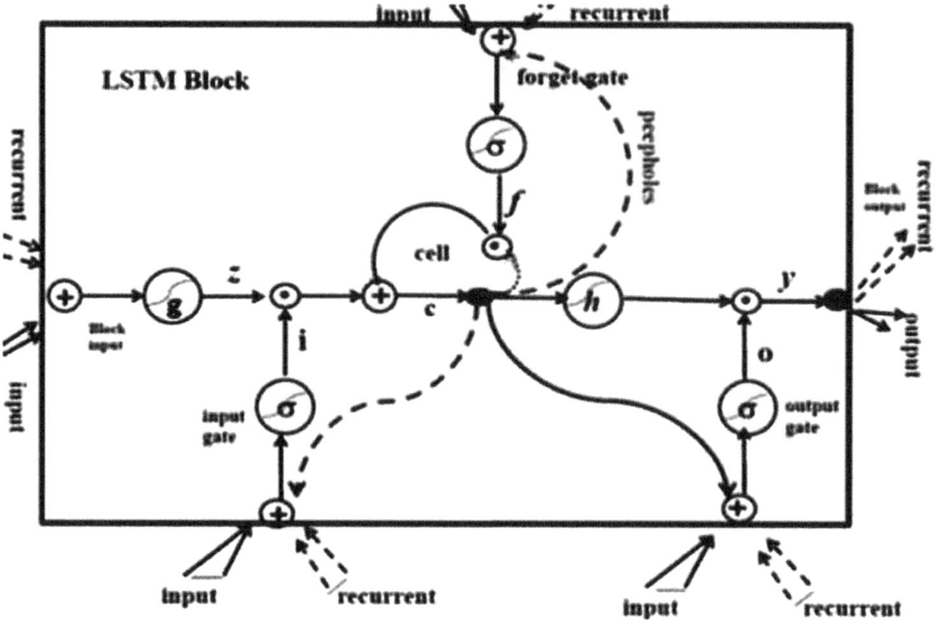

FIGURE 5.5 A LSTM block made up of various gates-input, forget, and the output gate.

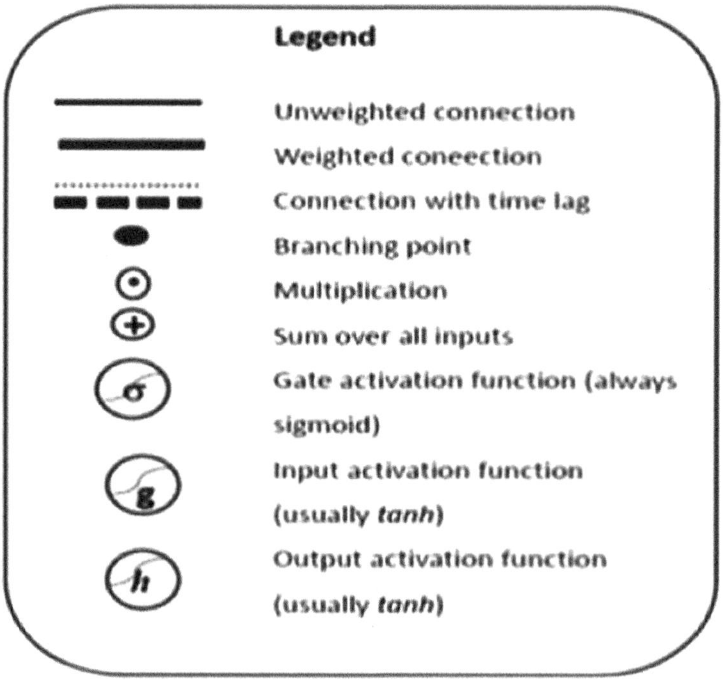

FIGURE 5.6 LSTM block model legends.

TABLE 5.4
Actual and Forecasted Values of Last Five Months using LSTM in Python

Niño (1+2) site						
Month	**Actual**	**Forecasted**	**CC**	**MAE**	**MSE**	**NSE**
Jan 2020	24.6	24.58	0.99	0.02	0.0004	0.9998
Feb 2020	26.29	26.89	0.99	0.6	0.36	0.9616
Mar 2020	26.29	26.83	0.96951	0.54	0.2916	0.9689
Apr 2020	25.69	25.58	1	0.11	0.0121	0.998
May 2020	24.22	24.37	1	0.15	0.0225	0.977
Niño 3 site						
Month	Actual	Forecasted	CC	MAE	MSE	NSE
Jan 2020	25.95	25.85	1	0.1000	0.0100	0.7732
Feb 2020	26.55	26.53	1	0.0200	0.0004	0.9994
Mar 2020	27.09	27.12	0.99	0.0300	0.00009	0.9995
Apr 2020	27.82	27.85	0.99	0.0300	0.00009	0.9998
May 2020	26.83	26.81	0.99	0.0200	0.0004	0.9997
Niño 3.4 site						
Month	Actual	Forecasted	CC	MAE	MSE	NSE
Jan 2020	27.22	27.24	1	0.0200	0.00004	0.9941
Feb 2020	27.25	27.27	1	0.0200	0.00004	0.9952
Mar 2020	27.25	27.31	1	0.0600	0.0036	0.9572
Apr 2020	27.62	27.61	0.998	0.0100	0.00001	0.9998
May 2020	28.26	28.31	0.999	0.0500	0.0025	0.9985
Niño 4 site						
Month	Actual	Forecasted	CC	MAE	MSE	NSE
Jan 2020	29.14	29.13	1	0.01	0.00001	0.9998
Feb 2020	28.92	28.91	1	0.01	0.00001	0.9997
Mar 2020	28.98	28.97	1	0.01	0.00001	0.9997
Apr 2020	29.11	29.12	1	0.01	0.00001	0.9998
May 2020	28.99	29.00	1	0.01	0.00001	0.9997

5.6 ERROR PARAMETERS USED IN THE PROPOSED OPTIMIZED ALGORITHMS AND TIME SERIES PLOTS

Along with regular error parameters for error evaluation like MSE, CC, MAE, we have tested the proposed algorithms for NSE, which finds good appreciation in hydro-based system error calculations. Regular error parameters may not be competent enough to project the efficiency of forecasting models and, hence, an altogether new symmetric index of agreement (λ) was proposed by Aniket et al. [46] to evaluate error performance and tested for Weather Research and Forecasting (WRF) model using Global Precipitation Measurement's (GPM) Integrated Multi-satellitE Retrievals for GPM (IMERG) and rainfall dataset (Figure 5.7).

Where yt = actual data, ft = forecasted data, myt = mean of actual data and mft = mean of the forecasted data

$$MSE = \frac{1}{2}\sum_{i=1}^{n}\left(y_t - f_t\right)^2 \tag{5.1}$$

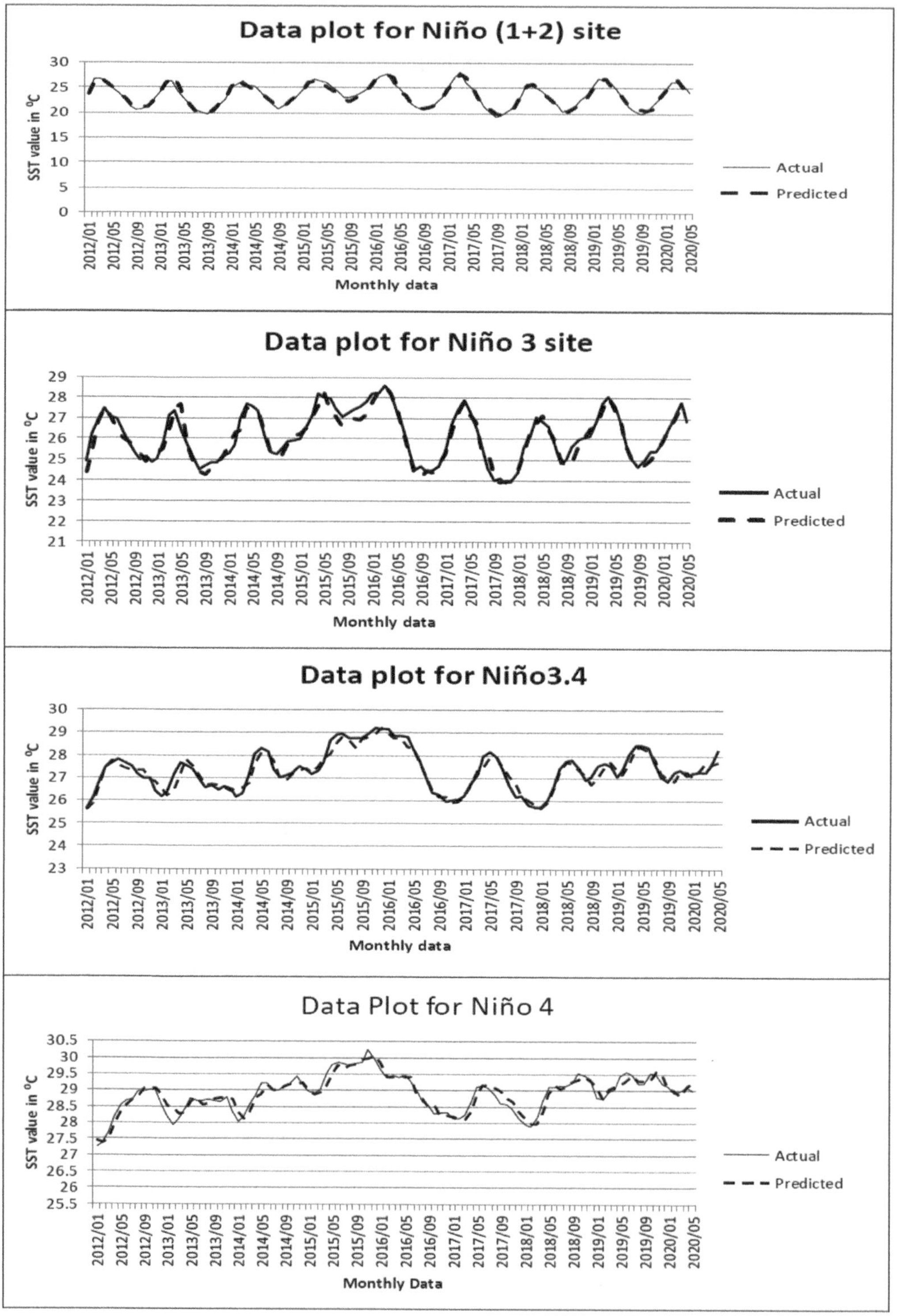

FIGURE 5.7 Time series plots of all the sites using NAR algorithms for the last 100 readings.

$$MAE = \text{mean}\left(abs\left(y_t - f_t\right)\right) \tag{5.2}$$

$$CC\left(\frac{\sum_{i=1}^{n}\left(y_t - m_{yt}\right)\left(f_t - m_{ft}\right)}{\sum_{i=1}^{n}\left(y_t - m_{yt}\right)^2 \sum_{i=1}^{n}\left(f_t - m_{ft}\right)^2}\right) \tag{5.3}$$

$$NSE = 1 - \left(\frac{\sum_{i=1}^{n}\left(y_t - f_t\right)^2}{\sum_{i=1}^{n}\left(y_t - m_{yt}\right)^2}\right) \tag{5.4}$$

5.7 OUTCOME

It may also be proposed to share critical information on the cloud gateway and keep local details at the local gateway. In this way, the traffic and storage can also be optimized.

The results very evidently show that such a system can very well be established. Predictive algorithms show results very close to the actual values. If the critical parameters are kept in check, then even small variations can be sensed and corrective action can be generated accordingly. For example, in Table 5.5, it is observed that for the Niño 3.4 and 4 sites, the skewness is negative, which means that the distribution has a longer left-handed tail and the probability of an unlikely event is high. With the initiative taken by NASA's Jet Propulsion Laboratory – Physical Oceanography Distributed Active Archive Centre (PODAAC) that has made the Group for high-resolution sea surface temperature (GHRSST) level-4 multiscale ultra-high resolution (MUR) data available on cloud, we will find cloud-based application programming interface (API) that would monitor and maintain data logs round the clock.

TABLE 5.5
A Comparative of all Critical Time Series Parameters for Every 500 Readings

Place	Max SST	Min SST	Mean SST	Variance	Skewness	Kurtosis
Niño(1+2)	28.55	19.11	23.11	4.72.	0.16	1.96
Niño(1+2)	28.15	18.71	23.28	5.03	0.17	1.82
Niño(1+2)	29.07	19.11	23.23	5.20	0.23	1.99
Niño 3	28.84	23.29	25.6	1.33	0.18	2.14
Niño 3	28.76	23.12	25.77	1.31	0.13	2.26
Niño 3	29.21	22.89	25.75	1.49	0.09	2.43
Niño 3.4	29.19	24.09	26.82	0.77	0.25	2.5
Niño 3.4	29.18	24.93	27.01	0.6	−0.10	2.73
Niño 3.4	29.18	24.41	27.00	0.83	−0.22	2.84
Niño 4	29.83	26.32	28.19	0.34	0.15	2.64
Niño 4	29.8	27	28.38	0.23	−0.31	3.04
Niño 4	29.63	26.54	28.43	0.39	−0.56	2.95

REFERENCES

[1] G. Mellor, *Introduction to Physical Oceanography*, Springer, 19 (1996).

[2] A. Gill, *Atmosphere and Ocean Dynamics*, Academic Press, New York (1982).

[3] National Climatic Data Center, National Center for Environmental Information, https://www.ncdc.noaa.gov, last accessed on the 15 December, 2020.

[4] F. Carbone, M.S. Landis, C. N. Gencarelli, A. Naccarato, F. Sprovieri, F. De Simone, I. M. Hedgecock, N. Pirrone, 'Sea surface temperature variation linked to elemental mercury concentrations measured on Mauna Loa', *Geophysical Research Letters*, 43 (2016).

[5] S. B. Mustapha, Pierre Larouche, Jean-Marie Dubois, 'Spatial and temporal variability of sea-surface temperature fronts in the coastal Beaufort Sea', *Continental Shelf Research*, 124, pp. 134–141 (2016).

[6] C. A. Stock, K. Pegion, G. A. Veechi, M. A. Alexander, D. Tommasi, N. A. Bond, P. S. Fratantoni, R. G. Gudgel, T. Kristiansen, T. D. O'Brien, Y. Xue, X. Yang, 'seasonal sea surface temperature anomaly prediction for coastal ecosystems', *Progress in Oceanography*, 137, pp. 219–236 (2015).

[7] P. K. Dinesh Kumar, Y. Steeven Paul, K. R. Muraleedharan, V. S. N. Murthy, P. N. Preenu, 'Comparison of long-term variability of Sea Surface Temperature in the Arabian Sea and the Bay of Bengal', *Regional Studies in Marine Science*, 3, pp. 67–75 (2016).

[8] A. Canadas, J. A. Vazquez, 'Common dolphins in the Alboran Sea: Facing a reduction in their suitable habitat due to an increase in Sea Surface Temperature', *Deep Sea Research Part II*, 141, pp. 306–318 (2017).

[9] M. Picone, A. Orasi, G. Nardone, 'Sea Surface Temperature monitoring in Italian Seas: Analysis of long term trends and short-term dynamics', *Measurement*, 129, pp. 260–267 (2018).

[10] K. Ae Park, E. Y. Lee, E. Chang, S. Hong, 'Spatial and temporal variability of sea surface temperature and warming trends in the Yellow Sea', *Journal of Marine Systems*, 143, pp. 24–38 (2015).

[11] L. Hu, M. He, 'Impacts of Sea Surface Temperature Anomaly to the coverage area and early appearance time of green tide in the Yellow Sea', *Conference: IGARSS IEEE International Geoscience and Remote Sensing*, pp. 4465–4468 (2014).

[12] R. Rajesh, G. S. Dwarakish, 'Satellite oceanography- a review', *International Conference On Water Resources, Coastal and Ocean Engineering (ICWRCOE 2015)*, Aquatic Procedia 4, pp. 165–172 (2015).

[13] R. Salles, P. Mattos, Ana-Maria D Iorgulescu, E. Bezerra, L. Lima, E Ogasawara, 'Evaluating temporal aggregation for predicting the sea surface temperature of the atlantic ocean', *Ecological Informatics*, pp. 1–14 (2016).

[14] A. Wada, N. Usui, K. Sato, 'Relationship to maximum tropical cyclone intensity to sea surface temperature and tropical cyclone heat potential in the North Pacific Ocean', *Journal of Geophysical Research*, 117, no. D11(June 2012).

[15] M.M. Ali, P. S. V. Jagadeesh, I. I. Lin and Je. Yuan Hsu, 'A neural network approach to estimate tropical cyclone heat potential in the Indian Ocean', *IEEE Geoscience and Remote Sensing Letters*, 9, no. 6, pp. 1114–1117 (2012).

[16] M. M. Ali, D. Swain, R. A. Weller: 'Estimation of ocean subsurface thermal structure from surface parameters: A neural network approach', *IEEE Geoscience and Remote Sensing Letters*, 31, no. 20 (October 2004).

[17] D. E. Rumelhart, G. E. Hinton, R. J. Williams, 'Learning representations by back-propagating errors', *Nature*, 323, pp. 533–536 (1986).

[18] W. W. Hsieh, B. Tang, 'Applying neural network models to prediction and data analysis in meteorology and oceanography', *Bulletin of the American Meteorological Society*, 79, no. 9, pp. 1855–1870 (1998).

[19] F. T. Tangang, W. W. Hsieh, B. Tang, 'Forecasting regional sea surface temperatures in the tropical Pacific by neural network models, with wind stress and sea level pressure as predictors', *Journal Of Geophysical Research*, 103, no. C4, pp. 7511–7522 (1998).

[20] F. T. Tangang, W. W. Hsieh, B. Tang, 'Forecasting the equatorial Pacific sea surface temperatures by neural network models', *Climate Dynamics*, 13, no. 2, pp. 135–147, (1997).

[21] B. Tang, W. W. Hsieh, A. H. Monahan, F. T. Tangang, 'Skill comparisons between neural networks and canonical correlation analysis in predicting the equatorial pacific sea surface temperatures', *Bulletin of the American Meteorological Society*, pp. 287–293 (2000).

[22] R. W. Reynolds, T. M. Smith, 'Improved global sea surface temperature analyses using optimum interpolation', *Journal of Climate*, 7, pp. 929–994 (1994).

[23] T. M. Smith, R. W. Reynolds, 'Improved extended reconstruction of SST (1854–1997)', *Journal of Climate*, 17, pp. 2466–2477 (2004).
[24] J. S. Kug, S. I. An, F. F. Jin, I. S. Kang, 'Preconditions for El Nino and La Nina onsets and their relation to the Indian Ocean', *Geophysical Research Letters*, 32, no. 5, pp. 1–5 (2005).
[25] S. H. Yoo, S. Yang, C. H. Ho, 'Variability of the Indian Ocean Sea surface temperature and its impacts on Asian-Australian monsoon climate', *Journal of Geophysical Research*, 111, no. D03, pp. 108–125 (2006).
[26] K. E. Trenberth, 'Recent observed lnterdecadal climate changes in the Northern Hemisphere', *American Meteorological Society*, 71, no. 7, pp. 983–993 (1990).
[27] D. J. Shea, K. E. Trenberth, 'A global monthly sea surface temperature climatology', *American Meteorological Society*, 5, pp. 987–1001 (1992).
[28] K. E. Trenberth, J. W. Hurrell, 'Decadal atmosphere-ocean variations in the Pacific', *Climate Dynamics*, 9, pp. 303–319 (1994).
[29] K. C. Tripathi, I. M. L. Das, A. K. Sahai, 'Predictability of sea surface temperature anomalies in the Indian Ocean using Artificial Neural Networks', *Indian Journal of Geo Marine Sciences*, 35, no. 3, pp. 210–220 (2006).
[30] K. C. Tripathi, S. Rai, A. C. Pandey, I. M. L. Das, 'Southern Indian ocean SST indices as early predictors of Indian summer monsoon', *Indian Journal of Marine Sciences*, 37, no. 1, pp. 70–76 (2008).
[31] S. B. Mohongo, M. C. Deo, 'Using Artificial Neural Networks to forecast monthly and seasonal sea surface temperature anomalies in the western Indian Ocean', *International Journal of Ocean and Climate Systems*, 4, no. 2, pp. 133–150 (2013).
[32] K. Patil, M. C. Deo, S. Ghosh, M. Ravichandran, 'Predicting sea surface temperatures in the North Indian ocean with nonlinear autoregressive neural networks', *International Journal of Oceanography*, 2013, 11 pages (2013).
[33] K. Patil, M. C. Deo, M. Ravichandran, 'Prediction of sea surface temperatures by combining numerical and neural techniques', *Journal of Atmospheric and Oceanic Technology*, 33, pp. 1715–1726 (2016).
[34] A. Wu, W. W. Hseih, B. Tang, 'Neural network forecasts of the tropical Pacific sea surface temperatures', *Neural Networks*, 19, pp. 145–154 (2006).
[35] https://climatedataguide.ucar.edu/climate-data/sst-data-hadisst-v11, last accessed on 26/11/2020
[36] Y. Sun, H. Song, A. J. Jara, R. Bie, 'Internet of Things and big data analytics for smart and connected communities', *IEEE Access*, 14, no. 8 (2015).
[37] Y. Huang, P. Gao, Y. Zhang, J. Zhang, 'A cloud computing solution for big imagery data analytics', *IEEE International Workshop on Big Geospatial Data and Data Science (BGDDS)*, Wuhan, China, (2018).
[38] S. Fang, L. D. Xu, Y. Zhu, J. Ahati, H. Pei, J. Yan, Z. Liu, 'An integrated system for regional environmental monitoring and management based on Internet of Things', *IEEE Transactions On Industrial Informatics*, 10, no. 2 (2014).
[39] S. Liu, L. Guo, H. Webb, X. Yao, X. Chang, 'Internet of Things monitoring system of modern eco-agriculture based on cloud computing', *IEEE Access* (2019).
[40] B. N. Lawrence, V. L. Bennett, J. Churchill, M. Juckes, P. Kershaw, S. Pascoe, S. Pepler, M. Pritchard and A. Stephens, 'Storing and manipulating environmental big data with JASMIN', *IEEE International Conference on Big Data*, pp. 68–75 (2013).
[41] A. C. Onal, O. B. Sezer, M. Ozbayoglu, E. Dogdu, 'Weather data analysis and sensor fault detection using an extended IoT framework with semantics, big data, and machine learning', *IEEE International Conference on Big Data (BIGDATA)*, pp. 2037–2046 (2017).
[42] E. Oyekanlu, 'Predictive edge computing for time series of industrial IoT and large scale critical infrastructure based on open-source software analytic of big data', *IEEE International Conference on Big Data (BIGDATA)*, pp. 1663–1669 (2017).
[43] A. Truskinger, M. C. Fields, P. Eichinski, M. Towsey, P. Roe, 'Practical analysis of big acoustic sensor data for environmental monitoring', *IEEE Fourth International Conference on Big Data and Cloud Computing*, pp. 91–98 (2014).
[44] E. Solaiman, R. Ranjan, P. P. Jayaraman, K. Mitra 'Monitoring Internet of Things application ecosystems for failure', *IT Pro September/October 2016, Published by the IEEE Computer Society*, pp. 8–11.
[45] H. Shalini, C. V. Aravinda, 'An IoT-based predictive analytics for estimation of rainfall for irrigation' chapter in springer book', *Advances in Artificial Intelligence and Data Engineering (AISC, volume 1133)*, pp. 1399–1413 (2021).

[46] A. Chakravorty, R. B. Gogoi, S. S. Kundu, P. L. N. Raju, 'Investigating the efficacy of a new symmetric index of agreement for evaluating WRF simulated summer monsoon rainfall over northeast India', *Meteorology and Atmospheric Physics*, Springer Nature, (2020)
[47] G. Venati, Ch. Srinivasrao, K. S. Reddy, K. L. Sharma, A. Rai, 'Soil health and climate change', *Climate Change and Soil Interactions* (2020).
[48] G. Saha and N. C. Chauhan, 'Numerical weather prediction using nonlinear auto regressive network for the Manaus region, Brazil', In *Proc. International Conference on Innovations in Power and Advanced Computing Technologies'17*, pp. 1–4 (2017).
[49] G. Saha, N. C. Chauhan, 'Dependency investigation of sea surface temperature on sea bottom temperature and sea surface salinity', In *Proc. International Conference on Innovations in Power and Advanced Computing Technologies'19*, March 2019, VIT, Vellore, pp. 1–9 (2019).
[50] G. Saha, N. Chauhan, 'Week ahead time series prediction of sea surface temperature using non linear auto regressive network with and without exogenous inputs', *Applications of Machine Learning, Algorithms for Intelligent Systems*, Springer Nature Singapore Pte Ltd., P. Johri et al. (eds.) pp. 235–256 (2020).
[51] D. Hanes, G. Salgueiro, P. Grossetete, R. Barton, J. Henry, 'IoT fundamentals- networking technologies, protocols, and use cases for the internet of things'. Ciscopress.com

6 Solar PV and HTC-PFM Device
A Scheme for Smart Poultry Farm

S.M. Masum Ahmed
Heriot-Watt University, Edinburgh, Scotland

Mohammad Zeyad
Universidad del País Vasco/Euskal Herriko Unibertsitatea, Bilbao, Spain

Md. Shehzad
Southern University, Chittagong, Bangladesh

CONTENTS

6.1 INTRODUCTION

Farming is one of the core revenue-generating sectors in several countries on earth. This has more of an impact on the economy than on other things. Moreover, food is the most important part of human life. In the national market, the farming industry has been making an excellent effort. Therefore, poultry farming has to be much more successful than ever. Increasing demand for chicken and egg intake has been constantly rising. Furthermore, priority must be given to the poultry sector. Besides,

DOI: 10.1201/9781003155577-8

a scheme for control and automation of chicken farms is important. Besides, in poultry farms, temperature and humidity control is very essential as chickens need a specific temperature and humidity for survival. Farmworkers encounter many challenges on their farms during harsh winter and warm summer seasons, although chickens require a normal temperature and humidity; the temperature range (T) is 20°C–25°C and the relative humidity (RH) range is 60%–80% [1, 2]. Even then, temperatures drop below the normal temperature in December, and temperatures in July climb just above normal temperature. To overcome these dilemmas, try to build such a system that will monitor and manage poultry farm loads by creating a conventional temperature for chickens.

There are nearly 100 breeder farms and hatcheries in Bangladesh, 8 grandparent stock farms, 70,000 industrial sheet and broiler farms, and more than 200 feed mills in 2019 [3]. So, a tremendous amount of electricity is needed in the poultry farm. People need to think about this energy consumption not only in Bangladesh but also at a global level. Global energy supplies such as fossil fuels, coal, and crude oil are depleting and will be exhausted in the coming years. Solar power is simply the leading alternative solution to satisfy existing and potential power demands [4–7]. Particularly, for this reason, renewable energy is vital for this sector instead of conventional fuel-based energy generation grid. Also, poultry farmers can earn extra money by selling extra electricity to the national grid. The current Bangladesh government has announced the development of smart cities across the nation that will soon be of great significance in smart agriculture solutions. This work, however, aims to establish a comfortable thermic atmosphere inside a poultry farm by using a smart poultry scheme and fulfilling the farm's electricity demand through a solar photovoltaic power plant that boosts renewable energy production.

6.2 LITERATURE REVIEW

Poultry farm monitoring devices are becoming popular due to their numerous benefits. In recent years, poultry farm monitoring devices are an essential requirement for farmers to keep poultry safe. The increasing interest in poultry technologies has created a need for a comprehensive literature survey.

Ahmad Ammar Nor Azlin and his team conducted a study that was based on the modular smart farm system. The focus of this research paper was mainly on electronics, embedded systems, and wireless technology for poultry farm monitoring integration. The system of control was divided into two main components: master and slave. The ATMega328p interface with different analog sensors, buzzer, relay output, passive and active modules, monetary push button and light indicator, LCD, included both the master and slave design process. Besides, to refine the output control system for increasing farm output, the PID controller was integrated. The device was successfully introduced and tested [8].

Minwoo, Jaeseok, and their team had displayed an outline that was based on the concept and deployment of a linked farm for a smart farming framework. A linked farm based on IoT systems has been seen in this article. The sensors and controls of the linked farm were supplied with an Internet link, and cube (a standard device software) was implemented for the IoT device. Also, for the management of the estate, an android program was introduced [9].

Ahmed A. Radhi suggested a thesis based on the design and implementation of a smart farm system. This paper had suggested a smart farm with an automated irrigation system. The system was developed with a programmable schedule in this automation irrigation system, automated tank level monitoring for irrigation storage water, and temperature calculation for farm-based microcontrollers with sensors and network servers. Finally, this system could be monitored and controlled by a network server [10].

Watcharin and their team have introduced a smart warning system that detects fan failure in the evaporative cooling system of the poultry farm project. The evaporating system malfunctions were triggered by power outages in the cooling fan in Chiang Mai, Thailand. To monitor the operation of the ventilator in the evaporative cooling system of the local poultry farm, a smart notification system has been developed. Infrared sensors have been used to recognize fan malfunctions. Subsequently, via a short letter, a phone call, and a LINE application, the data will be sent to the machine for analysis and alerted to the customer in three separate ways. Finally, a machine was mounted and checked at a poultry farm in the Mae Faek community, and this process took 45 days [11].

6.3 PROPOSED DESIGN

The key aim of this work is to create such a model of a smart poultry farm with on-site renewable energy production. Although, the concept intends to make poultry farming considerably more flexible and integrated. The conceptual design of the smart farm system is shown in Figure 6.1. Figure 6.1 illustrates the architecture of a poultry farm that operates via a solar Power system through which the electricity generation of a poultry farm can be sufficient and the climate can be managed smartly within a poultry farm using the HTC-FPM device that makes life very productive, pleasant, and comfortable for poultry farmers. However, with photovoltaic cells, solar panels capture radiation, produce direct current (DC) energy, and then transform using power electronics to accessible alternative current (AC) energy. Afterward, the AC power passes into the electrical panel of the chicken farm, and the power will be transmitted according to the needs of the chicken farm. Besides, the power grid is supplied with the extra power produced by the solar panel.

Solar PV includes all the components required to convert the energy from the sun and be able to be used with typical appliances. Usually, it consists of two major elements, an inverter, and a PV module. Also, batteries are connected to the system for energy storage purposes. The PV systems on top of the roof convert the incoming radiance into photo-generated electricity on a regular day with the sunshine. The grid-connected power converters used throughout the system also convert the

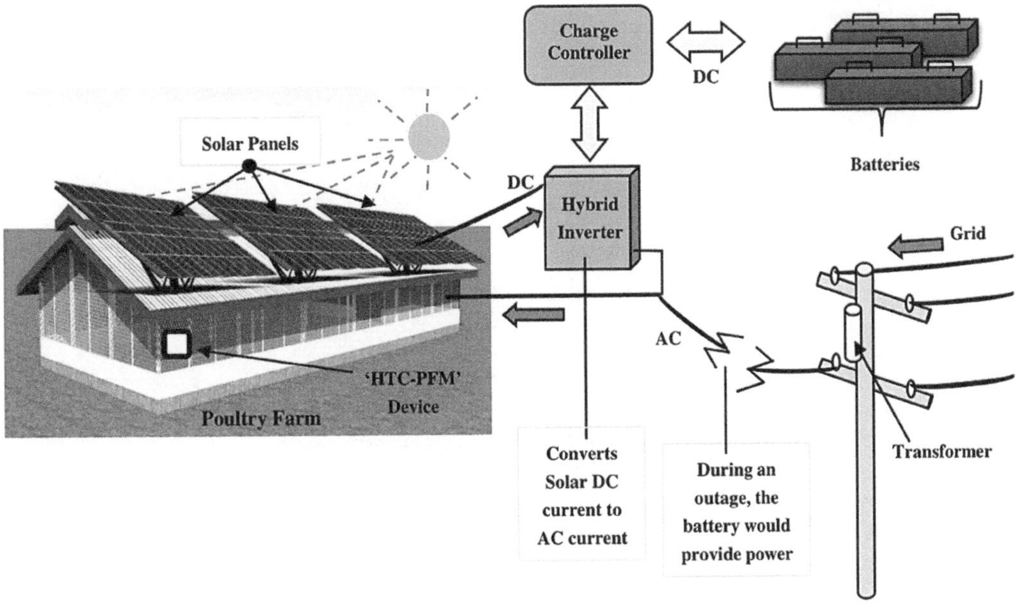

FIGURE 6.1 Working concept of smart poultry Farm system.

solar panels' DC output into available AC power continuously. The solar photovoltaic (PV) array should meet with the household's connected load. The solar photovoltaic (PV) system generates even higher power than what the load requires on quite a sunny day. The surplus power is supplied to the electrical grid in certain conditions. The mentioned system is a grid-connected PV system. In this system, two main components are available, i.e., an array of PV modules that are responsible for the power generation and a grid-connected inverter.

The customer will cover electric bills in this way in most nations. In comparison, the more direct sunlight the module consumes, the more energy is transformed into useful power. The new government of Bangladesh aims to develop smart cities around the country, which will soon maintain a large range of smart solutions.

6.4 SITE SELECTION

The location map for the Halishahar region is shown in Figure 6.2. Halishahar is situated at Chittagong in Bangladesh. The Latitude of Halishahar is 22.341 °N and the Longitude of Halishahar is 91.774 °E.

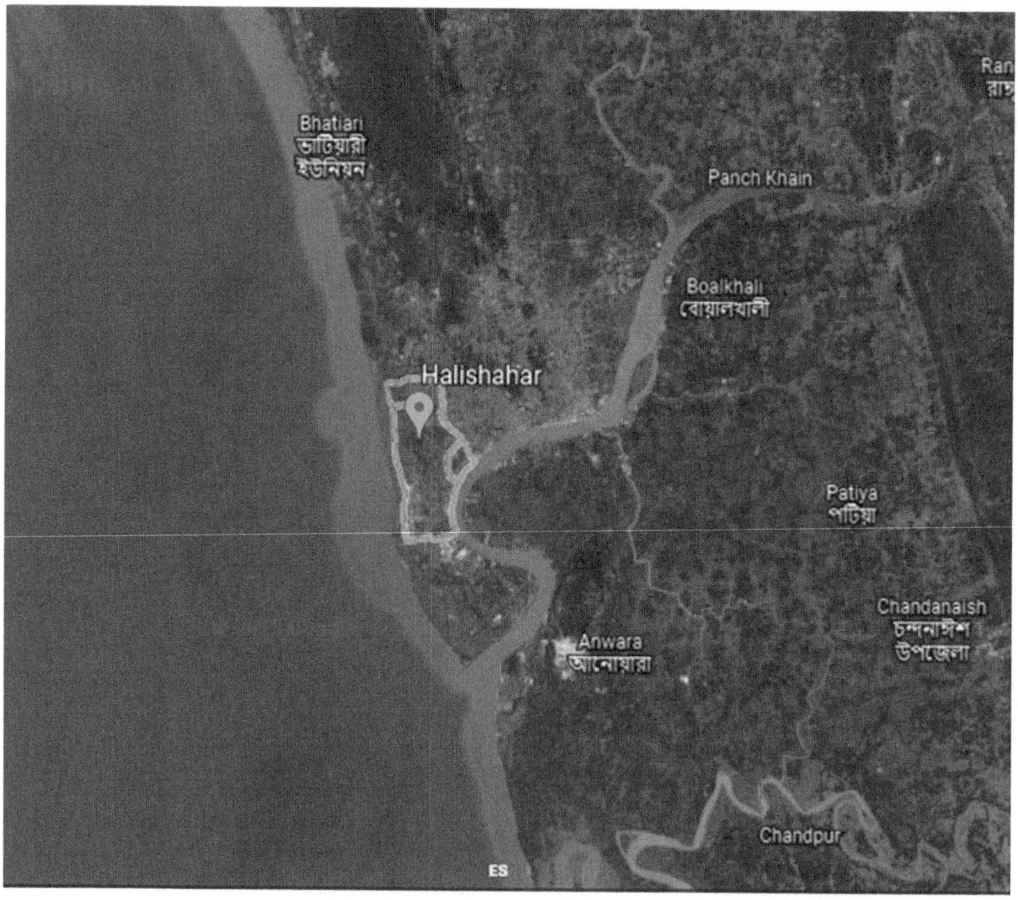

FIGURE 6.2 Selected site for smart poultry farm.

6.5 FEASIBILITY ANALYSIS

We estimated the most eminent temperature, most lowering temperature, relative humidity, and Solar Irradiance almost for 24 months, 2018 and 2019, in Halishahar after site selection. In fact, for feasibility analysis of 'HTC-FPM' devices, we have tested the most eminent temperature, most lowering temperature, and relative humidity. Also, for the feasibility study of solar PV, maximum temperature, minimum temperature, and solar irradiance were assessed.

Table 6.1 shows the feasibility analysis of the system.

Where, maximum temperature = T_{MAX},

Relative humidity = RH,

Minimum temperature = TMIN,

Solar irradiance = SI.

TABLE 6.1
Feasibility Analysis

Month	T_{MAX} (°C)	RH (%)	T_{MIN} (°C)	SI (kWh/m²/day)
Jan/2018	21.84	76.90	14.36	4.33
Feb/2018	25.56	76.45	18.19	4.85
Mar/2018	29.69	72.81	22.64	5.60
Apr/2018	29.90	78.58	25.04	5.79
May/2018	29.67	85.81	26.24	4.53
Jun/2018	29.69	88.67	27.28	4.47
Jul/2018	29.90	89.22	27.05	4.29
Aug/2018	30.16	88.15	26.89	5.31
Sept/2018	30.24	85.09	26.92	5.01
Oct/2018	29.25	77.54	24.75	4.36
Nov/2018	27.05	73.24	20.94	4.72
Dec/2018	23.66	74.97	16.73	3.84
Average – 2018	**28.05**	**80.62**	**23.08**	**4.76**
Jan/2019	23.67	68.68	15.26	4.51
Feb/2019	25.61	67.25	17.68	4.67
Mar/2019	28.28	72.89	21.20	5.54
Apr/2019	31.07	75.38	24.97	6.21
May/2019	31.27	82.80	27.37	5.75
Jun/2019	30.61	86.62	27.64	5.10
Jul/2019	29.77	89.29	27.28	4.13
Aug/2019	30.13	87.85	26.92	5.17
Sept/2019	30.20	85.58	26.89	4.54
Oct/2019	29.35	82.04	25.66	4.44
Nov/2019	27.67	76.99	22.33	4.31
Dec/2019	23.70	76.35	17.05	3.79
Average – 2019	**28.44**	**79.31**	**23.35**	**4.85**

6.6 'HTC-PFM' DEVICE IMPLEMENTATION

6.6.1 System Software Design

Figure 6.3 displays the flow map presenting the 'HTC-PFM' device algorithm for automatic temperature regulation and the relative humidity control system for the poultry farm. In ATmega328p, i.e., microcontroller (MCU), the system files will initially be imported. Specific work began to be carried out by the system, like checking the whole process, the necessary input voltage (V_I), current

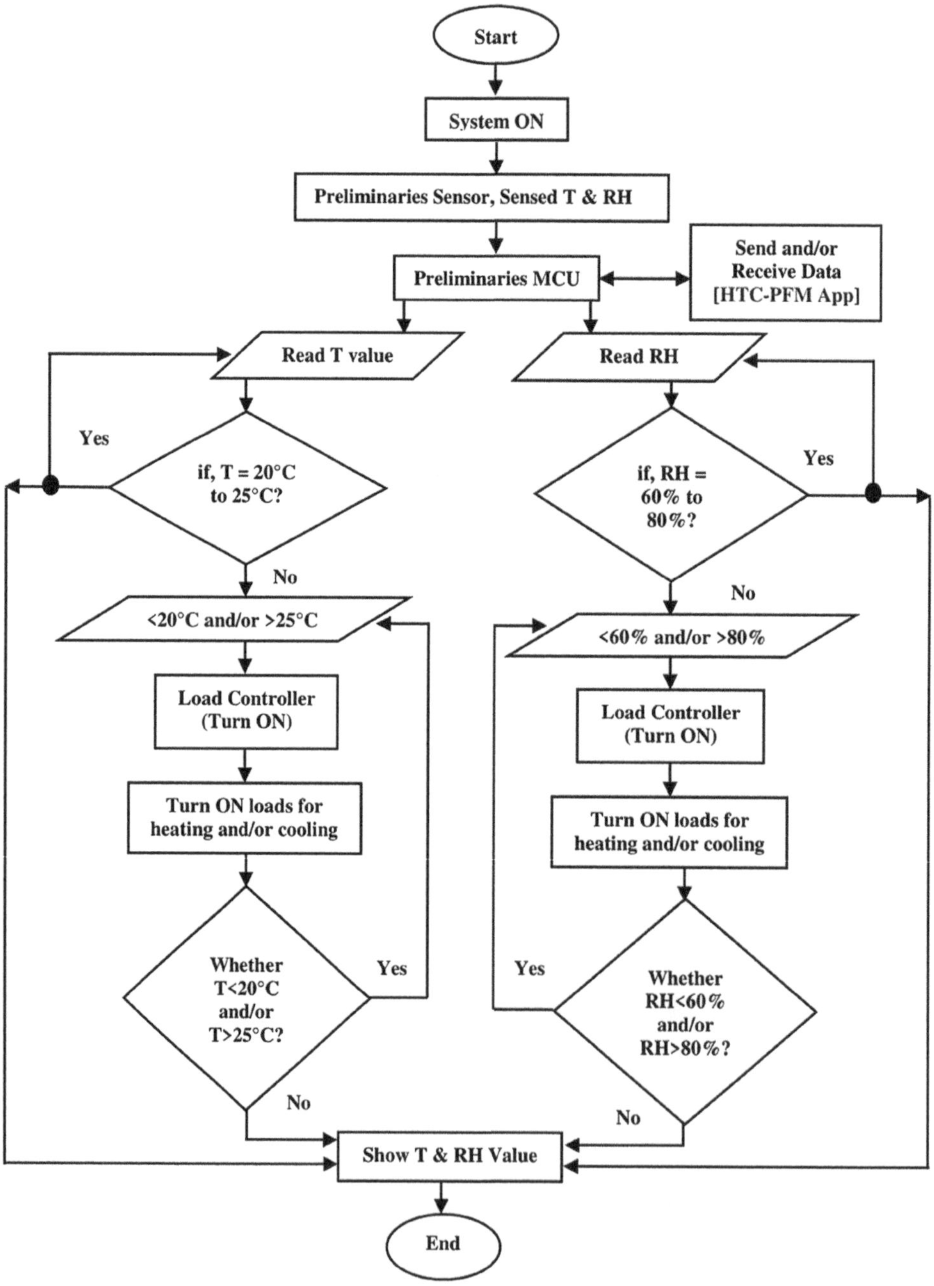

FIGURE 6.3 Algorithm flowchart of 'HTC-PFM' device.

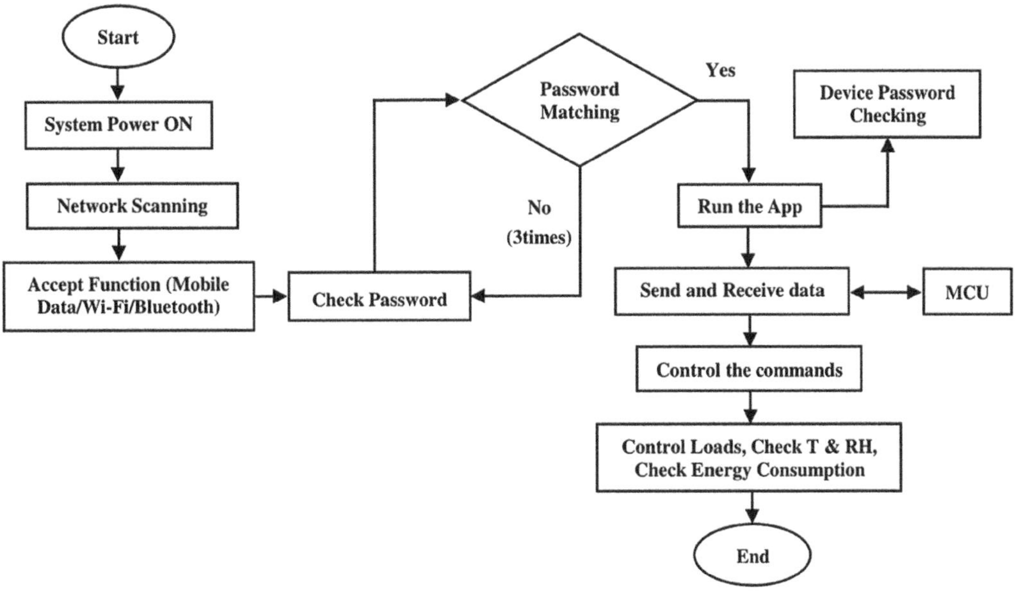

FIGURE 6.4 Algorithm flowchart of 'HTC-PFM' App.

(I), and so on. Every assignment was then re-established to execute commands. A voltage (V) and current (I) control framework was built in the graphical interface using the programming language C. The method introduces the hardware and software and then releases several task modules, beginning each module according to the initialization process known as priority. However, all the process is the same for Figure 6.3 and Figure 6.4.

Figure 6.4 demonstrates an algorithm flowchart of the 'HTC-PFM' App. Initially, the start-up process begins the scheme clock and performs the codes to initiate the interrupt operation. Then the scheme can be tested and the module phase can be triggered. Eventually, the scheme can be begun to perform a variety of operations. Using the ASSEMBLY language, the code was written and compiled using Arduino, which created a hex file that was burned with an IC burner.

6.6.2 System *Hardware Design*

To achieve the intent of the proposed work, at first, we designed such a type of device that can easily control the inside environment i.e., temperature and relative humidity of the poultry farms. The name of the poultry device is given as 'HTC-PFM' device, which stands for 'Humidity and Temperature Controlling for Poultry Farm Monitoring' device. However, by using the AM2302 sensor and MCU, we regulated relative humidity as well as temperature so that the goal of the proposed work achieve. The microcontroller can be called a CPU, memory, and peripherals, self-contained device, and can be used as an embedded system [12–14].

Figure 6.5 displays the combined block layout of the 'HTC-PFM' App and 'HTC-PFM' device. In this model, the microcontroller presents the 'MCU', which sent the command to the AM2302 sensor. Besides, the MCU operated as a mechanism to turn the loads on/off [15, 16]. The sensor to the relays (Relay1 & Relay2) to toggle the load controllers on/off and even the loads to change the relative humidity (RH) and temperature (T) transmits the next instruction. However, Relay1 and Relay2 were used for controlling the T and RH respectively. Also, a 4 * 4-matrix keypad was used to manually set the temperature and humidity. Finally, temperature and relative humidity were displayed on the LCD, which is controlled by the load. Contrariwise, MCU sends the same command to the 'HTC-PFM' App for operating the system from anywhere.

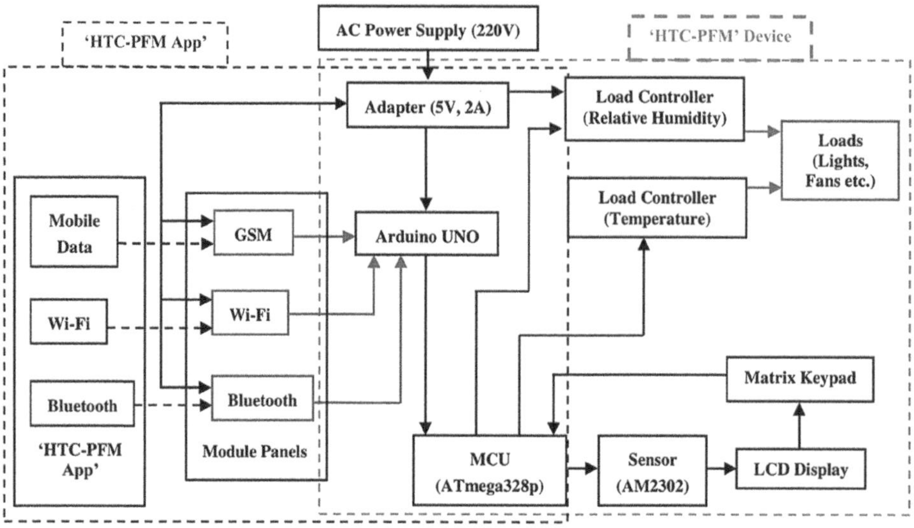

FIGURE 6.5 Combine block diagram of the 'HTC-PFM' App and device.

6.6.3 Design Prototype

Figure 6.6 shows the ON mode of the implemented 'HTC-PFM' device. Although, the device's keypad was adjusted to the normal temperature and relative humidity. By using the keypad, a user will change the set point. On the other side, for adjusting and testing the temperature and humidity, various functions of the keypad can be used.

Accessible functions are:

- F1 – Fixed temperature
- F2 – Fixed relative humidity
- F3 – Check temperature and relative humidity
- F4 – Check daily energy consumption

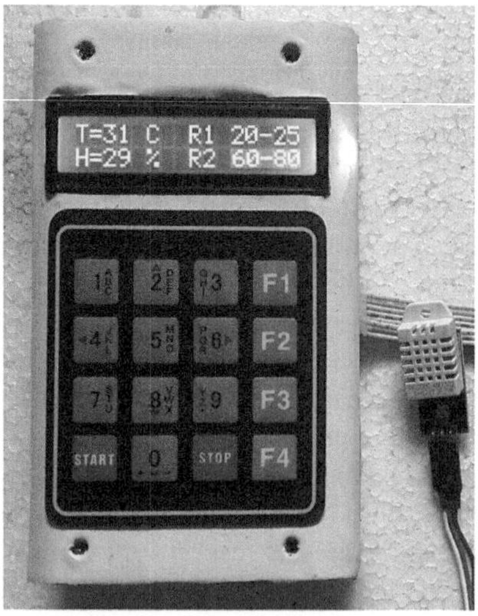

FIGURE 6.6 Design prototype of 'HTC-PFM' device.

There is no potential difference throughout this circuit at standard temperature, since there is no difference in the voltage. As a consequence, there is zero current running through the whole circuit and the system does not always change to ON. As the sensor detects the temperature, it transfers the signal (analog) into the MCU automatically. Using the successive approximation technique, this value (analog) is internally transformed to a value that is digital by the MCU. When the value of temperature and relative humidity is greater than the present value of temperature (20 Celsius–25 Celsius) and relative humidity (60%–80%), the microcontroller sends an order to the load controllers to turn on the appropriate loads within a specified range to change the temperature and relative humidity.

6.6.4 Implemented 'HTC-PFM' Application

The prime objective of the system is to use an Android-based smartphone app to introduce such a form of poultry farm network operating method that allows loads of poultry farms to be identified and controlled from everywhere and from any distance to turn a conventionalized farm into a smart poultry farm. There were different features in the Android program, including regulation of temperature and humidity. Figure 6.7 shows the 'HTC-PFM' app (Humidity and Temperature Controlling for Poultry Farm Monitoring Application) system design and working process. The 'HTC-PFM' model takes into consideration that the system will be an adjustable, resilient wireless application control mechanism with a highly confidential system that provides a user-friendly interface, which enables the user to add wireless connectivity to control remote devices.

The android application will meet the operating criteria specified:

- To control loads of poultry farms remotely by operating the suggested device from anywhere, an android-based 'HTC-PFM' app has been created. Besides, the design of the system requires the collection of a manual and automatic environment.
- To run the application, it needs to connect to Bluetooth/Wi-Fi/Mobile Data.

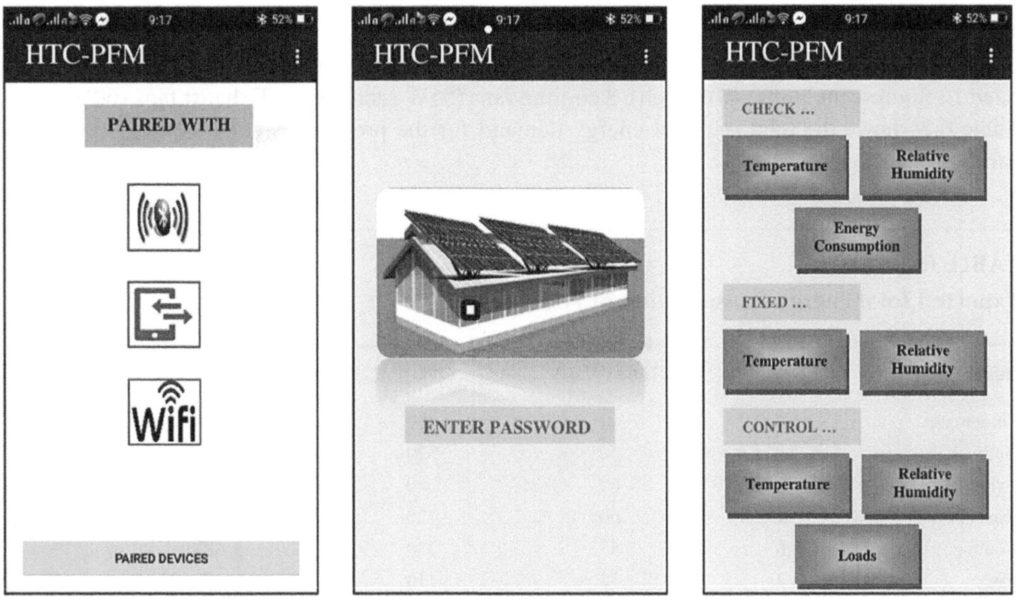

FIGURE 6.7 Device architecture and operation of the 'HTC-PFM' App.

- The application will request a code to be provided so that the user can set the code according to his or her wish. The application would then need a code from the user that is fixed to the device. If this matches the specified code, the request would be sent to the device for the passcode to be verified. The device will also be secured from accessing the whole network through this process. The application would be disabled for a certain period by the device if the user places the wrong password thrice consecutively. Additionally, at any point, the user will change the password. The software would be able to monitor the chosen loads for the poultry farms after entering the password. A customer protection scheme would introduce an interface that will help protect home appliances from suspicious people.
- It would also be necessary for the consumer to check the use of energy from the app regularly.

Based on the study of existing smart home app response platforms, this app's key criteria include the following:

- It is easy to install the proposed framework device and app without any effort. Also, it is very easy to run and track the machine. The system is intended to take into consideration that it is more customer and much more comfortable.
- Privacy, confidentiality, and pseudonymity of users: maintaining privacy and making it convenient for users to participate. In the scheme, a two-step password authentication method is provided. The app can also be blocked for 30 seconds by sequentially placing the incorrect password three times. The method, as well as the app, was meant to bear in mind that it is more private, discreet, and pseudonymous for the user.
- Between system users and emergency responders, there is a bi-directional interface process.
- Updating and display of reported geographic information in real-time.

6.7 REQUIRED ELECTRICITY DEMAND CALCULATION

Before constructing a solar PV power plant for a poultry farm, it is crucial to know the overall energy consumption of the poultry farm. For lighting, cooling, and heating of poultry farm, we need 12 fluorescent bulbs (40W each), 8 cooling fans (55W each), and 8 Exhaust fans (60W each). Table 6.2 shows the total required energy demand for the proposed solar PV plant for poultry farms.

TABLE 6.2
Expected Total Energy Consumption of Poultry Farm

Items Name	Quantity of the Items	Power per Time (Watt)	Total Power (Watt)	Time of Use (hour)	Total Energy (Watt)
Fluorescent	4	40	160	12 (6AM–6PM)	1920
Bulb	8	40	320	12 (6AM–6PM)	3840
Exhaust	6	60	360	12 (6AM–6PM)	4320
Fan	2	60	120	12 (6AM–6PM)	1440
Cooling	6	55	330	12 (6AM–6PM)	3960
Fan	2	55	110	12 (6AM–6PM)	1320
Total			**1400**		**15,480**

6.8 SPECIFICATION OF SOLAR PV POWER PLANT FOR POULTRY FARM

We need dimensions and sizes of solar panels, inverters, charge controllers, and batteries for the construction of a solar power plant for poultry farms. Hence, the requirements and sizing necessary for the proposed poultry farm solar PV plant are given below:

Equivalent hours of the sun = 6.8 hours/day

6.8.1 Specification for the Panel

The specification of the solar panel is among the most important aspects before the building of a solar Power plant [17, 18]. Besides, the specifications of the solar panel should be familiar with the specification, e.g., the power output of the solar panel, voltage at maximum power, short circuit current, and open circuit voltage.

The power output of the solar panel is 360W.

Voltage at maximum power, $V_{mpp} = 38.8\ V$

Short circuit current, $I_{sc} = 9\ A$

Open circuit voltage, $V_{oc} = 47.1\ V$

6.8.2 Required Solar Photovoltaic (PV) Panels

Minimum PV power required = [Total energy demand/Equivalent sun hours] * Account for system loss = [15480/6.8] * 1.2 = 2731.76 W

Number of Panels = Minimum PV power required/Size of Solar PV

$$= \frac{2731.76W}{360Wp} = 7.58$$

6.8.3 Sizing of Inverter

Minimal nominal power rating = Total power from the panels * Safety margin

$$= 2880\,W^{*}\,1.2 = 3456\,W$$

$$\text{Required inverter size} = \frac{3456W}{0.96} = 3600VA$$

6.8.4 Sizing of Charge Controller

The required size of charge controller = [Size of solar panel array/Maximum power voltage of the array] * 1.2 = [2880/38] * 1.2 = 90 A

For Parallel: Maximum current = I_{sc} * Number of panels = 9 A * 8 = 72 A

For Series: Maximum voltage = V_{oc} * Number of panels = 47 V * 8 = 376 V

6.8.5 Specifications for the Charge Controller

Maximum voltage (V) – 480 V

Maximum current (A) – 90 A

MPPT – Yes

6.8.6 Specifications for the Battery

Depth of discharge – 95%
Battery voltage (V) – 90 *V*
Battery capacity (Ah) – 40 *Ah*

6.8.7 Sizing of Battery

Minimum C_{batt} = [Total energy demand/(Depth of discharge * Operational voltage of the system)] * Account for system losses * Days of autonomy

$$= \left[15480 / \left(0.95^{*} 100 V\right)\right]^{*} 1.2^{*} 2 = 391 Ah$$

No. of batteries (series) = 100 *V*/90 *V* = 2 Batteries
No. of batteries (parallel) = 391 *Ah*/40 *Ah* = 10 Batteries
So, total no. of batteries = No. of batteries (parallel) * No. of batteries (series)

$$= 10^{*} 2 = 20 \text{ Batteries}$$

6.9 RESULTS

Table 6.3 demonstrates the capacity to know the accuracy of the AM2302 sensor. Parameter monitoring for data variance of different temperature and humidity conditions.

Table 6.4 reveals that the load controller (temperature control) will remain switched off only if the temperature is between 20 °C and 25 °C, and the load controller (relative humidity control) will remain switched off when the humidity is between 60% and 80% percent of the 'HTC-PFM' unit. Besides, real-time temperature and relative humidity data were collected for approximately 24 months in 2018 and 2019 in Halishahar, Chittagong, Bangladesh, using the 'HTC-PFM' unit.

TABLE 6.3
Checking Sensor (AM2302)

Air Temperature, T (°C)	Temperature [AM2302] T′ (°C)	Error, E = T′−T	Relative Error, $\frac{E}{T}$ ETx 100%	% of Error $\frac{E}{T'}$ ETx 100%
31.19	31.10	0.09	0.24	0.24
29.50	29.43	0.07	0.24	0.24
27.85	27.57	0.18	0.65	0.65
25.95	25.73	0.22	0.88	0.89
23.22	23.00	0.22	0.99	1.00
21.88	21.48	0.40	2.01	2.05
19.08	18.68	0.40	2.01	2.05
17.22	17.00	0.22	0.99	1.00
16.88	16.48	0.40	2.01	2.05
15.51	15.40	0.11	0.66	0.66

TABLE 6.4
'HTC-PFM' Device Monitoring Data

Different Conditions of T (°C)	Actual Time T (°C)	Different Conditions of RH (%)	Actual Time RH (%)	Condition of Load Controllers (T)	Condition of Load Controllers (RH)
Temperature: T; Relative Humidity: RH; ON✓ ; OFF✗ .					
	21.50		60		
20~25	23	60~80	70	✗	✗
	24.50		80		
	22		59		
20~25	23.50	<60	46	✗	✓
	25		33		
	20.50		81		
20~25	22.50	>80	86	✗	✓
	24		91		
	19.50		63		
<20	18	60~80	71	✓	✗
	16		77		
	30.50		65		
>25	28	60~80	70	✓	✗
	25.50		79		
	31		83		
>25	29	>80	88	✓	✓
	26		93		
	19		57		
<20	17	<60	41	✓	✓
	15		29		

6.10 CONCLUSION

In reality, the proposed poultry farm is specifically built for tropical countries such as Bangladesh. Moreover, the Solar PV power plant had been designed not only for reducing the usage of electricity from the main grid but also for increasing the usage of renewable energy from the proposed Solar PV power plant for poultry farms. After completion of the design of a poultry farm with Solar PV, it will increase the generation from renewable energy and a more dependable source where the main grid cannot provide electricity. Also, the construction of the 'HTC-PFM' App and the 'HTC-PFM' device Temperature and Relative Humidity Control Unit would boost the tracking system for poultry farms in different conditions like summer and winter. Additional features like an automatic feeder system, energy generation by the PV; HVAC (heating, ventilation, and air conditioning) System will be added to the 'HTC-PFM' App and device shortly. To enable the other appropriate automation to be operated within the poultry farm. However, the proposed scheme of a smart poultry farm with Solar PV power plant will make the poultry farmers' life more effective by selling extra amount of energy to the main grid and also employing a poultry farm controlling system the performance of poultry will be fine, the climate inside the poultry farm will be easier to run, making it more appealing and easier for poultry farmers to work. Also, the entire scheme would have a positive effect on the country's economic conditions.

REFERENCES

[1] Zeyad, Mohammad, Prodip Biswas, Susmita Ghosh, Md Tanvir Hassan Maruf, Md Shehzad, Md Ibrahim Hasan, and Sheikh Raihana Shoshi. "Design and Implementation of Temperature & Relative Humidity Control System for Poultry Farm." In *2020 International Conference on Computational Performance Evaluation (ComPE)*, pp. 189–193. IEEE, 2020.

[2] Zeyad, Mohammad, Prodip Biswas, Md Zakaria Iqbal, Susmita Ghosh, and Pronab Biswas. "Designing of Microcontroller Based Home Appliances Governor Circuits." *International Journal of Computer and Electrical Engineering (IJCEE)* 10, no. 2 (2018): 94–105.

[3] Sarker, Yousuf A., Sm Z. Rashid, Sabbya Sachi, Jannatul Ferdous, Bishan L. Das Chowdhury, Syeda S, and Mahmudul H. Sikder. "Exposure Pathways and Ecological Risk Assessment of Common Veterinary Antibiotics in the Environment through Poultry Litter in Bangladesh." *Journal of Environmental Science and Health, Part B* (2020): 1–8.

[4] Ahmed, SM Masum, Md Rahmatullah Al-Amin, Shakil Ahammed, Foysal Ahmed, Ahmed Mortuza Saleque, and Md Abdur Rahman. "Design, Construction and Testing of Parabolic Solar Cooker for Rural Households and Refugee Camp." *Solar Energy* 205 (2020): 230–240.

[5] Zeyad, Mohammad, SM Masum Ahmed, Anup Kumar Pramanik, Md Mustafizur Rahman, Md Tanvir Hassan Maruf, and Debashish Ghosh. "Performance Analysis and Scaling Behavior of Ultra-Scaled III-V (InAs) HEMTs System with 2-D Tunneling Effects on Leakage Current." In *2020 IEEE Region 10 Symposium (TENSYMP)*, pp. 48–51. IEEE, 2020.

[6] Ahmed, SM Masum, Foysal Ahmed, Shakil Ahammed, Md Rahmatullah Al-Amin, Md Nasimul Islam Maruf, Ahmed Mortuza Saleque, and Md Abdur Rahman. "Construction of a Parabolic Solar Cooker Using Mylar Tape for Rohingya Refugee Rehabilitation Program." In *2020 6th IEEE International Energy Conference (ENERGYCon)*, pp. 439–444. IEEE.

[7] Ahmed, SM Masum, Md Rahmatullah Al-Amin, Shakil Ahammed, Foysal Ahmed, Ahmed Mortuza Saleque, and Md Abdur Rahman. "Performance Analysis of Parabolic Solar Cooker with Different Reflective Materials." In *2019 International Conference on Robotics, Electrical and Signal Processing Techniques (ICREST)*, pp. 297–302. IEEE, 2019.

[8] Azlin, Ahmad Ammar Nor, Hasmah Mansor, Ahmad Zawawi Hashim, and Teddy Surya Gunawan. "Development of Modular Smart Farm System." In *2017 IEEE 4th International Conference on Smart Instrumentation, Measurement and Application (ICSIMA)*, pp. 1–6. IEEE, 2017.

[9] Ryu, Minwoo, Jaeseok Yun, Ting Miao, Il-Yeup Ahn, Sung-Chan Choi, and Jaeho Kim. "Design and Implementation of a Connected Farm for Smart Farming System." In *2015 IEEE SENSORS*, pp. 1–4. IEEE, 2015.

[10] Radhi, Lecturer Ahmed A., and Asst Lecturer Hayder Hassan Mohammed. "Design and Implementation of a Smart Farm System." *Association of Arab Universities Journal of Engineering Sciences* 24, no. 3 (2017): 227–240.

[11] Sarachai, Watcharin, Parot Ratnapinda, and Pitchayanida Khumwichai. "Smart Notification System for Detecting Fan Failure in Evaporative Cooling System of a Poultry Farm." In *2019 Joint International Conference on Digital Arts, Media and Technology with ECTI Northern Section Conference on Electrical, Electronics, Computer and Telecommunications Engineering (ECTI DAMT-NCON)*, pp. 296–299. IEEE.

[12] Zeyad, Mohammad, Susmita Ghosh, MD Rakibul Islam, SM Masum Ahmed, Prodip Biswas, and Eftakhar Hossain. "Design Proposal of an Automatic Smart MultiInsect (Mosquito) Killing System." In *2019 IEEE International Conference on Electrical, Computer and Communication Technologies (ICECCT)*, pp. 1–6. IEEE, 2019.

[13] Zeyad, Mohammad, and Susmita Ghosh. "Designing of a Low Cost Handy Cooling System." In *2018 4th International Conference on Electrical Engineering and Information & Communication Technology (iCEEiCT)*, pp. 557–560. IEEE, 2018.

[14] Zeyad, Mohammad, Susmita Ghosh, MD Rakibul Islam, SM Masum Ahmed, and Sheikh Raihana Shoshi. "Proposing a Technique of a Low Cost Automatic Cooling and Exhaust System for Old Age Home Kitchen." In *2019 IEEE International Conference on Electrical, Computer and Communication Technologies (ICECCT)*, pp. 1–5. IEEE, 2019.

[15] Zeyad, Mohammad, SM Masum Ahmed, Md Tanvir Hassan Maruf, Md Shehzad, and Md Abul Ala Walid. "Design & Implementation of a Micro-Controller based Home Appliances Controlling with Dual Verification Application System." In *2020 International Conference on Computational Performance Evaluation (ComPE)*, pp. 665–670. IEEE, 2020.
[16] Alam, Md Abrarul, and Mohammad Zeyad. "Smart Cities and Buildings: GSM Based Smart Electric Energy Meter Billing System." In *2019 IEEE International Conference on Power, Electrical, and Electronics and Industrial Applications (PEEIACON)*, pp. 1–4. IEEE.
[17] Zeyad, Mohammad, Susmita Ghosh, and SM Masum Ahmed. "Design Prototype of a Smart Household Touch Sensitive Locker Security System Based on GSM Technology." *International Journal of Power Electronics and Drive Systems* 10, no. 4 (2019): 1923.
[18] Ahmed, SM Maruf, SM Masum Ahmed, and Mohammad Zeyad. "An Approach of a Nearly Zero-Energy Building (nZEB) to Build an Official Zone with Micro-Grid." In *2020 6th IEEE International Energy Conference (ENERGYCon)*, pp. 662–667. IEEE.

7 Cloud IoT for Pollution Monitoring

A Multivariate Weighted Ensemble Forecasting Approach for Prediction of Suspended Particulate Matter

Tushar Saini and Gagandeep Tomar
Indian Institute of Technology Mandi, Mandi, India

Duni Chand Rana
Department of Environment, Science, and Technology,
Government of Himachal Pradesh, Shimla, India

Suresh Attri
Department of Environment, Science, and Technology,
Government of Himachal Pradesh, Shimla, India

Pratik Chaturvedi
Indian Institute of Technology Mandi, Defence Terrain Research Laboratory, Defence Research and Development Organization, New Delhi, India

Varun Dutt
Indian Institute of Technology Mandi, Mandi, India

CONTENTS

DOI: 10.1201/9781003155577-9

7.1 INTRODUCTION

Air pollution in the world causes severe health issues, where both urban cities and rural areas are affected by it (WHO, 2018). It was estimated that around 42 lakhs premature deaths worldwide were caused by air pollution in 2016 (WHO, 2018). Most of the deaths occurred in densely populated countries like China and India, where a high concentration of particulate matter of 2.5 microns or smaller ($PM_{2.5}$) was registered (OECD, 2016). Various studies have shown that prolonged exposure to pollutant $PM_{2.5}$ can cause short-term and long-term health effects (WHO, 2018). Furthermore, the $PM_{2.5}$ particle can even penetrate the lung barrier and then enter the blood system. In fact, $PM_{2.5}$ is not only responsible for health effects, but it also incurs enormous economic losses (OECD, 2016).

Given its vast impact on health and the economy, it is imperative to investigate new ways to reduce these impacts. One such method is forecasting air pollution via computational models that could make short- and long-term predictions with high accuracy. Such models could work on data collected from several IoT technologies and sensors and perform air pollution forecasting in the cloud. This forecasting of air pollution may likely help the government authorities and policymakers in making informed decisions. For example, agencies could use the forecast data to make crucial decisions like issuing permits to set up new industries, open new parks, and renovate damaged infrastructure.

Prior research has proposed particular individual and ensemble machine-learning models to predict particulate matter (Feng et al., 2020). For example, some researchers have proposed individual MLP models for forecasting air pollution (Feng et al., 2020). However, some researchers have tried an ensemble of multiple machine-learning models consisting of CNN models and LSTM models for forecasting air pollution. Similarly, reference (Ganesh et al., 2018) proposed an ensemble of three models, namely, gradient boosting, neural networks, and random forest, to forecast $PM_{2.5}$ concentrations. Although researchers have proposed particular individual and ensemble models for forecasting air pollution, a comprehensive evaluation of multivariate statistical, neural, spatial, and temporal models and their ensemble lacks literature.

This research's primary goal is to propose individual and ensemble multi-variate forecasting models of air pollution. Specifically, we evaluate a multi-variate statistical SARIMAX model, a neural multilayer perceptron (MLP) model, a spatial convolutional neural network (CNN) model, a temporal long short-term memory (LSTM) model, and a weighted ensemble model to predict $PM_{2.5}$ concentration over time. We rely upon real-world air-pollution data collected from the US Embassy in Beijing, China, for our evaluation. These data consist of dew, temperature, atmospheric pressure, wind speed, snow, rain, and $PM_{2.5}$ concentrations over time. This research work's primary novelty is that we perform a comprehensive evaluation of individual and ensemble statistical and machine-learning models on a large dataset. We believe that some of these models could be deployed in the cloud to perform real-time air-pollution forecasting.

In what follows, we first describe prior research work undertaken in the field of forecasting air-pollutant concentration and IoT technologies in the cloud. Next, we describe the dataset used for our analyses. Furthermore, we detailed different models and their parameters. Finally, we detail the results and discussion of forecasting air pollution via ensemble and individual multivariate models.

7.2 LITERATURE REVIEW

7.2.1 Role of IoT Technologies and Cloud for Air-Pollution Monitoring

Reference (Arora et al., 2019) investigated the use of IoT-based solutions for monitoring various air pollutants. Their research explored multiple sensors and IoT technologies for detecting general pollutants. However, this research was limited to the use of IoT technologies and cloud for air-pollution monitoring. Specifically, it did not explore forecasting methods for air pollution. Reference (Desai and Alex 2017) investigated the use of IoT and cloud technologies for monitoring carbon-monoxide and carbon-dioxide concentrations. An IoT device was proposed to capture CO and CO_2 parameters and then send the data to an Azure cloud server where data analyses were performed. However, these authors did not discuss forecasting models for CO and CO_2 concentrations. Reference (Guanochanga et al., 2018) implemented a secure low-cost, real-time air-quality monitoring system. Various sensors were connected to an Arduino microcontroller, which was connected to a Raspberry Pi. The Raspberry Pi acted as a gateway to send data to the webserver using the SFTP protocol. The developed system monitored five pollutants, namely, CO, CH_4, SO_2, H_2S, and NO_2. These authors did not explore machine-learning or statistical models for air-pollution forecasting in the cloud. Reference (Saha et al., 2017) explored an IoT-based technology to monitor the water temperature and PH levels. The device collected the temperature, the turbidity, and the PH level of water. Again, these researchers did not investigate forecasting models.

7.2.2 Machine Learning Models for Air-Pollution Monitoring

Reference (Ordieres et al., 2005) employed three multivariate neural network models, namely, MLP, square multilayer perceptron" (SMLP), and radial basis function (RBF), for forecasting daily average $PM_{2.5}$ concentrations using the mean $PM_{2.5}$, wind direction, humidity, wind speed, and atmospheric pressure. The data used by the researchers were collected on an hourly basis for over two years. However, only a small set of hyperparameters was varied over a short range. Also, the comparison was limited, and various other machine-learning and statistical models and their ensembles were not investigated.

Reference (Zhao et al., 2019) employed LSTM neural networks for forecasting of $PM_{2.5}$ and other pollutant concentrations over long and short time-periods. The data consisted of pollutants and five meteorological parameters (i.e., temperature, pressure, wind speed, wind direction, and humidity). The data set for the experiment was taken from the Microsoft Research's Urban Air project. However, only LSTMs were evaluated, and no comparison with other models was undertaken. Reference (Zhou et al., 2014) proposed an E-LSTM model with ensemble empirical mode decomposition (EEMD). The steps undertaken to build this model were the following: EEMD was used for "multi-modal feature extraction," LSTM was used for the feature learning, and inverse computation of EEMD" was used for estimated integration. Again, a comprehensive evaluation and comparison with other machine-learning models were absent. Furthermore, no benchmarking was undertaken, and a smaller number of hyperparameters were varied over a short range. Reference (Ferlito et al., 2019) used the UCI machine-learning repository's Beijing data and developed a single-layered LSTM model. Again, no benchmarking was present, and the models' parameters were also varied over a small range.

Reference (Li et al., 2020) proposed an ensemble of CNN-LSTM models for forecasting $PM_{2.5}$ concentration. The developed model worked in the following two steps: The CNN model was used for the feature extraction, while the LSTM model was used for forecasting. The ensemble model was compared with some of the well-known models like SVMs, MLPs, CNNs, and LSTMs. However, a comparison with any statistical model was not made. Furthermore, some of the hyperparameters in the ensemble model were set to constant values, and these parameters were not optimized over a range.

Reference (Thaweephol et al., 2019) employed a statistical SARIMAX model and a ma-chine-learning LSTM model for forecasting $PM_{2.5}$ levels and other pollutants. Data were provided by the Pollution Control Department, Thailand, and collected between 07/06/2017 and 30/06/2018. The pollutant parameters included $PM_{2.5}$, PM_{10}, NO, NO_2, NOX, and CO. Other parameters used were wind speed, wind direction, temperature, humidity, pressure, and rain. The grid-search method was used to fine-tune the hyperparameters in the models. But again, only two models (SARIMAX and LSTM) were compared, and several other models were not considered for benchmarking. Also, no ensemble approach was evaluated.

In this chapter, we overcome some of these literature gaps by considering a large class of machine-learning models. We also discuss how some of the proposed models could utilize IoT and cloud technologies for timely forecasting of air pollution.

7.3 METHODOLOGY

7.3.1 Data

The data used in this research were taken from the UCI machine-learning repository. The data were logged hourly and consisted of pollutant and meteorological parameters. The hourly $PM_{2.5}$ data were collected from the US Embassy in Beijing, while other meteorological parameters were collected from Beijing International Airport. The data was collected over five years, i.e., from 1 January 2010 to 31 December 2014. Thus, in total, there were nearly 43,000 data points. The data's pollutant parameter was $PM_{2.5}$, and other meteorological parameters were dew, temperature, atmospheric pressure, wind speed, snow, and rain. This research aimed to forecast the hourly $PM_{2.5}$ concentration by using the initial values of the hourly $PM_{2.5}$ concentration and the other six meteorological parameters.

Figure 7.1 shows the plot of all different parameters over time. We found that data parameters did not show any explicit or significant correlation between each other on preliminary analyses. However, the plot autocorrelation function (ACF) in Figure 7.2 showed that the data had a relationship between the current value and its lagged value. The influence of the lagged values decreased starkly from lag 1 to lag 40. As the ACF plot also derives the impact of previous lag periods, we also evaluated the partial autocorrelation function (PACF) to understand better the relationship between the current value and the lagged value. Figure 7.3 shows the PACF plot for data up to a lag of 50. As seen in Figure 7.3, there was a "strong correlation between the current value and the value lagged by one step". The rest of the lagged steps did not show any significant relationship. Thus, we drew the inference that the data had a strong relationship with the value at lag 1. The dataset was divided into two parts for training various machine-learning and statistical models, in the ratio of 80:20. Thus, 80% of the dataset was used for training models, whereas the remaining 20% of the dataset was used for testing the trained models.

7.3.2 Data Pre-Processing

The time-series data were logged over timesteps. All machine-learning models followed a supervised learning approach, where a set of predictors were used to forecast the $PM_{2.5}$ concentration. To train a supervised machine-learning model, we had to transform the time-series data into a supervised format. Thus, a time series "$p_t, p_{t-1}, p_{t-2}, p_{t-3}, \ldots, p_{t-n}$" was transformed into a supervised format in the following form:

$$p_t = f\left(p_{t-1}, p_{t-2}, p_{t-3}, \ldots p_{t-n}\right) \tag{7.1}$$

where p_t is the parameter value to be predicted and $p_{t-1}, p_{t-2}, p_{t-3}, \ldots, p_{t-n}$ are the values of the predicted lag observations of the variable on n prior timesteps. The number of lag observations n used to predict the observation at the current timestep was treated as the lookback period in different machine-learning algorithms. For different multivariate models, the y_t was the $PM_{2.5}$ parameter that was being

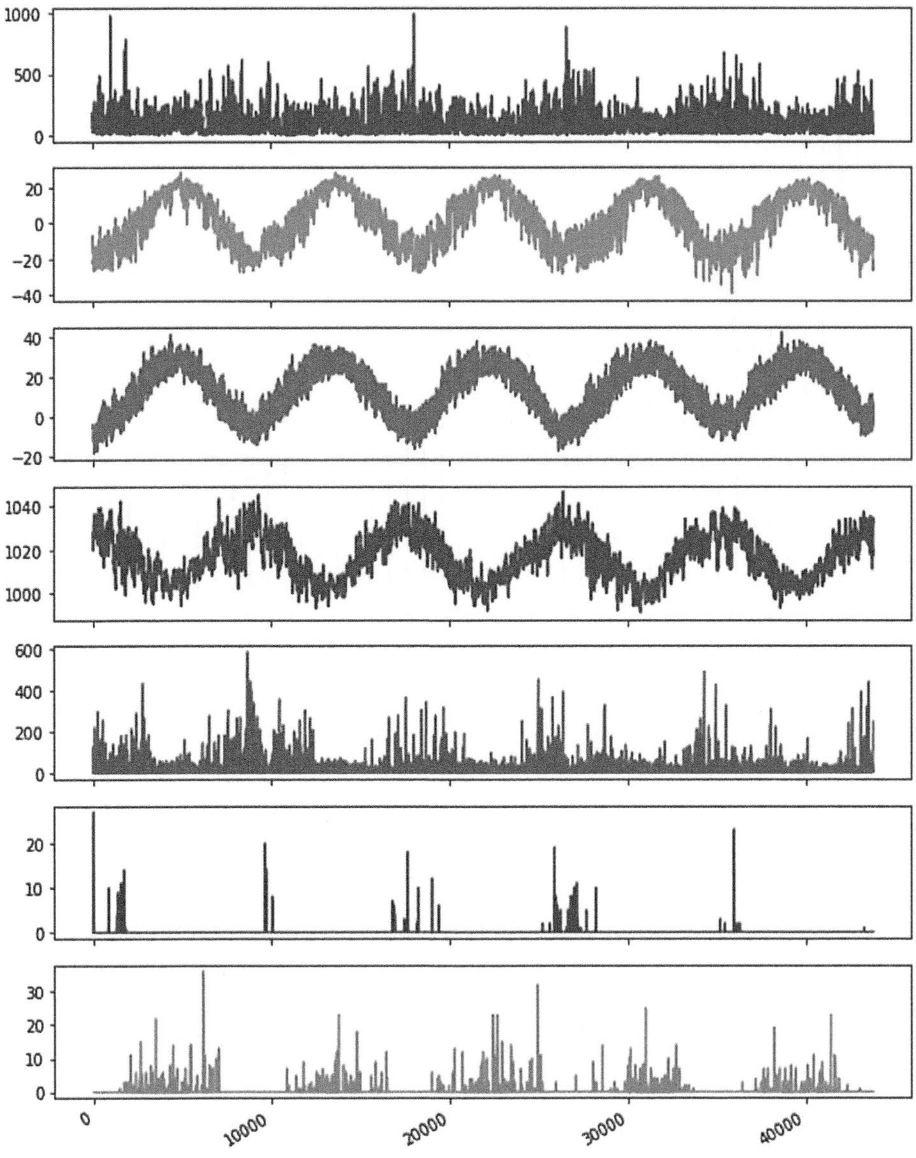

FIGURE 7.1 A plot of all parameters of the Beijing data set. Pollution refers to $PM_{2.5}$ concentration.

predicted, and $\gamma_{t-1}, \gamma_{t-2}, \ldots, \gamma_n$ represented the $PM_{2.5}$ parameter and other parameters lagged intervals. Thus, each row in the dataset may be represented as:

$$\begin{aligned}(PM_{2.5})_t = \{&(PM_{2.5})_1, \text{dew}_1, \text{temperature}_1, \text{pressure}_1, \text{wind speed}_1, \text{snow}_1, \text{rain}_1 \ldots\ldots \\ &(PM_{2.5})_{t-i}, \text{dew}_{t-i}, \text{temperature}_{t-i}, \text{pressure}_{t-i}, \text{wind speed}_{t-i}, \text{snow}_{t-i}, \text{rain}_{t-i}\}\end{aligned} \tag{7.2}$$

where, the data values for each timestamp 1 to t-i were defined by a set of seven parameters as shown in Equation 7.2.

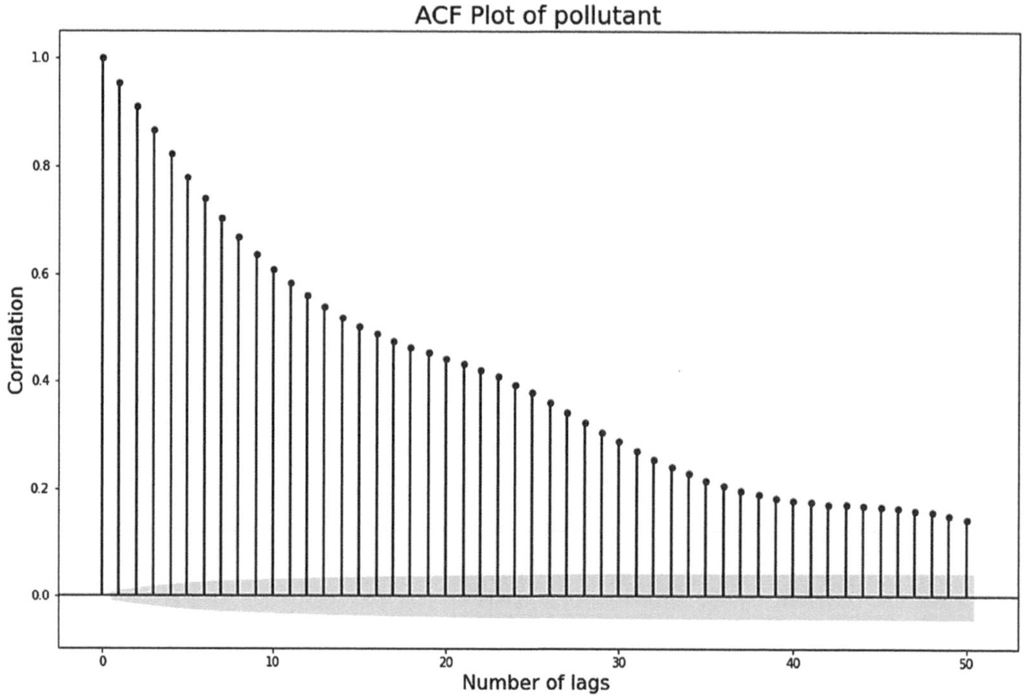

FIGURE 7.2 ACF plot for $PM_{2.5}$ concentration for lags up to 50.

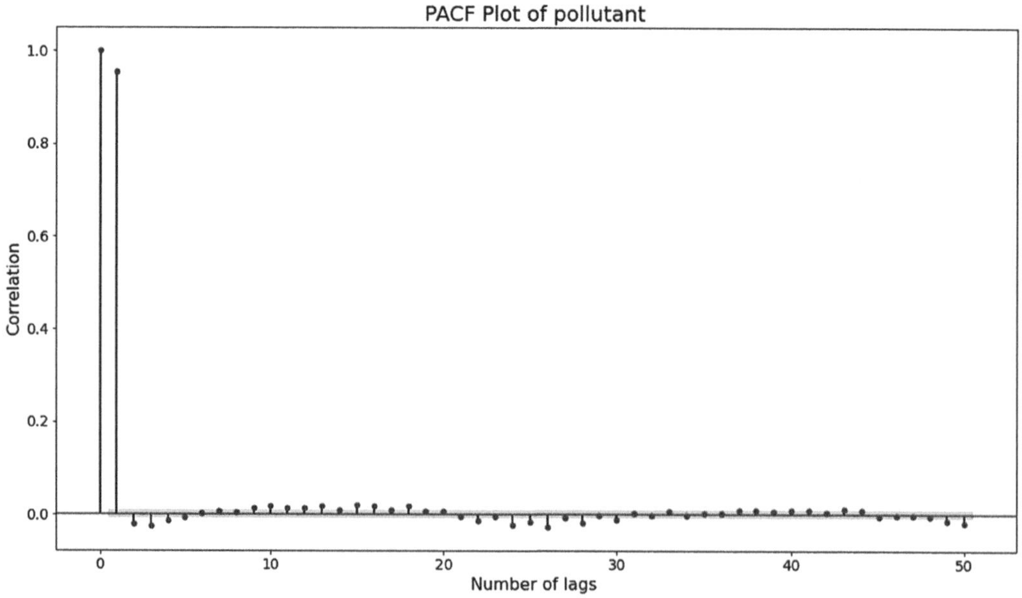

FIGURE 7.3 PACF plot for $PM_{2.5}$ concentration for lags up to 50.

7.3.3 Models

7.3.3.1 Multilayer Perceptron

"The MLP is a feedforward artificial neural network (ANN)". For learning the parameters of the model, it utilizes a technique called backpropagation (Leung and Haykin 1991). The backpropagation works by computing the loss function one layer at a time, iterating from the last layer to the first layer. With a non-linear activation function and multiple layers, the MLP can also fit non-linear data. An MLP model generally consists of at least three layers: an input layer, one (or more) hidden layer, and an output layer (Ramchoun et al., 2016). Initially, some random weights are assigned to each node of the layers, the node takes input from its previous layer (unless it is the input layer), multiply with the weight, and pass the values to the next layers. At the output layer, the error is calculated by comparing the predicted and actual values. The calculated error is then backpropagated to subsequent layers, and the weights of the nodes are updated (Leung and Haykin 1991). The hyperparameters calibrated for the MLP model were the lookback period, number of layers, nodes per layer, batch size, and epochs. The model's performance was determined by comparing the RMSE error between the forecasted and the actual values.

7.3.3.2 Long-Short Term Memory

LSTM is a type of recurrent neural network (RNN), capturing long-term dependencies in the data (Schmidhuber and Hochreiter 1997). Unlike a standard neural network, RNN-based models have a feedback connection (Sak et al., 2014). LSTM was explicitly designed to model long-term and temporal dependencies in the data (Sak et al., 2014). Like standard RNNs, LSTM has repeating modules of a neural network. These modules are made up of special units called memory blocks, which include self-connected cells, enabling them to capture the network's temporal state, and another special multiplicative unit called gates that regulate the information flow. Each of these blocks in the modules contains three gates, namely, an input gate, which regulates the flow of input activations; the output gate, which regulates the flow of cell activations into the rest of the network; and the forget gate, which is used for forgetting the cell's memory (refer to Figure 7.4) (Sak et al., 2014). The LSTM works in the same way as an MLP network, where it maps input values to an output value by calculating the weights of the network and unit activations. The hyperparameters varied in the LSTM model were lookback period, number of layers, nodes per layer, batch size, and epochs.

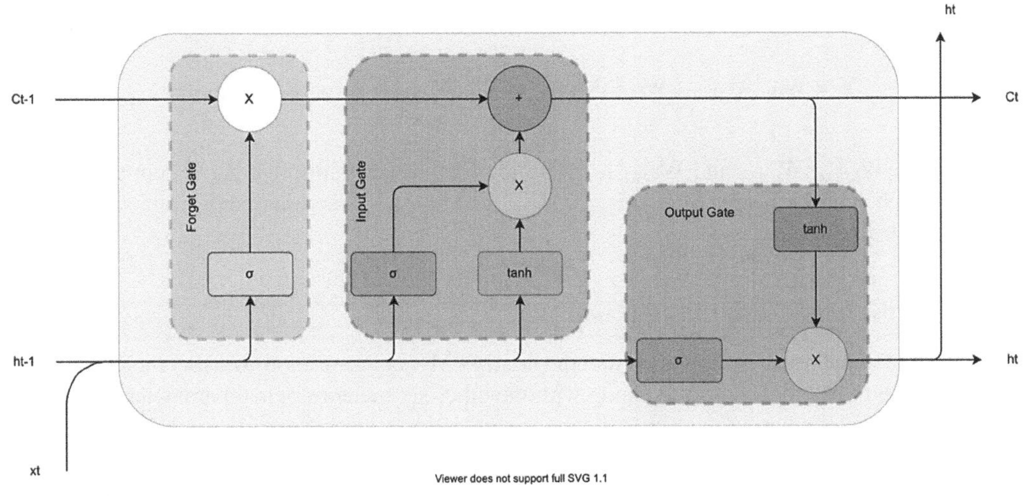

FIGURE 7.4 LSTM cell containing three gates, forget gate, input gate, and output gate.

7.3.3.3 Convolution Neural Network

CNN was first introduced in the year 1980 and later was improved by LeCun et al. (LeCun and Bengio 1995). CNN is better at learning local spatial relationships present in data. Each node in CNN is only connected to the local region in the input. This spatial scale of connection is referred to as the node's receptive field (Gu et al., 2018). A weighted matrix slides over the input and computes the Hadamard product between the input and the weight matrix. Due to local connectivity and a shared weight matrix, the learnable parameters are reduced to a fewer number. This reduction results in efficient training (Gu et al., 2018). The CNN is best suited to fit models with hidden information between the subsequent data points in the time series. The parameters varied included the lookback period, filters, kernel size, batch size, and epochs.

7.3.3.4 Seasonal Autoregressive Integrated Moving Average with Exogenous Variables

The SARIMAX is a statistical forecasting model for multivariate time-series data (Hyndman and Athanasopoulos 2018). Beyond the input and output time series, this model also considers exogenous variables and seasonality in its prediction. Seasonality is a characteristic of time-series data in which it experiences regular changes that recur every specific interval (Hyndman and Athanasopoulos 2018). SARIMAX model can capture the covariance between the target and exogenous variables. Standard SARIMAX model has eight hyperparameters, namely, p, d, q, P, D, Q, m, and trend t. Here parameters p, d, and q are the trend autoregression order, trend difference order, and trend moving average order. While parameters P, D, and Q are the seasonal autoregressive order, seasonal differencing order, and seasonal moving average order, m is the seasonality (several time steps for a single seasonal period) and, t is the trend. These hyperparameters were optimized in the SARIMAX model using a grid-search procedure.

7.3.3.5 Ensemble Model

Ensemble modelling is a technique in which we employ an ensemble of various models for forecasting (Kotu and Deshpande 2018). In this research, we ensembled all the models mentioned above, namely, MLP, LSTM, CNN, and SARIMAX. We used a weighted average method to assign weight to each model, where the weights defined the importance of each model in the calculation of the predicted value (Busemeyer and Diederich 2010). The higher the weight of a model, the more it contributed towards the calculation of the prediction. The weights provided the least error for the ensemble model while training data were chosen as the final weights in the model for testing. The following equation states how the final prediction was made in the ensemble model:

$$Y_t = W_{MLP}M_{MLP} + W_{LSTM}M_{LSTM} + W_{CNN}M_{CNN} + W_{SARIMAX}M_{SARIMAX} \tag{7.3}$$

where W_{MLP}, W_{LSTM}, W_{CNN}, and $W_{SARIMAX}$ were the four weights in range [0, 1] representing the weight of each model, whereas M_{MLP}, M_{LSTM}, M_{CNN}, and $M_{SARIMAX}$ represented the trained individual model's prediction itself.

7.3.4 Optimization of Model Parameters

The objective of the research was to predict the hourly $PM_{2.5}$ concentration by using the prior values of the collected $PM_{2.5}$ concentration along with the other six meteorological parameters. Table 7.1 shows the hyperparameters of each model, which were optimized using a grid-search method. In this research, we took the root mean squared error (RMSE) (Busemeyer and Diederich 2010) for determining the performance of the models. Hence, the parameter configuration that had the least RMSE value in the grid search was the one considered as the best configuration of parameters in a model. For the MLP model, the hyperparameters varied included lookback period (1, 2, 3, 5, 7, 9); number of layer (1, 2, 4, 6, 8, 16, 32, 64); nodes per layer (1, 3, 6, 12, 25, 50, 75); batch size (50, 75, 100);

TABLE 7.1
Hyperparameters and Their Ranges Used in Different Models

Model	Parameter	Range of Values
MLP	Lookback period	1, 2, 3, 5, 7, 9
	No of layers	1, 2, 4, 6, 8, 16, 32, 64
	Nodes per layer	1, 3, 6, 12, 25, 50, 75
	Batch size	50, 75, 100
	Epochs	50, 100
LSTM	Lookback period	1, 2, 3, 5, 7
	No of layers	1, 2, 4, 8, 16, 32
	Nodes per layer	25, 50, 75
	Batch size	50, 75, 100
	Epoch	50, 100
CNN	Lookback period	1, 3, 5, 7
	Filters	2, 4, 8, 16, 32, 64
	Kernel size	2, 3, 5
	Batch size	50,75, 100
	Epochs	50, 100
SARIMAX	p	0, 1, 2
	d	0, 1, 2
	q	0, 1, 2
	P	0, 1, 2, 4, 8, 16, 32
	D	0, 1, 2
	Q	0, 1, 2
	m	0, 1, 2
	t	NULL, n, c, t, ct
Ensemble Model	W_{MLP}	[0–1] in steps of 0.01
	W_{LSTM}	[0–1] in steps of 0.01
	W_{CNN}	[0–1] in steps of 0.01
	$W_{SARIMAX}$	[0–1] in steps of 0.01

and epochs (50, 100). For the LSTM model, the hyperparameter varied included lookback period (1, 2, 3, 5, 7); number of layer (1, 2, 4, 8, 16, 32); number of nodes per layer (25, 50, 75); batch size (50, 75, 100); and epochs (50, 100). For the CNN model, the hyperparameters included lookback period (1, 3, 5, 7); kernel size (2, 4, 8, 16, 32, 64); filters (2, 3, 5); batch size (50, 75, 100); and epochs (50, 100). For the SARIMAX model, the hyperparameters included p (0, 1, 2); d (0, 1, 2); q (0, 1, 2); P (0, 1, 2, 4, 8, 16, 32); D (0, 1, 2); Q (0, 1, 2); m (0, 1, 2); and t (NULL, n, c, t, ct). Lastly, for the ensemble model, the hyperparameters included WMLP [0, 1]; WLSTM [0, 1]; WCNN [0, 1]; and WSARIMAX [0, 1] in steps of 0.01.

7.4 RESULTS

Table 7.2 shows the RMSE values from different models in the training dataset. As seen in Table 7.2, the ensemble model had the lowest RMSE (23.84 $\mu g/m^3$). The MLP model performed the second best with an RMSE of 24.05 $\mu g/m^3$. Furthermore, LSTM and CNN had RMSEs of 27.22 $\mu g/m^3$ and 24.41 $\mu g/m^3$, respectively. The statistical model, i.e., SARIMAX, had the highest RMSE among all the models (60.98 $\mu g/m^3$).

TABLE 7.2
The RMSEs of Evaluated Models for the Training Dataset

Models	RMSE in the Training Dataset (in μg/m³)
MLP	24.05
LSTM	27.22
CNN	24.43
SAIRMAX	60.98
Ensemble Model	23.84

Table 7.3 shows the optimized hyperparameters for different models in the training dataset. As seen in Table 7.3, the MLP possessed the following hyperparameters: lookback period: 7, number of layers: 16, nodes per layer: 50, batch size: 75, and epochs: 50. For LSTM, the optimized hyperparameters included lookback period: 2, number of layers: 4, nodes per layer: 75, batch size: 75, and epochs: 50. For CNN, the optimized hyperparameters included lookback period: 7, filters: 16, kernel size: 2, batch size: 75, and epochs: 50. For SARIMAX, the optimized hyperparameters included p: 1, d: 0, q: 2, P: 1, D: 0, Q: 2, m: 0, and t: 'c'. Lastly, in the ensemble model, the optimized weight parameters included W_{MLP}: 0.29, W_{LSTM}: 0.58, W_{CNN}: 0.13, $W_{SARIMAX}$: 0. As can be inferred from these weights, the weight for SARIMAX in the ensemble was 0, i.e., it did not play any role in forecasting.

Table 7.4 shows the obtained RMSEs in different models in the test dataset. Again, the lowest RMSE was obtained for the ensemble model, which was 23.41 μg/m³. The MLP performed second

TABLE 7.3
Values of Optimized Hyperparameters for All the Experimented Models

Model	Optimized Value of Parameters
MLP	lookback period: 7, number of layers: 16, nodes per layer: 50, batch size: 75, epochs: 50
LSTM	lookback period: 2, number of layers: 4, nodes per layer: 75, batch size: 75, epochs: 50
CNN	lookback period: 7, filters: 16, kernel size: 2, batch size: 75, epochs: 50
SARIMAX	p: 1, d: 0, q: 2, P: 1, D: 0, Q: 2, m: 0, t: 'c'
Ensemble	W_{MLP}: 0.29, W_{LSTM}: 0.58, W_{CNN}: 0.13, $W_{SARIMAX}$: 0

TABLE 7.4
The RMSEs of Evaluated Models for the Test Dataset

Models	RMSE in Test Dataset (in μg/m³)
MLP	23.11
LSTM	26.14
CNN	23.79
SAIRMAX	58.24
Ensemble Model	23.41

best with an RMSE of 23.11 μg/m³. For LSTM and CNN, the obtained RMSEs were 26.14 μg/m³ and 23.79 μg/m³, respectively. Again, the SARIMAX performed the worst, and it had the highest RMSE of 58.24 μg/m³.

7.5 DISCUSSION AND CONCLUSION

Air pollution is a severe problem in the world. Of the 30 most polluted cities in the world, 21 were in India (OECD, 2016). Air pollution-related health problems are well known, and exposure to air pollution over a long period may cause pulmonary and cardiovascular diseases (WHO, 2018). Overall, it is crucial to monitor and develop forecasting methods to help authorities make informed decisions. This research's primary goal was to propose individual and ensemble multi-variate forecasting models of air pollution. Specifically, we evaluated multi-variate statistical (SARIMAX), neural (MLP), spatial (CNN), and temporal (LSTM) models and their weighted ensemble to predict the $PM_{2.5}$ concentration over time. We used an air-pollution data set from Beijing, China (provided by UCI machine-learning repository) for developing and training models. Our research results revealed that the MLP model performed better among individual models than the SARIMAX, CNN, and LSTM models. Furthermore, the weighted ensemble model, which was the weighted combination of all individual models, performed the best on both train and test datasets. The best RMSE value obtained in this research from the ensemble model was better than the ones cited in the literature on these data (Zhao et al., 2019; Ferlito et al., 2019; Li et al., 2020).

First, we found that the machine-learning models (MLP, CNN, and LSTM) outperformed the statistical model (SARIMA) by a large amount. The edge of machine-learning models over statistical models could be attributed to the capabilities of capturing non-linear relationships (in MLP and LSTM models), presence of memory (in LSTM models), and spatial capabilities (in CNNs models). These models could learn the non-linear relationships present between pollutant concentration and other variables in a better way due to these capabilities. These results also correspond well with prior research, where even machine-learning models like MLPs, LSTMs, and CNNs were found to predict air-pollution values (Zhao et al., 2019; Ferlito et al., 2019; Li et al., 2020).

Second, the weighted ensemble model, a linear combination of individual models, performed better than all other models. A likely reason for this finding could be that the ensemble model took the best out of the individual models' forecasts by weighting different individual predictions. These findings agree with the prior research, where ensemble models have performed in forecasting air-pollutant data (Zhou et. al., 2014; Li et al., 2020).

There are several implications of this research in the field of cloud IoT. First, the developed models could be deployed on the cloud, along with a real-time IoT-based air quality monitoring system (Sharma et al., 2020). The IoT-based system could provide real-time air quality information along with real-time forecasting to people. Second, the proposed models could also be trained on real-time incoming data from IoT technologies to make the models more accurate. This ecosystem of IoT technologies with cloud integration could help deploy highly accurate and reliable forecasts of air quality over a large geographical area. Various automated reports from the collected data could be generated for policymakers or even citizens, helping them make informed decisions. Based on the forecasts from the cloud's proposed models, warnings may be generated to mobile phones or other media. A timely warning can also help policymakers to understand the root cause of the problem. This warning may also allow policymakers to reduce air pollution by eliminating the likely sources of this pollution.

Future research may build upon this work and develop and compare models that can predict pollutant concentrations multistep ahead in time. Thus, models could forecast longer-term pollution values that are several steps ahead in time. Another aspect of future research could be comparing the models in this paper with classical machine-learning models like decision trees, k-nearest neighbour, and support vector machines.

ACKNOWLEDGMENT

This research work was made possible by a grant provided by the Department of Environment Science and Technology, Government of Himachal Pradesh, on the project IITM/DST-HP/VD/240 to Dr. Varun Dutt and Er. Pratik Chaturvedi. We are also grateful to the Indian Institute of Technology, Mandi, HP, India, for providing computational support, which made training models faster and efficient.

REFERENCES

Arora, Jhanvi, Utkarsh Pandya, Saloni Shah, and Nishant Doshi. "Survey-pollution monitoring using IoT." *Procedia Computer Science* 155 (2019): 710–715.

Busemeyer, Jerome R., and Adele Diederich. *Cognitive Modeling*. Sage, (2010).

Desai, Nitin Sadashiv, and John Sahaya Rani Alex. "IoT based air pollution monitoring and predictor system on Beagle bone black." In *2017 International Conference on Nextgen Electronic Technologies: Silicon to Software (ICNETS2)*, Chennai, India, pp. 367–370. IEEE, (2017).

Feng, Rui, Han Gao, Kun Luo, and Jian-ren Fan. "Analysis and accurate prediction of ambient PM2. 5 in China using Multi-layer Perceptron." *Atmospheric Environment* 232 (2020): 117534.

Ferlito, S., F. Bosso, S. De Vito, E. Esposito, and G. Di Francia. "LSTM Networks for Particulate Matter Concentration Forecasting." In *AISEM Annual Conference on Sensors and Microsystems*, pp. 409–415. Springer, Cham, (2019).

Ganesh, S. Sankar, P. Arulmozhivarman, and V. S. N. Rao Tatavarti. "Prediction of PM 2.5 using an ensemble of artificial neural networks and regression models." *Journal of Ambient Intelligence and Humanized Computing* (2018): 1–11.

Gu, Jiuxiang, Zhenhua Wang, Jason Kuen, Lianyang Ma, Amir Shahroudy, Bing Shuai, Ting Liu et al. "Recent advances in convolutional neural networks." *Pattern Recognition* 77 (2018): 354–377.

Guanochanga, Byron, Rolando Cachipuendo, Walter Fuertes, Santiago Salvador, Diego S. Benítez, Theofilos Toulkeridis, Jenny Torres, César Villacís, Freddy Tapia, and Fausto Meneses. "Real-Time Air Pollution Monitoring Systems Using Wireless Sensor Networks Connected in a Cloud-Computing, Wrapped Up Web Services." In *Proceedings of the Future Technologies Conference*, pp. 171–184. Springer, Cham, (2018).

Hyndman, Rob J., and George Athanasopoulos. *Forecasting: Principles and practice*. OTexts, (2018).

Kotu, V., and B. Deshpande. *Data Science* 2nd Edition 19–37. (2018).

LeCun, Yann, and Yoshua Bengio. "Convolutional networks for images, speech, and time series." *The Handbook of Brain Theory and Neural Networks* 3361, no. 10 (1995): 1995.

Leung, Henry, and Simon Haykin. "The complex backpropagation algorithm." *IEEE Transactions on Signal Processing* 39, no. 9 (1991): 2101–2104.

Li, Taoying, Miao Hua, and Xu Wu. "A hybrid CNN-LSTM model for forecasting particulate matter (PM2. 5)." *IEEE Access* 8 (2020): 26933–26940.

Liang, Xuan, Tao Zou, Bin Guo, Shuo Li, Haozhe Zhang, Shuyi Zhang, Hui Huang, and Song Xi Chen. "Assessing Beijing's PM2. 5 pollution: severity, weather impact, APEC and winter heating." *Proceedings of the Royal Society A: Mathematical, Physical and Engineering Sciences* 471, no. 2182 (2015): https://doi.org/10.1098/rspa.2015.0257.

OECD. "The economic consequences of outdoor air pollution." (2016). Retrieved from https://www.oecd.org/env/the-economic-consequences-of-outdoor-air-pollution-9789264257474-en.htm Last Visited (09/12/2020)

Ordieres, J. B., E. P. Vergara, R. S. Capuz, and R. E. Salazar. "Neural network prediction model for fine particulate matter (PM2. 5) on the US–Mexico border in El Paso (Texas) and Ciudad Juárez (Chihuahua)." *Environmental Modelling & Software* 20, no. 5 (2005): 547–559.

Ramchoun, Hassan, Mohammed Amine Janati Idrissi, Youssef Ghanou, and Mohamed Ettaouil. "Multilayer perceptron: Architecture optimization and training." *IJIMAI* 4, no. 1 (2016): 26–30.

Saha, Himadri Nath, Supratim Auddy, Avimita Chatterjee, Subrata Pal, Shivesh Pandey, Rocky Singh, Rakhee Singh et al. "Pollution control using internet of things (iot)." In *2017 8th Annual Industrial Automation and Electromechanical Engineering Conference (IEMECON)*, Chennai, India. pp. 65–68. IEEE, (2017).

Sak, Haşim, Andrew Senior, and Françoise Beaufays. "Long short-term memory based recurrent neural network architectures for large vocabulary speech recognition." *arXiv preprint arXiv:1402.1128* (2014).

Schmidhuber, Jürgen, and Sepp Hochreiter. "Long short-term memory." *Neural Computation* 9, no. 8 (1997): 1735–1780.

Sharma, Rishi, Tushar Saini, Praveen Kumar, Ankush Pathania, Khyathi Chitineni, Pratik Chaturvedi, and Varun Dutt. "An Online Low-Cost System for Air Quality Monitoring, Prediction, and Warning." In *International Conference on Distributed Computing and Internet Technology*, pp. 311–324. Springer, Cham, (2020).

Thaweephol, Kankamon, and Nuwee Wiwatwattana. "Long short-term memory deep neural network model for PM2. 5 forecasting in the Bangkok urban area." In *2019 17th International Conference on ICT and Knowledge Engineering (ICT & KE)*, Chennai, India. pp. 1–6. IEEE, (2019).

WHO. "Ambient (outdoor) air pollution." (2018). Retrieved from https://www.who.int/news-room/fact-sheets/detail/ambient-(outdoor)-air-quality-and-health Last Visited (09/12/2020)

Zhao, Jiachen, Fang Deng, Yeyun Cai, and Jie Chen. "Long short-term memory-Fully connected (LSTM-FC) neural network for PM2. 5 concentration prediction." *Chemosphere* 220 (2019): 486–492.

8 Energy Balance Indicators Calculation Software Solution for Energy Management Systems

Andrii Perekrest, Vita Ogar, Mykhailo Kushch-Zhyrko and Olga Gerasimenko
Kremenchuk Mykhailo Ostrohradskyi National University, Kremenchuk, Ukraine

CONTENTS

8.1 INTRODUCTION

The book *Cloud IoT: Concepts, Paradigms and Applications* aims to discuss and outline various aspects for the benefit of mankind. The past decade has been marked by the rapid development of the Internet of Things (IoT) and cloud computing. IoT is based on intelligent self-configuring nodes (also known as things) interconnected in a dynamic and globally shared network infrastructure. The basic idea of IoT is the pervasive presence of things that can understand, measure, draw conclusions, and even change the environment of collaboration. IoT is often supplemented by cloud computing. Cloud computing has virtually unlimited capabilities in terms of storage and processing power, speed, and is a more mature technology than IoT.

More recently, we have seen a trend toward increased use of cloud technology and IoT together, leading to a new paradigm known as cloud IoT. Cloud IoT is a scenario where IoT data is collected from nodes and processed in the cloud. Then the results of cloud processing are transmitted back to the IoT device for optimal performance. Cloud IoT has many noteworthy programs for using collaboration, standardization, and intelligence in social networks, as well as in home and work situations, such as smart living, smart governance, digital health, smart transport, smart cities, and more. Industries such as intelligent logistics, industrial automation, product and process automation, intelligent freight transport, intelligent security, intelligent environmental monitoring, green energy, risk management, pharmaceuticals, intelligent networks, and intelligent aerospace and aviation management.

DOI: 10.1201/9781003155577-10

Building energy monitoring and management systems helps collect and analyze real-time energy consumption. With real-time data, the system can effectively control and manage the energy consumption of buildings in order to achieve optimized energy consumption. In addition, the system can forecast the energy consumption trends of different buildings and make a realistic estimation of the energy consumption based on processing and analyzing the previous energy consumption data [1].

Devices such as low-power wireless sensor networks (WSNs) for environmental monitoring and novel smart meters for electric load profiling and recognition give the possibility of monitoring and characterization of energy consumption behavior of buildings and dwellings [2].

In this respect, there is a huge opportunity to improve the most competitive actors to offer more cost-effective, user-friendly, healthy, and safe products for buildings. In Europe, for instance, the area of energy management systems in buildings has only just started but is rapidly moving toward a technology-driven status with rising productivity [3].

The purpose of this book is to gather the current level of scientific and applied research of cloud IoT concepts, paradigms, and various applications. This book focuses on advanced graduate and postgraduate students, researchers, academics, and industry researchers. Thus, the authors are expected to try to maintain a balance between scientific rigor and practical significance.

8.2 METHODS FOR DETERMINING THE ENERGY EFFICIENCY OF BUILDINGS

For each functional component of the system, the heat required at the input is determined by adding the calculated heat loss in it and the heat at the outlet [4]. Specific heating energy consumption ($E_{PH,use}$), kW•h/m^2[kW•h/m^3] is calculated by the formulas for residential buildings

$$EP_{H,use} = Q_{H,use} / A_f ; \tag{8.1}$$

for public buildings

$$EP_{H,use} = Q_{H,use} / V , \tag{8.2}$$

where $Q_{H,use}$ – annual energy consumption of the building for heating, kWh;

A_f – air-conditioned (heated) area for a residential building, m^2;
V – air-conditioned (heating) volume for a public building (or its part), m^3.

Direction of calculation of the annual energy consumption is determined by energy requirements ($Q_{H,nd,i}$), kW•h to the power source ($Q_{H,gen,out,i}$), kW•h, and is opposite the flow of energy supplies in the system. The calculation is structured according to the components of the heat supply system (heat transfer, heat distribution, heat storage, heat generation) [5].

For each functional component of the system, the heat required at the input is determined by adding the calculated heat loss in it and the heat at the outlet.

Annual energy consumption for heating ($Q_{H,use}$), kW•h calculated as:

$$Q_{H,use} = Q_{H,gen,out,i} + Q_{H,gen,ls,i} , \tag{8.3}$$

where $Q_{H,gen,out,i}$ – the energy output from the subsystem of production/generation and accumulation of heat within i-th month, kW•h calculated by the formula (8.5); $Q_{H,gen,ls,i}$ – general heat losses of subsystems of production/generation and accumulation of heat within i-th month, kW•h calculated using the formula (8.4).

General subsystems heat production/generation and accumulation of heat within i-th month ($Q_{H,gen,ls,i}$), kW h calculated by the formula

$$Q_{H,gen,ls,i} = Q_{H,gen,out,i} \cdot \left(1 - \eta_{H,gen}\right) / \eta_{H,gen}, \tag{8.4}$$

where $\eta_{H,gen}$ – indicators of efficiency of subsystems of production/generation and accumulation of heat, accepted according to the data of values of seasonal efficiency of production/generation of heat [6].

If there is a heat supply source with an efficiency indicator specified in the technical documentation for equipment that differs from the tabular indicators [7–13], the value specified in the technical documentation for equipment is accepted.

The total energy output from the subsystem of production/generation and accumulation of heat ($Q_{H,gen,out,i}$), kW•h, is calculated as follows:

$$Q_{H,gen,out,i} = Q_{H,dis,in,i} = Q_{H,dis,ls,nrvd,i} + Q_{H,dis,out,i}, \tag{8.5}$$

where $Q_{H,dis,ls,nrvd,i}$ – unutilized heat distribution within the subsystem within i-th month, kW•h calculated by the formula (8.6); $Q_{H,dis,out,i}$ – energy out of the distribution subsystem within i-th month, kW•h calculated by the formula (8.9).

Unutilized heat distribution within the subsystem within i-th month, $Q_{H,dis,ls,nryd,i}$, kW•h calculated by the formula

$$Q_{H,dis,ls,nrvd,i} = Q_{H,dis,ls,nrbl,i} + \left(Q_{H,dis,ls,rbl,i} - Q_{H,dis,ls,rvd,i}\right), \tag{8.6}$$

where $Q_{H,dis,ls,nrbl,i}$ – unutilized heat loss kW•h calculated by the formula (8.7); $Q_{H,dis,ls,rbl,i}$ – recycling heat losses kW•h calculated by the formula (8.7); and $Q_{H,dis,ls,rvd,i}$ – utilized heat loss, kW•h calculated by the formula (8.8).

Heat losses of distribution subsystems located in all non-heating volumes are considered non-utilizable. Heat losses of distribution subsystems in all heated volumes are considered utilizable.

Heat losses at distribution subsystems within i-th month, kW•h calculated by the formula

$$Q_{H,dis,ls,i} = \Sigma \psi_{L,j} \cdot \left(\theta_{m,i} - \theta_{i,j}\right) \cdot L_j \cdot t_{op,an,i}, \tag{8.7}$$

where $\psi_{L,j}$ – is the linear heat transfer coefficient of the j-th pipeline, kW/(m•K), determined according to the typical values of the linear heat transfer coefficient Ψ, W/(m · K), for new and existing buildings listed in tables; $\theta_{m,i}$ – the average temperature of the coolant in the zone during the i-th month, °C; determined by the temperature schedule of regulation of the coolant under weather conditions at the average monthly ambient temperature of the month, which is determined in accordance with table A.2 [14–17]; $\theta_{i,j}$ – ambient temperature during the i-th month, °C; L_j – length of the j-th pipeline, m; $t_{op,an,i}$ – heating hours during the i-th month, hours; and j – is an index denoting pipelines with the same boundary conditions.

Recovered heat kW•h is calculated by formula

$$Q_{H,dis,ls,rvd,i} = Q_{H,dis,ls,rbl,i} \cdot 0{,}9 \cdot \eta_{H,gn,i}, \tag{8.8}$$

where $\eta_{H,gn,i}$ – dimensionless coefficient of gains utilization rate for heating during the i-th month is calculated in accordance with paragraph 12.2 [18–20].

The output energy of the distribution subsystems within the i-th month, ($Q_{H,dis,out,i}$), kW·h, which is equal to the input energy required for heat transfer subsystem during the i-th month ($Q_{H,em,in,i}$), kW·h is calculated by the formula

$$Q_{H,dis,out,i} = Q_{H,em,in,i} = Q_{H,em,out} + Q_{H,em,ls,i}, \tag{8.9}$$

where $Q_{H,em,out}$ – energy output of the heating transfer subsystem within i-th month, kW·h, is calculated by the formula (8.12); $Q_{H,em,ls,i}$ – the total heat losses of heat transfer/emission subsystems within the i-th month that are considered suitable for 100% recycling kW·h are calculated by the formula (8.10).

General heat losses of the heat transfer/emission subsystems for a particular month ($Q_{H,em,ls,i}$), kW·h, are calculated by the formula

$$Q_{H,em,ls,i} = \left(\frac{f_{hydr} \cdot f_{im} \cdot f_{rad}}{\eta_{em}} - 1 \right) \cdot Q_{H,em,out}; \tag{8.10}$$

$$\eta_{em} = \frac{1}{4 - \left(\eta_{str} + \eta_{ctr} + \eta_{emb} \right)}. \tag{8.11}$$

If the indicators of the components of the general level of efficiency of heating surfaces and hydraulic adjustment of systems ($f_{hydr}, f_{im}, f_{rad}, \eta_{em}$) in the technical documentation for equipment differ from the values of the indicators given in the appendix, the value is determined on the basis of equipment technical documentation [21–22].

The output energy of the heat transfer subsystem for the i-th month is equal to the energy consumption and is calculated by the formula

$$Q_{H,em,out} = Q_{H,nd,i} = \left(H_{tr,adj} + H_{ve,adj} \right) \cdot \left(\theta_{\text{int},set,H} - \theta_c \right) \cdot t - \eta_{H,gn} \cdot \left(\sum_k \Phi_{\text{int},mn,k} \cdot A_f + \sum_k \Phi_{sol,mn,k} \right) \cdot t, \tag{8.12}$$

where $Q_{H,nd,i}$ – heat to be submitted to the conditioned volume to maintain the temperature within a specified period of time, without taking into account the building heating systems, kW·h; $H_{tr,adj}$ – total heat transfer coefficient of the zone transmission, W/K; $H_{ve,adj}$ – total heat transfer coefficient by ventilation, W/K; $\theta_{\text{int},set,H}$ – the setpoint temperature of a zone of the building for heating, °C; θ_c – average monthly ambient temperature, °C; $\eta_{H,gn}$ – dimensionless coefficient of heat gains utilization; $\Phi_{\text{int},mn,k}$ – time-averaged heat flux from the k-th internal source, W/m²; $\Phi_{sol,mn,k}$ – time-averaged heat flux from the k -th source of solar radiation, W; t – duration of the month for which the calculation is made, hours.

Specific energy consumption for cooling ($EP_{C,use}$), kW·h/m² [kW·h/m³], is calculated by the formula

for residential buildings

$$EP_{C,use} = Q_{C,use} / A_f; \tag{8.13}$$

for public buildings

$$EP_{C,use} = Q_{C,use} / V, \tag{8.14}$$

where $Q_{C,use}$ – annual energy consumption of building for cooling kW•h.

Annual energy consumption for cooling ($Q_{C,use}$), kW h is calculated by the formula

$$Q_{C,use} = Q_{C,gen,out,i} + Q_{C,gen,ls,i}, \quad (8.15)$$

where $Q_{C,gen,out,i}$ – the energy output from the subsystem of production/generation and accumulation, kW•h; $Q_{C,gen,ls,i}$ – overall heat losses of the production/generation and accumulation subsystem kW•h.

General heat losses of production/generation and accumulation subsystems ($Q_{C,gen,ls}$), kW•h, are calculated by the formula

$$Q_{C,gen,ls} = Q_{C,gen,out} \cdot \left(1 - \eta_{C,gen}\right) / \eta_{C,gen}, \quad (8.16)$$

where $\eta_{C,gen}$ – is the efficiency index of the production/generation and accumulation subsystem, determined in accordance with the annual efficiency indicators (SEER) of individual refrigeration machines.

If the production/generation and storage subsystem consists of more than one type of generator/transformer, the calculations are performed separately for each part with the corresponding efficiency indicator [23].

The total energy output of the cooling production/generation and accumulation subsystems of ($Q_{C,gen,out}$), kW·h is calculated by the formula

$$Q_{C,gen,out} = Q_{C,dis,in} / \eta_{C,ac}, \quad (8.17)$$

where $Q_{C,dis,in}$ – the energy input of distribution subsystem kW•h;

$\eta_{C,ac}$ – the efficiency of automatic control/regulation, depending on the efficiency class of the control/regulation system the values are taken as follows: for class A systems – $\eta_{C,ac} = 0.99$; for class B systems – $\eta_{C,ac} = 0.93$; class C systems – $\eta_{C,ac} = 0.88$; for systems of class D – $\eta_{C,ac} = 0.82$.

In the absence of a cooling system in the building, in order to determine the energy efficiency of the building, a value of 0.93 is taken as the efficiency of automatic control/regulation ($\eta_{C,ac}$) and a value of 2.4 as the efficiency of the production/generation subsystem.

The input energy required for the distribution subsystem is determined by the formula

$$Q_{C,dis,in} = \sum_{i} Q_{C,dis,out,i} / 1000 + Q_{C,dis,ls}, \quad (8.18)$$

where $Q_{C,dis,ls}$ – the annual heat losses of the cooled air distribution subsystem kW•h; $Q_{C,dis,out,i}$ – output energy for the distribution subsystem during the i-th month, W•h.

$$Q_{C,em,out} = Q_{C,nd,i} = \left(H_{tr,adj} + H_{ve,adj}\right) \cdot \left(\theta_{\text{int},set,C} - \theta_c\right) \cdot t + \sum_{i=1}^{N} \left(\sum_{j=1}^{24} f_{ve,extra,j,k} H_{ve,extra,j,k} \left(\theta_{\text{int},set,C} - \theta_{e,j}\right) \right) - \eta_{C,gn} \cdot \left(\sum_{k} \$_{\text{int},mn,k} \cdot A_f + \sum_{k} \Phi_{sol,mn,k} \right) \cdot t, \quad (8.19)$$

where $Q_{C,nd,i}$ – the annual energy needs for cooling kW•h; $\theta_{\text{int},set,C}$ – setpoint temperature of the building area for cooling, °C; $f_{ve,extra,j,k}$ – the share of operation for a specific j-th hour of the i-th day of the month from the k-th element of additional ventilation (if night ventilation and/or natural cooling operates $f_{ve,extra,j,\kappa} = 1$, if not, $f_{ve,extra,j,k} = 0$); $H_{ve,extra,j,k}$ – total heat transfer coefficient due to additional ventilation (night ventilation and/or natural cooling) from the k -th element, W/K; $i = 1$ to N – calculation step in days (N = 31 till January); $j = 1$ to 24 – calculation step in hours; $\eta_{C,gn}$ – dimensionless utilization factor of cooling losses.

Annual losses of cooling distribution subsystem kW•h, are determined by the formula

$$Q_{C,dis,ls} = Q_{C,nd}\left(\left(1-\eta_{C,ce}\right)+\left(1-\eta_{C,ce,sens}\right)+\left(1-\eta_{C,d}\right)\right), \tag{8.20}$$

where $\eta_{C,ce}$ – the degree of utilization of heat transfer during cooling in the cooling system is taken in accordance with the indicators of the average annual coefficients of cooling systems; $\eta_{C,ce,sens}$ – the degree of explicit utilization of heat transfer during cooling in the cooling system. This value takes into account the undesirable dehumidification (energy for condensation) in the existing equipment of the cooling system; $\eta_{C,d}$ – the degree of utilization of the distribution subsystem.

Specific energy consumption of hot water supply ($EP_{dhv,use}$), kW•h/m^3 [kW•h/m^3], is calculated by formulas

for residential buildings

$$EP_{DHW,use} = Q_{DHW,use}/A_f; \tag{8.21}$$

for public buildings

$$EP_{DHW,use} = Q_{DHW,use}/V, \tag{8.22}$$

where $Q_{DHW,use}$ – the annual energy consumption of a building with hot water supply, kW h.

Annual energy consumption with hot water supply ($Q_{DHW,use}$), kW•h calculated as:

$$Q_{DHW,use} = \left(Q_{DHW,nd} + Q_{W,dis,ls} + Q_{W,dis,ls,col,m} + Q_{W,em,l}\right)/\eta_{gen}, \tag{8.23}$$

where $Q_{DHW,nd}$ – energy need for hot water supply kW•h; $Q_{W,dis,ls}$ – annual heat losses on hot water distribution subsystems kW•h;$Q_{W,dis,ls,col,m}$ – annual heat losses of hot water supply circulation circuit, kW•h; $Q_{W,em,l}$ – heat losses of water used in the water pumping kW•h; η_{gen} – efficiency of the subsystem of production/generation and accumulation of heat.

Energy consumption for hot water supply ($Q_{DHW,nd}$), kW•h is calculated by the formula

$$Q_{DHW,nd} = c_W \cdot V_W \cdot \left(\theta_{W,del} - \theta_{W,0}\right) \cdot a_x, \tag{8.24}$$

where c_W – is the specific heat capacity of water (kJ/kg•°C); $\theta_{W,del}$ – setpoint temperature of hot water supply, °C; $\theta_{W,0}$ – the average annual temperature of cold water, which is taken equal to 10°C; a_x – conversion factor, KJ, in kW•h, which is considered equal to 0.278•10^{-3} (kW•h/kJ); V_W – annual water consumption (kg), is calculated by the formula:

$$V_W = q_W \cdot n_m \cdot n_d \cdot \rho_W \cdot 10^{-3}, \tag{8.25}$$

where q_W – the average daily water consumption per year (l/day); n_m – the number of calculated units of hot water consumption; n_d – number of days of hot water supply system operation, days; ρ_W – density of water under normal conditions (kg/m^3).

Annual heat distribution subsystems hot water $Q_{W,dis,ls}$, kW·h, is calculated by the formula

$$Q_{W,dis,ls} = \Sigma \psi_{W,j} L_{W,j} \left(\theta_{W,dis,avg,j} - \theta_{amb,j} \right) t_W / 1000, \tag{8.26}$$

where $\psi_{W,j}$ – linear heat transfer coefficient of the pipeline, W/(m·K);

$L_{W,j}$ – length of the pipeline section, m; $\theta_{W,dis,avg,j}$ – average temperature of hot water in the pipeline section, °C; $\theta_{amb,j}$ – average temperature of the environment around the section of the pipeline or temperature of the heated or unheated room, °C; t_W – the period of use of hot water (hours/year), which is set when identifying the actual condition of the building; j – is an index denoting pipelines with the same boundary conditions.

Heat losses must be calculated separately for pipelines located in unheated volumes and heated volumes of the building.

Annual heat losses in the circulation circuit of HWS $Q_{W,dis,ls,col,m}$, kW·h are calculated by the formula

$$Q_{W,dis,ls,col,m} = Q_{W,dis,ls,col,on} + Q_{W,dis,ls,col,off}, \tag{8.27}$$

where $Q_{W,dis,ls,col,on}$ – heat losses in the pipelines during periods of circulation kW·h; $Q_{W,dis,ls,col,off}$ – heat losses in the pipelines during periods of absence of circulation, kW·h.

$$Q_{W,dis,ls,col,on} = \Sigma \psi_{W,j} L_{W,j} \left(\theta_{W,dis,avg,j} - \theta_{amb,j} \right) t_{W,on,j} / 1000; \tag{8.28}$$

$$Q_{W,dis,ls,col,off} = \Sigma \rho_W c_W V_{W,dis,j} \left(\theta_{W,dis,avg,j} - \theta_{amb,j} \right) n_{nom} / 1000, \tag{8.29}$$

where $\psi_{W,j}$ – is the linear heat transfer coefficient of the pipeline, W/(m·K);

$L_{W,j}$ – length of the pipeline section, m; $\theta_{W,dis,avg,j}$ – average temperature of hot water in the pipeline section, °C; $\theta_{amb,j}$ – average temperature of the environment around the section of the pipeline or temperature of the heated or unheated room, °C; $t_{W,on,j}$ – circulation period, hours/year; in case of the absence of accurate data is taken $t_{w,on}$ = 8760 hours; $\rho_W c_W$ – heat capacity of water is taken 1150 W·h/(m³·K); $V_{W,dis,j}$ – the volume of water contained in the section of the pipeline, m³ determined by the values of the length and diameter of the pipeline; n_{nom} – the number of operating cycles of the circulating pump during the year; in the absence of accurate data is taken n_{norm} = 1–2 cycles per day.

Heat losses of water used in the water pumping $Q_{W,em,l}$ kW·h is calculated by the formula

$$Q_{W,em,l} = Q_W \cdot \eta_{eq} / 100, \tag{8.30}$$

where Q_W – the annual energy needs for HWS kW·h; η_{eq} – gain equivalent, which takes into account the heat loss of water used in water collection, is taken according to the data of heat loss of water used in water collection in buildings without a circulation circuit.

The specific energy consumption during the ventilation supply ($EP_{V,use}$), kW·h/m³[kW·h/m³], kW·h/m²[kW·h/m³] is calculated by the formula

for residential buildings

$$EP_{V,use} = {Q_{V,use}}/{A_f}; \tag{8.31}$$

for public buildings

$$EP_{V,use} = \frac{Q_{V,use}}{V}, \tag{8.32}$$

where $Q_{V,use}$ – annual energy consumption in the building during ventilation kW•h.

Annual energy consumption during ventilation ($Q_{V,use}$), kW•h, is equal to power consumption of supply and exhaust ventilation fans ($Q_{V,sys,fan}$) and calculated by the formula

$$Q_{V,use} = Q_{V,sys,fan} = P_{el} \cdot t_w, \tag{8.33}$$

where t_w– time of operation of the ventilation system, h; P_{el} – electric power of the fan, kW, calculated by the formula:

$$P_{el} = \frac{SFP \cdot V_L}{3600}, \tag{8.34}$$

where SFP – is the specific power of the fan of the mechanical ventilation system, kW/(m^3/s). In the absence of a mechanical ventilation system, the calculation is not performed; V_L – volumetric airflow in the mechanical ventilation system, m^3/h.

Specific energy consumption for lighting ($EP_{W,use}$), kW•h/m^2 [kW•h/m^3], is calculated by the formula

$$EP_{W,use} = \frac{W_{use}}{A_f}, \tag{8.35}$$

where W_{use} – the annual amount of energy consumption for lighting, kWh, is determined by the formula:

$$W_{use} = W_L + W_P, \tag{8.36}$$

where W_L – the energy required to perform the function of artificial lighting in the building, kWh; W_P – energy required to charge the batteries of emergency lighting fixtures, and energy to control/regulate lighting in the building, kWh.

The amount of energy required to perform the function of artificial lighting in the building (W_L), kWh, is calculated by the formula

$$W_L = \left(P_N \cdot F_C\right) \cdot \left(\left(t_D \cdot F_o \cdot F_D\right) + \left(t_N \cdot F_D\right)\right) \cdot A_f / 1000, \tag{8.37}$$

where P_N – specific power of the installed artificial lighting in the building, W/m^2, is determined according to the design data or when detecting the actual condition of the building to provide lighting in accordance with regulatory values; F_C – constant brightness factor, which refers to the use of lighting installation in the functioning control of constant illumination of the zone and is calculated according to the indicators of standard values for the calculation of energy consumption for lighting;F_o – lighting utilization factor, which is the ratio of the total installed capacity of artificial lighting to the period of use of the zone, and is taken according to the tabular data [24], or calculated according to the actual power of lighting fixtures; F_D – coefficient of natural lighting, which is the ratio of the use of the total installed capacity of artificial lighting to the available natural lighting of the area; t_D – time of use of natural light during the year, h; t_N – time of use of artificial lighting during the year, h.

The energy required to provide battery power for emergency lighting fixtures and energy to control/regulate lighting in a building W_P, kW·h, is calculated as follows:

$$W_P = \left(P_{em} + P_{pc}\right) A_f, \tag{8.38}$$

where P_{em} – the total determined power density battery power emergency lighting fixtures, kW·h/m²;P_{pc} – total determined specific power of all control systems of zone lighting devices at the time when lamps are not used, kW h/m².

Primary energy is the sum of all sources of energy supply, including domestic production, imports, exports, and changes in reserves of primary energy sources, as well as transformations, own consumption by the energy sector, losses in transportation and distribution, etc. Calculated for each energy source and calculated by the formula

$$E_p = \sum E_{del,i} \cdot f_{p,del,i}, \tag{8.39}$$

where $E_{del,i}$– supplied energy, kW·h; $f_{p,del,i}$ – primary energy factor for the i-th energy carrier.

The supplied energy ($E_{del,i}$) is calculated by the formula

$$E_{del,i} = Q_{H,use} + Q_{C,use} + Q_{DHW,use} + EP_{V,use} + EP_{W,use}. \tag{8.40}$$

Specific indicator of primary energy consumption (e_p), kWh/m²

$$e_p = {E_p}/{A_f}. \tag{8.41}$$

According to Kumar et al. [25] the concept of greenhouse gas is a gas that traps the infrared radiation of the earth's surface, which leads to global warming on the planet. The mass of greenhouse gas emissions m_{CO2}, kg, is calculated from the supplied and exported energy for each energy carrier according to the formula

$$m_{CO_2} = \sum\left(E_{del,i} \cdot K_{del,i}\right) / 1000, \tag{8.42}$$

where $K_{del,i}$ – is the CO_2 emission factor for the *i*-th energy carrier, g/kWh.

8.3 PROCEDURE FOR ENERGY EFFICIENCY CERTIFICATION

The information required for the calculation of energy efficiency indicators of buildings is established on the basis of design documentation for the building. In the absence of design documentation, the relevant data are determined by the results of identifying the actual condition of the building [26].

The information needed to calculate the energy performance of buildings is:

1) local climatic conditions;
2) functional purpose, architectural-planning, and constructive decision of the building (characteristics of wall enclosing constructions, covering constructions, overlapping constructions, translucent enclosing constructions, external doors);
3) geometrical parameters of the building and determined actual values (total area and area external enclosing structures of the building, their thickness, air-conditioned (heated) area, air-conditioned (heated) volume, volume intended for ventilation, average height of the premises);

4) normative sanitary and microclimatic conditions of the building premises;
5) the presence of premises with different functional purposes in the building, the actual values of the air-conditioned area, air-conditioned volume, and volume for ventilation of such premises;
6) design features and geometric parameters of translucent enclosing structures, weaving material, type of glazing, the presence of sun protection devices, the value of the calculated thermal conductivity;
7) indicators of the reduced heat transfer resistance of opaque and translucent enclosing structures;
8) the estimated value of the time-averaged airflow for the building or its air-conditioned zones;
9) internal heat input;
10) solar heat input;
11) data on engineering systems of the building: information on the means of calculation of consumption of thermal and electric energy [27], use of gas or other energy sources installed in the building; information on the use of renewable energy sources or methods of heat recovery, passive solar systems and solar protection systems or the use of cogeneration with the establishment of characteristics and scope of application and performance indicators;
12) for heating systems: type of heating system (hydraulic, electric, air); hydraulic adjustment of the system (two-pipe, one-pipe, one-pipe with a constant hydraulic mode, one-pipe with a variable hydraulic mode); type of room air temperature control, temperature pressure; specific heat losses through external protections, specific heat losses through the surfaces adjacent to heating panels; type of heating system (floor, wall, ceiling); electric heating (direct, accumulative, accumulative with adjustment) configuration of air heating; technical parameters of the distribution system (insulation of pipelines, shut-off and control valves, type of regulation and level of regulation of the pump); generation parameters and type of energy carrier (natural gas, fuel oil, coal, wood pellets, wood chips);
13) for cooling systems: type of fan; compressor type; refrigerant; the presence of a pre-cooling system; availability of closers; control system class;
14) for hot water supply systems: type of system (without circulating circuit, with statically balanced circulating risers, with automatically circulating risers); technical parameters of distribution (number of sections, length of the pipeline, linear coefficient of heat transfer of pipelines, average temperature of hot water in the section of the pipeline); monthly or annual period of use, number of working cycles per day, circulation period, water intake;
15) for ventilation systems: type of mechanical ventilation (balanced, decentralized, other); specific power of fans; availability of systems for dehumidification, humidification, night cooling, heat recovery;
16) for lighting systems: number of lamps, their type and power; specific power of the installed artificial lighting in the building;
17) standard service life of fencing structures and elements;
18) energy balance of the building.

The obtained results of calculation of energy efficiency indicators of buildings, indicators of thermal characteristics of enclosing structures, energy efficiency indicators of engineering systems are compared with the minimum requirements for energy efficiency of buildings in accordance with Article 6 of the Law of Ukraine “On Energy Efficiency of Buildings”, requirements, characteristics of enclosing structures and requirements for energy efficiency of engineering systems (including equipment) of buildings.

Based on the results of the comparison, recommendations for improving the energy efficiency of the building are given, which are given in the energy certificate of the building, to ensure compliance with the minimum requirements for energy efficiency of buildings [28].

Ensuring the highest class of energy efficiency is considered in the recommendations for improving the energy efficiency of the building with the consent of the certification customer.

Recommendations are developed on the basis of the defined structure of energy consumption of the building and depending on values of components priority measures for reduction of such energy consumption are established.

The scope and list of energy-saving measures are determined on the basis of the type of energy used by the engineering systems of the building, which is a combination of all delivered energy and renewable energy produced on the territory of the building.

Recommendations for improving the energy efficiency of buildings should take into account local climatic conditions and be technically and economically effective.

8.4 STRUCTURE OF THE BUILDING ENERGY CERTIFICATE

The energy certificate shall contain the following information:

1) address (location) of the building;
2) information on the functional purpose and construction of the building – data on the geometric parameters of the building and applied design solutions, determined by the design documentation or the results of certification of energy efficiency of the building, namely: total area of the building, m^2; total volume, m^3; heated area of the building, m^2; heated volume of the building, m^3; number of floors (if the building consists of several different sections, the floors of each section are indicated consecutively); year of commissioning of the building; number of entrances;
3) photography – a photographic image of the facade of the building;
4) scale of energy efficiency classes – graphic color designation of existing energy efficiency classes (from high level "A" to low "G") in the following form: class A – dark green; class B – green; class C – turquoise; class D – light yellow; class E – dark yellow; class F – orange; class G – red.
   On the opposite of the relevant indicator of the energy efficiency class, the numerical value of the indicator of this class in accordance with the requirements of Article 5 of the Law of Ukraine "On Energy Efficiency of Buildings" is situated, kWh/m^2 or kWh/m^3;
5) energy efficiency class – contains a graphical designation by the arrow of the corresponding class of energy efficiency of the building (the letter designation is contained inside the arrow) according to the results of certification of energy efficiency of the building;
6) specific energy consumption for heating, hot water supply, cooling of the building – indicator of specific energy consumption for heating, hot water supply, cooling of the building, determined by the results of certification of energy efficiency of the building, indicating the numerical indicator and units, kWh/m^2 or kWh/m^3;
7) specific consumption of primary energy – graphic color and digital notation of the scale of energy consumption levels, on which the arrow indicates the level of primary energy consumption by the building, determined by the results of certification of energy efficiency of the building, kWh/m^2;
8) specific greenhouse gas emissions – graphical color and digital designation of the scale of levels of greenhouse gas emissions, on which the arrow indicates the level of greenhouse gas emissions of the building, determined by the results of certification of building energy efficiency, kg/m^2;
9) series and number of the energy auditor's qualification certificate – series and number of the energy auditor's qualification certificate, who composed the energy certificate;
10) actual or design characteristics of enclosing structures – data on geometric and thermophysical characteristics of individual enclosing structures, determined by the design documentation or by the results of certification of energy efficiency of the building, namely:

- types of fencing structures;
- value of heat transfer resistance of enclosing structures (existing reduced value and minimum requirements), $m^2 \cdot K/W$;
- area of separate enclosing structures, m^2;

11) description of the technical condition of enclosing structures – a description of the shortcomings of the structures identified during the energy efficiency certification and a description of their technical condition;
12) energy efficiency indicators and the actual specific energy consumption of the building – data on energy efficiency indicators of the building, namely:
    - specific energy consumption for heating, cooling, hot water supply (existing value and established minimum requirements), kWh/m^2 kWh/m^3 per year;
    - specific energy consumption for heating (existing value and minimum requirements), kWh/m^2 $kW \cdot h/m^3$ per year;
    - specific energy consumption for cooling (existing value and minimum requirements), kWh/m^2 kWh/m^3 per year;
    - specific energy consumption for hot water supply (existing value and minimum requirements), kWh/m^2 $kW \cdot h/m^3$ per year;
    - specific energy consumption of the ventilation system (existing value and minimum requirements), kWh/m^2 kWh/m^3 per year;
    - specific energy consumption for lighting (existing value and minimum requirements), kWh/m^2 $kW \cdot h/m^3$ per year;
    - specific consumption of primary energy (existing value and minimum requirements), kWh/m^2 $kW \cdot h/m^3$ per year;
    - specific greenhouse gas emissions, kg/m^2 per year;
13) energy consumption of the building – data on the estimated and actual energy consumption of the building per year, namely:
    - energy consumption of heating systems (actual consumption per year and estimated consumption for the year), thousand kWh, kWh/m^2, or kWh/m^3;
    - energy consumption of ventilation systems (actual consumption per year and estimated consumption per year), thousand kWh, kWh / m^2, or kWh/m^3;
    - energy consumption of hot water supply systems (actual consumption per year and estimated consumption per year), thousand kWh, kWh / m^2, or kWh/m^3;
    - energy consumption of cooling systems (actual volume of consumption per year and estimated volume of consumption per year), thousand kWh, kWh/m^2, or kWh/m;
    - energy consumption of lighting systems (actual consumption per year and estimated consumption per year), thousand kWh, kWh/m^2, or kWh/m^3;
    - actual consumption volumes are indicated on the condition that energy consumption meters are available for the relevant system. In the absence of such means of accounting, the actual indicators are not specified. For new construction objects, the energy consumption indicators of the building are not filled in;
14) the reasons for the deviation of the estimated consumption from the actual – data determined during the certification of energy efficiency of the building, which affect the discrepancy between the estimated and actual consumption of the building;
15) annual energy consumption of the building – a sector diagram of the annual energy consumption of the building with a division into the relevant types of annual energy consumption of the building;
16) actual or design characteristics of engineering systems of the building – data on engineering systems of the building, determined during the certification of energy efficiency of the building;
17) recommendations for ensuring (increasing the level) energy efficiency – data on measures to ensure (increasing the level) energy efficiency of the building, the implementation of

which will allow indicators of enclosing structures and engineering systems of the building to reach a level not lower than the minimum. Detailed information specified in the energy certificate, including the economic efficiency of the stated recommendations for ensuring (increasing the level) of energy efficiency of the building and/or its separate parts, is provided in the recommendation report;

18) additionally, indicate information on the possibility of obtaining more detailed information specified in the certificate, including information on the economic efficiency of the recommendations set out in the certificate to ensure (increase) the energy efficiency of buildings and/or their separate parts. Such information may be included in the recommendation report.

The size of the certificate can be changed depending on the amount of information indicated.

The extract from the energy certificate contains the following information:

1) address (location) of the building;
2) information on the functional purpose and construction of the building – data on the geometric parameters of the building and applied design solutions, determined by the design documentation or the results of certification of energy efficiency of the building, namely: total area of the building, m^2; total volume, m^3; heated area of the building, m^2; heated volume of the building, m^3; number of floors (if the building consists of several different sections, the floors of each section are indicated consecutively); year of commissioning of the building;
3) scale of energy efficiency classes – graphic color designation of existing energy efficiency classes (from high level "A" to low "G"). On the opposite of the corresponding indicator of the energy efficiency class is the numerical value of the indicator of this class, kWh/m^2 or kWh/m^3.
4) energy efficiency class – contains an arrow graphical designation of the corresponding class of energy efficiency of the building (the letter designation is contained inside the arrow), determined by the results of certification of energy efficiency of the building;
5) specific energy consumption for heating, hot water supply, cooling of the building – indicator of specific energy consumption for heating, hot water supply, cooling of the building, determined by the results of certification of energy efficiency of the building, indicating the numerical indicator and units, kWh/m^2 or kWh/m^3;
6) specific consumption of primary energy – graphic color and digital designation of the scale of energy consumption levels, on which the arrow indicates the level of primary energy consumption by the building, determined by the results of certification of building energy efficiency, kWh/m^2;
7) specific greenhouse gas emissions – graphical color and digital designation of the scale of levels of greenhouse gas emissions, on which the arrow indicates the level of greenhouse gas emissions of the building, determined by the results of certification of building energy efficiency, kg/m^2;
8) series and number of the energy auditor's qualification certificate – series and number of the energy auditor's qualification certificate, who composed the energy certificate.

8.5 BLOCK DIAGRAM OF THE PROCESS OF CALCULATING THE ENERGY CERTIFICATE OF THE BUILDING

Based on the abovementioned method of calculating the energy efficiency of buildings, a detailed block diagram of the calculation of the main items of the energy certificate of the building was made (Figure 8.1).

Immediately after ordering the energy certification of the building, it is proposed to provide a questionnaire with general questions about the construction of the building and about engineering

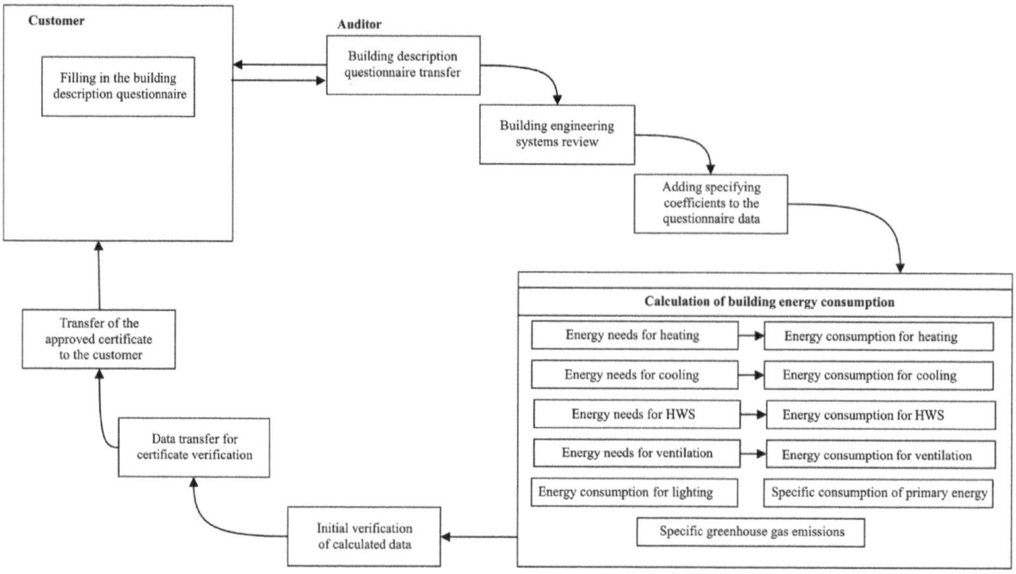

FIGURE 8.1 Stages of energy certification of the building.

systems, for the preparation of the necessary documentation by the customer. The next step for the auditor is an inspection of the condition of the building and engineering systems (inspection data in the form of a description of the technical condition of the enclosing structures and the actual characteristics of the engineering systems of the building are provided in the certificate). After clarifying the necessary information to determine the adjustment factors, the auditor proceeds to calculate the energy efficiency of the building, issue a certificate and provide recommendations for energy efficiency (together with the calculation of the payback period of these implementations).

The next step is the initial verification of the developed energy certificate. Each energy certificate is assigned a level of reliability based on the sum of the points in accordance with the results of comparing the values of its input, intermediate, and performance indicators, which calculate the energy efficiency of buildings in the established range.

The final step is the transfer of the prepared documentation for verification. The inspection is considered successful if the following conditions are met at the same time: as a result of the inspection, no changes in the energy efficiency class of the building have been established; each of the indicators of energy efficiency of the building, indicated in the energy certificate, does not differ by more than 5% from the calculation (Figure 8.1).

After acquainting with modern software and regulatory documentation, the main requirements for the developed software were established. They include:

- indication of building construction characteristics;
- choice of types of engineering systems (heating, cooling, hot water supply, etc.) of the building;
- construction of schedules of energy consumption needs and energy consumption by months;
- formation of data sets on the calculated indicators of energy efficiency;
- formation of recommendations for increasing the level of energy efficiency;
- formation of the energy certificate of the building;
- formation of an application with initial, intermediate, and effective indicators of energy efficiency of the building;
- formation of the initial inspection table and establishment of the certificate group.

These requirements are due to the regulatory documentation according to which the energy auditor independently selects the software [29–30]; however, it must pass some verification (compliance of the calculation elements). One of the important points of verification is the possibility of access to the intermediate results of the calculation for the possibility of their analysis and verification.

Schematically, the diagram can be divided into four stages. The first stage includes the entry of construction characteristics (heating area and volume, the area of enclosing structures, including around the world). The following is the calculation of energy needs for heating and cooling the building. At this stage, the auditor, based on the documentation and after a personal inspection of the systems, selects the parameters to clarify the calculated coefficients. The calculation is performed monthly and the calculated data are displayed in the form of tables and graphs on the screen. The third stage includes the calculation of energy consumption of building engineering systems (heating, cooling, hot water supply, ventilation, and lighting), primary energy, and greenhouse gas emissions.

As a result, after three stages, the final one is the formation of the energy certificate of the building in which the auditor only has to fill in the items of the description of real engineering systems and create recommendations for improving the energy efficiency class. Also, on the way out is the formation of an application for independent monitoring of certificates and a letter of initial verification with the provision of a level of reliability.

8.6 SOFTWARE DEVELOPMENT

The software was developed in LabVIEW [31–32]. The first tab is "Building Data" (Figure 8.2). The main page consists of calculation points for each system to facilitate the evaluation of system efficiency. Part of the calculation of transmission costs is to determine the thermal resistance. It is accepted that walls can contain up to four layers of materials. The auditor selects his material for each layer, choosing from a drop-down list that contains a certain set of standard data. The thermal conductivity is automatically loaded into LabVIEW from. Csv files using the Read From Spreadsheet File element (Figure 8.2).

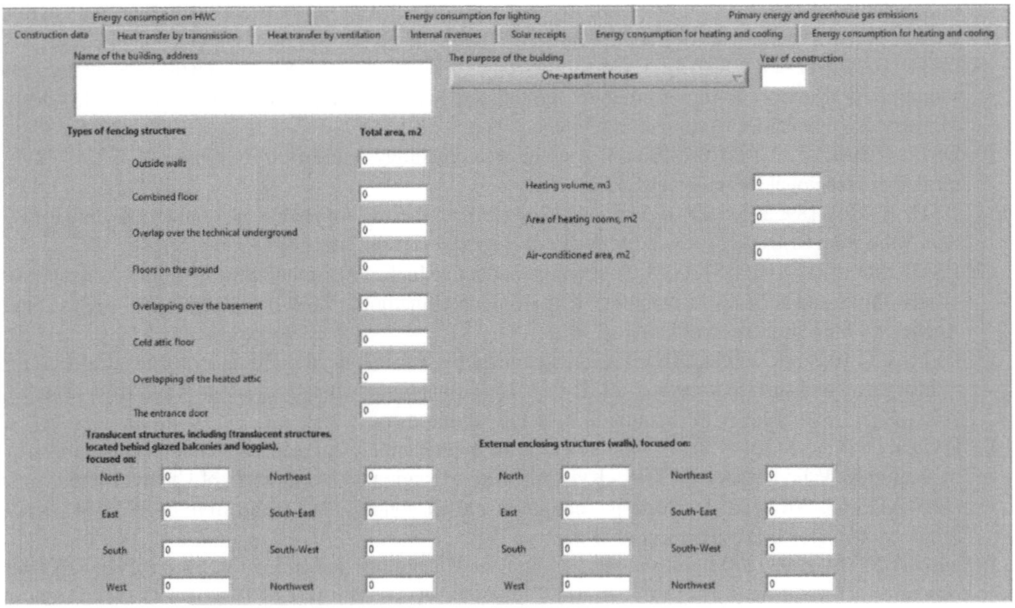

FIGURE 8.2 General view of the software and its first tab "Building Data."

8.7 CONCLUSIONS

Information-analytical, algorithmic, and software solutions, which provide practical implementation of solutions for energy audit of buildings and research of their energy consumption on the basis of heat balance on a monthly basis, were developed. The developed solutions logically divide the process of formation of energy certificate into stages represented by the tabs of the developed software. Benefiting the simplification, improving quality of the energy audit process and excluding human factor calculation mistakes facilitate the reduction of time required for processing the energy audit information.

REFERENCES

1. Wei, C., & Li, Y. (2011, September). Design of energy consumption monitoring and energy-saving management system of intelligent building based on the Internet of things. In *2011 International Conference on Electronics, Communications And Control (ICECC)* (pp. 3650–3652). IEEE.
2. Bottaccioli, L., Aliberti, A., Ugliotti, F., Patti, E., Osello, A., Macii, E., & Acquaviva, A. (2017, July). Building energy modelling and monitoring by integration of iot devices and building information models. In *2017 IEEE 41st Annual Computer Software and Applica-tions Conference (COMPSAC)* (Vol. 1, pp. 914–922). IEEE.
3. Moreno, M., Úbeda, B., Skarmeta, A. F., & Zamora, M. A. (2014). How can we tackle en-ergy efficiency in iot basedsmart buildings? *Sensors*, 14(6), pp. 9582–9614.
4. Perekrest A., Chebotarova Y. and Herasimenko O. (2016). Classification of requirements for ther-mal supply systems of civil buildings. *Electromechanical and Energy Saving Systems*, 4 (36). pp. 74–85.
5. DSN 3.3.6.042-99 (1999). Sanitary norms of microclimate of industrial premises. Valid from 01.12.1999 - K.: Ministry of Health of Ukraine, 12 p.
6. DSTU B EN 15251: 2011 (2012). Calculated parameters of the microclimate of the premises for the design and evaluation of energy performance of buildings in relation to the quality of wind, thermal comfort, lighting and acoustics. Valid from 01.01.2013 - Kyiv: Ministry of Regional Development of Ukraine, 71 p.
7. DBN B.2.6-31: 2016 (2017). *Thermal insulation of buildings*. Kyiv: Ministry of Regional Develop-ment of Ukraine, 31 p.
8. DSTU B EN ISO 7730: 2011 (2012). Ergonomics of the thermal environment. Analytical definition and interpretation of thermal comfort based on calculations of PMV and PPD and local ther-mal comfort criteria. Valid from 01.01.2013 - Kyiv: Ministry of Regional Development of Ukraine, 43 p.
9. DSTU BA.2.2-12-2015 (2015). Energy efficiency of buildings. Method of calculating energy consumption for heating, cooling, ventilation, lighting and hot water supply. Valid from 07/27/2015 - Kyiv: Ministry of Regional Development of Ukraine, 199 p.
10. DSTU-N B B.1.1.-27: 2010 (2011). Construction climatology. Valid from November 1, 2011 - Kyiv: Ministry of Regional Development, 123 p.
11. DSTU B B.2.3-189: 2013 (2013). Methods of selection of thermal insulation material for building insulation. Valid from 01.01.2014 - Kyiv: Ministry of Regional Development of Ukraine, 85 p.
12. DSTU ISO 10211-1: 2005 (2008). Thermally conductive inclusions in building structures. Calcula-tion of heat fluxes and surface temperatures. Part. 1. General methods. Valid from 01.03.2008 - Kyiv: State Agency for Standardization of Ukraine, 42 p.
13. DSTU ISO 10211-1: 2005 (2008). Thermally conductive inclusions in building structures. Calcula-tion of heat fluxes and surface temperatures. Part. 2. Linear heat-conducting inclusions. Valid from March 1, 2008 - Kyiv: State Agency for Standardization of Ukraine, 17 p.
14. DSTU-N B B.3.2-3: 2014 (2014). Guidelines for the implementation of thermal modernization of residential buildings. Valid from 01.10.2015 - Kyiv: Ministry of Regional Development of Ukraine, 40 p.
15. DBN B.2.5-67: 2013 (2013). Heating, ventilation and air conditioning. Valid from 01.01.2014 - Kyiv: Ministry of Regional Development of Ukraine, 174 p.
16. DBN B.2.5-39: 2008 (2009). Engineering equipment of buildings and structures. External networks and structures. Thermal networks. Valid from 09.12.2008 - Kyiv: Ministry of Regional De-velopment of Ukraine, 55 p.

17. DSTU-N B B.2.5-37: 2008 (2008). Guidelines for the design, installation and operation of auto-mated systems for monitoring and management of buildings and structures. Valid from 18.02.2008 - Kyiv: Ministry of Regional Development, 174 p.
18. DSTU B EN 15232: 2011 (2012). Impact of automation, monitoring and management of buildings. Valid from 01.04.2012 - Kyiv: Ministry of Regional Development of Ukraine, 115 p.
19. DSTU B B.2.5-44: 2010 (2010). Design of heating systems for buildings with heat pumps. Valid from 02.02.2010 - Kyiv: Ministry of Regional Development of Ukraine, 56 p.
20. DSTU B EN 15459: 2014 (2014). Energy efficiency of buildings. Procedure for economic evaluation of building energy systems. Valid from 14.07.2014 - Kyiv: Ministry of Regional De-velopment of Ukraine, 86 p.
21. DSTU B.A.2.2-12-2015 (2015). Energy efficiency of buildings. Method of calculating energy consumption for heating, cooling, ventilation, lighting and hot water supply. Valid from 27.07.2015 - Kyiv: Ministry of Regional Development of Ukraine, 199 p.
22. Perekrest, A., Shendryk, V., Pijarski, P., Parfenenko, Y., & Shendryk, S. (7 August 2017) "Complex information and technical solutions for energy management of municipal ener-getics", Proc. SPIE 10445, Photonics Applications in Astronomy, Communications, Indus-try, and High Energy Physics Experiments 2017, 1044567; doi: 10.1117/12.2280962.
23. A. Perekrest, I. Konokh and M. Kushch-Zhyrko, (2019). "Administrative Buildings Heating Automatic Control Based on Maximum Efficiency Criterion," *2019 IEEE International Confer-ence on Modern Electrical and Energy Systems (MEES)*, Kremenchuk, Ukraine, pp. 202–205, doi: 10.1109/MEES.2019.8896517.
24. A. Perekrest, M. Kushch-Zhyrko, V. Ogar, O. Zalunina, O. Bilyk and Y. Chebotarova, (2020). "Key Performance Indicators Assessment Methodology Principles Adaptation for Heating Sys-tems of Administrative and Residential Buildings," *2020 IEEE Problems of Automated Electrodrive. Theory and Practice (PAEP)*, Kremenchuk, Ukraine, pp. 1–4, doi: 10.1109/PAEP49887.2020.9240784.
25. Sampath Kumar, V. R., Khamis, A., Fiorini, S., Carbonera, J. L., Olivares Alarcos, A., Habib, M., Goncalves, P., Li, H., & Olszewska, J. I. (2019). Ontologies for Industry 4.0. *The Knowledge Engineering Review, 34.*
26. van der Vegte, W. F.. & Vroom, R. W. (2013). Vroom Considering cognitive aspects in de-signing cyber-physical systems: an emerging need for transdisciplinarity. In *International Workshop on the Future of Transdisciplinary Design*, pp. 41–52.
27. Gerritsen, B. H. M. & Horváth, I. (2013). Current Drivers and Obstacles of Synergy in Cyber-Physical Systems Design. *Proceedings of the ASME 2012 International Design Engineering Tech-nical Conferences and Computers and Information in Engineering Conference.* 2, pp. 1277–1286.
28. Dobrovolska, O. (2009). Ontologies in Computer Science: A Philosophical Analysis. Abstract of the dissertation for the degree of Candidate of Philosophical Sciences in the specialty 09.00.09 - *Philosophy of Science.* Kharkiv, 19 p.
29. Tymchuk, Sergii, Abramenko, Ivan, Zahumenna, Katerina, Shendryk, Sergii, & Shendryk, Vira. (2020). Determination of the Sampling Interval of Time Series of Measure-ments for Automation Systems. doi: 10.1007/978-3-030-46817-0_55.
30. Boiko, Olha, Shendryk, Vira, Shendryk, Sergii, & Boiko, Andrii. (2020). MES/ERP In-tegration Aspects of the Manufacturing Automation. doi: 10.1007/978-3-030-40724-7_2.
31. Pavlenko, Petro, Shendryk, Vira, Balushok, Kostyantyn, & Doroshenko, Stanislav. (2019). Data Integration Technology of Industrial Information Systems. doi: 10.1007/978-3-030-22365-6_25.
32. A. Perekrest, Y. Chebotarova and O. Herasimenko, (2017). "Information and analytical set of tools for assessing efficiency of the civil buildings heating modernization," *2017 International Conference on Modern Electrical and Energy Systems (MEES)*, Kremenchuk, pp. 216–219. doi: 10.1109/MEES.2017.8248893.

Part III

Smart Living

9 A Comparison of Cloud-IoT-Based Frameworks of Identification and Monitoring of Covid-19 Cases

Sargam Yadav
Dublin Business School, Dublin, Ireland

Abhishek Kaushik
Adapt Centre, Dublin City University, Dublin, Ireland

Mahak Sharma
The Maharajah Sayajirao University of Baroda, Baroda, India

CONTENTS

DOI: 10.1201/9781003155577-12

9.1 INTRODUCTION

Coronavirus is an infectious disease caused by a newly discovered SARS-CoV-2 strain. The current number of cases as reported by WHO as of 24 December is over 79 million (Worldometers.info, 2020a). Most people who come in contact with the virus might not be severely affected, with some experiencing only mild to moderate respiratory illness. They will also not require any special treatment and might recover autonomously (World Health Organization, 2020). This majority may however serve as carriers of the virus for people who are more at risk. This demographic includes the elderly and those with underlying medical conditions such as respiratory ailments, diabetes, cancer, and so on (World Health Organization, 2020).

The current Covid-19 pandemic has called into question the efficacy of healthcare systems worldwide. The ill-prepared healthcare system puts healthcare professionals and essential workers at higher risk. Several novel ideas involving cloud computing and IoT are being proposed to detect and combat Covid-19 until a reliable vaccine becomes available to the public. Some of these measures include predictive modelling of Covid-19 growth and spread (Qin et al., 2020), monitoring the at-risk patients, self-determination of symptoms, and many more.

The SARS-CoV2 virus originated in Wuhan, China, as a consequence of which travel was banned from and to Wuhan city on 23 January 2020 (Guo et al., 2020). Manual contact tracing has proven ineffective in controlling the spread of the virus due to the delays in tracing and contacting the exposed individuals (Avitabile et al., 2020). Also, the duration of exposure and the location of contact are harder to trace in case the individuals are not familiar with each other. This results in prevention of quarantine of the individuals that may be infected but do not show any symptoms. Digital contact tracing is then the obvious alternative for preventing the spread of Covid-19 in addition to social distancing, until the vaccine becomes more readily available to the public. Figure 9.1 shows the procedure for manual contact tracing. User A is infected and comes in contact with a few other people. User B caught the infection and passed it onto User C. Manual tracing requires tracing everyone who has come in contact with an infected person, which could be tedious.

The outbreak of the new coronavirus (Covid-19) has claimed the lives of close to a million people worldwide (Guo et al., 2020). There has been a lot of research poured into figuring out a solution for Covid-19. Several alternative scenarios have been explored in order to alleviate the pressure that is being put on healthcare officials, physicians and essential employees. This article first introduces the types of architecture that are currently being used for building contact-tracing applications and their respective advantages and limitations. Then, it highlights the basic concepts of cloud computing, Internet of Things and cloud-IoT applications in healthcare. Then it discusses the proposed architecture for the cloud-IoT-based framework for testing and restricting the spread of the coronavirus.

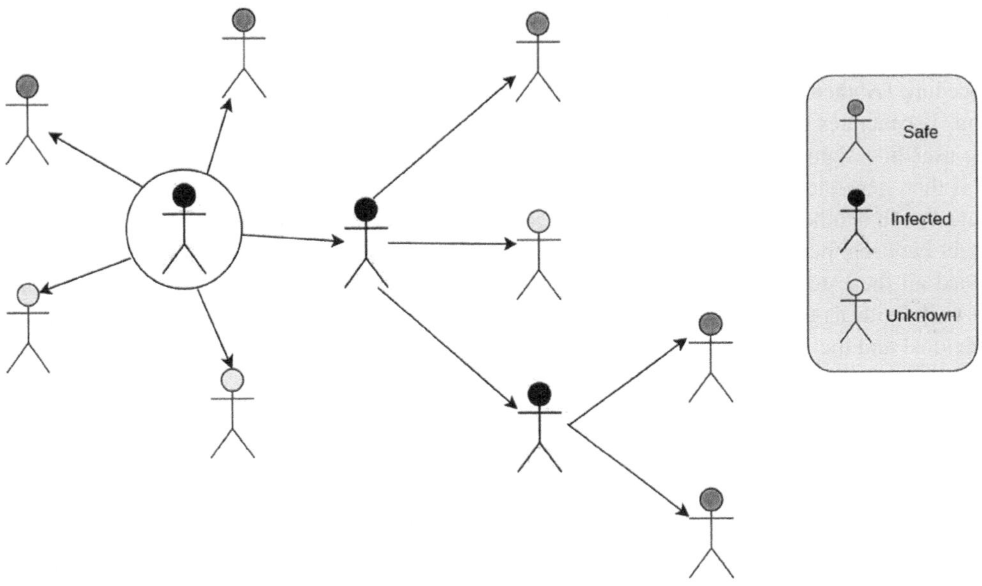

FIGURE 9.1 Manual contact tracing.

9.2 SYSTEM ARCHITECTURE FOR APPLICATIONS

Three types of architectures are used for developing data collection protocols for tracing applications, with the main concerns being user security and privacy. The three system architectures are centralized, decentralized and the hybrid approach which combines the features of both (Ahmed et al., 2020). Figure 9.2 provides the summary of events that occur in a contact-tracing architecture at a high level. It shows the possible spread of the virus from one person to another. The right side shows the workings of a contact-tracing app for one user.

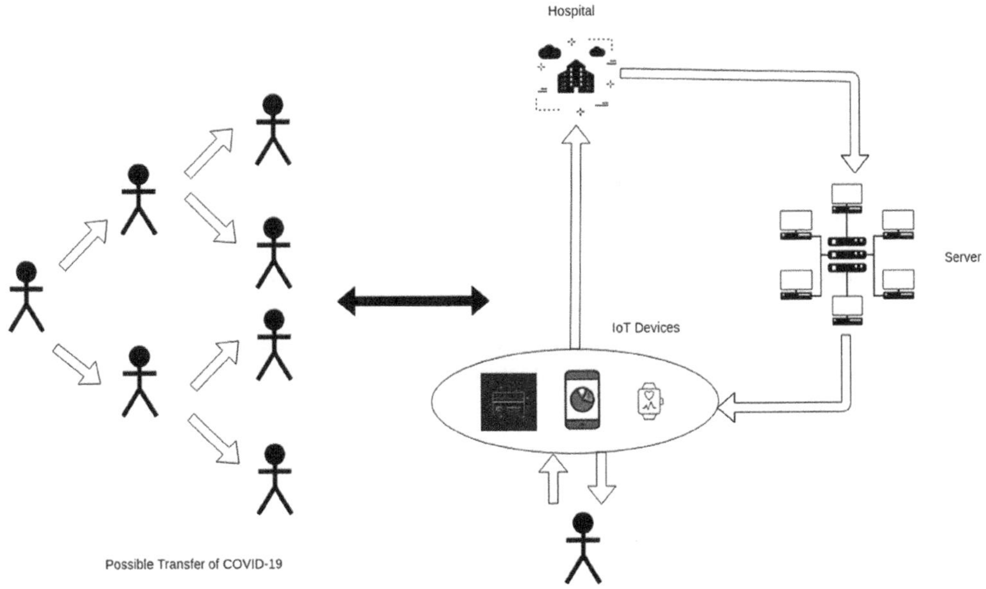

FIGURE 9.2 A generic overview of contract tracing architecture.

9.2.1 Centralized Architecture

In a centralized architecture, the central server performs most of the functions in the contact-tracing procedure (Ahmed et al., 2020). It stores the personally identifying information in an encrypted form. It generates a temporary ID for each user and provides notifications for each user device. The user first signs up for the application by registering through the central server. A temporary ID is then generated for each device to preserve the privacy of the user. When the user comes in contact with another user who has the application installed on their phone, an encounter message is sent between the two smartphones. If a user tests positive for coronavirus, they can volunteer to upload all their stored encounter messages to the central server, which then maps the temporary IDs to individuals to identify at-risk contacts (Ahmed et al., 2020). The true identity of the infected individual and the others at-risk that came in contact can be identified by a health professional by providing a secure one-time authentication password.

9.2.2 Decentralized Architecture

In a decentralized architecture, the server has minimal involvement in the contact-tracing process. The user devices do most of the heavy lifting by handling the core functionalities. Anonymous identifiers are generated at user devices and the exposure notifications are processed on individual devices instead of a centralized server (Ahmed et al., 2020). In this approach, there is no need to pre-register before use. Thus, there is no personally identifying information stored in the server. There are random seeds generated by each device when it encounters another device. The lifetime of the random seeds is about a minute, in which the seeds are exchanged with other devices that encounter them. Private Automated Contact Tracing PACT (Rivest et al., 2020) protocol is used as a basis for the decentralized architecture. If a user has tested positive for coronavirus, they can volunteer to upload their seeds and the time-stamp information to a central server. All the chirps are not uploaded as this would hamper bandwidth utilization. The central server acts as a bulletin board to record the seeds of the infected users. Other users can reconstruct the chirps with the use of timestamps to analyse if they have been exposed. However, no personally identifying information can be derived from these chirps.

9.2.3 Hybrid Architecture

The hybrid architecture does not put the entire load of all the functions on either the server, like the centralized structure, or the user's device, like the decentralized structure. The functions are divided among the server and the devices. The devices handle the generation of temporary IDs and their management. This part of the contact tracing remains decentralized (Ahmed et al., 2020). Performing risk analysis and sending out notifications remain a task for the central server. The hybrid architecture is based on the DESIRE protocol (Avitabile et al., 2020). It has some advantages and disadvantages over both decentralized and centralized architectures. In a decentralized structure, the server is unaware of any at-risk patients and does not have any data to perform risk analysis. Hybrid architecture also provides better privacy and anonymity as compared to the other two. Figure 9.3 provides a classification of the apps according to their incorporated architecture.

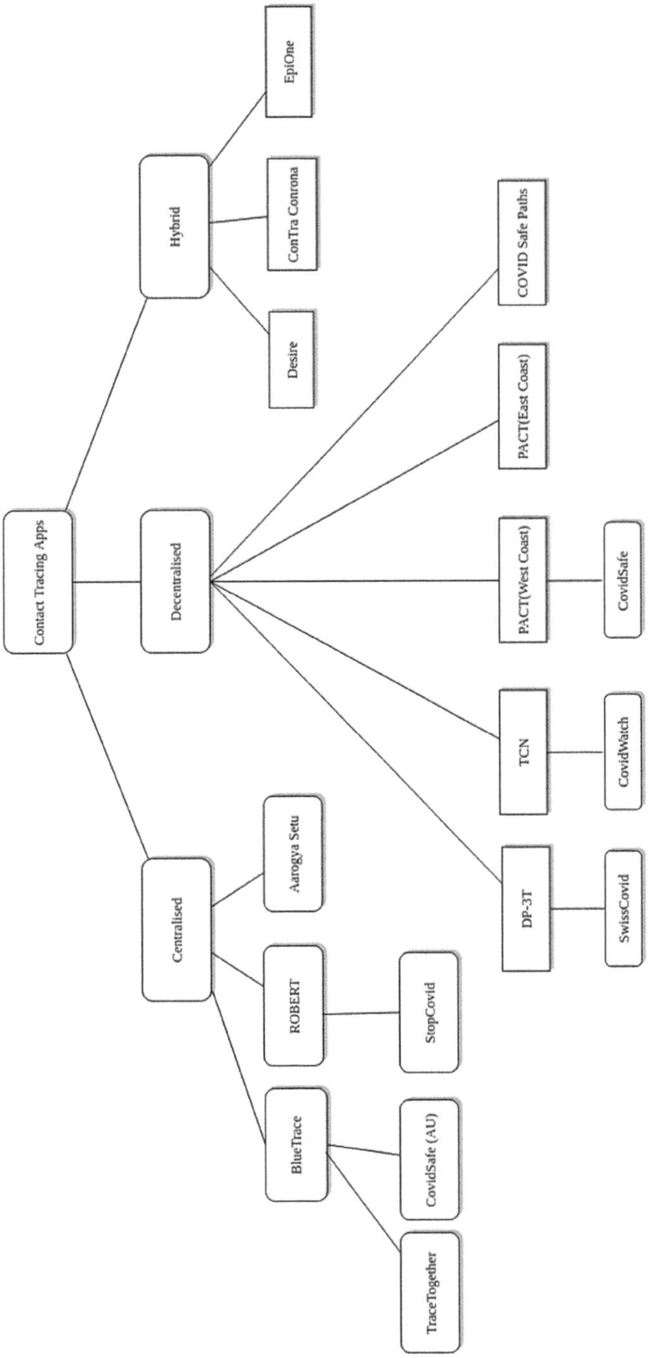

FIGURE 9.3 Classification of contact-tracing apps based on architecture.

9.3 OVERVIEW OF THE APPLICATIONS FOR CONTACT TRACING

There could be several parameters that could be used for comparing contact-tracing apps:

- The duration of time in which the user data that has been stored is destroyed. The data should be deleted either manually or automatically in a reasonable amount of time.
- The transparency of an application is of great importance. The policies and design should be publicly available, and the code base should be open-sourced.
- The data collected during contact-tracing should be retained and used for other purposes such as law enforcement.
- The underlying technology used to build the app, such as GPS, Bluetooth, and other standard APIs should be openly stated.

9.3.1 Aarogya Setu

Aarogya Setu was developed by the National Informatics Center under the Ministry of Electronics and Information Technology, Government of India. The first confirmed case of Covid-19 in India was on the 30 January 2020 (Reid, 2020). Since then, there has been an exponential growth in the number of cases and deaths. The current number of cases in India is close to 10 million (Worldometers.info, 2020b). The app is developed for both Android and iOS, with the source code made available. It is available in 12 Languages (Government of India, 2020), with more options on the way. It makes use of Bluetooth technology and GPS to alert a user when they are in the vicinity of a person who has been infected by Covid-19.

The application requires to be downloaded onto the smartphone. The user then provides login information and fills out several personal details such as age, gender, foreign travel history, and previous illnesses. The app informs people if they cross paths with someone who is Covid-19 positive through the use of Bluetooth and location-generated social graphs. It detects and tracks the user's movements and sends a notification if another smartphone nearby has the app installed. The app is divided into four sections: Your Status (risk of getting Covid-19), Self-Assessment Test, Covid-19 Updates (local and national), and E-Pass (movement pass in case of emergencies). The application provides a Self-Assessment Test, after the completion of which the user is assigned a color-coded risk level: Green for 'Safe', Yellow for 'Moderate Risk', and Orange for 'High Risk'. At high risk, the user is advised to contact the help-line number provided. Instructions on how to self-isolate in case symptoms develop are also provided (Government of India, 2020).

9.3.2 TraceTogether

TraceTogether is an app launched by the Singaporean Government. It was one of the first apps to be launched to the public and provides the source code of the reference domain, OpenTrace (Bay et al., 2020b). TraceTogether has been developed by the Ministry of Health, SG United, and GovTech Singapore (Stevens and Haines, 2020). It is primarily a contact-tracing app which relies on Bluetooth-enabled smartphones to interact with and collect data about other smartphones nearby. The cryptographically generated temporary IDs and the duration of contact among smartphones are to be stored in the user's phone for up to 21 days (Choudhury, 2020). If a user tests positive for Covid-19, the smartphone can then be used to trace everyone the user was in contact with. The people exposed can then effectively be quarantined. The app was very-well received, with over

620,000 sign-ups within the first three days. TraceTogether has two entities: the users and Ministry of Health of the Government of Singapore, assuming all the users of the TraceTogether App trust the Ministry of Health (Abeler et al., 2020). The users do not need to share their data involuntarily if they haven't been in contact with anyone infected with Covid-19.

9.3.3 CovidSafe

CovidSafe is another contact-tracing app that follows the BlueTrace protocol released by the Australian government in April. It works on Bluetooth technology to check if any nearby phones also have CovidSafe installed on them. The source codes for both Android and iOS were made public in June 2020 (Australian Government, 2020). It is similar to TraceTogether in many aspects. CovidSafe uses 2 hours instead of 15 minutes, as recommended in the BlueTrace protocol specifications, which makes it more vulnerable to replay attacks. However, CovidSafe provides a little more security by not downloading the TempIDs frequently. It makes use of Amazon AWS Servers locally available.

9.3.4 Apple/Google Exposure Notification

Apple Inc. and Google Inc. have recently teamed up to design a contact-tracing system to reduce the pressure on health officials by proposing the privacy-preserving contact tracing project. An exposure notification system using decentralized architecture is being developed with several versions already having been deployed. The design was inspired by the privacy-preserving DP-3T (Han et al., 2012) and TCN protocols. The framework is a double-edged sword. In one case, it can open up several opportunities as both Apple and Google have widespread reach in their user-base. On the other hand, the system is also open to several possible attacks which could introduce false-negatives or be used to spy on individuals (Michael and Abbas, 2020).

9.3.5 Corona-Warn-App

The Corona-Warn-App is a Covid-19 contact-tracing app that is being used for digital contact tracing in Germany. It was developed by SAP and Deutsche Telecom and commissioned by the German Government (Braun, Haffner, and Woodcock, 2020). The app works on privacy-preserving technologies with a decentralized approach inspired by the DP-3T and TCN protocols (*Open-Source Project Corona-Warn-App*, 2020). Despite initial concerns over data security, the app has been downloaded by over 14 million people as of July 2020. The app has also been made open-source. The app is available for iOS and Android devices and works with Bluetooth. The device collects pseudonymous data from other devices in the vicinity. The data is then stored locally on the device and cannot be accessed by the authorities too. The app claims to be in strict compliance with General Data Protection Regulation (GDPR) policies for privacy and security concerns.

The app collects nearby identifiers, which are generated by the Exposure Notification Framework (Wilson et al., 2020). The proximity identifiers are valid for only about 10 minutes and are being scanned by other devices which are using Bluetooth Low Energy (BLE) technology. The identifiers are stored as cryptographic hashes and are discarded automatically after a certain period of time. The app is continually in the process of improvement. For this reason, data from various sources is extensively being incorporated into the development process (Table 9.1).

TABLE 9.1
Summary of Contact-Tracing Applications

Application and Country	Architecture	Protocol Used	Privacy Concerns	Attacks Possible
Aarogya Setu, India	Centralized	Aarogya Setu Data Access and Knowledge Sharing Protocol	Social graph easy to construct, Collection of Bluetooth and location data, single server for data	Replay, Relay, Wireless Tracking, Location confirmation, *Enumeration*, DoS
TraceTogether, Singapore	Centralized	BlueTrace	Social graph easy to construct	Replay, Relay, Wireless tracking, Location confirmation, DoS, Linkage, Carryover
CovidSafe, Australia	Centralized	BlueTrace	Social graph easy to construct	Replay, Relay, Wireless tracking, Location confirmation, DoS, Linkage, Carryover
StopCovid, France	Centralized	ROBERT	Very few notifications produced, only 2.4 millions downloads	Replay, Relay, DoS, Linkage
SwissCovid, Switzerland	Decentralized	DP-3T	Identification of user, False positive	Replay, Relay, Enumeration, DoS, Linkage, Carryover
CovidWatch, University of Arizona DP-3T (unlinkable)	Decentralized	TCN	(unknown)	Replay, Relay, DoS, Linkage
CovidSafe, PACT (West Coast), University of Washington	Decentralized	PACT	(unknown)	Limited Replay, Relay, Wireless Tracking, Enumeration, DoS, Linkage

9.4 PRIVACY CONCERNS

The contact-tracing applications have been downloaded across the world at varying degrees. This highlights that there is an issue with Covid testing and tracing apps. The issues and concerns with respect to these applications are as follows:

9.4.1 Common Concerns

Government surveillance, dataveillance, and digital spying were all concerns that were voiced by citizens upon the release of the application. The user's smartphone is at a higher risk of exploitation by an attack, which would result in the expulsion of all data, regardless of the architecture used. Other than that, the encounter data stored in smartphones is not considered sensitive, as it cannot be used to directly identify the user and contacts.

9.4.2 Concerns with Centralized Architecture

In case of centralized contact-tracing applications, the data collected could be misused. In a centralized architecture, the servers have access to all types of data: PII of participants, contact advertisement messages and social/proximity graphs (Cho, Ippolito, and Yu, 2020). If the servers are compromised by the attack of a malicious user, the data of all individuals and their contacts could be compromised. Therefore, extra precautions should be taken to keep the centralized architectures protected. Maintaining a secure server encompasses preventing a malicious attacker from introducing false negatives and false positives into the system, thus ensuring the system's integrity and availability. The attack could be motivated politically, ideologically, or financially.

In a centralized architecture, the server is considered as trusted. All the user's PII and the security keys to decrypt/encrypt TempIDs are stored in the server. There is a great risk of data theft if the server is compromised. This type of environment would require the use of appropriate authentication and access control mechanisms. The system could be at risk if a malicious user exploits un-authenticated BLE contact information exchanged between devices. They could then spread erroneous contact information by relaying or replaying (Villalba and Lleida, 2011).

9.4.3 Concerns with Decentralized Architecture

In a decentralized architecture, user devices can perform risk analysis and this information is not uploaded to the main server. The server lacks complete statistical knowledge to perform risk analysis and identify at-risk individuals and clusters. Risk analysis and notifications are sensitive tasks and should be handled by proper authorities (Ahmed et al., 2020). De-anonymization attacks are also a risk as the data from infected users is retained only at the server. In a decentralized architecture, the list of seeds is accessible by everyone on the public server. The chirps can then be calculated to pinpoint an infected user.

9.4.4 TraceTogether

There are several privacy concerns associated with the use of TraceTogether, as pointed by Asghar and Farokhi (4AD). The installation may not be voluntary. There has been no data released providing evidence regarding the assistance the app has provided in reducing the spread of the virus. Users of the app also have to place a significant amount of trust in the Ministry of Health, since it is a centralized architecture. This may be due to the political regime and cultural status of Singapore.

9.4.5 Aarogya Setu

The privacy policy currently states that the data is to be shared only with the Government of India for tracing purposes. If a user has tested positive or has a foreign travel history, then the data is stored in the Indian Council of Medical Research (ICMR). There are several privacy concerns with the Aarogya Setu app. The personal information of a user can be determined and tracked by malicious users. Their true identity could then be used to determine their socioeconomic status and religion. Publicly available health records on an individual can also lead to discrimination against the individual. The architecture lacks a comprehensive personal data protection framework, and it can be easy to cause violation (Government of India, 2020). There is no governing legislation, terms of service, and privacy policy account for data security issues. It is one of the few apps that allows the government to collect both location and Bluetooth data (Sharma, 2020). There is also a single server that stores the data of several users, which can allow the access and sharing of personal data. Hackers have been able to access the exact location data of infected patients. Also, the validity of the Aarogya Setu data access and knowledge sharing protocol (Chunduru, 2020) might expire before the end of the pandemic.

9.5 TYPES OF ATTACKS

The different types of cyber-attacks are displayed in Figure 9.4 with the apps they are most likely to target. The applications are enlisted regarding each of the attacks that could potentially affect them.

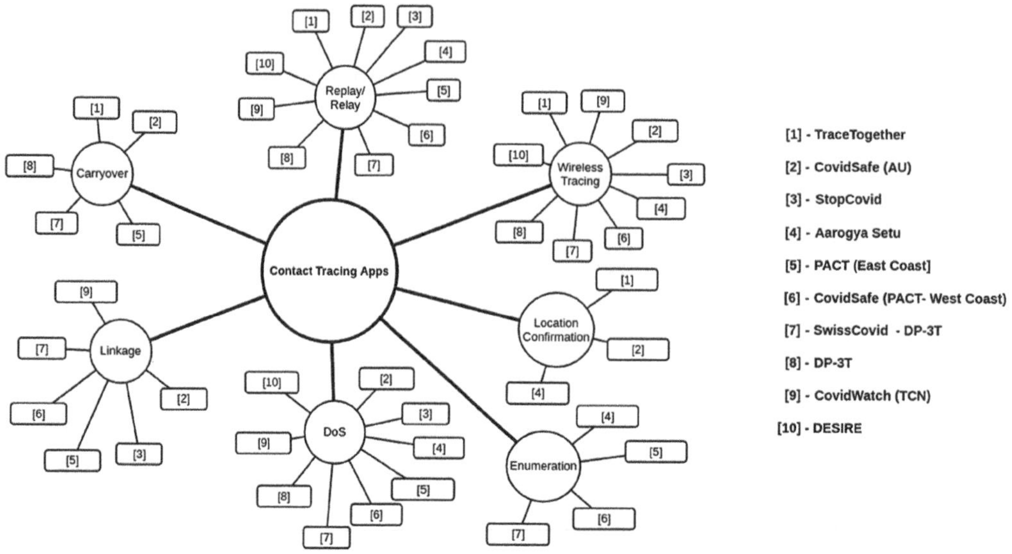

FIGURE 9.4 The susceptibility of various apps to different types of attacks.

9.5.1 Replay Attack

A replay attack occurs when an unauthorized user captures network traffic and then sends the communication to its original destination, acting as the original sender (Sun et al., 2020). To prevent replay attacks from succeeding, timestamps and sequence numbers could be attached to the message. This allows authentication systems to accept only network packets that contain the appropriate timestamp or sequence numbers. If the timestamp is beyond a certain time, then the packet is discarded.

9.5.2 Denial of Service (DoS)

The main idea of a DOS attack is to make a certain service unavailable. It can be used to shut down a system or a network. Since every service is actually running on a machine, the service can be made unavailable. DoS attack works by flooding the target server with traffic, therefore causing a crash. In case of Covid-19 apps, a DoS attack would try to take up as many resources as possible and sending out fake encounter messages to drain out the battery of users, as explained by Bay et al. (2020a)

9.5.3 User Enumeration

User enumeration can be used by a malicious party to determine the number of people that have been infected with Covid-19 (Ahmed et al., 2020). The attack is usually brute-force and it attempts to identify all the users of the system. In case of contact-tracing apps, the data could have been shared by the user through the app. Apps using the Hybrid architecture are not susceptible to this type of attack as the ID of the infected person is not made visible.

9.5.4 Linkage Attacks

In a deanonymization or linkage attack, the identity of a user could be revealed through the information voluntarily shared by the user (Ahmed et al., 2020). Some background information (zip code, gender, etc) could be combined with the information that is voluntarily shared to harm the user.

Personal user information could be compromised and be made available without the user's consent. Hybrid architecture is the safest from this attack, since the user ID is not shared with other users.

9.5.5 User Abuse

The use of the app in any misleading or destructive manner by the user would also reduce the effectiveness of the app. This was the case with a user who created high congestion by collecting 99 mobile phones down an empty road (Baldwin, 2020).

9.5.6 Carryover Attack

A carryover attack would be the extension in privilege for tracking another's user device. The messages are sent out via Bluetooth could have longer lives and may become vulnerable and provide the attacker with longer access to the user's device. This could be prevented by anonymizing the user's device ID every few seconds (Ahmed et al., 2020).

9.5.7 Trolling Attacks

Trolling attacks can take the form of spread of misinformation or fear mongering that a certain group of individuals might be infected by one individual (Gaus, 2012). This would result in people panicking and rushing to their nearest hospitals to get tested for Covid-19. This would result in the loss of a lot of healthcare resources. A patient genuinely in need for healthcare may not be able to receive it at that point. A trolling attack would prove especially harmful for a tracing application, as it could lead to the release of personal identities of a lot of people.

9.5.8 Bluejacking

Bluejacking is the act of sending several unsolicited messages to another Bluetooth device. It can be used to attack devices within a range of 10 metres. The model number of the sender's phone is displayed in the messages sent. There are software available to perform this type of attack. Any device with Bluetooth functionality available and switched on is susceptible to this type of attack. Users may have to turn off their phones if they wish to take counter measures. The trade-off to be made between user privacy and prevention of Covid-19 has been discussed in the article (Karen Hao, 2020).

9.5.9 BlueSnarfing

BlueSnarfing will allow the attackers to access a Bluetooth-enabled device and transfer data such as caller privilege contact list, calendar, email, pictures and video. (Bay et al., 2020a). This is a severe security weakness and users must not download a file without authentication. This attack can take place even when the device is set to non-discoverable. Only recognized devices should be connected to via Bluetooth.

9.5.10 Ransomware

In a Ransomware attack, the user is locked out of an important account or a device. The attacker then demands a certain sum of money to release the device. During the pandemic, apps such as CovidLock parades as a legit contact-tracing app (Saleh, 2020). They then lock the phone and resets the password. It can then use the data for malicious purposes unless a sum of $100 is paid up. In order to avoid being attacked by ransomware, installation of an antivirus is necessary. Also, try to avoid untrustworthy websites (Bay et al., 2020a).

9.5.11 Bluebugging

Bluebugging is a more serious form of attack than Bluejacking and BlueSnarfing. The attacker is able to gain total access and control the victim's page. Bluebugging takes advantage of the phone when it's in discovery mode. Some attacks take advantage of a flaw inherent in the firmware of older Bluetooth devices to gain access to the victim's day. To employ a countermeasure, the phone may be set to invisible mode. Also, do not join any open WiFi networks. In general, apps that focus on Bluetooth-based solutions are more susceptible to Bluejacking, BlueSnarfing, and Bluebugging. Similarly, apps that rely on GPS-based systems are more vulnerable to Jamming Attack and Spoofing Attack. Most other attacks are more widely applicable (Bay et al., 2020a).

9.6 APPROACH FOR PROSPECTIVE SOLUTION

There are several limitations to the contact-tracing apps that are made available by governments all across the world. The wide adoption of the apps must direct at their effectiveness, yet there has been no data published that shows the number of users that tested positive and measures that were taken for isolation. Also, the various drawbacks and vulnerabilities of the various apps have been highlighted in this paper. We aim to integrate cloud-based solutions, a diagnostic app for at-home diagnosis, Blockchain technology and IoT devices. Artificial Intelligence models could be used for predictive models and testing purposes. The article by Gupta et al. (2020) also highlights the use of data science concepts such as classification, association, rule mining and clustering to analyse Covid-19 spread. Expected cases for a three-week duration were predicted using a Regression model and SEIR model, providing a rather accurate prediction.

Authors (Vaishya et al., 2020) identified seven major areas where AI could assist in preventing or treating Covid-19. These areas are early detection and diagnosis, monitoring the treatment, contact tracing, projection of cases and mortality, development of drug and vaccines, reducing the workload on healthcare workers, and prevention. Computer vision could provide a better reading of other symptoms. Ulhaq et al. (2020) have provided a hierarchical taxonomy of the application areas of computer vision in dealing with Covid-19. These include diagnosis (X-Ray), prevention and control, and clinical treatment and management.

The conceptual framework adopted for our purposes is inspired by the study conducted by Alam (Alam, 2020). A cloud-IoT-based framework has been proposed which could be downloaded as an app on the user's phone once implemented. In addition to the current contact-tracing measures, we also suggest the inclusion of a diagnostic tool which is capable of diagnosing Covid-19 fairly well based on cough samples, body temperature, EEG, etc. The main components and terminology associated with the architecture have been discussed below.

9.7 CLOUDIOT IN HEALTHCARE

Cloud computing is an on-demand delivery of a huge number of IT resources and computer applications via the internet with a pay-as-you-go pricing. Velte et al. (2011) highlight in their book that cloud computing can deliver services and provide the framework for your business and provide fast access to IT resources at minimal cost.

Internet of Things (IoT) is the collection of millions of devices all over the world with connection to the internet. Collection and sharing of data are constantly happening over these devices. IoT can help tackle the current situation by gathering useful information, allowing remote monitoring of infectious and at-risk patients, contact tracing, etc. Installation of useful applications and the use of IoT devices can reduce the reaction time of the testing and subsequent treatment to be provided to the patient. It can also help limit the spread of the virus to others. Touch and distance monitoring applications are being extensively used in Asian countries. This is particularly due to the shortage of healthcare professionals, the lack of a suitable infrastructure to deal with a pandemic and the unwillingness of some individuals to be tested and quarantined. As suggested by Darwish et al. (2019), the cloud-IoT paradigm combines cloud computing and Internet of Things technologies to complement the advantages of both. Botta et al. (2016) highlight the complementary advantages of both cloud computing and IoT such as computational and storage capabilities, virtually unlimited resources, ubiquitous coverage, and convenient service delivery via the internet. The physical presence of IoT devices allows the diversification of cloud services, which in turn overcome the storage and other technological constraints of IoT. There are several applications for cloud-IoT paradigms, such as proactive prognosis, reduction of healthcare costs, availability of personalized treatment (Hassanalieragh et al., 2015), and more.

The main hurdle in combating Covid-19 is the scarcity of testing models available. The main strategies for protection against Covid-19 are social distancing and self-isolation. Many infected people do not contact the government for one reason or another. The pandemic has already spread to an extent where it cannot be controlled by simple laboratory testing.

9.7.1 Proposed Architecture

The proposed architecture takes into account the scarcity of testing and treatment facilities. There is a limited availability of testing facilities worldwide. These factors combined have been the reason that many countries are not able to deal with the coronavirus effectively. If a person is heading to the healthcare facility for a test, they are getting further exposed or exposing others with Covid-19. The tests require a long time to produce a result and the testing and healthcare facilities are overwhelmed, adding more workload. The medical staff is also at a higher risk due to multiple points of exposure. Many existing tests are not accurate as they produce high positives and negatives. Thus timely, safely, and cost-effective testing is a mandate in combating Covid-19.

A novel approach to use cough for its distinct latent features to perform a preliminary diagnosis of Covid-19 was proposed by Imran et al. (2020). This could provide us with a means to test for Covid by just observing cough sounds through our smartphones. We wish to incorporate this functionality in our existing model which is derived from the architecture proposed by (Alam, 2020). The idea to use cough sounds for diagnosis and screening of pulmonary diseases was proposed by Infante et al. (2017). The engine runs on a cloud server and the front-end serves as an app. The cough sounds are first recorded, then signal processing and mathematical transformations are performed (Imran et al., 2020). Covid-19 had been shown to produce a distinct cough which seldom overlaps with those of other respiratory ailments. The author (Imran et al., 2020) attempts to capture the pathomorphological changes caused by Covid-19 in the respiratory of alive patients through X-rays and CT-scans. Autopsy reports of dead bodies are also included. Three parallel classifiers are trained with the outcomes consolidated by an automated mediator. There is a limited amount of sample data used, due to lack of availability. The data includes 1838 cough sounds and 3597 non-cough environmental sounds. Further, there are 130 pertusses, 70 Covid-19, 247 normal cough samples. The classification is performed in two separate steps. As more data becomes available, the model can be trained to increase accuracy. To counter the lack of data, a deep domain knowledge-based approach can be used. The model could be further improved by adding more breathing sounds and adding more background data about the individual. Smart, intelligent and active food packaging are also in trend for use to kill the microbes by the use of active agents (Sharma et al., 2020). Also, the enhancement in nanotechnology helps to monitor and study the transmission of microbes from one surface to another (Sharma et al., 2019). The use of biomarkers that can be measured by wearable sensors like ambient sensors such as infrared cameras or wearable sensors. There are several other methods to utilize the sensors in smartphones without the need for additional hardware. Monitoring physiological monitoring from optical recordings with a mobile phone for sleep apnea in children has been proposed by researchers. Mobile phones can accurately monitor several physiological

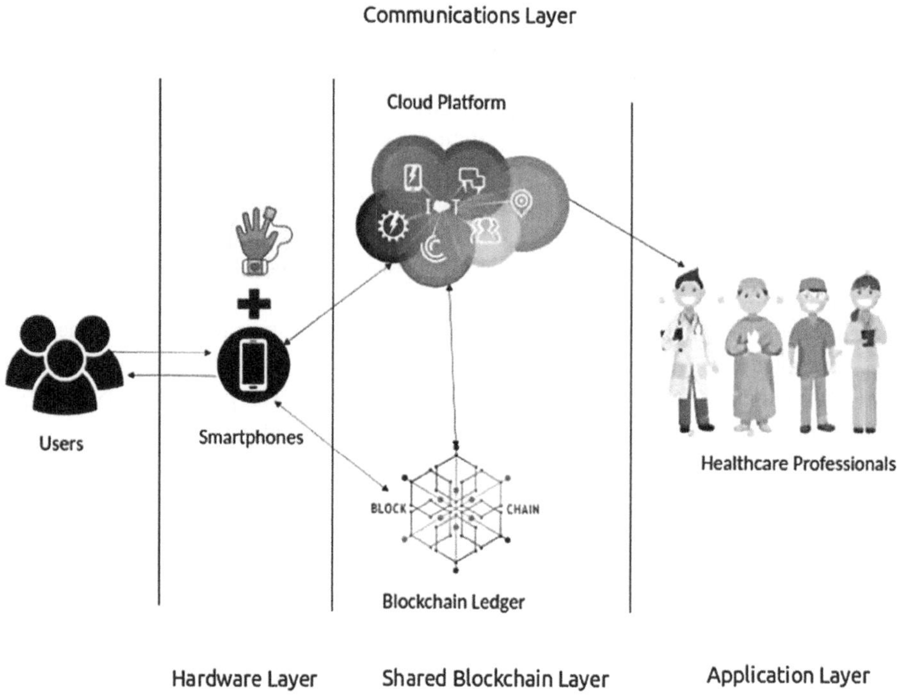

FIGURE 9.5 Proposed framework.

variables by recording and analysing the varying colour signals of a fingertip placed in contact with an optical sensor. Heart rates and breathing rates through measuring the green band of the video signal have shown results which are comparable with their respective standards. It can also evaluate the decreases in oxygen saturation levels. These sensing faculties could be integrated into the Covid-19 diagnostic tool that is being proposed. In future, if another pandemic breaks through, we can be better prepared in providing the necessary diagnostic tools through the use of cloud computing and artificial intelligence.

Figure 9.5 shows the four layers of the proposed architecture. The framework is based on the cloud-IoT framework proposed by supplemented with the tools necessary to provide a reasonable positive diagnosis at home. It aims to improve the effectiveness of patient interaction with health specialists. There have been vaccines in development since March, and Thanh Le et al. (2020) have shown a timeline of the vaccine development. Currently, there are 172 countries and many candidate vaccines are being tested, with some having reached Phase-3 trials (World Health Organization, 2020). However, the vaccines are yet to show results or side effects. Thus, we must also broaden our efforts towards technological solutions. The patient must always go to a testing facility if they show symptoms and not simply rely on the testing methods provided in the app.

9.7.1.1 Hardware Layer

The hardware layer will consist of hardware nodes that can monitor body temperature, blood saturation levels through the use of a pulse oximeter, and consistently irregular breathing patterns through the use of EEGs. These measures could be obtained through smartphones, medical devices and wearable devices such as biosensors. Symptoms data collection for all confirmed and contact cases is also suggested by Otoom et al. (2020) in their proposal for an IoT framework for early identification. It could also collect user information such as travel and contact history.

9.7.1.2 Communication Layer

The cloud system stores the travel logs and social interactions of a person to further limit the spread of coronavirus. Cloud-IoT-based systems have also been suggested by Neagu et al. (2017) in the provision of healthcare systems. Communicating through cloud services and applications would also ensure that people maintain social distancing and only visit the doctor if absolutely necessary.

9.7.1.3 Shared Blockchain Ledger

An additional Shared Ledger is introduced into the framework in order to preserve the patient's confidentiality. Author (Alam, 2019) explains the role of Blockchain technology in IoT as a measure to store the transactions among the various IoT nodes. Blockchain technology is a secured technology which can be used only by people who are authenticated to communicate with the IoT device. The Blockchain Ledger could keep track of all the suspected and confirmed Covid-19 cases, which can then be used by the applications to trace social interactions of an infected party. The Blockchain Ledger serves as a safe and reliable database of medical records. It can provide faster assessment of large amounts of health records from more users.

Study (Saxena and Verma, 2020) discusses the potential applications of Blockchain technology in public health care systems. Interoperability is a serious issue in incorporating technological measures into health care facilities. This might result in the loss of electronic health data (EHR). Other issues that may come up are privacy and security of the EHR. Blockchain technology is secured against these by using public key encryptions and P2P architecture. The investigations (Linn and Koo, 2016) point out some of the limitations which make the cryptocurrency protocols not suitable for application to healthcare facilities. Private-led Blockchains would be able to provide the necessary privacy, scalability and security.

9.7.1.4 Application Layer

Applications provide you with the status of others you are interacting with. This is crucial for contact tracing. It also keeps your Covid status updated on the basis of your travel logs and social interactions. The potential of smartphones for diagnosing and recognizing related health issues has been explored in this paper. It also allows patients to be more involved in their treatment procedures and make more informed choices. It also allows for greater transparency and secure transmission of electronic data.

The app could then be deployed on smartphones to gather user health data. After sufficient use, we can then test the accuracy of predictions and further improve upon the models.

9.8 CONCLUSION AND FUTURE WORK

The Covid-19 pandemic has led to several changes in the way people do things all over the world. Despite the severe precautions taken by governments around the world, the number of cases continues to rise. Contact-tracing apps have been a huge help for health professionals and authorities quickly determine that might have been exposed to the virus or are at a higher risk. Though the apps have helped in limiting the spread of coronavirus, but they also have structural and security concerns, The apps themselves have come under scrutiny regarding their architecture, data sharing and storing policies. The anonymization of user data and the introduction of false positives/negatives are also a huge concern. The article discusses the various types of architectures that could be adopted for building such an application, along with examples of apps that currently exist based on the architecture. The advantages and shortcomings of each of the architecture are highlighted. An alternative approach to build a cloud-IoT Blockchain-based framework is also proposed to overcome some of these privacy and security concerns. With regards to the future scope of the applications, better handling of patient data and availability of testing facilities will prove monumental in combating coronavirus. Overall, the need for a durable and widely available healthcare has become a necessity.

REFERENCES

Abeler, J., Bäcker, M., Buermeyer, U., & Zillessen, H. (2020) 'Covid-19 contact tracing and data protection can go together', *JMIR mHealth and uHealth, 8*(4), e19359.

Ahmed, N. et al. (2020) 'A survey of covid-19 contact tracing apps', *IEEE Access*. doi: 10.1109/ACCESS.2020.3010226.

Alam, T. (2019) 'Blockchain and its role in the Internet of Things (IoT)', *arXiv preprint arXiv:1902.09779*.

Alam, T. (2020) 'Internet of things and blockchain-based framework for coronavirus (Covid-19) disease', Available at SSRN 3660503.

Asghar, H. and Farokhi, F. (n.d.) *TraceTogether and Australian recommendations*.

Australian Government (2020) *CovidSafe, GitHub*. Available at: https://github.com/AU-CovidSafe (Accessed: 24 December 2020).

Asghar, H., Farokhi, F., Kaafar, D., & Rubinstein, B. (2020). On the privacy of TraceTogether, the Singaporean COVID-19 contact tracing mobile app and recommendations for Australia. *Melbourne School of Engineering, Technology and Society, 6*. Available at: https://eng.unimelb.edu.au/ingenium/technology-and-society/on-the-privacy-of-tracetogether,-the-singaporean-covid-19-contact-tracing-mobile-app,-and-recommendations-for-australia (Accessed: 24 December 2020).

Avitabile, G. et al. (2020) 'Towards defeating mass surveillance and SARS-CoV-2: The Pronto-C2 fully decentralized automatic contact tracing system', *Cryptology ePrint Archive*.

Baldwin, R. (2020) *Artist Creates Fake Traffic Jam with Google Maps App*. Available at: https://www.caranddriver.com/news/a30754804/google-maps-hack-smartphones/ (Accessed: 24 December 2020).

Bay, J., Kek, J., Tan, A., Hau, C. S., Yongquan, L., Brack, S., et al. (2020a) 'Applicability of mobile contact tracing in fighting pandemic (Covid-19): Issues, challenges and solutions', *Computer Science Review, 38*(April), 1–22. doi: 10.1016/j.cosrev.2020.100307.

Bay, J., Kek, J., Tan, A., Hau, C. S., Yongquan, L., Tan, J., et al. (2020b) 'BlueTrace: A privacy-preserving protocol for community-driven contact tracing across borders', *Government Technology Agency, Singapore*.

Botta, A. et al. (2016) 'Integration of cloud computing and Internet of Things: A survey', *Future Generation Computer Systems*. doi: 10.1016/j.future.2015.09.021.

Braun, P., Haffner, S., and Woodcock, B. G. (2020) 'Covid-19 pandemic predictions using the modified Bateman SIZ model and observational data for Heidelberg, Germany: Effect of vaccination with a SARS-CoV-2 vaccine, coronavirus testing and application of the Corona-Warn-App', *International Journal of Clinical Pharmacology and Therapeutics, 58*(8), 417–425.

Choudhury, S. R. (2020) 'Singapore says it will make its contact tracing tech freely available to developers', *CNBC*. (Accessed: 6 November 2020).

Chunduru, A. (2020) *Validity of Aarogya Setu's Data Access and Sharing Protocol extended by six months - Medianama*. Available at: https://www.medianama.com/2020/11/223-meity-data-access-protocol-extension/ (Accessed: 24 December 2020).

Darwish, A. et al. (2019) 'The impact of the hybrid platform of internet of things and cloud computing on healthcare systems: Opportunities, challenges, and open problems', *Journal of Ambient Intelligence and Humanized Computing*. doi: 10.1007/s12652-017-0659-1.

Gaus, A. (2012) 'Trolling Attacks and the Need for New Approaches to Privacy Torts', *University of San Francisco Law Review, 47*(2). Available at: https://repository.usfca.edu/usflawreview/vol47/iss2/6 (Accessed: 8 December 2020).

Government of India (2020) *nic-delhi/AarogyaSetu_Android: Aarogya Setu Android app native code, GitHub*. Available at: https://github.com/nic-delhi/AarogyaSetu_Android (Accessed: 24 December 2020).

Guo, Y. R., Cao, Q. D., Hong, Z. S., Tan, Y. Y., Chen, S. D., Jin, H. J., and Yan, Y. (2020) 'The origin, transmission and clinical therapies on coronavirus disease 2019 (Covid-19) outbreak–an update on the status', *Military Medical Research, 7*(1), 1–10.

Gupta, R. et al. (2020) 'Analysis of covid-19 tracking tool in India: Case study of Aarogya Setu mobile application', *Analysis of Covid-19 Tracking Tool in India: Case Study of Aarogya Setu Mobile Application*.

Han, J. et al. (2012) 'Privacy-preserving decentralized key-policy attribute-based encryption', *IEEE Transactions on Parallel and Distributed Systems*. doi: 10.1109/TPDS.2012.50.

Hao, Karen. (2020) *Coronavirus is forcing a trade-off between privacy and public health | MIT Technology Review, MIT Technology Review*. Available at: https://www.technologyreview.com/2020/03/24/950361/coronavirus-is-forcing-a-trade-off-between-privacy-and-public-health/ (Accessed: 24 December 2020).

Hassanalieragh, M. et al. (2015) 'Health monitoring and management using Internet-of-Things (IoT) sensing with cloud-based processing: Opportunities and challenges', In *Proceedings - 2015 IEEE International Conference on Services Computing, SCC 2015*. doi: 10.1109/SCC.2015.47.

Imran, A., Posokhova, I., Qureshi, H. N., Masood, U., Riaz, S., Ali, K., and Nabeel, M. (2020) 'AI4Covid-19: AI enabled preliminary diagnosis for Covid-19 from cough samples via an app', *arXiv preprint arXiv:2004.01275*.

Infante, C., Chamberlain, D., Fletcher, R., Thorat, Y., and Kodgule, R. (2017, October). 'Use of cough sounds for diagnosis and screening of pulmonary disease', In *2017 IEEE Global Humanitarian Technology Conference (GHTC)* (pp. 1–10). IEEE.

Le, T. T., Andreadakis, Z., Kumar, A., Roman, R. G., Tollefsen, S., Saville, M., and Mayhew, S. (2020) 'The covid-19 vaccine development landscape', *Nature Reviews Drug Discovery, 19*(5), 305–306.

Linn, L. A., and Koo, M. B. (2016) 'Blockchain for health data and its potential use in health it and health care related research', In *ONC/NIST Use of Blockchain for Healthcare and Research Workshop. Gaithersburg, Maryland, United States: ONC/NIST* (pp. 1–10).

Neagu, G., Preda, Ş., Stanciu, A., and Florian, V. (2017, June). 'A cloud-IoT based sensing service for health monitoring', In *2017 E-Health and Bioengineering Conference (EHB)* (pp. 53–56). IEEE.

Open-Source Project Corona-Warn-App (2020) Available at: https://www.coronawarn.app/en/ (Accessed: 24 December 2020).

Otoom, M., Otoum, N., Alzubaidi, M. A., Etoom, Y., and Banihani, R. (2020) 'An IoT-based framework for early identification and monitoring of Covid-19 cases', *Biomedical Signal Processing and Control, 62*, 102149.

Qin, L. et al. (2020) 'A predictive model and scoring system combining clinical and CT characteristics for the diagnosis of Covid-19', *European Radiology*. doi: 10.1007/s00330-020-07022-1.

Reid, D. (2020) *India confirms its first coronavirus case, CNBC*. Available at: https://www.cnbc.com/2020/01/30/india-confirms-first-case-of-the-coronavirus.html (Accessed: 24 December 2020).

Rivest, R. L. et al. (2020) 'The PACT protocol specification', *The PACT Protocol Specification, 1*, 1–13. Available at: https://pact.mit.edu/wp-content/uploads/2020/04/The-PACT-protocol-specification-ver-0.1.pdf

Saleh, T. (2020) *CovidLock: Mobile Coronavirus Tracking App Coughs Up Ransomware*. Available at: https://www.domaintools.com/resources/blog/covidlock-mobile-coronavirus-tracking-app-coughs-up-ransomware (Accessed: 24 December 2020).

Saxena, D., and Verma, J. K. (2020) 'Blockchain for public health: Technology, applications, and a case study', In *Computational Intelligence and Its Applications in Healthcare* (pp. 53–61). Academic Press.

Sharma, S., Barkauskaite, S., Jaiswal, A.K., and Jaiswal, S., (2020) Essential oils as additives in active food packaging. *Food Chemistry, 128403*.

Sharma, S., Jaiswal, S., Duffy, B., and Jaiswal, A. K. (2019) Nanostructured materials for food applications: Spectroscopy, microscopy and physical properties. *Bioengineering, 6*(1), 26.

Sharma, U. (2020) *Understanding Aarogya Setu: Navigating privacy during a pandemic proves to be tricky | LSE Covid-19*. Available at: https://blogs.lse.ac.uk/covid19/2020/07/02/understanding-aarogya-setu-privacy-during-the-pandemic-may-be-compromised/ (Accessed: 24 December 2020).

Stevens, H., and Haines, M. B. (2020) 'Trace together: Pandemic response, democracy, and technology', *East Asian Science, Technology and Society*. doi: 10.1215/18752160-8698301.

Sun, R., Wang, W., Xue, M., Tyson, G., Camtepe, S., and Ranasinghe, D. (2020) 'Vetting security and privacy of global covid-19 contact tracing applications', *arXiv preprint arXiv:2006.10933*.

Ulhaq, A. et al. (2020) *Computer Vision for Covid-19 Control: A Survey*.

Vaishya, R. et al. (2020) 'Artificial Intelligence (AI) applications for Covid-19 pandemic', *Diabetes and Metabolic Syndrome: Clinical Research and Reviews*. doi: 10.1016/j.dsx.2020.04.012.

Velte, A. T. T. J. V. et al. (2011) 'Cloud grid and high performance computing: Emerging applications', *Journal of Chemical Information and Modeling*.

Villalba, J., and Lleida, E. (2011) 'Preventing replay attacks on speaker verification systems', In *Proceedings - International Carnahan Conference on Security Technology*. doi: 10.1109/CCST.2011.6095943.

Wilson, A. M. et al. (2020) 'Quantifying SARS-CoV-2 infection risk within the Google/Apple exposure notification framework to inform quarantine recommendations 2 3 4', *medRxiv, 85721*, 2020.07.17. 20156539. doi: 10.1101/2020.07.17.20156539.

World Health Organization (2020) *Coronavirus disease (Covid-19)*. Available at: https://www.who.int/emergencies/diseases/novel-coronavirus-2019 (Accessed: 24 December 2020).

Worldometers.info (2020a) *Coronavirus Update (Live): 79,434,342 Cases and 1,744,373 Deaths from Covid-19 Virus Pandemic - Worldometer, Dover, Delaware, U.S.A.* Available at: https://www.worldometers.info/coronavirus/ (Accessed: 24 December 2020).

Worldometers.info (2020b) *India Coronavirus: 10,145,006 Cases and 147,097 Deaths Worldometer*. Available at: https://www.worldometers.info/coronavirus/country/india/?fbclid=IwAR3vXqWzA-HvgEi7f1N8sWZLzJhV00jTro07fRabirWIi44F3F4PI5eNOXM (Accessed: 24 December 2020).

10 Telemedicine, Telehealth, and E-health

A Digital Transfiguration of Standard Healthcare System

Siddharth Singh
Faculty of Pharmaceutical Sciences, PDM University, Bahadurgarh, India

Pankaj Kumar
College of Engineering Studies, University of Petroleum and Energy Studies, Dehradun, India

Faisal Rehman
Faculty of Pharmacy, DIT University, Dehradun, India

Poonam Vashishta
Faculty of Pharmaceutical Sciences, PDM University, Bahadurgarh, India

CONTENTS

DOI: 10.1201/9781003155577-13

10.1 INTRODUCTION

According to the American Telemedicine Association [ATA], telemedicine is the delivery and sharing of medical information used for the better health of patients from one location to another via the mode of electronic communication. The Greek and Latin words, "*Tele*" or "*mederi*" means "distance" and "to heal" respectively. The term "telemedicine" was invented by the World Health Organization in 1970 and defined as the transferring of approved information related to healthcare services with the help of information and communication technologies for various purposes like injuries, treatment, prevention, diagnosis of diseases, and so on for the better patient health. This health information may comprehend various types of medical data like images, sound files, live audio and videos between doctors and patients or between two same professionals and patient's medical records from sources like telemetry or electronic patients' records [1–4] (Figure 10.1).

The people in rural areas always struggle to get good quality healthcare in urgency because medical experts are mostly located in dense urban areas. This telemedicine technology brings in great potential and minimizes the problems of rural areas people by offering its administration into multiple ways like emails, smartphones, video calling, and other telecommunications modes.

If we look at the historical life of telemedicine, it is using telecommunication in a new aspect to explore its potential in the medical world. Throughout Europe, heliographs and bonfires were used for the exchange of information on the bubonic plague. Besides, a list of casualties was sent by telegram together with medical supplies during the civil war.

In the early 1960s, sophisticated biomedical telemetry and telecommunication technologies were developed and used by the National Aeronautics and Space Administration [NASA]. The physiological functions like blood pressure heart rate, body temperature, and respiration rate were tracked by NASA researchers. In 1964, the Norfolk State Hospital and the Nebraska Psychiatric Institute in Omaha made the first practical clinical use of video interaction. The medical center at Massachusetts General Hospital at Boston's Logan Airport was connected in 1967.

For improving the health aspect in the rural population, Lister Hill National Center for Biomedical Communication selected the 26 sites in Alaska in 1971 by using ATS-1, which was launched in 1966. Space technology applied to Rural Papago Advanced Health Care performed one of the earliest attempts in the world of telemedicine between 1972 and 1975. It was built by NASA for providing

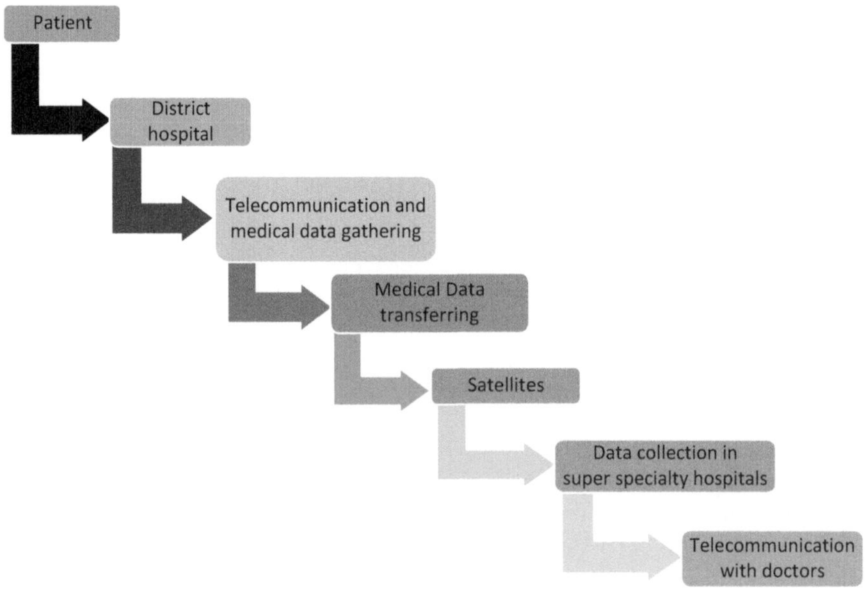

FIGURE 10.1 A basic concept of telemedicine.

quality healthcare to the Papago Indian Reservation in Arizona with the aim to offer healthcare or medical treatment to astronauts and Papago tribe.

Interactive audio networks for serving educational program and medical data transmission has been working and moved, since 1977 by the telemedicine center at the Memorial University of Newfoundland. By the early 1900s, modern telemedicine started to transmit heart rhythms over a phone in the Netherlands, and the 1920s radio consulting centers were eventually distributed across Europe.

Use of telemedicine programs exhibited a good impact by decreasing hospitalizations for mental health by more than 40%, hospitalizations for heart failure by 25%, and hospitalizations for diabetes and chronic obstructive pulmonary diseases by about 20% in 2012 and supported 677,000 veterans with nearly 2.1 million telemedicine appointments [2, 4, 5] (Figure 10.2).

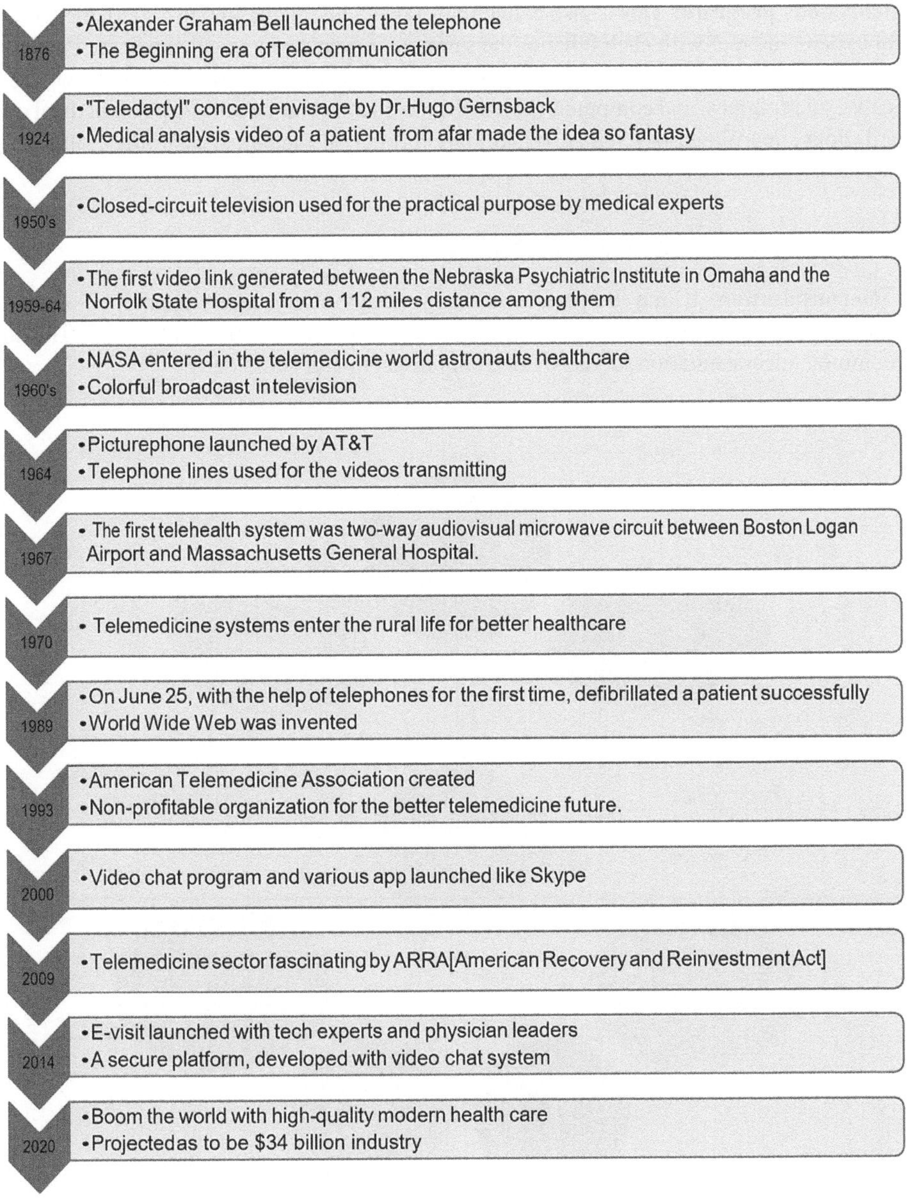

FIGURE 10.2 Telemedicine history flowchart.

10.1.1 Telemedicine Programs

These programs are divided into two main domains:

- Asynchronous program
- Synchronous program

Asynchronous program: This is also known as store and forward telemedicine in which medical data like photographs, videos, patient information, or its history and other health relating data are exchanged in this event by email and other modes. The data is transferred to medical experts for the analysis because the program is not live and use in non-emergent situations. Some examples of this domain are teleradiology, teledermatology, and telepathology.

Synchronous program: This is also called real-time telemedicine in which both the patient and medical experts interact with each other at the same time. Synchronous telemedicine is considered to be an interactive and two-way live interaction program in various ways like video conferencing, audio calls, smartphones, and computers with webcams that served various types of medical analysis like cardiology, neurology, psychiatry, rehabilitation, internal medicine, neurology, obstetrics, etc (Figure 10.3).

10.1.2 Domains under Telemedicine Technology

- **Teleconsultation:** It may be performed in two ways; it can either happen between two same medical professionals or between patients and one or more medical experts. The most common teleconsultation mode is video conferencing and audio calls.

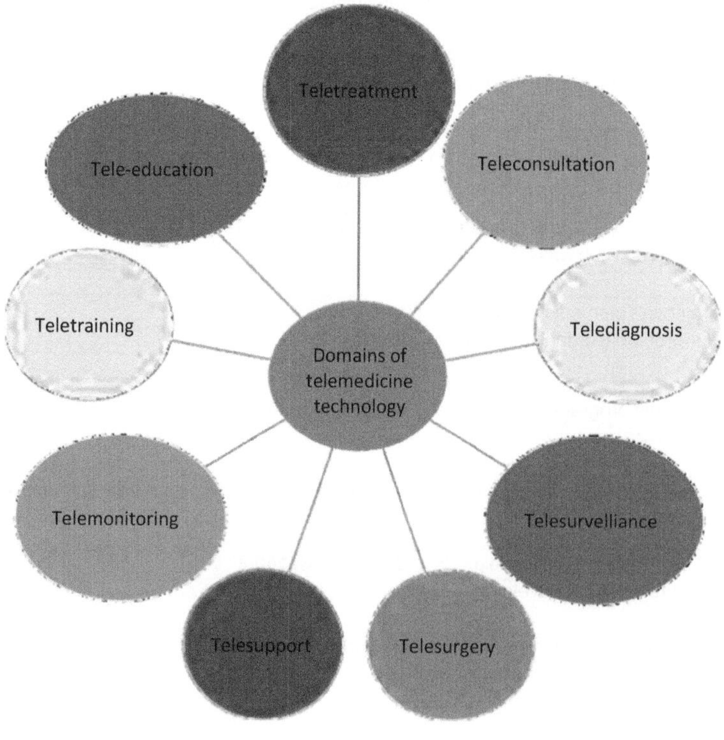

FIGURE 10.3 Telemedicine technology domains.

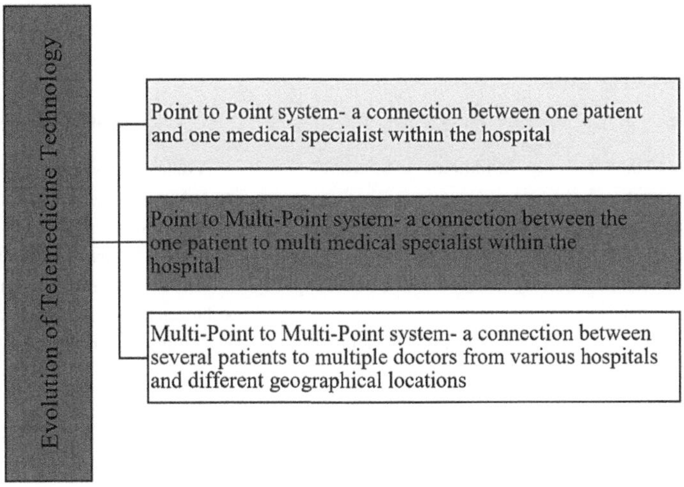

FIGURE 10.4 Telemedicine technology evolution.

- **Tele-education:** It serves and promotes medical education or knowledge at a low cost by providing outstanding material via online mode, which is useful for academic students, medical experts, and the public society.
- **Telemonitoring:** Telecommunications are used to obtain frequent or repetitive information about a patient's condition. Telecommunications monitoring the procurement process can be manual and patient information-related documents send via the phone, fax, or computer/modem network. Instead, the processing can be fully automated to provide continuous data either in synchronous [real time] or asynchronous [store and forward] mode.
- **Telesurgery:** It consists of two smart approaches, one is telementoring in which surgeons perform a surgical procedure at a remote location by a medical specialist via video and audio with the help of satellite connections from different locations. Telepresence surgery is another smart mode in which surgical procedures are performed by the robotics arm called a movement scaling technique.
- **Telesurvelliance:** Monitoring the spread of diseases to determine progression patterns and identification or evaluation of various case reporting of diseases.
- **Telesupport:** Natural disasters always cause a painful impact on the people and harm us physically so hard, which may cause death. This technology supports and serves medical emergencies [2, 6] (Figure 10.4) & (Table 10.1).

10.1.3 Telemedicine Information Types

Nevertheless, in telemedicine, the medical data are transmitted to the remote doctor first in electrical pulses. Techniques for translating smell and taste sensations into electric signals are still in the experimental stage, and the back process is more complicated and cannot be understood easily, even though the sensation of touch can be effectively transformed into electrical equivalents. ASC II, Unicode text, and numerical data in the electronic reports or medical analysis records directly transfer in digital formats. While medical audio can be transferred by the public switched telephone network, the quality of images is checked by its pixel size and different colors used in picture depiction and analysis of videos among the doctor or patients must have clarity and with National Standard Committee (NTSC) and Phase Alternating Line (PAL) formats [4] (Figure 10.5).

TABLE 10.1
Telemedicine Pros and Cons

Pros of Telemedicine	Cons of Telemedicine
• Serves medical care to the rural areas. Minimizes the time and healthcare cost of patients • Serves medical emergencies in disasters • Connects to abroad and within country medical specialist • Makes better professional education for students and medical experts • Creates awareness in society • Increases information technology uses with multiple benefits in medical care Performs surgeries via robotics • Makes connections between medical experts from different geographical areas • Patient records, diagnostic images, and clinical data transferred via satellite modes • Makes medical monitoring possible where the patient cannot be transferred It allows healthcare equity and standardization, both in individual member states and across regions and continents	• A deterioration of the doctor-patient connects • The breakdown of healthcare • Professionals relations • Decline in quality of healthcare • Institutional and operational difficulties • Discontinuity in patient care • Reimbursement laws and difficult policies

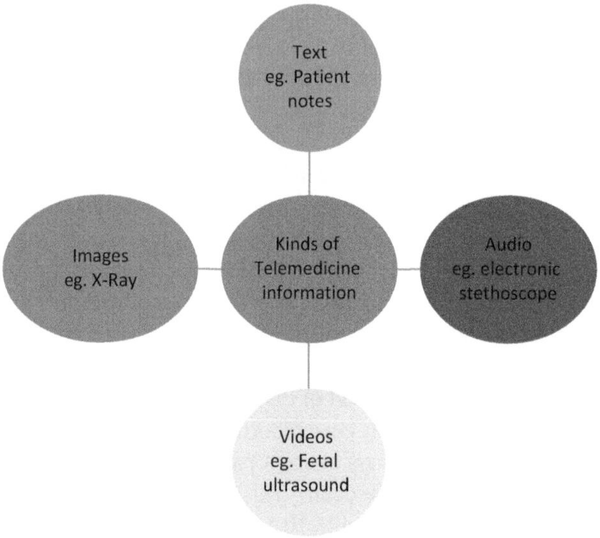

FIGURE 10.5 Telemedicine information types.

10.1.4 Telemedicine Service System

- **Network system:** It connects the medical caring workplaces from different locations such as rural areas and suburban areas hospitals by network consolidation to provide better health to the society.
- **End-to-end connection:** VSAT connectivity or private networking system used by hospital units to deliver the medical services directly to health facilities providers to ambulatory care units.
- **Point patient to administrative centers:** These links serve the facility like a cardiac, pulmonary, pacemaker, and other services for better patient observation from medical care points.

- **Web-based platform for e-health services:** This process offers various services via the internet approach.
- **Software for smartphones:** This is one of the most powerful and popular routes to serve medical care services to patients and medical experts.
- **Home connections medical care provider:** This depends upon the video process in which care providers or home health nurses directly connect to the specialist and with the hospitals. These services have great use in old-age homes.

10.1.5 Telemedicine in India

The telemedicine programs are favored by most reputed organizations such as the Department of Technology, Apollo healthcare, Asia heart consultation, state governments, and the NEC telemedicine program for North-Eastern states. ISRO Telemedicine project was launched in 2001 and connected urban, rural, suburban, medical colleges, and information units to a specialist hospital in different geographical locations via Indian satellites. A brief diagrammatic representation of the telemedicine smart approach in India is given below. In India currently 78 district and rural hospitals are connected to 22 specialist hospitals with help of ISRO networking systems from different states such as Jammu and Kashmir, Ladakh, Andaman and Nicobar Islands, Lakshadweep Islands, North-Eastern States, and other mainland states [8, 9, 10].

10.1.6 Applications of Telemedicine

- The population risk factors are described and identified with its help.
- It is useful for the treatment in telepediatrics, which deals with cardiac diseases, neuro diseases, etc.
- It has great potential in in-home telehealth services for rural areas and suburban areas.
- It serves sensitive care to newborn babies.
- It monitors disease at different levels such as within the states and globally.
- It contributes to the planning, analysis, and efficacy of specific treatment approaches.
- It delivers valuable statistics on risk factor profiles on specific populations at risk.
- It serves medical knowledge to the students, medical experts, or physicians and the public society.
- It helps in medical treatment by connecting the patient and medical experts from miles with the help of telecommunications.
- It maintains health behavior in society for a long time.
- It establishes and ensures healthy practices in society.
- It can be a very important tool for medical care evaluation and surveillance.
- It emphasizes self-care and home care for rural areas communities and gets relief from medical issues.
- It is easily accessible to the rest of the population of the entire country, including rural, suburban, and urban areas.
- Provides an opportunity for interaction among the medical specialist and practitioner.

10.1.7 Telemedicine Challenges

- **Medical experts view:** E-medicine is not entirely convinced or understood by physicians.
- **Fear and unfamiliarity of patients:** Patients lack confidence in the outcome of e- medicine.
- **Economic inability:** Because the costs of software and networking are too high and rendering, telemedicine financially unfeasible at times.
- **Absence of basic facilities and services:** There is lack of resources such as electricity, information technology, primary health services, etc.

- **Alphabetization and linguistic complexity:** Education rate among the population is an important factor.
- **Scientific limitation:** Software and hardware need to updated for a better future of e-medicine.
- **Quality features:** E-medicine also needs to mature with the help of different types of software and hardware. We need advanced biological sensors and more bandwidth support for the correct diagnosis and pacing of data [2, 8].

10.1.8 Future of Telemedicine

Only if it is seen as cost-effective will telemedicine move from the pilot phase into sustainable mainstream. It means that it must prove how money is saved compared to comparable, similar facilities, and modern quantifying approaches such as access extension, quality of care, and patient satisfaction have to be identified. As a basic tool, telemedicine must be classified as primary, secondary, and tertiary healthcare. For better healthcare, developing countries and commercial industries make a beneficial contribution to public health. One of the most futuristic approaches of telemedicine depends upon the internet because it provides endless offers to deliver telemedicine knowledge to the students, medical experts, and public society [11].

10.2 TELEHEALTH

Telehealth includes the distribution of services and data related to health through electronic data and telecommunications systems. It enables communication and care, guidance, reminders, education, intervention, tracking, and distant admissions to the patient/clinician long-range [12, 13, 14]. Sometimes telemedicine is used synonymously or is used to define distant clinical facilities such as diagnosis and tracking in a more restricted context. Telehealth can bridge the gap when rural environments, absence of transportation, absence of movement (i.e. in the aged or restricted), reduced financing, or absence of staff limit admission to care, as well as supplier distance learning, inter-practitioner conferences, oversight and presentations, internet information, and integration of health data organization and healthcare organization. Telehealth might comprise two clinicians debating a case via a video discussion; mechanical surgery performed by remote admission; physical therapy performed through digital surveillance tools, live feeds, and mixtures of applications; tests transmitted by a greater expert between interpretation centers; home tracking by continuous transmission of patient health information; and client to practice. Telehealth is discussed with telemedicine interchangeably at times. In its scope, the Administration of Health Resources and Services differentiates telehealth from telemedicine. According to them, Telemedicine defines one distant clinical facility, such as analysis and tracking, while telehealth involves preventive, promotional, and remedial maintenance. This involves the overhead-stated non-clinical apps, such as management and supplier education and which type offers telehealth services in the preferred modern language. However, telemedicine is used by the WHO to define all elements of healthcare, including defensive care [15, 16, 17]. The American Telemedicine Association makes interchangeable use of the terms "telemedicine" and "telehealth," while it recognizes that telehealth is occasionally used extra widely aimed at distant development without effective clinical procedures. Another associated word, used especially in the UK, is e-health, and in Europe as the canopy term for telehealth, digital medical annals, and other health information skill elements [18].

10.2.1 Method and Processes

Telehealth needs a powerful, reliable link to broadband. As the infrastructure for broadband has improved, the use of telehealth has become more widespread. Healthcare suppliers often start telehealth with a requirements evaluation that evaluates privations that could be enhanced by telehealth as per transportable time, cost, or leisure job. Traitors can ease the shift, such as technology businesses.

- **Store and forward:** Telemedicine store-and-forward includes obtaining health information (such as MRI pictures) and formerly conveying this information toward a clinician or medical professional at a suitable moment for off evaluation. It does not involve both sides to be present simultaneously. Radiology, dermatology, and pathology are prevalent specialisms conducive to asynchronous telemedicine. A part of this transmission should be a correctly organized medical record preferably in electric form. The "store-and-forward" method needs that the doctor depends instead on a physical examination of a past report and audio/video data.
- **Remote monitoring:** Remote surveillance, also called self-monitoring or testing, allows a patient to be monitored remotely using multiple technical types of equipment. This technique is used mainly for long-lasting disease management or particular circumstances by way of cardio disease, asthma diabetes mellitus. These facilities could deliver similar fitness results for traditional personal interactions with patients, provide patients with higher satisfaction, and can be rate-operative. Instances include night-time dialysis done at home then enhanced combined leadership.
- **Actual-time communicating:** Automatic discussions stay feasible by communicating telemedicine facilities that deliver real-time connections between all patients and doctors. Audiovisual conferencing has been for multiple reasons in a broad variety of scientific fields and environments, including patient leadership, diagnosis, counseling, and tracking [19–24].

10.2.2 Telehealth Types

- **Telenutrition:** Telenutrition relates to the use by a nutritionist or dietician of audiovisual conferencing/telephony to provide online discussion. On the telenutrition portal, patients or customers transfer their essential statistics, diet logs, food images, etc. that were formerly used by nutritionists or else dieticians to evaluate their present wellbeing situation. Nutritionists or else dieticians could check previous traditional targets for their particular patron/patients besides tracking their growth through survey-up discussions regularly. Telenutrition portals can assist clients/patients to seek distant advice from the finest nutritionist or dietician available worldwide for themselves and/or their families. This can remain highly obliging for aged/divan galloped patients whom canister check their nutritionist after home relief.
- **Telenursing:** It states to the usage of telecommunications and data technology to deliver healthcare nurture facilities whenever there is a wide physical remoteness between nurse and patient. It is a component of telehealth as a sector and has numerous contact opinions with other remedial and non-remedial apps, such as in place of telediagnosis, teleconsultation, and telemonitoring. Telenursing achieves important growing rates in many nations owing to numerous variables: a concern to reduce health maintenance expenses, an escalation in the amount of aging and regularly ill populations, and a rise in healthcare attention to remote, village, and small or sparingly occupied areas. Telenursing can address growing nursing shortages, decrease remoteness and minimize travel duration, and maintain patients out of the hospital, among its advantages. Between telenurses, a higher degree of job gratification has been recorded.
- **Telepharmacy:** Telepharmacy is the provision of pharmaceutical maintenance to patients anywhere they would not have straight contact with a pharmacist through telecommunications. It is an example of the broader telemedicine singularity as applied in the pharmacy sector. Telepharmacy facilities comprise surveillance of drug therapy, counseling of patients, previous approval and replenishment approval for prescribed drugs, and tracking

of formal obedience through videoconferencing. Distant delivery of medicines through automatic packaging and tagging technologies can also be considered as a telepharmacy example. Telepharmacy amenities can be provided at pharmacy retail locations or through hospitals, nursing homes, or extra features for healthcare. The word may also refer videoconferencing uses in pharmacies for other determinations, similarly offering services to pharmacists and pharmacists remotely.

- **Teledentistry:** Teledentistry involves the usage of IT and telecommunications for oral care, discussion, teaching, and government knowledge (comparing telehealth and telemedicine). Teledentistry provides a simpler, less expensive, and less scary approach to speak with dentistry. Teledentistry also helps general dentists in the specialized effort and enhance facilities for underserved communities, for example in rural or less developed regions.
- **Teleneurology:** It characterizes the use of mobile innovation to convey distant neural consideration, including stroke care, Parkinson's illness, epilepsy, and so forth. Utilizing teleneurology gives the opportunity to upgrade access to medicinal services for millions around the globe, since those living in city settings to those living in far-off, town settings. Verification shows that individuals with Parkinson's ailment favor their nearby clinician to have private associations with a far-off authority. Such locally established consideration is reasonable yet needs web access and recognition. A randomized estimated investigation of 2017 "cybernetic house calls" or video visits with individuals determined to have Parkinson's sickness shows persistent inclination following one year for the removed authority versus their nearby clinician. Teleneurology for patients with Parkinson's sickness is found to be economical than in-person visits by diminishing vehicle and travel time.

  Latest systematic review explains both the constraints and prospective advantages of teleneurology in improving maintenance for patients with long-lasting CNS conditions, particularly in small-income countries. Bleached, profoundly instructed, and innovatively proficient people are the biggest clients of telehealth administrations for Parkinson's illness rather than national minorities in the United States.
- **Teleophthalmology:** It provides appreciation care through online/digital health follow by telecommunications facilities. Teleophthalmology apps nowadays include access to eye experts for patients in distant fields, showing, diagnosis, and tracking of ophthalmic diseases, as well as distant teaching. Teleophthalmology can assist to decrease disparities by offering distant, low-cost screening tests for low-income and uninsured patients, such as diabetic retinopathy screening. In Mizoram, India, a hilly region with bad roads, more than 10,000 patients were treated by teleophthalmology between 2011 and 2015. Ophthalmic assistants examined these patients close by, but the operation was performed on selection after eye surgeons viewed the patient pictures online at the clinic six–twelve hours away. For example, instead of a regular of five journeys, a single cataract operation was needed for surgery unaccompanied, as even post-operation care such as stitch removal and local eyeglasses were performed. Traveling cost savings were enormous, etc. [25–36].

10.2.3 Majors Trends

Telehealth is a contemporary type of delivery of fitness care. Through contemporary telecommunications systems involving wireless communication techniques, telehealth disruptions are away from traditional healthcare distribution. To guarantee the care of medical consultants and patients, traditional health is regulated through policy. As a result, as telehealth is an innovative type of delivery of health maintenance that is today gaining impetus in the medical industry, numerous organizations have begun to establish the usage of telehealth in the policy. The Medical Board has a declaration on telehealth on its web in New Zealand. This shows that the medical council foresaw the significance of telehealth in the health scheme and began to implement telehealth lawgiving for professionals together with the government.

For specialist therapy, the traditional use of telehealth facilities has remained. However, a model shift has occurred and telehealth is no longer regarded as a specialist facility. This growth has guaranteed that many obstacles to admission are removed as medical practitioners can use wireless message systems to offer healthcare. In rural societies, this is obvious. Professional care can be some detachment away for people residing in rural areas, especially in the following main city. Telehealth eliminates this obstacle as health practitioners can use wireless communication technologies to perform medical consultations. However, this method depends on internet access to both sides. Telehealth enables the patient to be controlled between visits to the doctor's office, which can enhance the health of the patient. Telehealth also enables patients to gain access to knowledge not available in their local region. This capacity to monitor patients remotely allows patients to remain longer at their accommodation and avoid unwanted hospital time.

A significant development in telehealth is the technical progression of wireless communication devices. This enables patients to personally monitor their health circumstances and does not depend on healthcare practitioners as much. Besides, patients are more prepared to remain on their therapy strategies as they are more capitalized and involved in the procedure, sharing choice-making.

10.2.4 Telehealth Advantages

Telemedicine can benefit patients in inaccessible groups besides distant areas who could obtain care from physicians or experts far away. Current advances in moveable teamwork technology can let healthcare practitioners share data and discuss patient problems in various places as if they were in the same position. Distant patient intensive care using moveable innovation can diminish the prerequisite for outpatient visits and permit separated solution and drug control, potentially impressively bringing down the general pace of clinical consideration. It may likewise be alluring for patients with confined adaptability, for example, Parkinson's illness-affected person. Telemedicine could likewise promote medical teaching by making it easier for employees to monitor professional's cutting-edge areas and impart best performance. Telemedicine can also eradicate the possibility of broadcast between patients and medical employees of infectious diseases or parasites. This is especially a matter of concern for MRSA. Also, some patients in a physician's office who feel awkward may do better. White-coat syndrome, for instance, can be prevented. It is also a consideration for affected persons who remain home-destined and would then need an emergency vehicle to transfer them to a hospital (Figure 10.6).

10.2.5 Telehealth Disadvantages

While many medicine branches have long wanted to fully embrace telehealth, here are some jeopardies and walls that prevent the complete merger of telehealth into the finest practice. To twitch with, it remains uncertain whether a doctor could completely grant permission behind the "hands-on" knowledge. While telehealth is expected to substitute numerous appointments and additional health encounters, it cannot up till now completely substitute a physical inspection, mainly in diagnosis, recovery, and neural health. Telemedicine downsides include telephone and data organization equipment costs and medical staff practical training that will use it. Digital medical treatment often involves a possible reduction in humanoid interaction between health specialists and patients, an augmented danger of failure due to the unavailability of a licensed physician, and enhanced dangerousness of compromising confidential medical detail by electronic processing and transmission. In addition, possibly low quality of transmitted data, by means of photographs or patient growth reports, and limited admittance to appropriate medical material are quality declaration dangers that may threaten the reporting doctor's performance and continuity of patient care. Certain obstacles to telemedicine adoption include a vague permissible rule for certain telemedical activities and trouble in obtaining repayment from insurers or management agendas in certain regions. The failure to start treatment immediately is another downside of telemedicine. For instance, a patient

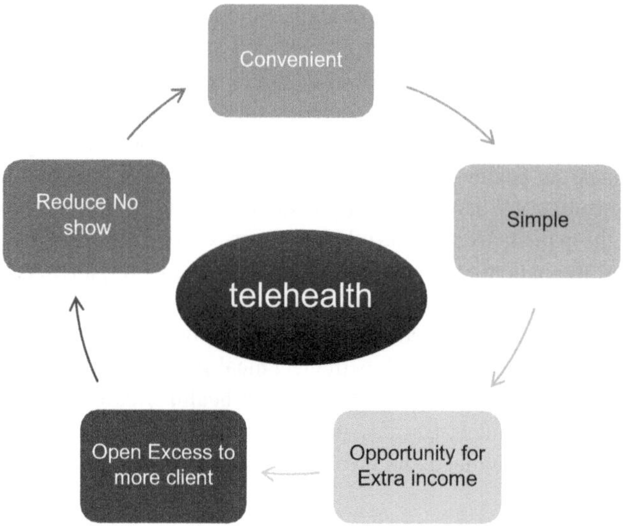

FIGURE 10.6 Telehealth benefits.

with bacterial contamination can receive an antibiotic hypodermic vaccine and detect any reaction before the antibiotic is administered as a tablet.

10.2.6 Growth of Telehealth for the Past Nine Years

In recent years, the development and acceptance of telehealth plans that have brought healthcare facilities by telecommunications and web-based technologies have expanded significantly. Telehealth adoption by big owners has become almost omnipresent due to health programs that provide telehealth to all its employees.

The rising interest in telebehavioral treatment and psychological/behavioral health agendas made existing via mobile and video visits is a singularity of concern. In reality, 56% of leaders of the Business Group give their workers these amenities [37–45] (Figure 10.7).

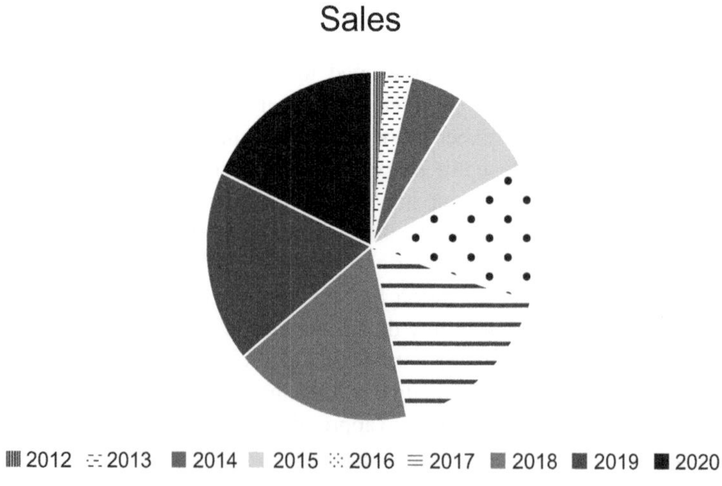

FIGURE 10.7 showing the growth of telehealth from 2012 to 2020 (data a took national business group on health/tower Watson best annual practices in healthcare survey).

10.3 E-HEALTH

Everyone is thinking about e-health today, but few people have a clear picture description of this relatively new terminology. This term had appeared before 1999 to be a common "buzzword" used to describe not only "Digital Pharmacies" but nearly everything that is linked to computer technology and medicine. E-Health defines the implementation of ICT throughout the spectrum of functions that impact the healthcare sector. The word e-health includes a variety of aspects, including health, technology, and trade. The term was first used not by scholars but by business leaders and marketers. They developed and used this concept according to other "e-words" including e-commerce, e-business, and e-solutions to bring the expectations, ideals, fervor (and hype) around e-commerce (electronic commerce) into the health environment and to explain the new potential that the internet has for the healthcare sector. For example, Intel named e-health as a "coordinated effort" between healthcare and high-tech leaders; to make good use of the advantages of collaboration-healthcare is an area of research at the crossroads of medical information technology, education, and businessmen relating to health services and data provided or distributed through the internet and related advances in technology. In a broader sense, the word describes not only technological development but also a mindset, a way of rational, an insolence, and a contribution to multinational networked thinking to improve healthcare nearby, territorially, and internationally through information and communication technology [46] (Figure 10.8).

10.3.1 Areas of E-health

E-business: Involve the online purchase processes among providers of healthcare and manufacturers, online processing of electronic applications, insurance company compliance authorization, and customer purchasing of prescription medicines and health insurance.

Consumer marketing: Requires internet application to view institutional data attracting and providing new patients and current patients with information on health and data unique to the diseases.

Organizational management: It involves publishing employee details on the company website, providing education-related programs, listing job advertisements, and announcing health benefits services to workers. It also involves operational procedures such as supervision of accounts and strategic design.

Clinical customer service: Provides connection to medical services data through electronic health records (EHRs), which allow patients to perform their health risk assessments and include email communications between patient and doctor. Communication via email will provide patients with internet access the ability to email their questions and receive answers from their physicians. This method of electronic interaction and facilitation of patient-to-healthcare experiences (Figure 10.9).

FIGURE 10.8 Areas of e-health.

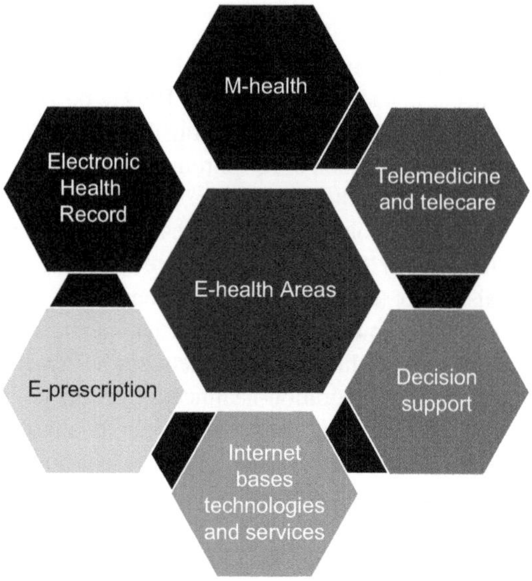

FIGURE 10.9 Different function of E-health.

10.3.2 Challenges for E-Health

An effective, scalable e-health system is facing various challenges.

Incentivization: Incentivizing all interested stakeholders are a major challenge and raises the issue of who is going to pay the bill because the value for construction, medical drugs, salaries for physicians, and other operating costs could be very high. Therefore, these costs need to be shared between different entities.

Cost Containment: It is expensive to provide healthcare to the population, and additional capital expenditure would be needed to implement ICT. Costs need to be handled in such a way as to reduce the overall healthcare cost. This could be done if there is more funding for ICT in the overall healthcare budget. An e-health plan will have to build a large number of users to cover costs.

Information Exchange: The transfer of health information needs to be driven by request, with appropriate systems control and tracking in place. The goal is to inspire and enable key stakeholders – patients, providers of healthcare, insurance companies, and the government extract and move the right information from the process.

Adoption and Resistance: In the world, clinicians and physicians are hesitant to completely embrace e-health. Correct methods need to be used in the right way so that both patients and physicians feel contented with e-health activities. Organizations need to not only plan the best technical solutions, but they also need to ensure they are easy to understand and can use. Success will require multiple public awareness programmers on the assistance of e-health.

Staffing at Different Levels: E-health is not all about the introduction of technology. It must also have a human interface that is visible, usable, and well-qualified. It is very important to get the exact people to use these tools to deliver adequate healthcare facilities. Therefore, the right people need to be employed and properly trained so that they are prepared to perform the chore of providing healthcare to remote zones.

Evaluation: It is the procedure that an independent third-party investigator has to do and be honest. Benchmarks need to be set to monitor progress. These can be taken from regional project greatest practices and prominent initiatives in further countries like Sweden and Singapore. For this purpose, an independent panel could be formed to provide ratings. The resulting assessment would deliver a nonstop learning loop to educate the e-health process itself as well.

Power Sharing: The whole healthcare system ought to be such that it could be regulated by both the central government and the state. Control, accountability, incentives, and risks need to be well established in advance to prevent any conflicts of curiosity.

Managing Information: The composed data should remain enriched with mass media (containing audio, photo, text, etc.). Using various software systems, this data should be properly stored, available, redeemable, safe, and legible from distant locations. To prevent duplication of records, "one patient and one record" must be introduced. To achieve this goal, creative and gainful health IT solutions need to be developed.

Education: E-Health is not only about providing healthcare services when someone is unwell, but it should also be used to encourage proactive treatment to improve living standards and minimize intermediate to long-term healthcare expenses. This will also support in improving the advanced production elsewhere in society and enable it. But this includes getting persons into the system and humanizing them about the unlike prevention actions to prevent disease outbreaks such as H1N1 or other periodic diseases [47].

10.3.3 The Ten Most Common E's in "E-Health"

As such, the "E" in e-health not only stands for "electronic" but also suggests a variety of other "es" that might better explain what e-health is all about.

Efficiency: One of e-health's potentials is to improve healthcare effectiveness, thereby reducing expenses. One way of reducing budgets would be to reduce duplicity or needless analytical or clinical procedures, enhance contact opportunities between healthcare foundations, and engage patients.

Enhancing quality of care: Growing competence means not individual dropping costs but also a refining class in the meantime. E-health can expand the value of healthcare, for example through enabling correlations between dissimilar providers, involving customers as a supplementary quality guarantee force, and directing patient flows to the best quality providers.

Evidence-based: E-health initiatives must be grounded on the suggestion, in the sense that their efficacy and feasibility would not be predicted but completely by hard scientific evaluation. There's a motionless portion of work to do.

Empowerment of consumers and patients: Through creation of medicine information centers and private electrical records available to patients on the net, e-health unlocks novel doors for patient-centered care and empowers patient-centered evidence-created choice.

Encouragement: From a new patient healthcare professional association to a genuine partnership where decisions are taken in a shared way.

Education: Digital specialists (ongoing medical education) and customers (health tutoring, personalized preventive data, and consumer information).

Enabling: The discussion of information and interaction between healthcare institutions in a standard way.

Extending: Healthcare coverage beyond its traditional limits. This remains intended in topographical intelligence as well as in a theoretical sense. E-health empowers customers to effortlessly get health services online from universal earners. These facilities can range from simple guidance to more multifaceted interferences or products such as pharmaceuticals.

Ethics: E-health includes a novel mode of communication between patient and doctor and introduces new tests and risks to ethical issues such as digital expert practice, informed consent, confidentiality, and fairness.

Equity: One of the potentials of e-health is to form healthcare services more affordable, but at the same time, there is a significant risk that e-health may extend the divide among the "rich" and the "poor." Those who don't have the money, knowledge, and admission to computers and networks can't make good use of computers. As a result, these patient groups (which really advantage greatest from health information) are the slightest likely to profit from improvements in information technology, unless political action guarantees fair admission for all. The numerical division currently exists among city and village communities, between privileged and underprivileged, between young and old, and between men and women [48].

10.3.4 Pros and Cons of (E-Health)

It underpins a wide-extending healthcare system in accomplishing productivity and cost decreases in the allotment of personnel and assets; however, it can likewise, as the report contends, improve the nature of administration, and give progressively conspicuous value in access to think about patients who may as of now have had issues with a vis-à-vis specialist now ready to get care. Categories of e-Health include digital health (v-Health), in which medicinal services suppliers collectively provide medicinal services administration at all, and mobile health (m-Health), in which patients themselves may access services directly through the use of a wireless network via their device's default functions or a mobile application specifically designed. Medical professionals have the most exciting and valuable prospects for developing e-Health technology in the fields of connectivity and data gathering. Tablets and smartphones were duplicated as devices for healthcare as well as information-sharing resources. For both group meetings and collection of data or information, video conferencing is used. Healthcare professionals are always linked to the software and computer systems of their hospital and can consult or share data or information when they need it. On account of intensive medical information, the problems that emerge for all data frameworks with respect to information wellbeing, information uprightness, and security are especially intense. Nevertheless, these issues do not seem to dissuade most forthcoming patients. Despite the fact that the investigation found that a couple of respondents had utilized v-Health or m-Health administrations, when they turned out to be increasingly open, there was solid energy for utilizing these online administrations, especially for others under the watchful eye of the respondents. Moreover, the larger part of respondents were happy to utilize email for nonurgent issues, for example, the reordering of prescriptions, their certainty bolstered by a safe system and a record of correspondences. As the examination brings up, comparative administrations as of now work in the United States, where doctor visits have been diminished by 25%, and doctors say that patients are gaining more influential trust in practices that are willing to employ the new technology advancement. The meaning of v-Health and m-Health afterward introduced a lot of situations to choose if solid subtleties would hose the energy. Although the greater part of the respondents were happy to utilize the administrations recorded, they were "warily idealistic," with the nature of care and secrecy being their principal concerns. There was likewise noteworthy worry about losing an individual relationship with a doctor, maintaining a stable environment, and the potential for persistent misuse on account of electronic prescription reestablishments. The biggest obstacle to e-Health is seeking accurate and reliable information or data for customers. E-Health's two main metrics, data reliability, are source integrity and completeness of the information. Health data given on a basis that is not reliable is harmful to product results, according to the recommendation of medical experts. Therefore, if health data and details are accurate, the user is likely to be fooled into making wrong decisions. The comprehensiveness of health information is considered only the most significant single factor for choice-making in healthcare. Due to mental, economic, and cultural barriers, the most disadvantaged people in our culture may be less able to benefit from e-Health. Such barriers include the level of literacy, social differences, language differences, technology exposure, and shortcomings in education. E-Health programs can only be extended by concerted efforts to address these obstacles and meet the needs and aspirations of a wide range of society [49–51].

10.4 CONCLUSION

Adverse drug events and patient injury are often triggered by medication system mistakes such as overdose, drug interactions, or contraindications. Information systems and clinical decision support systems provide means by automatic controls and accessibility of all appropriate data to prevent such medication errors. Although technical means are accessible in theory, the transmission of data on prescription and dispensed medicines among several healthcare suppliers remains a challenge in many nations. Another significant issue is increasing the burden on practitioners due to which they are unable to provide patients with adequate time. The idea of telemedicine helps patients and medical practitioners to solve this issue. Telemedicine is a medicinal practice that uses technology to provide medical care to remote areas. A doctor at one place utilizes a telecommunications infrastructure to provide remote site care to a patient. Telemedicine techniques were described as alternatives to the problems of providing health services equitably, cost-effectively, and efficiently. How telemedicine mediates the sensory aspects of medical care and the connection between doctor and patient can be significant contributors to telemedicine's achievement. Telehealth generally relates to the techniques and services of electronics and telecommunications used in the provision of care and services at a distance. Telehealth is well defined from telemedicine on the grounds that it identifies with a more extensive territory than telemedicine for far-off medicinal services offices. Telemedicine explicitly identifies with remote medical facilities, while telehealth may allude to non-clinical remote administrations. Medicines are significant part of healthcare and enable many conditions to be prevented and treated. Drug mistakes and drug-related issues (DRP) are common, however, and cause patients suffering and significant social expenses. In the medication management phase, e-medication, defined as information technology (IT), can improve quality, effectiveness. E-Medication is the PC-based electronic age, transmission, and clinical prescription filling rather than paper and faxed prescriptions. E-Medication empowers a medical specialist, drug specialist, nurses, or physician collaborator to utilize advanced software for digital prescription to convey a new prescription or reestablishment approval electronically to a network drug store or postal drug store.

REFERENCES

1. Https://thesource.americantelemed.org/resources/telemedicine-glossary accessed by October.05.2019.
2. Dasgupta, A. and Deb, S., 2008. "Telemedicine: A new horizon in public health in India." *Indian Journal of Community Medicine: Official Publication of Indian Association of Preventive & Social Medicine*, 33.1, 3.
3. Aziz, Hassan A., and Hiba Abochar. "Telemedicine." *Clinical Laboratory Science* 28.4 (2015): 256–259.
4. Coiera, Enrico. "Essentials of telemedicine and telecare." *Bmj* 324.7345 (2002): 1104.
5 Mahar, Jamal H., J. G. Rosencrance, and Peter A. Rasmussen. "Telemedicine: Past, present, and future." *Cleveland Clinic Journal of Medicine* 85.12 (2018): 938–942.
6. Hjelm, N. M. "Benefits and drawbacks of telemedicine." Journal of telemedicine and telecare 11.2 (2005): 60–70.
7. https://evisit.com/resources/10-pros-and-cons-of-telemedicine/ accessed by October.07.2019
8. Khandpur, R. S. *Telemedicine technology and applications (mHealth, TeleHealth and eHealth)*. PHI Learning Pvt. Ltd, 2017.
9. https://www.isro.gov.in/applications/tele-medicine accessed by October.07.2019.
10. http://www.televital.com/downloads/ISRO-Telemedicine-Initiative.pdf accessed by October.09.2019.

11. https://www.nrtrc.org/content/articlefiles/White%20Papers/The%20Future%20of%20Telehealth.pdf accessed by October.09.2019.
12. Telehealth. The Health Resources and Services Administration accessed by October.06.2019.
13. Shaw, Donald K. "Overview of telehealth and its application to cardiopulmonary physical therapy." *Cardiopulmonary Physical Therapy Journal* 20.2 (2009): 13.
14. Masson, Maxime. "Benefits of TED talks." *Canadian Family Physician* 60.12 (2014): 10801080.
15. Mashima, Pauline A., and Charles R. Doarn. "Overview of telehealth activities in speechlanguage pathology." *Telemedicine and e-Health* 14.10 (2008): 1101–1117.
16. Miller, Edward Alan. "Solving the disjuncture between research and practice: telehealth trends in the 21st century." *Health Policy* 82.2 (2007): 133–141.
17. 2010 Opportunities and developments I Report on the second global survey on e-health I Global Observatory for e-health series - Volume 2: TELEMEDICINE" (PDF). 13 January 2011. Retrieved 25 March 2016 accessed by October.11.2019.
18. What is Telemedicine?. Washington, D.C.: American Telemedicine Association. Archived from the original on 8 May 2013. Retrieved 21 August 2011 accessed by October.11.2019.
19. What is Telehealth? The Center for Connected Health Policy accessed by October.11.2019.
20. Sachpazidis I (10 Jul 2008). Image and Medical Data Communication Protocols for Telemedicine and Teleradiology (dissertation) (PDF) (Thesis). Darmstadt, Germany: Department of Computer Science, Technical University of Darmstadt. Retrieved 14 Aug2018 accessed by October.11.2019.
21. Salehahmadi, Zeinab, and Fatemeh Hajialiasghari. "Telemedicine in Iran: Chances and challenges." *World Journal of Plastic Surgery* 2.1 (2013): 18.
22. Pierratos, Andreas. "Nocturnal hemodialysis: Dialysis for the new millennium." *Cmaj* 161.9 (1999): 1137–1137.
23. Koutras, Christos, et al. "Socioeconomic impact of e-health services in major joint replacement: A scoping review." *Technology and Health Care* 23.6 (2015): 809–817.
24. Fatehi, Farhad, et al. "Clinical applications of videoconferencing: A scoping review of the literature for the period 2002–2012." *Journal of Telemedicine and Telecare* 20.7 (2014): 377383.
25. Johnson, Gareth J. "McGraw-Hill concise encyclopedia of engineering." *Reference Reviews* (2006).
26. Cayten, C.G. and Schwartz, G.R. eds., 1992. *Principles and practice of emergency medicine*. Lea & Febiger.
27. Rogove, Herbert J., et al. "Barriers to telemedicine: Survey of current users in acute care units." *Telemedicine and e-Health* 18.1 (2012): 48–53.
28. Rawat, G., 2018. Tele nursing. *International Journal Keywords* accessed by October.12.2019.
29. Google Glass connects breastfeeding moms with lactation help. Inquisitr. Inquisitr. Retrieved 12 June 2014 accessed by October.13.2019.
30. Clark, Glenn T. "Teledentistry: What is it now, and what will it be tomorrow?" *Journal of the California Dental Association* 28.2 (2000): 121–127.
31. Dorsey, E. Ray, et al. "Teleneurology and mobile technologies: The future of neurological care." *Nature Reviews Neurology* 14.5 (2018): 285.
32. Beck, C.A., Beran, D.B., Biglan, K.M., Boyd, C.M., Dorsey, E.R., Schmidt, P.N., Simone, R., Willis, A.W., Galifianakis, N.B., Katz, M. and Tanner, C.M. National randomized controlled trial of virtual house calls for Parkinson disease. *Neurology*, 89.11, (2017): 1152–1161.
33. Ben-Pazi, H., et al. "The promise of telemedicine for movement disorders: an interdisciplinary approach." *Current Neurology and Neuroscience Reports* 18.5 (2018): 26.
34. Telemedicine-Based Eye Examinations Enhance Access, "Reduce costs, and increase satisfaction for low-income and minority patients with diabetes. Agency for healthcare research and quality." 2013-07-17. accessed by October.12.2019.
35. Remote Retinal Screening Facilitates Diagnosis and Treatment of Retinopathy for Poor and/or Uninsured Patients With Diabetes in Rural California. Agency for Healthcare Research and Quality. 2012-10-03. accessed by October.12.2019.
36. Phukan R, Mehta M.R., Gogia S. "Results and problems in executing teleophthalmology." *Indian Journal of Medical Informatics* 8.2 (2014): 32–33.
37. "Telehealth company sues Indiana for ban on online eye exams." *TimesUnion.com*. accessed by October.12.2019.

38. Altharthi, M.S. Telehealth practice in eight countries: New Zealand, Australia, the USA, Canada, UK, Malaysia, China and India: a thesis presented in partial fulfillment of the requirements of degree of Master in Information Science at Massey University, Albany campus, Auckland, New Zealand (Doctoral dissertation, Massey University). 2012.
39. García-Rojo, Marcial. "International clinical guidelines for the adoption of digital pathology: A review of technical aspects." *Pathobiology* 83.2–3 (2016): 99–109.
40. Gu, Yulong, Jim Warren, and Martin Orr. "The potentials and challenges of electronic referrals in transforming healthcare." *The New Zealand Medical Journal* 127.1398 (2014): 111–118.
41. Keshvari, Hamid, et al. "Survey determinant factors of telemedicine strategic planning from the managers and experts perspective in the health department, isfahan university of medical sciences." *Acta Informatica Medica* 22.5 (2014): 320.
42. Laxman, Kumar, Sharanie Banu Krishnan, and Jaspaljeet Singh Dhillon. "Barriers to adoption of consumer health informatics applications for health self management." *Health Science Journal* 9.5 (2015): 1.
43. Possemato, Kyle, et al. "Healthcare utilization and symptom variation among veterans using behavioral telehealth center services." *The Journal of Behavioral Health Services & Research* 40.4 (2013): 416–426.
44. Darkins, Adam, et al. "The design, implementation, and operational management of a comprehensive quality management program to support national telehealth networks." *Telemedicine and e-Health* 19.7 (2013): 557–564.
45. Maheu, Marlene, Pamela Whitten, and Ace Allen. *E-Health, Telehealth, and Telemedicine: A guide to startup and success*. John Wiley & Sons, 2002.
46. Vockley, M. "The rise of telehealth:'triple aim,'innovative technology, and popular demand are spearheading new models of health and wellness care." *Biomedical Instrumentation & Technology*, 49.5(2015): 306–320.
47. Kvedar, J., Coye, M.J. and Everett, W. "Connected health: A review of technologies and strategies to improve patient care with telemedicine and telehealth." *Health Affairs*, 33.2 (2014): 194–199.
48. Bardsley, M., Steventon, A. and Doll, H. "Impact of telehealth on general practice contacts: Findings from the whole systems demonstrator cluster randomised trial." *BMC Health Services Research*, 13.1(2013): 395.
49. Cartwright, Martin, et al. "Effect of telehealth on quality of life and psychological outcomes over 12 months (Whole Systems Demonstrator telehealth questionnaire study): Nested study of patient reported outcomes in a pragmatic, cluster randomised controlled trial." *Bmj* 346 (2013): f653.
50. Hjelm, N.M. Benefits and drawbacks of telemedicine. *Journal of Telemedicine and Telecare*, 11.2 (2005): 60–70.
51. https://www.businessgrouphealth.org/topics/engagement/telehealth/ accessed by October.12.2019.

11 The Smart Accident Predictor System using Internet of Things

Ganesh Khekare
Department of Computer Science & Engineering, Parul University, Vadodara, Gujarat, India

Pushpneel Verma
Bhagwant University Ajmer, Ajmer, India

Seema Raut
G H Raisoni Institute of Engineering & Technology, Nagpur, India

CONTENTS

11.1 INTRODUCTION

Transportation in urban smart cities can benefit a lot. Due to smart transportation, the on-road number of travelers has reduced in smart cities, which also helps the government to reduce costs and provide efficient services to people in terms of safety and protection.

Fastest travel in smart cities between sources to destination has become possible due to embedded and unguided technologies. It provides useful information regarding current traffic scenarios to government authorities to take necessary action for smooth traffic flow.

Smart cities require an intelligent transportation network (ITN) system for traffic management. It consists of:

- a system that manages traffic flow in the smart city intelligently;
- an alert system that gives an idea about the current traffic flow and provides the shortest path from source to destination and also alerts about accidents, jams, roadblocks, etc;
- a system having a single pass that allows travelers to go anywhere in the smart city through any transportation facility. Amount will automatically be deducted from the card.

DOI: 10.1201/9781003155577-14

The number of accidents has increased vastly in the past decade (Bodhankar et al., 2019). Developed countries with innovative infrastructure are unable to control the death rate caused due to accidents. Lower and middle economical countries have more accidents. In countries like Pakistan, almost 20 people lose their lives per day due to road accidents.

As per the data provided by Pakistan Bureau in the public domain around 10,000 accidents were confirmed, in which 5,000 deaths occurred. It becomes important to focus on-road safety for developing countries. Advancement of the Internet of Everything (IoE) boosted the concept of an intelligent transportation system and promoted the concept of smart cities. Through the global positioning system, it has become possible to identify the position of current transportation position. Nowadays, most automobiles come with an in-built global positioning system setup. Fog computing helps to save the large amount of data generated in real time. The extension of IoT and a significant use of sensors made things much easier.

Developing countries (Alvi et al., 2020) focus on creating an intelligent transportation system that will save travel time and reduce the driver's headache as well as pollution. Decision-making in real-time scenarios plays a major role in the intelligent transportation system. Government organizations are focusing on the infrastructure systems that will identify accidents red zone and after-accident intimation system to provide quick relief. Sometimes, sensors are also damaged so they are unable to identify the situation. Overall identification and avoidance of road accidents and their cause become a tedious job (Khan et al., 2018).

So rather than focusing on what to do after accidents, it is always better to prevent them before happening. To minimize the number of accidents, a smart predictor system is required which collects data from all the resources through the Internet of Things, transferred through the cloud, and after processing that data provides the ultimate solution in terms of the best safest path.

The predictor system proposed in this manuscript provides the best route to avoid red zone or accident-prone areas during rush hours. Our proposed system uses a machine-learning algorithm to train the system using DBSCAN algorithm with negative sampling to make future predictions.

The rest of the article is organized as follows: Section 11.2 describes the literature review. In Section 11.3, proposed methodology is explained. In Section 11.4, experimental setup and discussion of the results are done, and in Section 11.5 conclusion is made with future scope.

11.2 LITERATURE REVIEW

The need for IoT-Based Smart City Infrastructure:

- Garbage collection: Garbage collection and maintenance is a big issue in metro cities. Smart city infrastructure provides better management of this to reduce the garbage and maintain cleanliness in the smart city.
- Enriched life – Better communication and getting information at the right time will ease the overall travel fatigue, which improves quality of life (Chen et al. 2016).
- Minimized pollution – It becomes easier to use public transport as an accurate timetable is provided through the digital medium. Also, it provides the shortest congestion-free paths for vehicles, resulting in reduced pollution. Through an intelligent transportation system, it becomes easier to share personal vehicles as well as public transports (Khekare 2014).
- Green City: Smart city infrastructure also provides the facility to maximize the use of natural resources like solar energy plants, biogas plants, etc., to operate remotely.
- Individual traveling safety and security – In case of any on-time emergency, it would be helpful to maintain a smooth traffic flow. It provides the monitoring of the whole city. Parking is also a big issue in smart cities; infrastructure will help to improve it.
- Remote Places – Market in the smart city gives scope to android applications for business purposes. People in the city can easily know what things are trending in the market (Khekare et al. 2019).

11.2.1 Transportation in Smart City: Advantages and Real-Life Solutions

Smart cities improve their performance by using a smart transportation system. It consists of the following:

- Data processing systems that gather information regarding the current traffic scenario. By using this system, traveling will become easier and more efficient.
- Innovative transportation method that modified the current methods of transportation and has come up with an innovative one. The way android applications have come up like Uber and Ola, which makes transportation easier for the traveler as well as the driver. Vehicle sharing, rental, outstation, and fuel consumption have become efficient by this. Public transport becomes more organized.

11.2.2 Components of Smart City Transportation

Various components related to technical as well as organizational issues make transportation in the city convenient. The basic three components are as follows: Advanced Traffic Management Systems (ATMS), interconnected vehicles, and Mobility as a Service (MaaS) systems, Temurnikar et al. (2020).

11.2.3 Interconnected Vehicles

Advanced vehicles come with the Internet of Things (IoT) unit, which enables roadside infrastructure to analyze current traffic scenarios; this is called vehicle to infrastructure (V2I) system. Sometimes, these vehicles also communicate with nearby units like street lights, pedestrians, and highway IoT boards.

There is vehicle to vehicle (V2V) infrastructure in which vehicles are connected to form an ad-hoc network that helps to transfer data without infrastructure. It typically forms vehicular ad-hoc network (VANET), Khekare et al. (2021). They use wireless technology to communicate.

There is also a vehicle to pedestrian (V2P) system, which provides information regarding nearby pedestrians to avoid accidents.

11.2.4 Mobility as a Service (MaaS)

Mobility as a Service (MaaS) system provides solutions to public transports. It also provides a solution to privately rented vehicles. Through various android applications, it becomes easier to book a vehicle and travel as you desire. Vehicle sharing becomes easier. Through a single application, you can monitor and analyze the traffic of a complete metro city, Khekare et al. (2020).

11.2.5 Advanced Traffic Management System (ATMS)

It gives on-time solutions to traffic problems like managing traffic signal waiting time concerning real-time scenarios, providing the shortest congestion-free path. The main advantage of ATMS is that it provides live traffic scenarios. It also warns if the distance between two vehicles becomes less, Ricardo et al.

Accidents are very common nowadays. Infrastructure is redefining and on-road speed of vehicles is increasing. Accident-prone areas are increasing. Millions of people lose their life due to accidents. To avoid and predict road accidents is not a difficult thing. Accidents occur due to various factors like driver's laziness, road conditions, driving speed, current traffic scenario, car condition, environmental conditions, etc. By analyzing the historical data, the system can predict the causes and try to overcome them in future days.

Various countries provide their accidental data to researchers so that analysis can be done and conclusion can be made, Ryan et al. (2020).

In transformation of Chinese economic condition, development is elaborated. Sudden changes in traffic changes cause more accidents. In China, as per the government reports in 2006, the overall accident impact on highways is around 15%. Looking at history, SVM and Bayesian models are frequently used to see or predict accidents. In this system, data from Shanghai is used to train the system. Safety is equally important in industries also. In industries, crashes occur considering various factors. So multilevel security using the Internet of Things and cloud will serve the purpose. In Fumagalli et al. (2017), the location-based accident tracing system is implemented. The constant radar system is used to find out the location of the vehicle, the impact of the accident decided then, proper action is taken. Considering the history data behavior, appropriate future result is generated. After each iteration, accuracy of the result increases.

In Djahel et al. (2015), the accident-prone areas are identified and the speed limit is kept low as up to 20 km/hr in accident-prone areas. Accidents that occur in these areas are called high-density crashes. Once the accident occurs, the traffic demand for that road increases due to a jam. So more visibility is required regarding accident-prone areas to avoid them. In emergency cases, Chatbots are developed to make people aware of the impact of accidents and the level of damage done. How much more time is required to travel due to accidents, Nitya et al.?

The available rollover systems for transportation mainly focus on body straight but time has come to focus on injury criteria as well. A 3D belt system is invented to hold back passengers to the seat. Another problem with the travel system is the sudden change in weather. No accurate prior intimation is provided regarding the bad weather. The number of accidents in daylight is much more than the number of accidents and pedestrians have more risk at the night. Crash depletion methods are mostly used.

The cause of most accidents is driver's laziness, Ding et al. (2018). Even a blink of an eye at the wrong time may cause a hazardous effect. The unit is required to identify the laziness of the driver and intimate him/her on time. The unit mounted on the vehicle will blow the alarm in case laziness of the driver is identified. Also, the unit will provide the ultimate solution concerning the driver's condition like how much time he/she must rest. This kind of system will reduce the chances of accidents, Kirimtat et al. (2020).

The concept of deep learning is used to avoid accidents in prone areas. In Gohar et al. (2018), a system is proposed based on deep learning to avoid accidents. The large amount of data generated through the traffic scenario is handled so nicely in this system. It provides the result in a quick time. This system uses an eye recognition system. The accuracy of this system is not up to the mark. Parameters that this system considers are not appropriate to give the best results. To minimize the number of accidents, the smart predictor system is required, which collects data from all the resources through the Internet of Things devices, and through cloud computing, data is processed to provide the ultimate solution in terms of safest route, Wang et al. (2020).

11.3 METHODOLOGY

The predictor is implemented by using the Internet of Things and machine learning concept, which will predict future accidents. The superior way to get this target is by making predictors available online in the public domain. This predictor is capable of doing the following things:

- To provide the optimal congestion-free path from source to destination.
- To allow the user to select the path considering the time factor and which is not an accidental red zone on that particular timing.

11.3.1 Information Gathering and Data Processing

The inverse function is used to find out the desired output. The inverse problem in mathematical model has three factors: inspectional data (dins), an underlying natural law (OF), and model variables of interest (V). It consists of method variables as v € V, which creates the inspectional data (dins):

$$\text{dins} = \text{OF}(\text{v})$$

Our data consists of 14 years of accidental data available on the official website of the Ministry of Road Transport and Highways of the Government of India in the public domain. This data consists of various columns like the type of accident, year, state, number of accidents as per 3 hours span in a day, etc. Let's consider traveler has to do round trip i.e. traveler starts from point X and go to Y, then after some time return journey is done via the same route i.e. now starting point is Y and ending point is X. Though the considerations look impractical, it is validated well in the result section, made acceptable through well logic. Around 57% of data is of round trips and around 92% data of round trips satisfies our consideration during the simulation. Considering this ridership information, a new dataset is created.

A new structure of the database is created, which is referred to as "vehicle movement," which satisfies our assumption regarding the round trip that consists of two tuples: start time and end time, both at origin o.

$$\text{T}_\text{v}^\text{o}(\text{d}) = (\text{Tslo})(\text{Telo})$$

Where, v, o, d, Ti, and Te indicate vehicle, station ID (origin), date, start time, and end time, respectively.

Then the ridership data for a particular date and origin o is denoted by

$$\text{R}^\text{o}(\text{d}) = \sum_\text{v} \text{T}_\text{v}^\text{o}(\text{d}).$$

Now let us suppose, to calculate ridership data for the years 2018 and 2019, the equation becomes

$$\text{R}(2018{,}2019) = \sum_\text{d}\sum_\text{o}\sum_\text{v} \text{T}_\text{v}^\text{o}(\text{d}),$$

where 2018 and 2019 are the years for which you wish to calculate ridership. Round trip must be considered rather than a one-way trip which is explained in the next section. A tuple of a vehicle transit called data structure for the round travel of a vehicle is defined as

$$(\text{T}_\text{v}^{\text{O}_0}(\text{d}) \mid (\text{T}_\text{v}^{\text{O}_1}(\text{d}) = (\text{Tslo}_0)(\text{Telo}_0) \mid (\text{Tslo}_1)(\text{Telo}_1)$$

Whereas the starting point of the tuple is the transit entry of travel from point O0 to point O1 and the next element is the exact opposite of that which is the return trip. Our target is to rebuild Tv(d) for every traveler record, R is the metro subway inspectional data, which requires identification of each travel.

The average distribution of outdoor duration time (ODT) of traveler is denoted by $A\left(T_v^o\right)$, which represents the median of transit data in terms of vehicles. It depends on the origin point and the endpoint of travel and is known as the measure of vehicles and denoted as $TvO_0(d)$.

Assume a vehicle starts its journey from point X at time h_X^s and reaches its destination Y at time h_Y^e. After waiting for some time at station Y, again it becomes ready for the next travel, so it becomes ready at station Y at time h_Y^s and travels to destination X and reaches at time h_X^e. Then in this case, measure of ODT is denoted as $ODT = h_X^e - h_X^s$

The major problem here is to accurately identify which passenger enters the station at what time. During return journey, the same vehicle data which is considered on the first trip must be taken. In short in heavy traffic to uniquely identify the vehicles in both ways journey is important. This is done by providing unique ID to each vehicle which will remain permanent in the entire journey. If this is not done, the authenticity of data is not guaranteed.

Normalized matrix Ω is represented by the equation,

$$\Omega = \begin{matrix} w_{0,0} & \cdots & w_{0,n} \\ \cdots & \cdots & \cdots \\ w_{n,0} & \cdots & w_{n,n} \end{matrix}$$

where n is the total number of elements and $w_{i,j}$ is weighted function represented by

$$w_{i,j} = \frac{\alpha_{i,j}}{\sum_n \sum_m \alpha_{m,n}}$$

So, $\alpha_{i,j}$ from Ω is denoted as

$$\alpha_{ij} = F * w_{ij}$$

where F indicates the underline natural value.

11.3.2 DBSCAN Data Clustering

After analyzing the dataset available for Indian accidents, it is observed that accidents happen almost in every city perhaps on every road. Some roads are accidents prone. They become the red zone. The road accidental data taken for analysis is of the last 14 years 2006 to 2019 of India. After analyzing the data, the area in which more accidents occur is converted into clusters. The cluster has been defined with an area size of 50 meters each.

DBSCAN algorithms are taken into consideration because it is quickly responsive, it forms the cluster very easily, and it's robust to outliners as compared to other machine learning algorithms available. The accidents happening outside the cluster area are considered outliners. So the main focus is on the area which is more accident-prone, perhaps on the states in which more accidents occur.

11.3.3 Negative Sampling

There is a various red zone for accidents to occur. It is not that it will be accident-prone all the time. Some sharp turns come under the red zone. It must be analyzed under what conditions it must be activated as dangerous and traveling on these roads is avoided. In the rainy season also some sharp turns become tricky to travel. Time is also important. Parameters must be set so that user requirements must be fulfilled. Some may give importance to time and others may be to safety. So it becomes a binary classification problem. We need to predict the perfect combination of various parameters (like environmental conditions, time to travel, and safety) to activate the red zone. Data with accidents is available but data of non-accident is not available. So the data of positive sampling is there but negative sampling needs to generate data of non-accidents. How to generate negative samples based on positive samples is already discussed in the previous section. It generates four negative entries after every one positive entry for the cluster. With the preprocessing step, now ready to move toward the experimental setup, results, and discussion.

11.4 EXPERIMENTAL SETUP AND RESULTS

The complete data is divided in the ratio 60:40 as a training data set and testing data set. The supervised learning method is applied to the data set. Python's scikit-learn library is used as a platform for data testing training and result generation. Generalized classification models like support vector machine algorithms, random forest, and logistic regression are used to process the data. The random forest model performs well on our dataset as per the parameters set. The prediction model performance is analyzed, and the area under curve and receiver operating characteristic curve is generated. Then, this scikit-learn model is provided as a website using Flask, which is a python-based web platform creator. On the Flask application, we can provide the source and destination points of travel. It provides the desired result for a model trained. Google Maps API also plays a major role in this. For creating a cluster in simulation a circle is drawn having a radius of 50 meters. Darksky function is used to create the same. A binary prediction is done to provide final results to activate the red zone or not. Multiple times iterations are performed to get accurate results.

For positive sampling, the data provided by the Indian Ministry of Road Transport and Highways in the public domain is taken. This data gives the state-wise report of accidents that occurs in India every year. Data for 14 years is available. It is segregated in the form of three-hour span throughout the day. Through experimental status, this positive sampling data is analyzed.

Figure 11.1 shows a road accident analysis of 11 states in India, which are more accident prone. The x-axis represents the state name, the y-axis represents the number of tragedies occurred, and the z-axis represents time duration. Each time slot has three hours span, in this way whole day is divided into eight-part time slots. As clear from the graph, two-time slots have a maximum number of accidents i.e. 15–18 hours (day) and 18–21 hours (night). This time zone will be considered as a red zone while applying negative sampling.

After analyzing segregated data from various angles, following conclusions are made.

Considering another aspect, second graph for year-wise analysis for 14 years of accidental data for the state of Maharashtra is generated as shown in Figure 11.2. The x-axis shows the year, the y-axis shows the number of accidents occurred, and the z-axis represents time duration. Again from the graph, it is clear that the red zone timing is 15–18 hours (day) and 18–21 hours (night). On average, the numbers of accidents are almost the same. In the year 2012, the number of accidents has gradually higher.

Average of all 14 years data is taken as shown in Table 11.1 and Figure 11.3 graph is plotted. In Figure 11.3, the x-axis represents the state whereas the y-axis represents the number of accidents. Look at the linear average it is gradually increasing. Tamil Nadu has the highest number of accidents per year.

After generating the negative samples and applying DBSCAN clustering as discussed in the methodology, random negative samples are generated by using the predictor system. The red zone has been identified based on accidents and timings through simulation based on machine learning perception. Data is collected through various Internet of Things devices. Data is processed, analyzed, and stored using cloud computing concept. While providing a path to the vehicles, these red

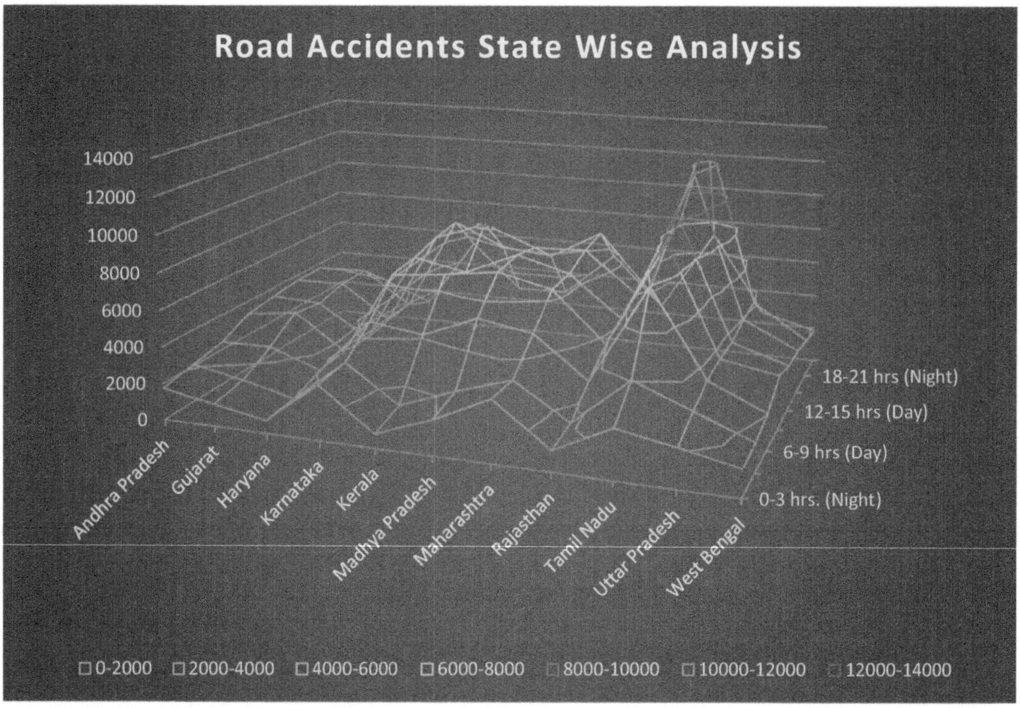

FIGURE 11.1 Road accidents state-wise analysis India.

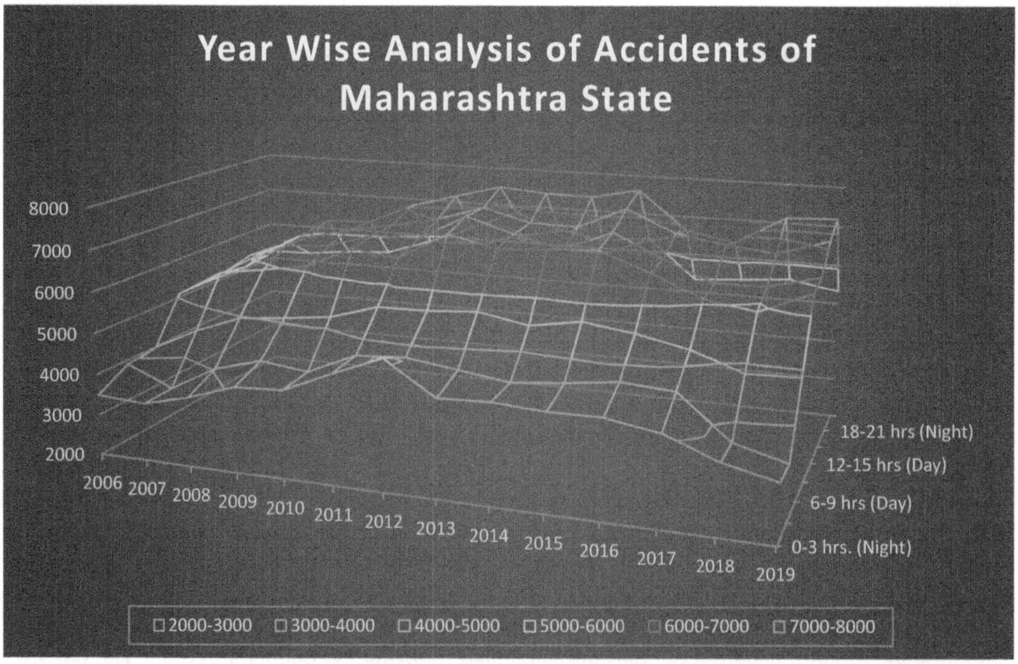

FIGURE 11.2 Year-wise analysis of accidents of Maharashtra state.

TABLE 11.1
State-Wise Actual Average Number of Accidents

Sr. No.	State	Average Accidents Per Year
1	Andhra Pradesh	37,625
2	Gujarat	2,008
3	Haryana	9,423
4	Karnataka	41,769
5	Kerala	37,012
6	Madhya Pradesh	28,143
7	Maharashtra	45,830
8	Rajasthan	23,118
9	Tamil Nadu	60,862
10	Uttar Pradesh	19,609
11	West Bengal	13,527

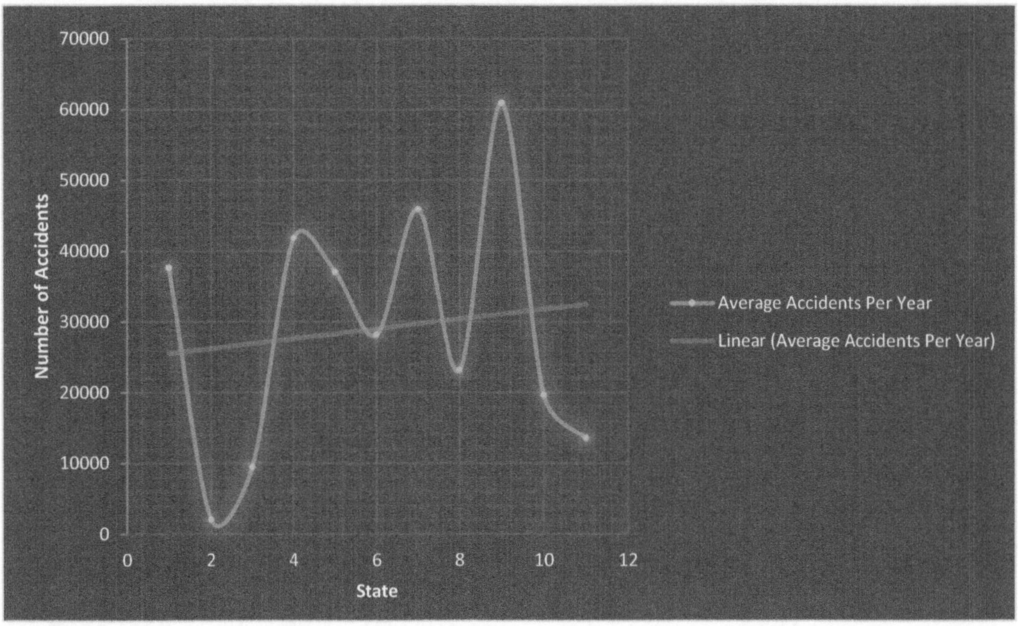

FIGURE 11.3 State-wise average accidents per year.

zones are avoided by the predictor system. Random samples are generated and various iterations are performed. Based on the trace file generated, following results have been generated as shown in Figures 11.4–11.6.

In Figure 11.4, x-axis shows the state name, the y-axis shows the number of accidents that occurred, and the z-axis represents time duration. By comparing Figure 11.4 with Figure 11.1, the state-wise analysis is done and it is observed that by the proposed system, the number of accidents has been highly reduced. The red zone has been avoided during peak hours.

In Figure 11.5, the x-axis shows the year, the y-axis shows the number of accidents occurred, and the z-axis represents time duration. As compared to Figure 11.2 in Figure 11.5, the number of accidents has been dropped gradually.

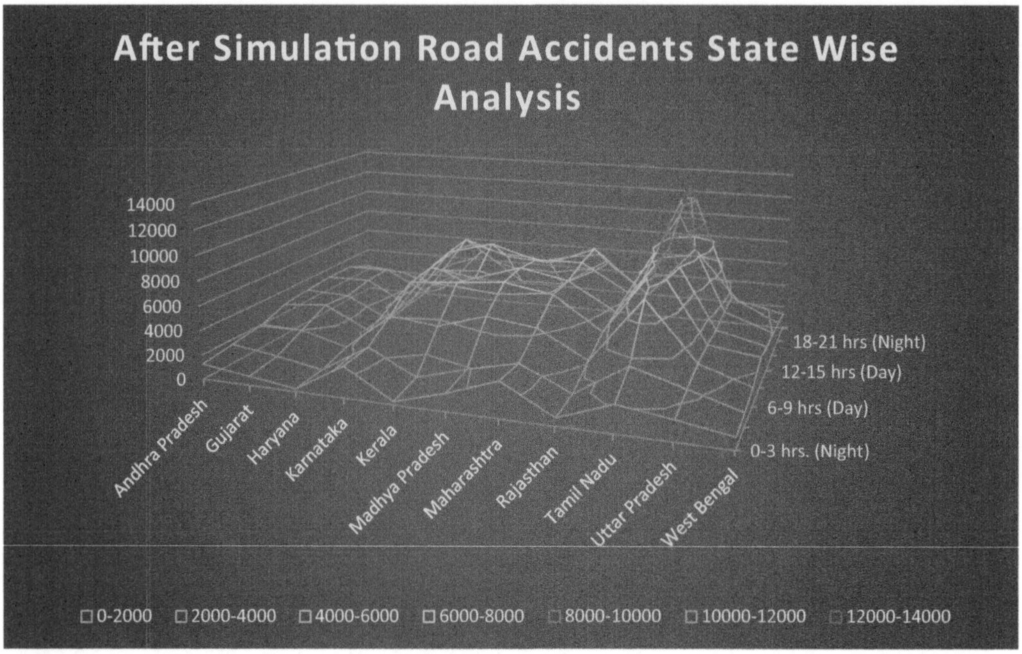

FIGURE 11.4 After simulation state-wise analysis of road accidents.

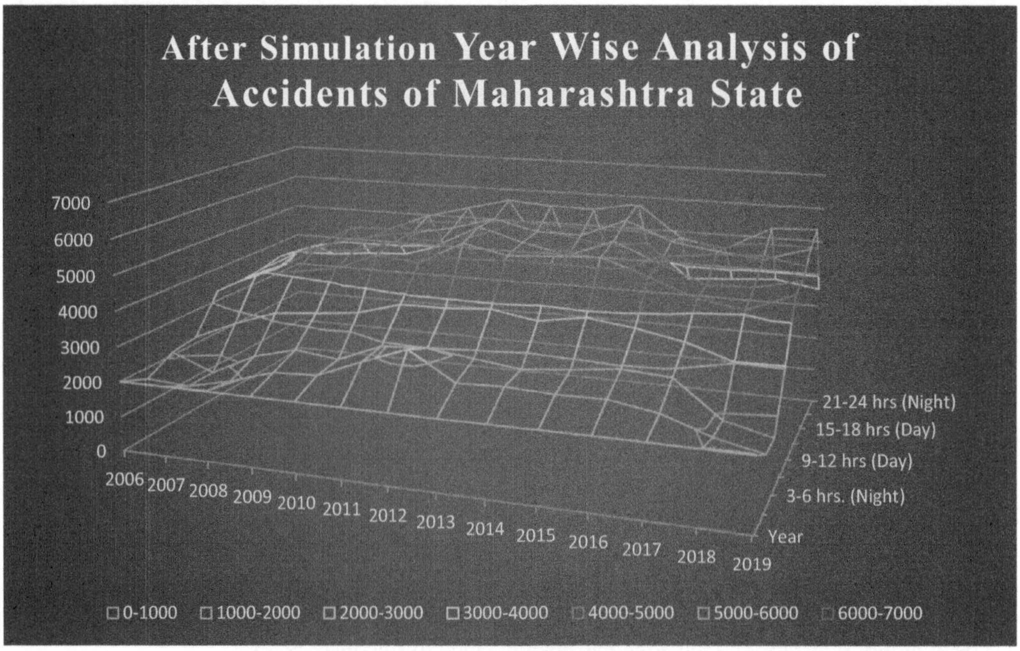

FIGURE 11.5 After simulation year-wise analysis of Maharashtra state.

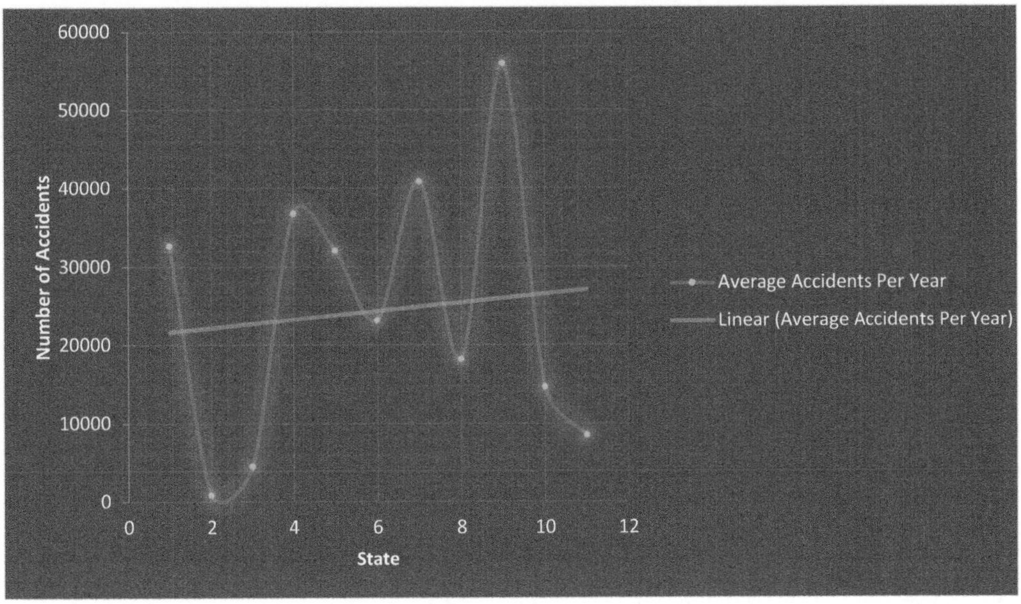

FIGURE 11.6 After simulation state-wise average accidents.

TABLE 11.2
State Wise Average Number of Accidents after Performing Simulation

Sr. No.	State	Average Accidents Per Year
1	Andhra Pradesh	32,625
2	Gujarat	824
3	Haryana	4,423
4	Karnataka	36,769
5	Kerala	32,012
6	Madhya Pradesh	23,143
7	Maharashtra	40,830
8	Rajasthan	18,118
9	Tamil Nadu	55,862
10	Uttar Pradesh	14,609
11	West Bengal	8,527

In Figure 11.6, the x-axis shows the state whereas the y-axis displays the number of accidents. The data obtained after simulation is shown in Table 11.2 and from that data graph 6 has been generated. After comparing our results with Figure 11.3, which is data of only positive sampling, almost a 17% reduction in accidents is observed by applying the proposed method.

11.5 CONCLUSION

The survey of issues faced by smart city transportation in developing countries is done in this paper. The increased number of accidents with the development in the transportation sector is bothering to common human beings as well as governments. The accidental data of the Indian 11 states are analyzed. The unique predictor system is proposed, which provides the route avoiding the red and accident-prone zones. This system provides routes to the driver with the least accident-prone areas considering the time factor. The proposed system uses the concept of Internet of Things, cloud computing, and machine-learning-based DBSCAN algorithm to train the system considering negative sampling. From simulation results, it is clear that the linear average of the number of accidents is reduced by almost 17%. The modification in the algorithm considering various factors of accidents remains for the future scope.

REFERENCES

Alvi, U., M. A. K. Khattak, B. Shabir, A. W. Malik, and S. R. Muhammad. 2020. "A Comprehensive Study on IoT Based Accident Detection Systems for Smart Vehicles." *IEEE Access*, 8: 122480–122497. doi: 10.1109/ACCESS.2020.3006887.

Belhajem, Ikram, Yann Ben Maissa, and Ahmed Tamtaoui. 2018. "Improving Vehicle Localization in a Smart City with Low Cost Sensor Networks and Support Vector Machines." *Mobile Networks and Applications*, 23: 854–863. doi 10.1007/s11036-017-0879-9.

Bhatti, Fizzah, Munam Ali Shah, Carsten Maple, and Saif Ul Islam. 2019. "A Novel Internet of Things-Enabled Accident Detection and Reporting System for Smart City Environments." *Sensors*, 19(2071). doi: 10.3390/s19092071.

Bodhankar, P. A., R. K. Nasare, and Yenurkar, G. 2019. "Designing a Sales Prediction Model in Tourism Industry and Hotel Recommendation Based on Hybrid Recommendation." In *3rd International Conference on Computing Methodologies and Communication (ICCMC)*, Erode, India. pp. 1224–1228. doi: 10.1109/ICCMC.2019.8819792.

Chen, L.-B., W.-J. Chang, J.-P. Su, J.-Y. Ciou, Y.-J. Ciou, C.-C. Kuo, and K. S.-M. Li. 2016. "A Wearable-glasses-based Drowsiness-fatigue Detection System for Improving Road Safety." In *Proceedings of the 2016 IEEE 5th Global Conference on Consumer Electronics (GCCE'16)*, pp. 401–402.

Ding, H., X. Li, Y. Cai, B. Lorenzo and Y. Fang. 2018. "Intelligent Data Transportation in Smart Cities: A Spectrum-Aware Approach." *IEEE/ACM Transactions on Networking*, 26(6): 2598–2611. doi: 10.1109/TNET.2018.2871667.

Djahel, S., R. Doolan, G. Muntean, and J. Murphy. 2015. "A Communications-Oriented Perspective on Traffic Management Systems for Smart Cities: Challenges and Innovative Approaches." *IEEE Communications Surveys & Tutorials*, 17(1): 125–151. doi: 10.1109/COMST.2014.2339817.

Fumagalli, E., D. Bose, P. Marquez, L. Rocco, A. Mirelman, M. Suhrcke, and A. Irvin. 2017. *The High Toll of Traffic Injuries: Unacceptable and Preventable*; World Bank Group: Washington, DC, USA.

Geyik, B., and M. Kara. 2020. "Severity Prediction with Machine Learning Methods." In *International Congress on Human-Computer Interaction, Optimization and Robotic Applications (HORA)*, Ankara, Turkey, pp. 1–7. doi: 10.1109/HORA49412.2020.9152601.

Gohane, S. P., and G. S. Khekare. 2015. "Reconfiguration of Industrial Embedded System in WSN." In *2015. IEEE 9th International Conference on Intelligent Systems and Control (ISCO)*, Coimbatore, pp. 1–5. doi: 10.1109/ISCO.2015.7282284.

Gonzalez, Ricardo Alirio, Roberto Escobar Ferro, and Daríoo Liberona. 2020. "Government and Governance in Intelligent Cities, Smart Transportation Study Case in Bogotá Colombia." *Ain Shams Engineering Journal*, 11: 25–34.

Jackson, L., and R. Cracknell. 2018. *Road Accident Casualties in Britain and the World*; House of Commons Library: London, UK.

Ingwersen, Peter, and Antonio Eleazar Serrano-Lo´pez. 2018. "Smart City Research 1990–2016." *Scientometrics*, 117: 1205–1236. doi: 10.1007/s11192-018-2901-9.

Khan, A., F. Bibi, M. Dilshad, S. Ahmed, Z. Ullah, and H. Ali. 2018. "Accident Detection and Smart Rescue System using Android Smartphone with Real-Time Location Tracking." *International Journal of Advanced Computer Science and Applications*, 9: 341–355.

Khekare, G. S. 2014. "Design of Emergency System for Intelligent Traffic System Using VANET." In *International Conference on Information Communication and Embedded Systems (ICICES2014)*, Chennai, pp. 1–7. doi: 10.1109/ICICES.2014.7033910.

Khekare, Ganesh, Urvashi T. Dhanre, Gaurav T. Dhanre, and Sarika S. Yede. 2019. "Design of Optimized and Innovative Remotely Operated Machine for Water Surface Garbage Assortment." *International Journal of Computer Sciences and Engineering*, 7(1): 113–117. doi: 10.26438/ijcse/v7i1.113117.

Khekare, Ganesh, Pushpneel Verma, Urvashi Dhanre, Seema Raut, and Shahrukh Sheikh. (2020). "The Optimal Path Finding Algorithm Based on Reinforcement Learning," *International Journal of Software Science and Computational Intelligence (IJSSCI)*, 12: 4, accessed (December 21, 2020), doi: 10.4018/IJSSCI.2020100101.

Khekare, Ganesh, Pushpneel Verma, Urvashi Dhanre, Seema Raut, and Ganesh Yenurkar. (2021). "Analysis of Internet of Things Based on Characteristics, Functionalities, and Challenges," *International Journal of Hyperconnectivity and the Internet of Things (IJHIoT)*, 5: 1, accessed (December 21, 2020), doi: 10.4018/IJHIoT.2021010103.

Kirimtat, A., O. Krejcar, A. Kertesz, and M. F. Tasgetiren. 2020. "Future Trends and Current State of Smart City Concepts: A Survey," *IEEE Access*, 8: 86448–86467.doi: 10.1109/ACCESS.2020.2992441.

Moneeb, Gohar, Muhammad Muzammal, and Arif Ur Rahman. 2018. "SMART TSS: Defining Transportation System Behavior Using Big Data Analytics in Smart Cities." *Sustainable Cities and Society*, 41: 114–119.

Naomi, J. F., and S. Robini 2019. "Hybrid Autoscaling for Cloud applications using an Efficient Predictive technique in Private Cloud." *Indian Journal of Science and Technology*, 12(8): 1–7.

Nithya, M., and N. Pooranam. 2018. "Secure e-payment System Using Cryptography and Stegnography with Two-fish Algorithm." *Journal of Advanced Research in Dynamical and Control Systems*, 12: 1072–1075.

Ryan, C., F. Murphy, and M. Mullins. 2020. "End-to-End Autonomous Driving Risk Analysis: A Behavioural Anomaly Detection Approach." *IEEE Transactions on Intelligent Transportation Systems*. doi: 10.1109/TITS.2020.2975043.

Shin, Hyunkyung. 2020. "Analysis of Subway Passenger Flow for a Smarter City: Knowledge Extraction from Seoul Metro's 'Untraceable' Big Data". *IEEE Access*. doi: 10.1109/ACCESS.2020.2985734.

Temurnikar, Ankit, and Sanjeev Sharma. 2013. "Secure and Stable VANET Architecture Model." *International Journal of Computer Science and Network*, 2: 37–43.

Temurnikar, A., P. Verma, and J. Choudhary. 2020. "Securing Vehicular Adhoc Network against Malicious Vehicles using Advanced Clustering Technique." In *2nd International Conference on Data, Engineering and Applications (IDEA)*, Bhopal, India, pp. 1–9, doi: 10.1109/IDEA49133.2020.9170696.

Wang F., Zhang M., Wang X., Ma X., and J. Liu. 2020. "Deep Learning for Edge Computing Applications: A State-of-the-Art Survey." *IEEE Access*, 8: 58322–58336. doi: 10.1109/ACCESS.2020.2982411.

12 An Efficient Lightweight Location Privacy Scheme for Internet of Vehicles (IOVs)

Intyaz Alam, Sushil Kumar, and Manoj Kumar
School of Computer and Systems Sciences, JNU, New Delhi, India

CONTENTS

12.1 INTRODUCTION

Due to a drastic increment in the number of automobiles on the road, several traffic critical issues such as accidents and threats are increasing. Internet of Vehicles (IOV) consists of mobile nodes (MNs) that are embedded in vehicles and linked in a self-organized way to transmit information among vehicles and roadside units [1]. It is used for high-level road safety applications, optimized traffic management where data exchange is possible with the help of vehicle-to-vehicle (V2V), and vehicle-to-infrastructure (V2I) wireless communication. During V2V communication, vehicles available in the communication range are communicated to share road conditions and traffic information for reducing the chances of a severe accident. Since it is used in safety-critical applications (safety of vehicle drivers and passengers), the security protocol must include privacy, availability, data consistency, authentication, traffic congestion, and non-repudiation [2–3]. Intelligent transportation systems (ITS) [4] are built on top of IOV. It resolves traffic-security-associated issues by combining communication technologies with traffic information for efficient and secure communication of information. IOV improves the responsiveness of various traffic-related events. IOV nodes (VNs) are classified as on-board units (OBU) and road side units (RSU). OBU are the radio devices installed on vehicles, and RSU are placed along the roadside to constitute the network infrastructure and are controlled by a network operator. Since large-scale IOVs use dynamic ad-hoc network topology with fast-moving vehicles, the existing secure communication protocols are ineffective. IOV-specific communication protocols seem to be an effective solution for vehicular environments since they efficiently provide crucial traffic information, accident sites, and road conditions to alleviate the accident problems. The protection allied application protocols in IOVs are "WSMP by WAVE, CALM FAST by ISO, and C2CNet by C2C consortium." Vehicular communications facilitate traffic management and improve the traveling experience with navigation with a high risk if no security measurement is considered. WAVE is the admired architecture of IOVs provided by IEEE [4–6].

DOI: 10.1201/9781003155577-15

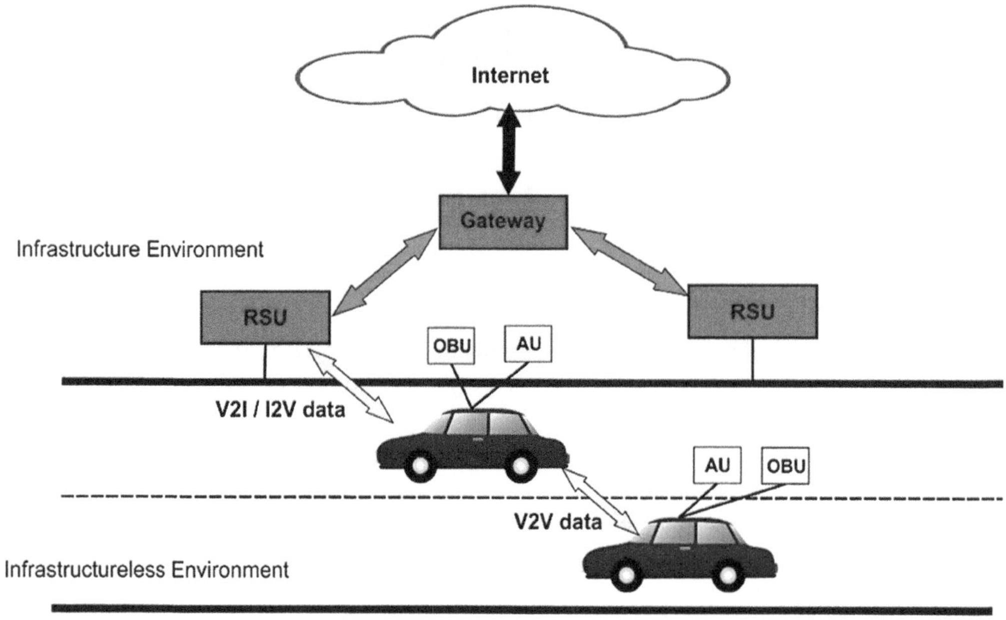

FIGURE 12.1 General IOV system [5].

Figure 12.1 shows the design of broad IOV system. The characteristics of IOVs include high mobility, driver safety and optimized traffic flow, direct interaction of vehicles with each other, vulnerability to attacks due to dynamic network topology, recurrent network disconnection, no power constraint, and limited transmission power. Several researchers have discussed various security and location privacy schemes for IOVs [6–8]. Researchers are interested in developing security and location privacy schemes for IOVs since it enhances road safety and optimizes traffic flow by transmitting various safety messages (SM) among vehicles. The robust security algorithms will provide the driver and passenger safety with security services such as authentication, availability, data integrity, privacy, and non-repudiation [9]. IOV properly utilizes the communication system and vehicle resources to reduce traffic congestion as well as limit (control) the unlikable events caused by severe traffic accidents. Figure 12.2 lists the major advantages, challenges, and applications of IOVs.

12.1.1 Motivation

Due to the high mobile nature of IOV, security, and locations privacy (LP) are the most critical challenges since it is vulnerable to various kinds of security threats [10–11]. However, we provide a list of IOV attacks and their defense techniques using Figure 12.3, but some uncovered greedy behaviors need to be resolved to improve security [12–17]. These attacks affect the functioning of other applications, degrade the security level, and malfunction comfort applications. The attacks on the IOV communication are privacy attack, eavesdropping attack, and certificate replication attack. Moreover, the attacks on safety applications are DoS attack, jamming attack, betrayal attack, and platooning attack. These attacks are related to channel allocation. There are two types of attacks in IOV: insider attack and outsider attack [18–20]. Insider attacks cannot be detected and defended by cryptographic solutions. Trust-based security solutions are an efficient way to catch such insider behaviors. However, cryptographic solutions can defend external attacks very well with some computational overhead [21–24].

In IOVs, the vehicle location and user identity are not closed, and vehicle LP can be tracked by unregistered vehicles. To maintain the vehicle security and privacy (ID, location), pseudonyms

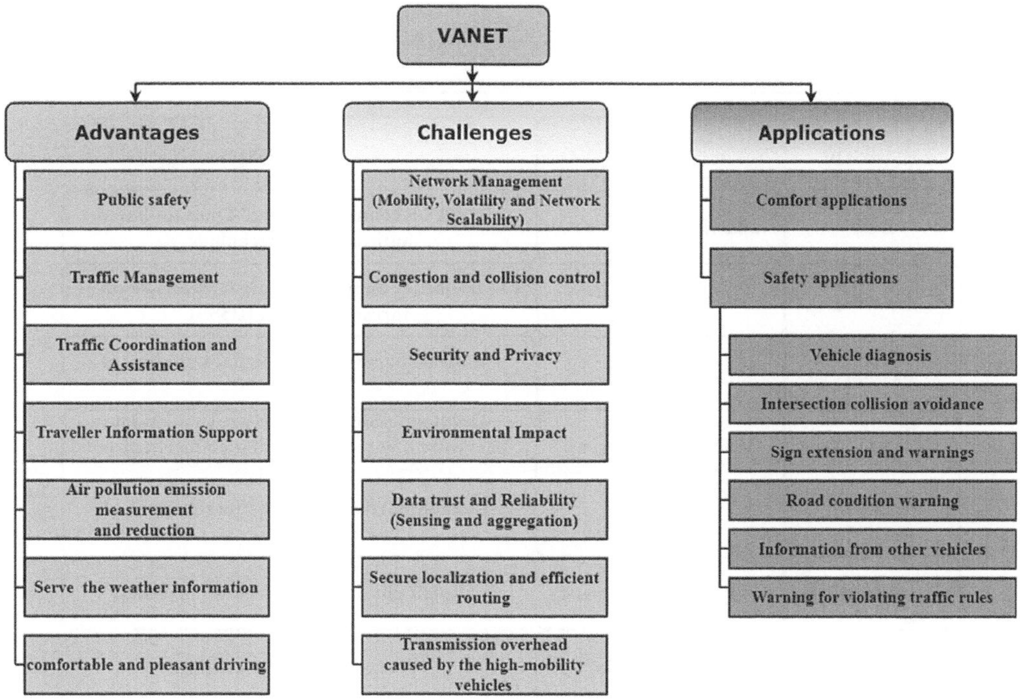

FIGURE 12.2 Advantage, challenges, and applications of IOVs [25–30].

are being used effectively [25]. However, vehicle location plays a vital role in IOVs since all other applications and associated algorithms work after obtaining traffic-related information from vehicles [26]. Furthermore, access control is also a challenging issue in IOVs for which various levels are predefined. Data exchange and data security are also important issues since they require many resources and broadcast sensitive safety messages [27]. These communication messages provide safety in locating and tracking vehicles and creating a location privacy risk in the dynamic ad-hoc environment. For efficient communication, sensitive safety messages should not be altered by the attacker. In case the attacker changes the private information, it should be detected as soon as possible to minimize the risk. An attacker changes his or her behavior to disturb the IOV for personal benefits [28–29]. The process of illegitimately getting private information of vehicles is called an attack on privacy. These attacks are classified as identity revealing and location tracking [30].

It affects driver privacy and puts passengers at risk since vehicles and drivers are related to each other. The main purpose of these attacks is automobile thefts or abductions. To avoid such risks of unauthorized location tracking, the transmitted message containing sensitive information must include verifiable identity and other accurate data. There are various location privacy schemes such as anonymity-based approaches, policy-based approaches, and regulatory approaches [31–32]. Each approach has some merits and demerits. The remaining work is divided into three more sections; namely, the literature review is discussed in Section 11.2, and the projected location privacy scheme is discussed in Section 11.3. At last, we summarize the paper and provide the future scope of the work.

Security attacks and their countermeasures in VANETs

Attack type	Compromised services	Countermeasures
DOS	Availability, authentication	Use the bit commitment and signature-based authentication technique
Jamming	Availability	Use frequency hopping technique, direct-sequence spread spectrum (DSSS)
Malware	Availability	Reliable hardware and digital signature of software
Broadcast tampering	Availability, integrity	Cryptographic primitives are enabled for prevention, but a nonrepudiation mechanism may exist
Blackhole, grayhole	Availability	Reliable hardware and digital signature of software
Eavesdropping	Confidentiality, integrity	Exploit physical layer security protocols
Traffic analysis	Confidentiality	Use encryption techniques
Man-in-the-middle	Authentication, confidentiality, integrity	Robust authentication technique such as digital certificates
Sybil	Availability, authentication	Deployment of central validation authority (VA), location and position verification
Tunneling	Integrity	Reliable hardware and digital signature of software and sensors
Message tampering	Availability, authentication	Zero-knowledge schemes for authenticate message
Replay	Authentication, integrity, nonrepudiation	Message authentication, using digital signature scheme

FIGURE 12.3 IOV attacks and their defense techniques [3–10, 25–34].

12.2 RELATED WORK

This section discusses the current work on location privacy-preserving (LP-preserving) in IOVs. Moreover, we discuss the methods with their advantage for efficient privacy-preserving.

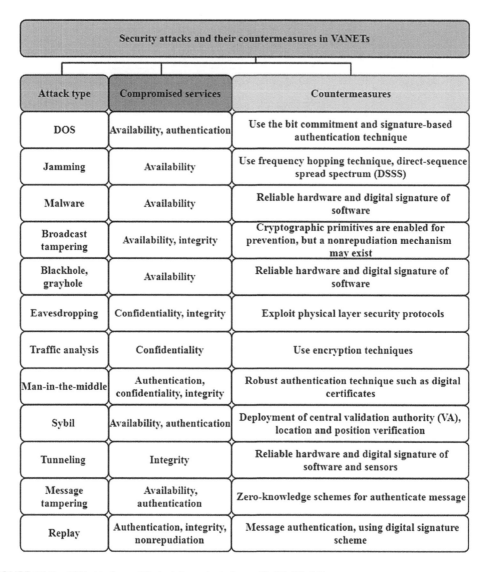

Sampigethaya et al. [1] proposed a robust LP scheme for IOV, known as AMOEBA to enhance user LP. AMOEBA uses group navigation of vehicles to achieve LP and simulate the system in streets and freeways with two passive adversary models. AMOEBA discussed several protocols such as group join and formation protocol, group operation protocol, group leaving protocol, probe data collection, and group leader rotation. Emara et al. [2] discussed a methodology to determine the secure level of privacy-preserving by incorporating an empirical vehicle tracker in IOVs. Monte Carlo analysis is also used to investigate the impact of the proposed approach on a safety application. Mei et al. [10] projected "a collaboratively hidden location privacy scheme for IOVs" to deal with the Privacy and liability using a modification of ring signature. The modified ring signature scheme authenticated all communication messages, and rings are formed using a distributed approach. The research gap of the proposed scheme is that it is not implemented on NS-2. Song et al. [11] suggested a "wireless location privacy protection in vehicular ad-hoc networks" based on vehicle density. The proposed scheme provides location privacy of vehicles by "utilizing the neighboring vehicle density as a threshold to change the pseudonyms." The suggested scheme defines some density zones and computes total delay as well as delay distribution of vehicles in a density zone. With this changed pseudonyms and vehicle delay model in some predefined density zones, location tracking becomes more complicated for attackers. Kaushik et al. [16] provide a "review of different approaches for privacy scheme in IOVs." Furthermore, authors discuss the protocol stack for IOVs and focus on WAVE with approved frequency band 5.9 GHz. Moreover, the authors examined the attributes (confidentiality, authentication, access control and availability, privacy, non-repudiation, data integrity) of secure network. In addition, the authors discussed the attack on privacy in IOVs. The main purpose of the attack on privacy is identity revealing and location tracking. The author discusses several privacy-preservation schemes, such as anonymous signing protocol, group signature scheme, digital signatures, mix zone method, and random encryption periods, to achieve privacy in IOVs. Al-Ani et al. [17] suggested an "adjusted location privacy scheme for IOV safety applications" based on a novel silent period concept. The authors discuss the shortcomings of ordinary silent-period-based schemes in which an accident may happen because a vehicle stops sharing its speed, location, and direction information. The author tries to maintain a least amount of silent period for fulfilling both purposes (location privacy, reduce the chance of accidents). The author says that if the silent period is long then it could lead to accidents. The authors compare three silent-period-based privacy schemes (CAPS, RSP, and SLOW) and analyze the silent period's effect using PREXT simulator. Zhang et al. [29] suggest a "TPPR: A trust-based and privacy-preserving platoon recommendation scheme in IOV" to diminish traffic congestion and raise travel comfort. The trust-based concept is used to select reliable vehicles and avoid malicious vehicles. Paillier cryptosystem and pseudonyms are used to preserve the privacy of vehicles.

Trust and authentication are employed to identify the applicable vehicles. Its efficiency is better against sophisticated attacks in IOVs. Ghane et al. [30] presented a data-adaptive system known as "preserving privacy in the internet of connected vehicles that scales the noise with respect to the data correlation." Ali et al. [31] present "issues, challenges, and research opportunities in intelligent transport system (ITS) for security and privacy" and discuss the solutions and limitations. These issues arise in ITS due to mobile nature, high speed, sparse and dense scenarios, bandwidth limitation, decentralization, and malicious attackers. ITS security and privacy schemes are classified into group signature-based schemes, pseudonym-based schemes, and hybrid schemes. Pseudonym-based schemes are further classified into symmetric and asymmetric cryptographic schemes. Moreover, the authors discussed the cloud with ITS. Cheng et al. [32] discuss a "location prediction model based on the Internet of vehicles for assistance to medical vehicles" based on the long short-term memory (LSTM) and deep belief nets (DBN). The suggested model considers driving environment, vehicle's attributes, and road information as well as the association between the factors that persuade vehicle driving behaviors and vehicle positions.

12.3 PROPOSED WORK

When a "vehicle wants to send a safety message SM, it encrypts the message, the current time, and the expiration time using its private key and then it broadcasts this message in its vicinity along with some other necessary parameters. The destination node verifies the signature. If successful, the destination decrypts the message using the public key of the sending vehicle. When CCA receives a complaint of malevolent behavior of some vehicle having pseudonym xyz, the CCA sends a Find Request to all the CAs. This request includes the malevolent pseudonym. As stated earlier, each CA maintains a list of IDs and their corresponding pseudonyms. The CAs check for

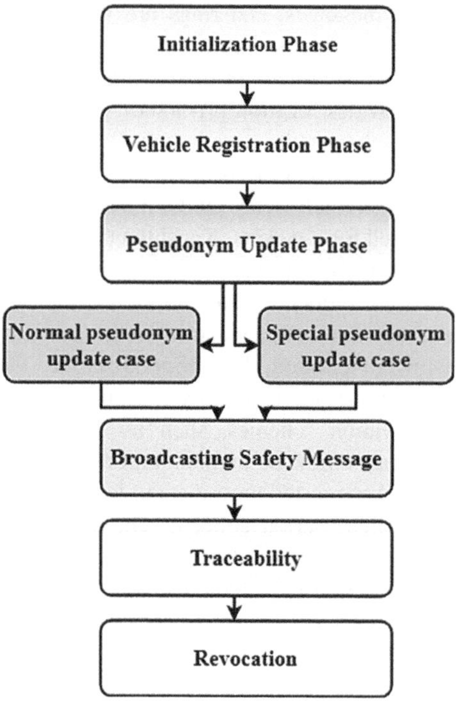

FIGURE 12.4 Flow chart of proposed scheme.

the pseudonym xyz in their databases. The one that finds it reverts back the corresponding ID to the CCA. The search for the malevolent pseudonym is done in linear time, which minimizes the computational overhead." Figure 12.4 represents the steps of proposed scheme. When "the CCA makes a determination to revoke a vehicle, it will inquire for the present pseudonym of this vehicle. For this, the CCA circulates the ID of the vehicle to all CAs in the network. Each CA that has communicated earlier with this vehicle will reply a triplet containing vehicle ID, corresponding pseudonym, and update date. The present pseudonym of this vehicle is the one that has the most recent update date. Once the CCA figures out the present pseudonym of this vehicle, it sends this present pseudonym along with the ID to all CAs. Each CA maintains a revocation list that includes the IDs of the revoked vehicles.

When a vehicle approaches a CA for updating its pseudonym, the CA checks for the ID (contained in the pseudonym update request) in the revocation list and if it finds it, the CA interrupts the pseudonym update process and ultimately the current pseudonym and signature will expire. Then, each CA circulates the present pseudonym of the revoked vehicle to all the vehicles in its vicinity. Each vehicle maintains a list of revoked pseudonyms. Hence, a revoked vehicle will not be able to communicate with other vehicles."

12.4 CONCLUSION AND FUTURE WORK

IOVs help in enhancing road safety and optimize traffic flow by transmitting various safety messages among vehicles. This paper presents an ID-based cryptosystem and pseudonym-based location privacy-preserving approach in IOVS. In future, we will assess the performance of the presented method using simulator in mobile environment. Moreover, we will add trust concept to improve security along with privacy.

REFERENCES

[1] Sampigethaya, K., Li, M., Huang, L., and Poovendran, R. 2007. AMOEBA: Robust location privacy scheme for VANET. *IEEE Journal on Selected Areas in Communications*, vol. 25, no. 8: 1569–1589.

[2] Emara, K., Woerndl, W., and Schlichter, J. 2015. On evaluation of location privacy preserving schemes for VANET safety applications. *Computer Communications*, vol. 63: 11–23.

[3] Emara, K., Woerndl, W., and Schlichter, J. 2015. CAPS: Context-aware privacy scheme for VANET safety applications. In *Proceedings of the 8th ACM Conference on Security and Privacy in Wireless and Mobile Networks*, (June): 1–12.

[4] Zidani, F., Semchedine, F., and Ayaida, M. 2018. Estimation of Neighbors Position privacy scheme with an Adaptive Beaconing approach for location privacy in VANETs. *Computers and Electrical Engineering*, vol. 71: 359–371.

[5] Kumar, G., Saha, R., Rai, M. K., and Kim, T. H. 2018. Multidimensional security provision for secure communication in vehicular ad hoc networks using hierarchical structure and End-to-End authentication. *IEEE Access*, vol. 6: 46558–46567.

[6] Gasmi, Rim, and Makhlouf Aliouat. 2019. Vehicular Ad Hoc NETworks versus Internet of Vehicles-A Comparative View. In *2019 International Conference on Networking and Advanced Systems (ICNAS)*. IEEE.

[7] Lu, R., Lin, X., Luan, T. H., Liang, X., and Shen, X. 2011. Pseudonym changing at social spots: An effective strategy for location privacy in vanets. *IEEE Transactions on Vehicular Technology*, vol. 61, no. 1: 86–96.

[8] Chen, Y. M., and Wei, Y. C. (2012). SafeAnon: A safe location privacy scheme for vehicular networks. *Telecommunication Systems*, vol. 50, no. 4: 339–354.

[9] Emara, K. 2017. Safety-aware location privacy in VANET: Evaluation and comparison. *IEEE Transactions on Vehicular Technology*, vol. 66, no. 12: 10718–10731.

[10] Mei, Y., Jiang, G., Zhang, W., and Cui, Y. 2014. A collaboratively hidden location privacy scheme for VANETs. *International Journal of Distributed Sensor Networks*, vol. 10, no. 3: 473151.

[11] Song, J. H., Wong, V. W., and Leung, V. C. 2010. Wireless location privacy protection in vehicular ad-hoc networks. *Mobile Networks and Applications*, vol. 15, no. 1: 160–171.

[12] Chen, Y. M., and Wei, Y. C. 2013. A beacon-based trust management system for enhancing user centric location privacy in VANETs. *Journal of Communications and Networks*, vol. 15, no. 2: 153–163.

[13] Eckhoff, D., Sommer, C., Gansen, T., German, R., and Dressler, F. 2010. Strong and affordable location privacy in VANETs: Identity diffusion using time-slots and swapping. In *2010 IEEE Vehicular Networking Conference* (December): 174–181.

[14] Taha, S., and Shen, X. 2013. A physical-layer location privacy-preserving scheme for mobile public hotspots in NEMO-based VANETs. *IEEE Transactions on Intelligent Transportation Systems*, vol. 14, no. 4: 665–1680.

[15] Sun, Y., Zhang, B., Zhao, B., Su, X., and Su, J. 2015. Mix-zones optimal deployment for protecting location privacy in VANET. *Peer-to-Peer Networking and Applications*, vol. 8, no. 6, 1108–1121.

[16] Kaushik, S. S. 2013. Review of different approaches for privacy scheme in VANETs. *International Journal of Advances in Engineering and Technology*, vol. 5, no. 2: 356.

[17] Al-Ani, R., Zhou, B., Shi, Q., Baker, T., and Abdlhamed, M. 2020. Adjusted location privacy scheme for VANET safety applications. In *NOMS 2020–2020 IEEE/IFIP Network Operations and Management Symposium* (April): 1–4.

[18] Carianha, A. M., Barreto, L. P., and Lima, G. 2011. Improving location privacy in mix-zones for VANETs. In *30th IEEE International Performance Computing and Communications Conference* (November): 1–6.

[19] Wei, Y. C., Chen, Y. M., and Shan, H. L. 2011. Beacon-based trust management for location privacy enhancement VANETs. In *2011 13th Asia-Pacific Network Operations and Management Symposium*. (September): 1–8.

[20] Luo, B., Li, X., Weng, J., Guo, J., and Ma, J. 2019. Blockchain enabled trust-based location privacy protection scheme in VANET. *IEEE Transactions on Vehicular Technology*, vol. 69, no. 2: 2034–2048.

[21] Khacheba, I., Yagoubi, M. B., Lagraa, N., and Lakas, A. 2018. CLPS: Context-based location privacy scheme for VANETs. *International Journal of Ad Hoc and Ubiquitous Computing*, vol. 2, no. 2: 141–159.

[22] Ren, D., Du, S., and Zhu, H. 2011. A novel attack tree based risk assessment approach for location privacy preservation in the VANETs. In *2011 IEEE International Conference on Communications (ICC)* (June): 1–5.

[23] Wang, S., Yao, N., Gong, N., and Gao, Z. 2018. A trigger-based pseudonym exchange scheme for location privacy preserving in VANETs. *Peer-to-Peer Networking and Applications*, vol. 11, no. 3: 548–560.

[24] Sheikh, M. S., and Liang, J. 2019. A comprehensive survey on VANET security services in traffic management system. *Wireless Communications and Mobile Computing*.

[25] Manvi, S. S., and Tangade, S. 2017. A survey on authentication schemes in VANETs for secured communication. *Vehicular Communications*, vol. 9: 19–30.

[26] Sheikh, M. S., Liang, J., and Wang, W. 2019. A survey of security services, attacks, and applications for vehicular ad hoc networks (VANETS). *Sensors*, vol. 19, no. 16: 3589.

[27] Sheikh, M. S., Liang, J., and Wang, W. 2020. Security and privacy in vehicular Ad Hoc network and vehicle cloud computing: A survey. In *Wireless Communications and Mobile Computing*.

[28] Ogundoyin, S. O. 2017. An efficient, secure and conditional privacy-preserving authentication scheme for vehicular ad-hoc networks. *Journal of Information Assurance and Security*, vol. 12, no. 5.

[29] Zhang, C., Zhu, L., Xu, C., Sharif, K., Ding, K., Liu, X., and Guizani, M. 2019. TPPR: A trust-based and privacy-preserving platoon recommendation scheme in VANET. *IEEE Transactions on Services Computing*.

[30] Ghane, S., Jolfaei, A., Kulik, L., Ramamohanarao, K., and Puthal, D. 2020. Preserving privacy in the internet of connected vehicles. *IEEE Transactions on Intelligent Transportation Systems*.

[31] Ali, Q. E., Ahmad, N., Malik, A. H., Ali, G., and Rehman, W. U. 2018. Issues, challenges, and research opportunities in intelligent transport system for security and privacy. *Applied Sciences*, vol. 8, no. 10: 1964.

[32] Cheng, J., Yan, H., Zhou, A., Liu, C., Cheng, D., Gao, S., and Cheng, D. 2019. Location prediction model based on the Internet of vehicles for assistance to medical vehicles. *IEEE Access*, no. 8: 10754–10767.

[33] Khan, T., Singh, K., Abdel-Basset, M., Long, H. V., Singh, S. P., and Manjul, M. 2019. A novel and comprehensive trust estimation clustering based approach for large scale wireless sensor networks. *IEEE Access*, vol. 7: 58221–58240.

[34] Khan, T., and Singh, K. 2019. Resource management based secure trust model for WSN. *Journal of Discrete Mathematical Sciences and Cryptography*, vol. 22, no. 8: 1453–1462.

13 Energy-Efficient Privacy-Preserving Vehicle Registration (ENTRANCE) Protocol for V2X Communication in VANET

N. Sasikaladevi, K. Geetha, and S. Aarthi
SASTRA Deemed University, Thanjavur, India

C. Mala
National Institute of Technology, Trichy, India

CONTENTS

13.1 INTRODUCTION

With the technology improving manifold day by day, the interest in Vehicular Ad-Hoc Networks (VANETs) is also increasing proportionally. This is mainly due to the wide range of applications it can offer, ranging from traffic management to infotainment services. Real-time communication

DOI: 10.1201/9781003155577-16

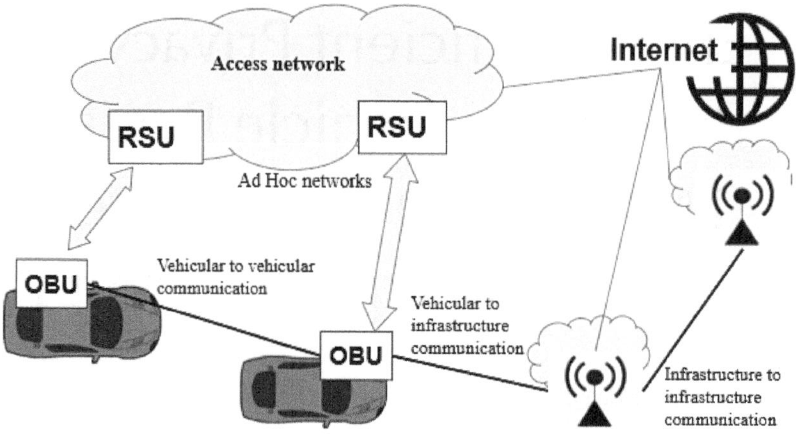

FIGURE 13.1 Simple architecture of VANET.

between vehicles for a better driving experience and safety can be achieved with the help of VANET [1, 2]. This communication includes their present status, weather conditions, and traffic, which provide the driver with a more efficient and safer driving experience.

Every vehicle in a VANET contains an On-Board Unit (OBU), which facilitates communication between Vehicle and Road Side Unit (RSU). Vehicles in a VANET communicate through Dedicated Short-Range Communication (DSRC) systems. DSRC [3] allows high throughput and secure communication between the On-Board Units of the vehicles and supports the communication among the surrounding environments. And different modes of communication in VANET include R2V, V2V, and V2R. In R2V, communication takes place between RSU and a vehicle. While in V2V, communication is between two vehicles, and V2R is the communication between Vehicle and Road Side Unit. With the help of the communications explained above, drivers can come to a proper conclusion about the driving environment and take the necessary action required.

In Figure 13.1, three communications that take place in VANET are illustrated properly. Here RSU forms the ad hoc network for the communication between vehicles and access networks. OBUs in vehicles are used to communicate with other vehicles or infrastructure domains to avoid collisions and promote cooperative driving.

In a VANET, vehicles form the majority of nodes that group together to form networks without any prior knowledge of each other. Hence, vehicles are the most vulnerable part of VANETs that can be easily exploited if no proper security measures are taken [4].

13.2 RELATED WORK

A number of researchers have proposed many privacy-preserving schemes [5] in the past decade. It includes schemes based on pseudonyms, ID-based schemes, group-signature-based methods, and symmetric cryptography-based approaches. In *The Journal of Computer Security* [6], Hubaux and Raya described the privacy and security requirements of VANET and also proposed the pseudonym-based privacy-preserving algorithm. After that, many researchers have followed the work of Hubaux and Raya to propose several group signature and pseudonym-based approaches.Williams et al. suggested a modification in RSA cryptographic primitive [7] to reduce the computational complexity and Key length. Public key infrastructure (PKI) is used to implement pseudonym-based schemes. Certificates generated by PKI are appended with the message signed by corresponding private keys. This certificate holds pseudo-identity and the relation between each certificate and pseudo-identity is known only to the certification authority (CA). In order to secure cryptographic parameters stored in OBU, Raya et al. [2] proposed a tamper-proof device (TPD) or hardware security module (HSM). TPD is implemented on OBU of vehicles used for mutual authentication with their own timestamps. But this approach suffers from communication and storage overhead due to pseudonym-based certificates. Another major drawback of this scheme is certificate revocation list (CRL). Certificates are needed for each vehicle to identify the authorized identities. So, CRL must be disseminated to all the authenticated vehicular nodes to avoid communication with unauthorized identities. While revoking a particular vehicle, all other certificates issued already to that particular vehicle need to be revoked. It significantly grows the size of CRL exponentially. Therefore, extra overhead is included in the management of certificate revocation lists.

Zhang et al. [8] proposed the scheme to ensure conditional anonymity using realistic TPD in the place of ideal TPD. Sun et al. proposed a scheme by introducing a hash chain for reducing the CRL and using a proxy re-signature method to advance the time needed to update the CRL. Later, a conditional privacy-preserving model is proposed by Lu et al. A vehicle in the network needs to get a pseudonym key from RSU, which is valid only for the short term. Therefore, this approach necessitates omnipresent deployment of RSU. But, the big drawback of the approach is that the trusted authority requires updating CRL frequently and distributing it to all RSUs. Later, Rajput et al. introduced a hierarchical pseudonym-based model, where CA issues primary pseudonyms to each vehicle and RSU issues secondary pseudonyms. An identity-based verification method is proposed by Zhang et al., which generates certificates based on pseudo-identity and its corresponding private key with the help of TPD.

Sungeetha et al. [9] framed a novel shared key protocol using the public key cryptography. For decentralized wireless ad hoc networks. Although this protocol is executed in a distributed heterogeneous wireless sensor network with bandwidth utilization, it leads to a high cost for V2V communication. Lightweight authentication protocol (LEAP) [10] ensures the high security and low cost for communication using hyper elliptic curve genus 2 cryptography. Furthermore, this protocol is not resistant to Pollard-rho's attack (square root attack). Godse et al. [11] explains the cost analysis of the elliptic curve cryptography with various parameters, which is used to attain the low computation cost. Edward et al. [12] list out the various factors of using public key cryptography in VANET. Manivannan et al. [13] describe a framework for addressing various issues like confidentiality, authenticity, and secure communication in communication models of VANET architecture. Ghassan Samara proposes a new model for lane changing and prediction for V2V communication in *Egyptian Informatics Journal* [14]. This model concentrates only on V2V communication.

Although there are various models used before for the security in VANET architecture, they are concerned with the active adversary; here, we propose a model that provides high resistance for both active and passive adversaries.

13.3 ENTRANCE SYSTEM MODEL

The system model consists of two entities: TA and the vehicles.

- **Trusted authority (TA):** It is responsible for generating key pairs, that is, private and public keys for each participating vehicle and issuing secret certificates. TA is a trusted third-party agent.
- **Vehicles:** Each and every vehicle in the network is equipped with an on-board unit (OBU) and tamper-proof device (TPD). OBU is used to gather the data collected from various sensors of the vehicle and transmit this sensitive information for V2V and V2R using radio frequency and Bluetooth modules. OBU assists to make communication between RSUs and vehicles, while TPD implemented within the OBU makes sure that OBU is not compromised.

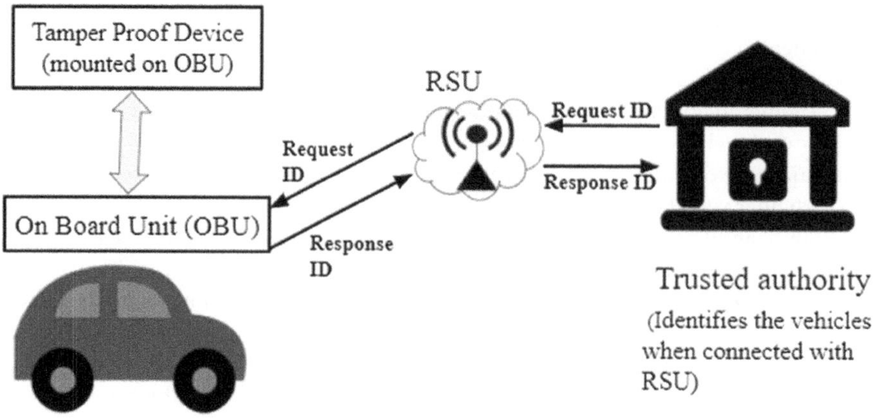

FIGURE 13.2 ENTRANCE System model.

Figure 13.2 illustrates the simple communication between the vehicles and trusted authority. When the vehicle is connected by the access network, trusted authority identifies the vehicle and requests it to communicate the ID of the vehicle. After receiving the request by TA, OBU sends its own ID to the TA. This communication must be secure; otherwise, it will be hacked by an adversary. After getting an ID from the OBU, TA generates the unique key pairs for the vehicle using the elliptic curve Diffie-Hellman algorithm. The notations used in the proposed scheme are depicted in Table 13.1.

TABLE 13.1
Notations and Its Definitions Used in ENTRANCE Scheme

Notation	Definition
TA	Trusted authority
RSU	Road side unit
V_i	i^{th} vehicle
TPD	Tamper-proof device of vehicle
OBU	On-board unit of vehicle
ID_X	Real identity of x
PWD	Vehicle's biological password
(P_X, Q_X)	Two distinct large secret odd primes of x
n_X	Number generated by x; $n_X = P_X . Q_X$
N_X	Nonce of the entity x
SA_X	Security association denotes a set of choices that are accepted by an entity x
G	A generator point of selected elliptic curve whose order is n
Ra_X	Random value chosen by an entity x
{x}_SK	A session key and x is encrypted and integrity-protected using internal keys
(PID , R , S)	A secret certificate issued by trusted authority
KE_X	mult (G , Ra_X) is a Diffie-Hellman value
Hash (.)	A secure hash function
PRF (.)	A pseudorandom function whose output is indistinguishable from that of a truly random function.
mult (.)	An arithmetic multiply function
Vehicle List	In this list, real identities of each vehicle along with its corresponding pseudo identities are stored known only by TA
Revocation List	It stores the pseudo identities of revoked vehicles along with revocation time

13.3.1 Assumptions

The following assumptions are made before proceeding with the proposed scheme.

- The trusted authority (TA) can be completely trusted, that is, it can never be compromised.
- A vehicle can be compromised thereby enabling an intruder to send and receive the messages. But the secret parameters within the TPD are safe.
- The communication between TA and RSUs is done with the help of a secure channel. But all other communications are done in an insecure channel.
- The TPD present in the vehicle will have its own unique key pair assigned for it at the time of installation.

13.4 PROPOSED ENTRANCE SCHEME

13.4.1 Certificate Generation by Trusted Authority

Trusted authority (TA) generates the secret certificate and issues it to the vehicle V_i. The steps carried out to produce a secret certificate are as follows:

1. Let $R_j = 0$ and pseudo-identity be PID_j.
2. Computes a = Hash (PIDj, R_j) and checks if $a(P_{ta}-1)/2 = 1 \pmod{P_{ta}}$ and $a(Q_{ta}-1)/2 = 1 \pmod{Q_{ta}}$.
3. If not, $R_j = R_j + 1$ and again does the calculation and verifies it.
4. Computes four modular square roots $X_{1,2,3,4}$ of $X_2 = a \pmod{N_{ta}}$ with the help of P_{ta} and Q_{ta}based on the equation $R_{1,2,3,4} = \pm . Q_{ta} . Q_{ta}* \pm . P_{ta} . P_{ta}* \pmod{N_{ta}}$ where $= a(P_{ta} + 1)/4 \pmod{P_{ta}}$, $= a(Q_{ta} + 1)/4 \pmod{Q_{ta}}$, $P_{ta}* = P_{ta}-1 (\mathrm{mod}\ Q_{ta})$, $Q_{ta}* = Q_{ta}$-1mod Pta and selects the smallest square root as S_j.
5. Then outputs (PID_j , R_j , S_j) and halts.

13.4.2 Vehicle Registration Phase

Whenever a vehicle enters into VANET, trusted authority identifies the vehicle and requests the vehicle's id by sending a message REQUEST ID. Vehicle reacts to the trusted authority request by sending its own real identity, that is, RESPOND ID V. After receiving IDv from the vehicle, TA agrees on a security association (SA) by accepting some set of choices used for the negotiation of the cryptographic algorithms.

Based on ECC Diffie-Hellman Key Exchange, trusted authority computes the public key mult (G,RaT) by selecting a random value RaT and the base point $G = (x_1 , y_1)$. A base point G in elliptic curve $E_p(a,b)$ with order n. Selected integer RaT value should be less than n. A nonce Nt is generated by TA and must be fresh to avoid replay attacks. Trusted authority computes the key exchange message by combining security association, public key, and the nonce, that is, SAt . mult (G , RaT) . Not and sends it to the vehicle. Vehicle also computes the key exchange message SAt . mult (G , RaV) . Nv by agreeing on the security association chosen by TA and sending it to the TA. RaV value should also be less than n and Nv must be fresh.

Now both the TA and vehicle computes the session key SK = PRF (Nt . Nv . mult (mult (G , RaT) , RaV)) = PRF (Nv . Nt . mult (mult (G , RaV) , RaT)). Both TA and vehicle compute digital signatures { TA . { SAt . mult (G , RaT) . Nt . Nv}_inv (Kt) }_SK , { V . { SAt . mult (G , RaV) . Nv . Nt}_inv (Kv) }_SK signed by its private key and encrypted with the session key respectively and exchanged with each other. It ensures mutual authentication and also avoids attacks like man-in-the-middle attack, message modification attack, and replay attack.

When authentication becomes successful, the vehicle sends the ID and password encrypted by the session key to the TA, that is, { (IDv , PWD) }_SK. After receiving login credentials from

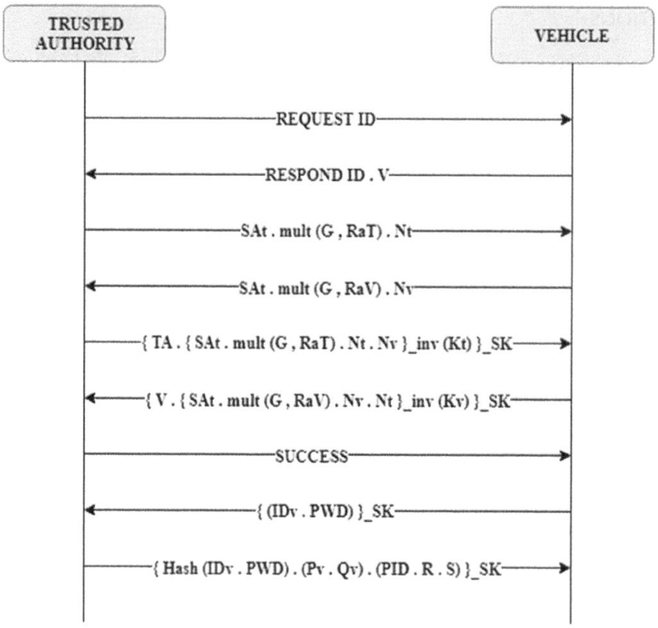

FIGURE 13.3 Vehicle registration.

the vehicle, TA computes the secret certificate (PID . R . S) based on the secret parameters P_{ta} , Q_{ta} chosen by TA. The secret certificate will be enclosed in a message that contains hashed login credentials and secret parameters for the vehicle chosen by TA, that is, { Hash (IDv . PWD) . (Pv . Qv) . (PID . R . S)}_SK.

In Figure 13.3, the vehicle is registered by trusted authority (TA) by the request-response model. Trusted authority gets the ID and password to authenticate the vehicle and turn it into an authorized identity.

13.4.3 RSU Registration Phase

Trusted authority identifies the RSU location and requests the RSUs id by sending a message REQUEST ID. RSU reacts to the trusted authority request by sending its own real identity, that is, RESPOND ID. RSU. After receiving IDr from the RSU, TA agrees on a security association (SA) by accepting some set of choices used for the negotiation of the cryptographic algorithms.

Based on ECC Diffie-Hellman Key Exchange, trusted authority computes the public key mult (G , RaT) by selecting a random value RaT and the base point G = (x_1 , y_1). A base point G in elliptic curve $E_p(a,b)$ is with the order n. Selected integer RaT value should be less than n. A nonce Nt generated by TA and must be fresh to avoid replay attacks. Trusted authority computes the key exchange message by combining security association, public key, and the nonce, that is, SAt . mult (G , RaT) . Nt and sends it to the RSU. RSU also computes the key exchange message SAt . mult (G , RaR) . Nr by agreeing on the security association chosen by TA and sending it to the TA. RaR value should also be less than n and Nr must be fresh.

Now both the TA and RSU compute the session key SK = PRF (Nt . Nr . mult (mult (G , RaT) , RaR)) = PRF (Nr . Nt . mult (mult (G , RaR) , RaT)). Both TA and RSU compute digital signatures { TA . { SAt . mult (G , RaT) . Nt . Nr}_inv (Kt) }_SK , { RSU . { SAt . mult (G , RaR) . Nr . Nt}_inv (Kr) }_SK signed by its private key and encrypted with the session key respectively and exchanged with each other.

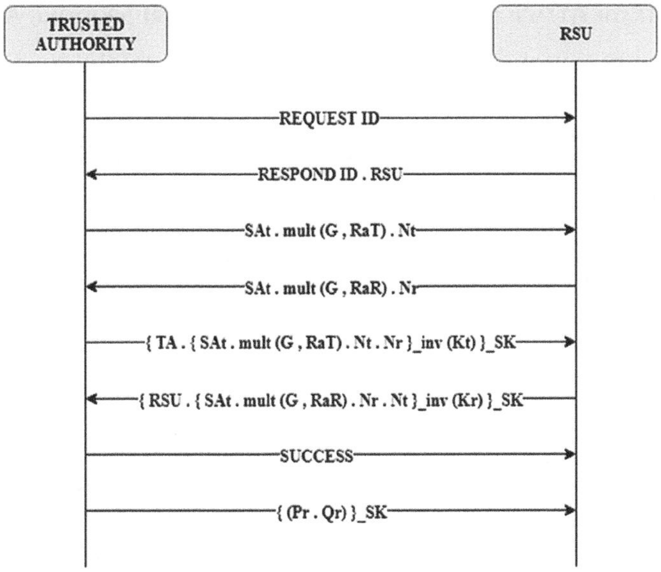

FIGURE 13.4 RSU registration.

It ensures mutual authentication and also avoids attacks like man-in-the-middle attack, message modification attack, and replay attack. When authentication becomes successful, TA sends the secret parameters (Pr , Qr) to the RSU chosen by TA and encrypted with the session key, that is, { (Pr . Qr) }_SK.

Figure 13.4 explains the registration of access networks (RSU) by the trusted authority(TA) to avoid any malicious access network to gain access to the VANET.

13.5 INFORMAL ANALYSIS

In the informal analysis, the description of major attacks is given along with the explanation of how our proposed authentication protocol provides resistance against such security attacks.

13.5.1 Man-in-the-Middle Attack

To perform man-in-the-middle attack, the intruder should capture transitions in mutual key exchange phase, that is, (SAt, mult(G, RaT), Nt) and (SAt. mult(G, RbV). Nv). Then, he will send the modified contents to both parties like (SAt, mult(G, RaT_M), Nt_M) and (SAt, mult(G, RaV_M), Nv_M). Later, both parties perform digital signature verification, which is encrypted with the session key, that is, SK = (Hash(Nt. Nv. mult(mult(G, RaT), RbV))) = (Hash(Nv. Nt. mult(mult(G, RaV), RaT))). Since, the intruder is unable to calculate the session key without the knowledge of RaT, RaV. It is computationally hard to calculate session keys only with key exchange transitions. Since digital signatures are encrypted with the session key, intruders are unable to modify the contents in the digital signatures. Any change in the digital signature will not match during signature verification. This avoids man-in-the-middle attack.

13.5.2 Eavesdropping Attack (or) Network Sniffing

In eavesdropping, the intruder tries to secretly listen to the private conversation and also capture the keys, that is, (SAt, mult(G, RaT), Nt) and (SAt, mult(G, RaV), Nv) exchanged by both parties. It is computationally infeasible to calculate the session key, that is, SK = (Hash(Nt. Nv. mult(mult(G, RaT), RbV))) = (Hash(Nv. Nt. mult(mult(G, RaV), RaT))). Since every transition after mutual key exchange is encrypted with the session key, it is impossible to capture what's inside the encrypted message.

13.5.3 Masquerade Attack (or) Impersonation Attack (or) Spoofing Attack

In order to perform this attack, the intruder needs to generate a valid message and the message should contain the valid signature (like {V.{Sat. mult(G, RaV). Nv. Nt}_inv(Kv)}_SK) signed with a private key by the corresponding entity, it may be a vehicle (or) RSU (or) the trusted authority. It is difficult for an adversary to produce such a signature without knowing the private key (like inv(Kv)). Even if the intruder tries to generate the message by using its own private key (like inv(Ki)), the entities on the other end verify the signature by decrypting it with the sender's public key. Since the message is generated by an intruder, other entities like RSUs, vehicles, and trusted authority are unaware about the intruder's public key; they fail to decrypt the signature and conclude that it is a masquerading attack.

13.5.4 Replay Attack (or) Playback Attack

In the registration phase, any entity (vehicles or RSU or trusted authority) before communicating with the other entities chooses a random value called Nonce (Nx represents the random nonce value chosen by entity "x") and it acts as a timestamp. Once an adversary intercepts and replays an intercepting message, the corresponding vehicle or RSU will be aware of the replay attack by verifying the current nonce Nx with the nonce value of the previously received messages. If the current nonce Nx matches with the nonce value of the previously received messages, then such a message is assumed to be a replayed message and it is discarded. Therefore, the adversary is unable to clear the verification challenge due to the freshness of Nx.

13.5.5 Message Modification Attack

It's impossible for an adversary to perform a message modification attack on an encrypted message without an equivalent key to decipher them. Since, every transition after mutual key exchange is encrypted with session key (SK = (Hash(Nt. Nv. mult(mult(G, RaT), RbV))) = (Hash(Nv. Nt. mult(mult(G, RaV), RaT)))), which is computed by both the sender and the receiver, it is impossible to alter the contents in the encrypted message.

If an intruder tries to modify the messages before key exchange, the contents will not match with the digital signatures. Digital signatures are verified by both the sender and the receiver after key exchange; any modification during key exchange can be found here.

13.5.6 Brute Force Attack

If the intruder tries to find the secret session key (SK = (Hash(Nt. Nv. mult(mult(G, RaT), RbV))) = (Hash(Nv. Nt. mult(mult(G, RaV), RaT)))), by trying with all possible combinations of values (Nonce and Random values chosen by the sender and receiver). But since we are using a large generator value ("G"), it is highly difficult for the intruder to get to know about the session key. Even if he manages to crack the session key ("SK"), by the time he does so the key would be invalid because we are making use of disposable session keys, which vary from session to session. Hence, brute force attack is not possible.

13.5.7 Denial of Service Attack (DoS)

In DoS attack, the attacker may prevent the secure communication between TA and vehicles (or) TA and RSUs (or) RSUs and vehicles. When a vehicle tries to establish a secure session key with the TA, it sends its identity along with its nonce, by signing with its own private key("inv(Kv)") and sending it as (mult(G, RaV). Nv. Nt)_inv(Kv). If an attacker tries to bombard the TA with a series of messages, TA can verify the signature of that message, by matching it with the public signature of the vehicle ("Kv"). Once the key pair (inv(Kv), Kv) match is found, the TA will put that vehicle in the revocation list("RL"), thereby preventing the TA, and not accepting any further messages from that vehicle. Thus, it avoids DOS attacks.

13.5.8 Flaw Attack

In flaw attack, the attacker tries to trick the other authorized entities (like vehicle, RSU, and trusted authority) to accept the message component (instead of hash, entities are tricked to accept text (or) message (or) natural number as a message component) of one type as a message of another. Flaw attack can be successfully prevented by "tagging" types of each field of a message like a hash component ("Pseudo Random Function"), which is concatenated with a "Hash function" tag).

13.5.9 Key Replication Attack

In a key replication attack, the intruder tries to replicate the private key of an entity (like vehicle, RSU, and trusted authority), and it is used to encrypt the private conversation between other entities. It certainly takes a lot of time for the intruder to find the private key of a particular entity. Since we are making use of disposable keys like session keys (SK = (Hash(Nt. Nv. mult(mult(G, RaT), RbV))) = (Hash(Nv. Nt. mult(mult(G, RaV), RaT)))) for every new session, even if an intruder is able to find the encryption key of the previous session, it would go in vain.

13.6 EXPERIMENTAL SETUP

The simulation of our proposed scheme is performed on SPAN v1.6 on a 4GB Ubuntu system with an i3 processor. The protocol has been coded in high-level protocol specification language (HLPSL) and then run on the SPAN [8, 15] for the simulation.

Figure 13.5 illustrates the initial setup of SPAN v1.6 in the i3 processor. Here, we have various tools and options to execute the high-level protocol specification language.

13.6.1 Simulation Results

The simulation results of the proposed lightweight authentication scheme clearly depict that the proposed protocol is safe and secure against an intruder. The simulation result is a sequence diagram, which tells us that an intruder who tries to eavesdrop on the message transfer between the TA and the vehicle will be unsuccessful in his attempts.

Figure 13.6 shows that the proposed model is successfully verified using SPAN. And it is safe to be used in VANET architecture to avoid passive adversaries eavesdropping on any communication. The intruder simulation for the vehicular registration in the proposed scheme is illustrated in Figure 13.7.

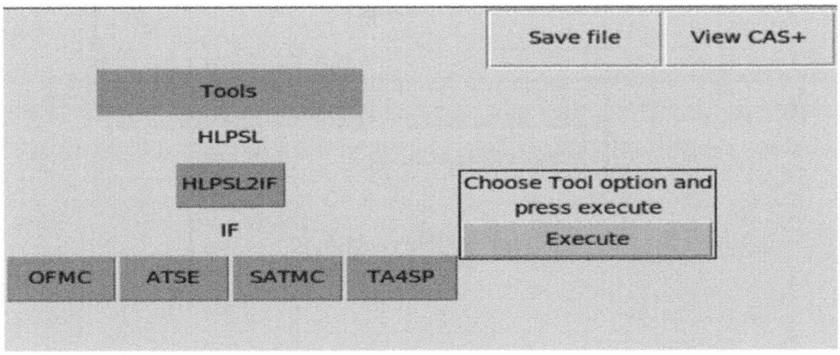

FIGURE 13.5 Security protocol animator (SPAN).

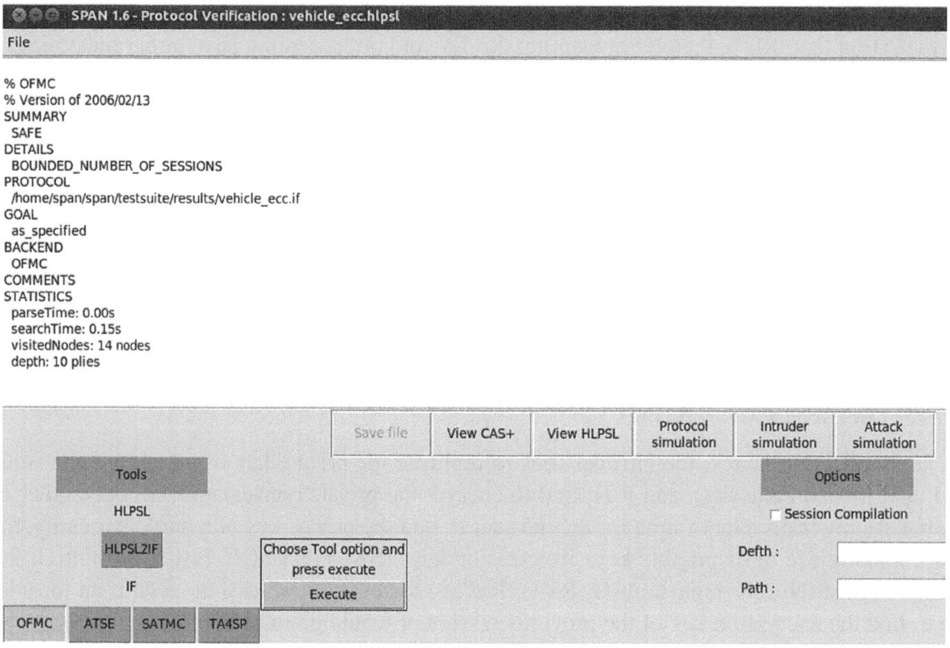

FIGURE 13.6 AVISPA output for vehicle registration.

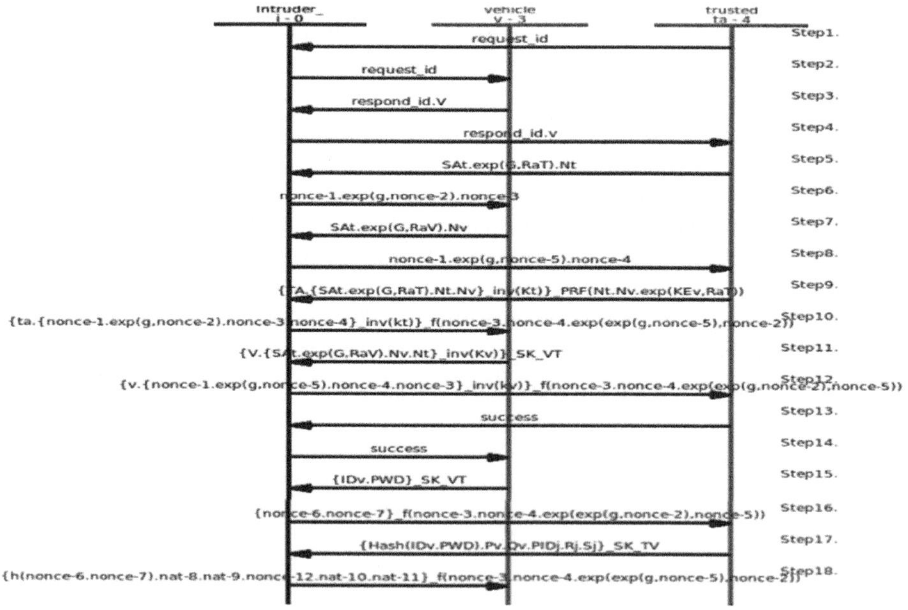

FIGURE 13.7 AVISPA intruder simulation for vehicle registration.

13.7 CONCLUSION

The proposed ENTRANCE protocol is a secured lightweight key distribution scheme recommended for VANET by using elliptic curve Diffie-Hellman (EC-DH). The proposed scheme prevents eavesdropping of the messages between the TA and the vehicle in a VANET. The informal security analysis of the proposed scheme proves that it resists from the following attacks namely man-in-the-middle Attack, eavesdropping attack (or) network sniffing, masquerade attack (or) impersonation attack (or) spoofing attack, replay attack (or) playback attack, message modification attack, brute force attack, denial of service attack (DoS), flaw attack, and key replication attack. The simulation results in the AVISPA show that the proposed scheme makes it difficult for the intruder to eavesdrop on the messages.

ACKNOWLEDGMENTS

This part of this research work is supported by the Department of Science and Technology (DST), Science and Engineering Board (SERB), Government of India under the TARE grant (TAR/2020/000259).

REFERENCES

1. Lin Yao, Jie Wang, Xin Wang, Ailun Chen, Yuqi Wang, V2X routing in a VANET based on the hidden Markov model, *IEEE Transaction on Intelligent Transportation Systems* 19, no. 3 (2018) 889–899.
2. Xu Yang, Xun Yi, Ibrahim Khalil, Yali Zheng, Xinyi Huang, Surya Nepal, Xuechao Yang, Hui Cui, A lightweight authentication scheme for vehicular ad hoc networks based on MSR, *Vehicular Communication* 15 (2019) 16–27.
3. D. Jiang, V. Taliwal, A. Meier, W. Holfelder, R. Herrtwich, Design of 5.9 GHZ DSRC-based vehicular safety communication, *IEEE Wireless Communications* 13 (2006) 36–43.
4. M.N. Mejri, J. Ben-Othman, M. Hamdi, Survey on VANET security challenges and possible cryptographic solutions, *Vehicular Communications* 1 (2014) 53–66.
5. M. Raya, P. Papadimitratos, J.-P. Hubaux, Securing vehicular communications, *IEEE Wireless Communications* 13 (2006) 8–15.
6. M. Raya, J.-P. Hubaux, Securing vehicular ad hoc networks, *The Journal of Computer Security* 15 (2007) 39–68.
7. H. Williams, A modification of the RSA public-key encryption procedure (Coresp.), *IEEE Transactions on Information Theory* 26 (1980) 726–729.
8. AVISPA www.avispa-project.org IST-2001-39592 AVISPA v1.1 User Manual.
9. Akey Sungheetha, and Rajesh Sharma. Novel shared key transfer protocol for secure data transmission in distributed wireless networks. *Journal of Trends in Computer Science and Smart Technology (TCSST)* 2, no. 02 (2020) 98–108.
10. N. Sasikaladevi, D. Malathi, Privacy preserving lightweight authentication protocol (LEAP) for WBAN by exploring Genus-2 HEC, *Multimedia Tools and Applications* 78, no. 13 (2019). https://doi.org/10.1007/s11042-019-7149-8.
11. Sachin Godse, A computational analysis of ECC based novel authentication scheme in VANET, *International Journal of Electrical and Computer Engineering* 8, no. 6 (2018) 5268. https://doi.org/10.11591/ijece.v8i6.pp5268-5277.
12. Edward David Moreno, Leila C.M. Buarque, Florêncio Natan, Gustavo Quirino and Ricardo Salgueiro, Impact of asymmetric encryption algorithms in a VANET, *Journal of Computer Sciences* 11, no. 12 (2015) 1118–1131.

13. D. Manivannan, Shafika Showkat Moni, Sherali Zeadally, Secure authentication and privacy-preserving techniques in Vehicular Ad-hoc NETworks (VANETs), *Vehicular Communications* 25 (2020) 100247, ISSN 2214-2096.
14. Ghassan Samara, Lane prediction optimization in VANET, *Egyptian Informatics Journal*, (2020), ISSN 1110-8665, https://doi.org/10.1016/j.eij.2020.12.005.
15. B. Blanchet, An efficient cryptographic protocol verifier based on prolog rules. In: *Proc. CSFW 2001*. IEEE Computer Society Press, Los Alamitos (2001).

Part IV

Security

14 Emotion Independent Face Recognition-Based Security Protocol in IoT-Enabled Devices

Bannishikha Banerjee
PP Savani University, Surat, India

Geetali Saha
G. H. Patel College of Engineering and Technology, Anand, India

CONTENTS

14.1 INTRODUCTION: BACKGROUND AND DRIVING FORCES

As the industry and the society get revolutionized under the influence of specific demand-driven approaches, it's the Internet of Things (IoT) that envelops our everyday life. It follows us everywhere, be it the smart cars on the roads, the home automation devices at our house or the smart sensors at the office/workplace. Ericsson in the year 2010 had predicted that IoT-enabled devices would reach a count of 50 billion by the year 2020, and the same was seconded by Cisco in the year 2011. However, the ground truth is a meagre count of 9 billion only. So, what about the missing 41 billion devices? Apart from stunted growth in Edge Computing and Mobile Network Operators, it is the secured cloud connectivity that has failed to mitigate the risks involved in terms of security which is a constant challenge to this development. There is, however, no domain [1] that is spared of the influence of IoT, and hence it is vital to ensure strong protocols be embedded in such applications (Figure 14.1).

And there is nothing better than user biometrics [2] that can better represent the unique identity of an individual, major among them being face recognition, fingerprint, hand/palm print, iris detection

DOI: 10.1201/9781003155577-18

FIGURE 14.1 The extent of IoT penetration in our day-to-day life activities.

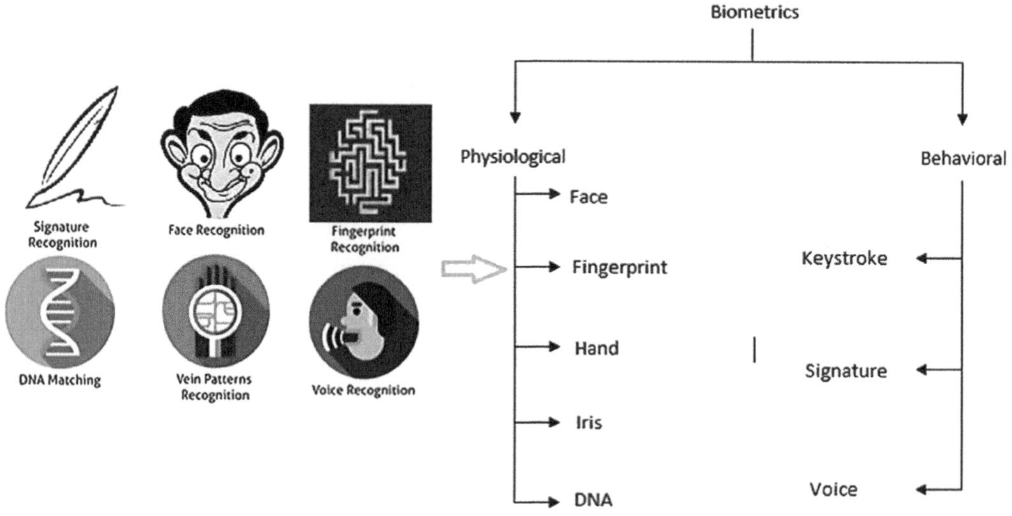

FIGURE 14.2 The various biometrics that are in use in the present era.

and DNA-based detection, which is broadly classified as physiological-based biometrics. Among these, the face recognition-based approach [3–5] is the most popular one contributed largely due to technological development and social mindset. Apart from that, we have the voice recognition, signature and keystroke-based systems that represent the behavioural approach. Among these, the signature-based approaches [6], using the ANN, are the most popular as they carry the most personal touch and various neural and deep learning techniques. Further, histogram of oriented gradients (HOG), Handwritten Signature Recognition (HSR), and multiple classifiers have enhanced the practical feasibility of the same as explained by Aravinda et al. in [7]. As much as these biometrics have certain advantages, so is it equally true that they are also subjected to various drawbacks. However, our frontal faces as a biometric find unbiased acceptance both in the social and research group (Figure 14.2).

Almost all biometric-based applications involve the use of a stored template that is compared with the processed feature extracted template and then matched to evaluate its authenticity. However, with emerging technologies, correct recognition also becomes challenging. Every stage right from preprocessing to matching needs rigorous implementation (Figure 14.3).

Challenges start surfacing as an image of the face is clicked in various lit conditions, with or without spectacles, under different emotional influences. As of late, recognition of facial images is significantly

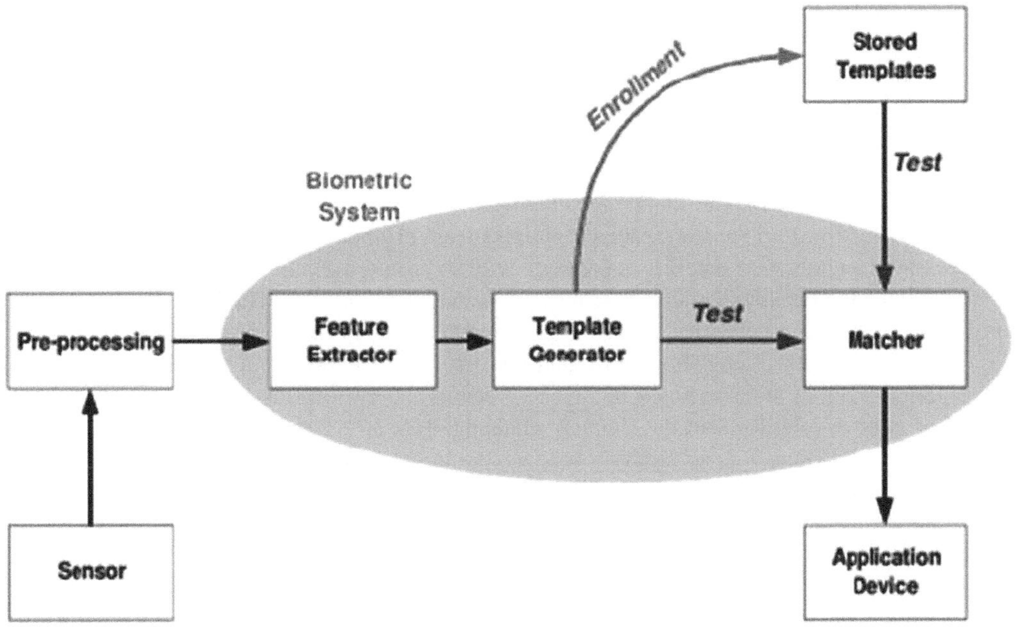

FIGURE 14.3 The basic block diagram of biometric-based recognition systems.

acknowledged by scientists working in biometrics, design systems and those in the visual perception network [3, 4]. The AI and PC researchers are progressively working towards facial domain-based system acknowledgement. This beyond normal interest among analysts working in miscellaneous fields is propelled by our wonderful capability to interpret individuals via their appearance both in the real and virtual world. Also, there are prospects for an enormous number of businesses, security and measurable applications, based largely upon physiognomy acknowledgement and innovations. A variety of applications involving such acknowledgements include scanning, security-based control, ID photos for passports, motor vehicle licenses, reproduction of facial images, facial aging applications and many more have provided thriving options for many business and administrative offices [8].

14.2 EMOTION DETECTION

Live outward appearance acknowledgement intends to characterize a live caught picture into a few essential feelings, for example, glad, irate, appal, dread, pitiful, unbiased and shock. Given a live vision, the mainstream outward appearance acknowledgement pipeline with a visual piece of information mostly incorporates three stages, to be specific causing pre-preparing, extraction and order. Programmed outward appearance acknowledgement has as of late pulled in expanding consideration in the scholarly community and industry because of its wide scope of uses, for example, full of feeling registering, smart conditions and multimodal human-PC interface [9]. In spite of the fact that extraordinary advancement has been made as of late, outward appearance, acknowledgement in the wild remains a difficult issue because of huge head present, enlightenment fluctuation, impediment, movement obscure and so on. Particularly, outline pre-preparing alludes to confront location, arrangement, brightening normalizing, etc. Highlight extraction or video portrayal is the critical piece of outward appearance acknowledgement which encodes edges or groupings into minimized element vectors. These component vectors are accordingly taken care of into a classifier for forecasting. Highlight extraction strategies for video-based outward appearance acknowledgement can be generally partitioned into three sorts in particular, static-based techniques, spatial-fleeting techniques and math-based strategies. Recognition of emotions derived from still image-based feature extractions could be either hand crafted or simulated [5, 10–13]. For the hand-made highlights, Littlewort et al. [10] proposed to utilize a bank of 2D Gabor channels to remove facial highlights for video-based outward appearance acknowledgement. For facial component extraction, Shan et al. [5] utilizes nearby paired examples and histograms. For the educated highlights, Yichuan et al. [11] used the profound convolutional neural organization for highlight extraction, thereby winning the FER2013. A few champs in the sound video feeling acknowledgement assignment of EmotiW2016 and EmotiW2017 just utilize static facial highlights from profound convolutional neural organizations prepared on huge face datasets or prepared with staggered oversight [12, 13] Spatial-transient strategies intend to display the fleeting or movement data in recordings. The long short-term memory [14, 15] is the most generally utilized spatial-fleeting strategy for video-based outward appearance acknowledgement. Long short-term memory gets data from groupings by misusing the way that highlight vectors are associated in an interpretable pattern towards progressive information. The same is broadly utilized in the EmotiW challenge [16, 17]. C3D, initially created for video activity acknowledgement, is additionally mainstream in the EmotiW challenge. Math-based techniques [18] intend to display the movements of central issues in faces which just influence the math areas of facial milestones in each video outlines. In Jung et al. [19], the authors have proposed a profound worldly appearance-math network which first on the other hand connects the x-directions and y-directions of the facial milestone focuses from each edge after standardization and afterward links these standardized focuses over the long run for a one-dimensional direction sign of each grouping. A picture-like-guide is developed by Yan et al. [18] through extending all the standardized facial point directions in a succession together as the contribution of a convolutional neural organization. Among all the above strategies, static-based techniques are better than the others as per a few victor arrangements in EmotiW challenges. To acquire a video-level outcome with differed outlines, a casing total activity is fundamental for static-based techniques. For outline accumulation [20], link the n-class likelihood vectors of 10 fragments to shape a fixed-length video portrayal by outline averaging or outline extension. Numerous outward appearance acknowledgement techniques resort to multi-dimensional parameterization followed by weak models. In this unique situation, Mliki et al. [21] proposed a technique that can screen the power variety of outward appearance and to lessen the grouping disarray between outward appearances of classes. The methodology utilizes the vector field convolution technique to portion facial component shapes. Likewise, Cotret et al. [22] proposed a wavelet-based face acknowledgement technique hearty against face position and light varieties for continuous applications. Wang et al. [23] proposed an appearance acknowledgement strategy dependent on proof hypothesis and nearby surface where the facial picture is isolated into districts with significant acknowledgement highlights, and the local binary patterns (LBP) textural highlights of the areas are separated. Ongoing works demonstrated how profound learning models could be applied to outward appearance acknowledgement, Liu et al. [24] introduced a novel boosted deep belief network (BDBN) for playing out the three preparing stages iteratively in a brought together loopy system. Burkert et al. [25] proposed a CNN design for outward appearance acknowledgement. Mollahosseini et al. [26] likewise proposed a profound neural organization design to address the outward appearance acknowledgement issue over various notable standard face datasets.

Bargal et al. [12] proposed a factual encoding module to total edge includes that figure the mean, difference, least and limit of the casing highlight vectors. One restriction of these current collection strategies is that they disregard the significance of edges for outward appearance acknowledgement. Motivated by the consideration system [27] of machine interpretation and the neural conglomeration networks [28] of video face acknowledgement, Meng et al [9] proposed the frame attention networks to adaptively total casing highlights. The frame attention networks is intended to learn self-consideration portions and connection consideration parts for outline significance thinking in a start to finish design. The self-consideration pieces are straightforwardly gained from outline highlight, while the connection consideration portions are found out from the linked highlights of a video-level anchor highlight and casing highlights. Shan et al. [9] proposed Frame Attention Networks, it shows better execution looked at than other convolutional neural organization-based strategies with just facial highlights and accomplishes best in class execution on CK+. Zhang et al. [29] proposed a novel profound neural organization-driven facial element learning model that utilizes a few layers to describe the comparing connection between the SIFT, including vectors and their relating elevated level semantic data. Sun et al. [30] extricated facial tourist spots from a fixed number of SIFT highlights utilized as an information lattice to CNN engineering. The framework size is X × Y where X is the quantity of scale-invariant component change highlights, and Y is the size of each element. In addition, Sun et al. [30] proposed a combination of scale-invariant component change and profound convolution, the creators utilized partial least squares relapse and straight SVM to prepare these highlights. At that point, the yield from all classifiers is joined with the combination organization. In another contribution by Eng et al. in [31], HOG-based SVM method to recognize the expression on face is implemented and tested for the KDEF and JAFFE datasets providing a success rate of 80.95% and 76.19%, respectively. In *Proceedings of the IEEE International Conference on Computer Vision* [32], a profound learning procedure is received. The thought is to join two models; in the primary profound organization worldly appearance highlights from picture arrangements are removed. Then, worldly calculation highlights from fleeting facial milestone focuses are extricated constantly by profound organizations. The Islam et al. in [33] proposed a novel method of taking inter vector angles (IVA) as mathematical highlights, which end up being scale-invariant and individual autonomous. An element repetition decreased convolutional neural organization is introduced by Xie et al. [34].

Thirumalai et al. [35] proposed another variation of RSA called the memory efficient multi-key age plot. For delicate information, their plan helps in trading the data between cloud to IoT and IoT to IoT gadgets. This plan reuses the Rivest, Shamir, and Adleman plot with a Diophantine type of the nonlinear condition. He et al. [36] proposed a private cloud stage design that incorporates six layers as indicated by the particular necessities. This stage uses the message line as a cloud motor, and each layer subsequently accomplishes relative autonomy by this inexactly coupled methods for correspondences with the distribute/buy in system.

Chen et al. [37] examined another strategy that utilizes an entropy-based element extraction measure combined with Reed-Solomon mistake adjusting codes that can create deterministic piece successions from the yield of an iterative single direction change.

14.3 GENETIC APPROACH

We target identification of individual images taken from frontal cameras, where variations in the emotions could lead to erroneous detection. We have selected genetic approach to perform the encryption and decryption on the image which is to be transferred on the network. The image pixels are extracted and stored in a matrix; this is done using NumPy in Python. Then the pixel bits are swapped with a different bit to perform mutation. Mutation is done by 1s complement. In the odd pixel vector, perform 1s complement. For even pixel vector leave it as it is. Then the pixels are rearranged to perform crossover.

The following flowchart shows the steps used in encryption of the images (Figure 14.4).

To achieve crossover in the mutated image, we use Table 14.1. In order to ensure smooth functioning, we divide the image pixel vectors into 4-bit blocks. And then we perform the following crossover operation with the 2-bit (dibit) blocks of key.

Various standard datasets are commonly available for testing and training upcoming algorithms-most common among them being the UCI standard database and the Yale Face dataset. Apart from that, there are competitions that address this kind of applications, most popular among them being the series of EmotiW, the latest being EmotiW2020.

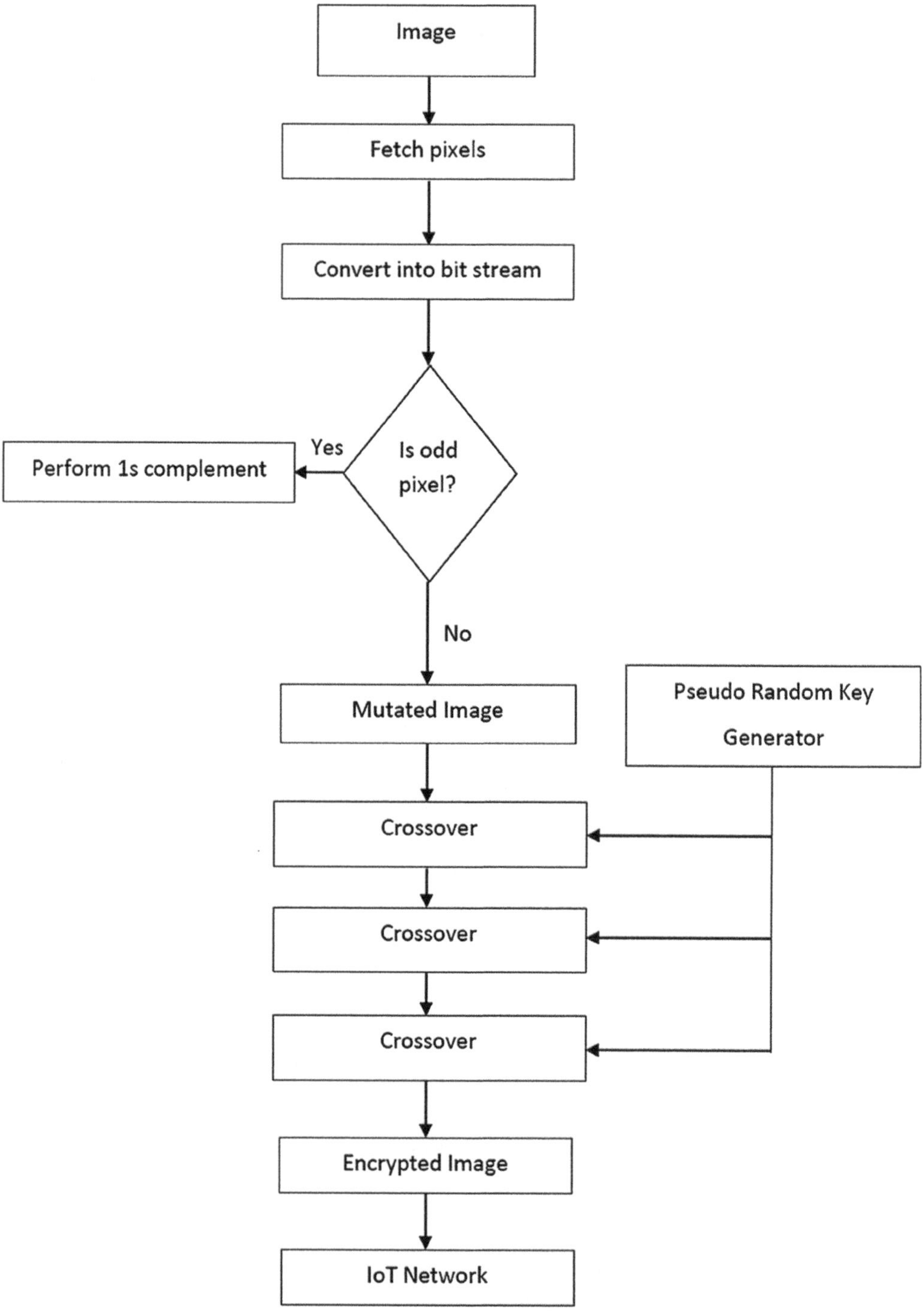

FIGURE 14.4 The flowchart of the proposed model with encryption using genetic approach.

TABLE 14.1
Crossover Table

Crossover		Image Bits															
		0000	**0001**	**0010**	**0011**	**0100**	**0101**	**0110**	**0111**	**1000**	**1001**	**1010**	**1011**	**1100**	**1101**	**1110**	**1111**
Key	00	0010	1100	0100	0001	0111	1010	1011	0110	1000	0101	0011	1111	1101	0000	1110	1001
	01	1110	1011	0010	1100	0100	0111	1101	0001	0101	0000	1111	1010	0011	1001	1000	0110
	10	0100	0010	0001	1011	1010	1101	0111	1000	1111	1001	1100	0101	0110	0011	0000	1110
	11	1011	1000	1100	0111	0001	1110	0010	1101	0110	1111	0000	1001	1010	0100	0101	0011

14.4 TRAINING

The model has been tested with approximately 60 unique appearances obtained from the standard Yale Face Dataset. Major challenging faces having poor lit facial images, images with spectacles, beard and extreme emotions are handpicked to test the proposed system. The model is prepared with various outward appearances of a similar individual. The model distinguishes various mindsets so that the biometric model is appropriately ready to recognize the individual's face paying little heed to their mindset. The model gets pictures utilizing Haar highlight-based course classifiers. Haar cascade utilizes AI-based methodology, where the course work is prepared from a ton of positive and negative pictures [38].

The following are the accompanying advances:

- Haar highlight selection
- Creating integral images
- Adaboost training
- Cascading classifiers

14.5 HAAR HIGHLIGHT SELECTION

A Haar include assesses contiguous rectangular locales at a particular area in a discovery window, summarizes the pixel powers in every district and ascertains the contrast between them (Figures 14.5–14.7).

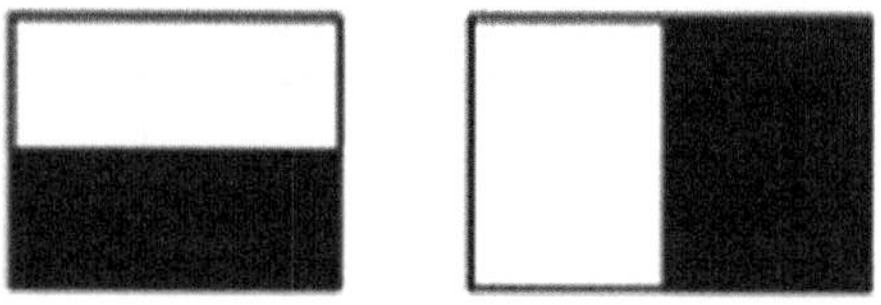

FIGURE 14.5 Edge features.

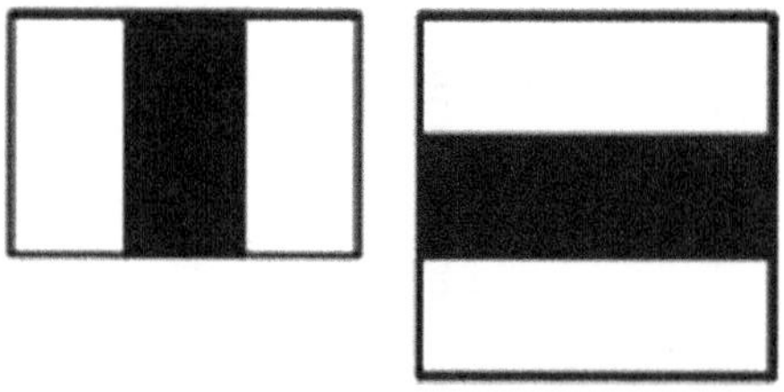

FIGURE 14.6 Line features.

FIGURE 14.7 Four rectangle feature.

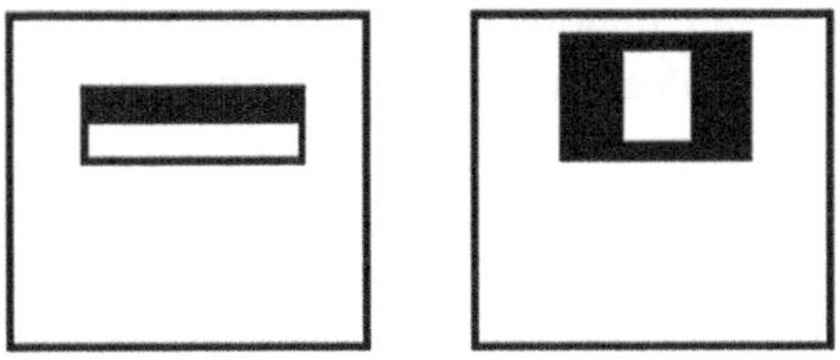

FIGURE 14.8 Eyes and nose detection.

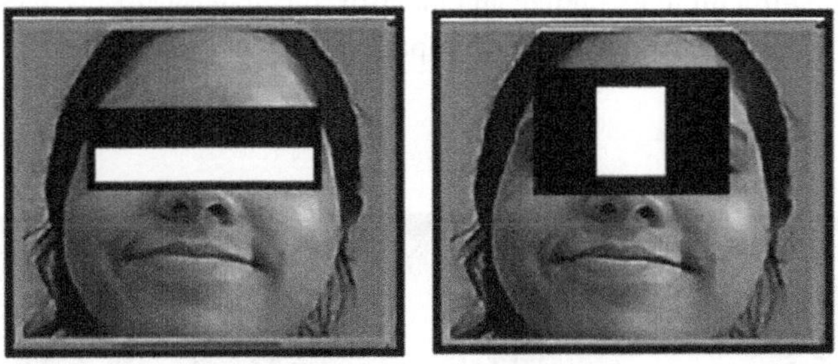

FIGURE 14.9 Creating integral image.

14.6 CREATING INTEGRAL IMAGES

Subsequent stage is incorporating Haar highlights with the facial pictures. The principal highlight centres around the property that the district of the eyes is regularly hazier than the area of the nose and cheeks. The subsequent component choose depends on the property that the eyes are hazier than the scaffold of the nose (Figures 14.8, 14.9).

14.7 ADABOOST TRAINING

The above preparing strategy depends on essential element extraction. To choose the best fit out of thousands of highlights is through Adaboost preparing which both chooses the best highlights and prepares the classifiers that utilize them. This calculation develops a solid classifier as a straight blend of weighted powerless classifiers.

14.8 CASCADING CLASSIFIER

The course classifier comprises an assortment of stages, where each stage is a troupe of feeble students. The frail students are basic classifiers called choice stumps. Each stage is prepared utilizing a procedure called boosting. Boosting gives the capacity to prepare an exceptionally exact classifier by taking a weighted normal of the decisions made by powerless learners [39] (Figure 14.10).

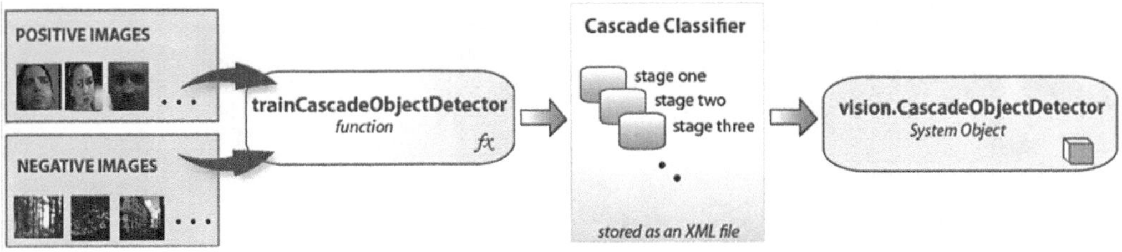

FIGURE 14.10 Cascading classifier.

Initially, we tested our proposed algorithm with standard Yale Face dataset. Then, we took all possible emotions for a single individual and tried to verify the success rate of emotion identification (Figure 14.11).

Performing mutation on Figure 14.12 results in the following figure.

Next, we performed a triple crossover on the mutated image results in the following figure (Figure 14.14).

The confusion matrix shows the performance analysis of the model on the single individual (Table 14.2).

Thereafter, we identified challenging faces from the entire database and had a collection of 64 facial images that are difficult to recognize and identify. Taken in sets of two each, this is the matrix of 4 × 8 faces, having variations in the images captured by frontal cameras.

FIGURE 14.11 Few faces from the Yale Face dataset.

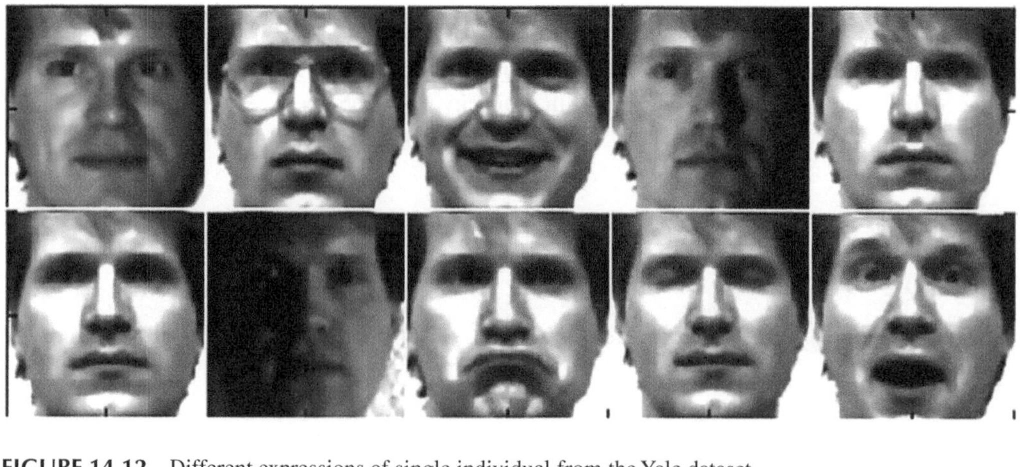

FIGURE 14.12 Different expressions of single individual from the Yale dataset.

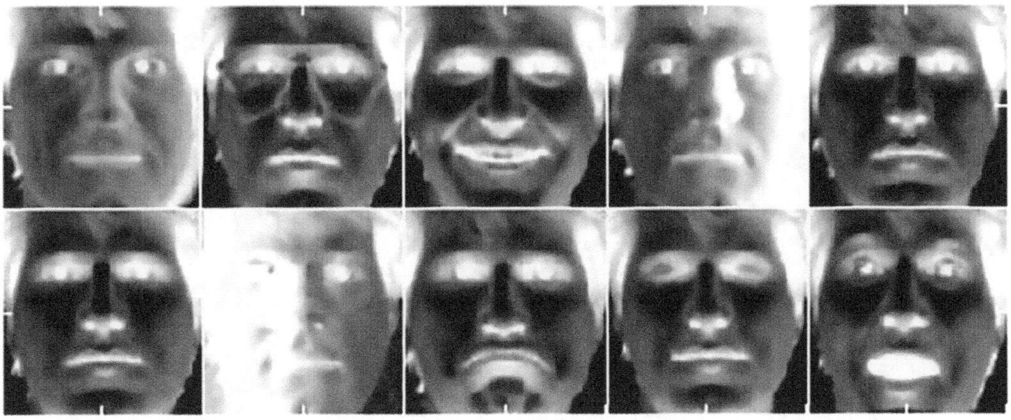

FIGURE 14.13 Mutated image of Figure 14.12.

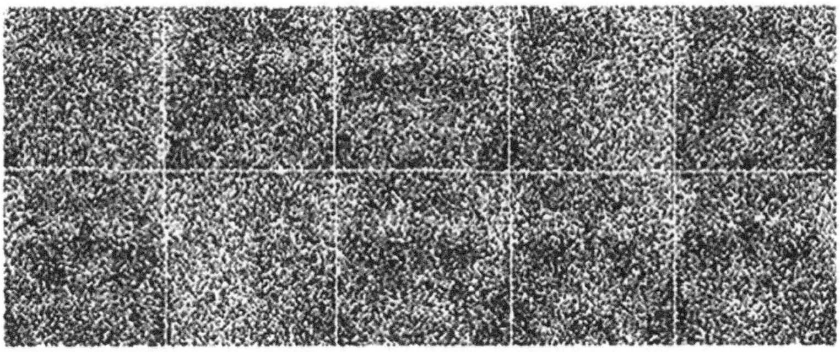

FIGURE 14.14 Triple crossover image of the mutated image of Figure 14.13.

TABLE 14.2
Confusion Matrix of Yale University Dataset; Single Individual

Accuracy	Predicted Expression					
Actual Expression	Expression	Alert	Daydreaming	Drowsy	Yawning	Sleeping
	Alert	100	–	–	–	–
	Daydreaming	11	89	–	–	–
	Drowsy	–	9	90	–	1
	Yawning	–	–	–	100	–
	Sleeping	–	–	2	–	98

Performing mutation on Figure 14.15 results in the following figure.

Performing a triple crossover on the mutated image results in the following figure (Figure 14.17).

The following confusion matrix shows the performance analysis of these few handpicked images of Yale University dataset (Table 14.3).

The confusion matrix is generated to check the accuracy of the result. In the above table, it is observed that when the user is alert, our system is resulting in an alert almost 90% of the time. For yawning it is 100% accuracy. For daydreaming, it is 89% accuracy. For drowsy, it's 88% accuracy. We can conclude that the prediction percentage of our system is optimum.

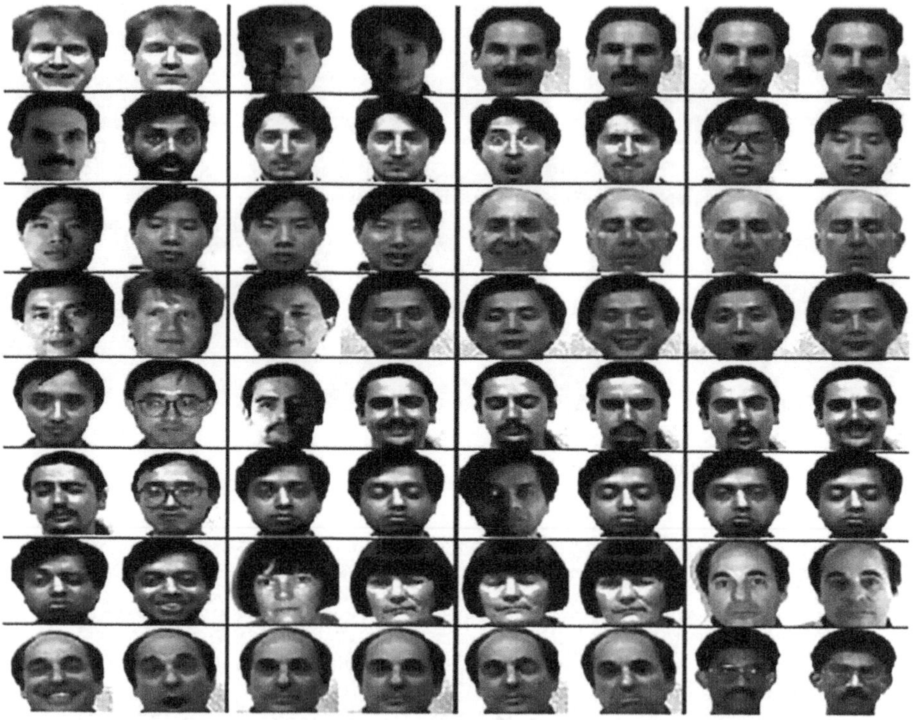

FIGURE 14.15 Challenging faces from the Yale dataset.

FIGURE 14.16 Mutated image of the images of Figure 14.15.

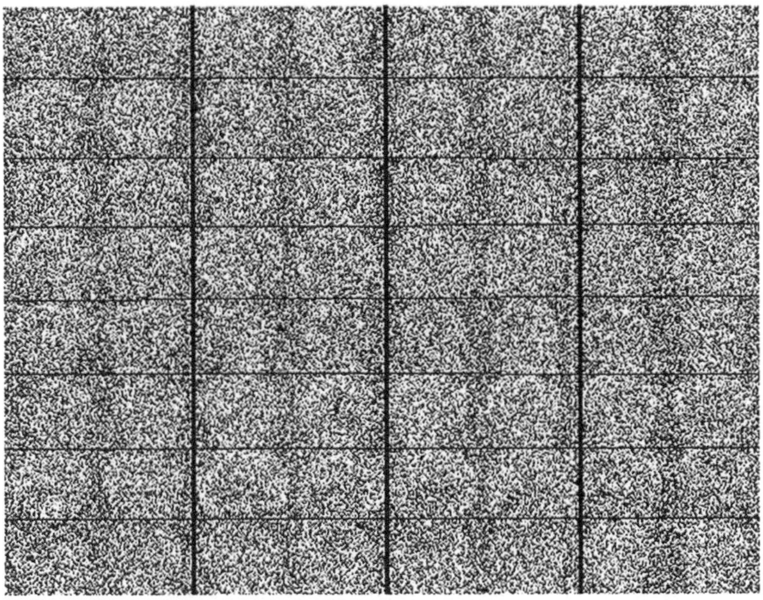

FIGURE 14.17 Triple crossover image on the image of Figure 14.16.

TABLE 14.3
Confusion Matrix of Yale University Dataset; Handpicked Challenging Cases

Accuracy	Predicted Expression					
Actual Expression	Expression	Alert	Daydreaming	Drowsy	Yawning	Sleeping
	Alert	90	2	1	–	–
	Daydreaming	8	89	–	–	3
	Drowsy	–	2	88	–	10
	Yawning	–	–	–	100	–
	Sleeping	–	5	11	–	84

14.8.1 Model Testing for User

Using the above-mentioned steps, the faces are captured using OpenCV. Feature extraction includes identification of eyes, nose and mouth to conclude the expression (Figures 14.18, 14.19).

The model has been trained with different facial expressions so that it can recognize faces regardless of the different moods of the person (Figure 14.20).

The images are fetched from OpenCV, then it is converted to grayscale using Python. Then mutation and crossover are performed on the image to achieve the resulting image (Figures 14.21, 14.22).

A is the original image. It is converted to grayscale using python resulting in B. Mutation is done in which for odd pixel vector, perform 1s complement. For even pixel vector leave it as it is. This results in C. Then crossover is done for 1 time and we receive D. Repetition of crossover provides a higher butterfly effect. We have found that three-level crossovers are the most optimum. The following confusion matrix shows the performance analysis of the model on our facial image (Table 14.4).

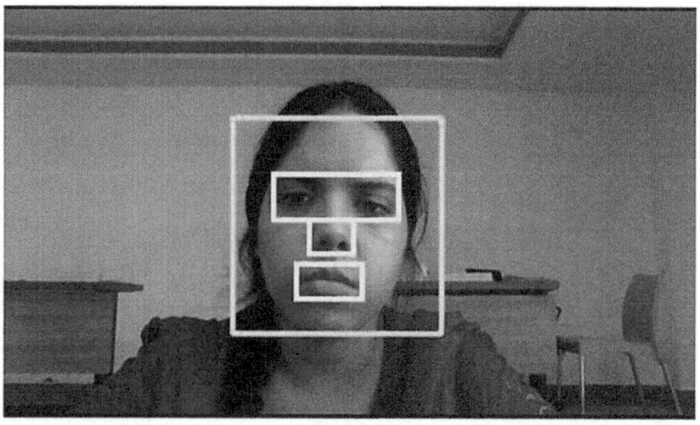

FIGURE 14.18 Feature extraction.

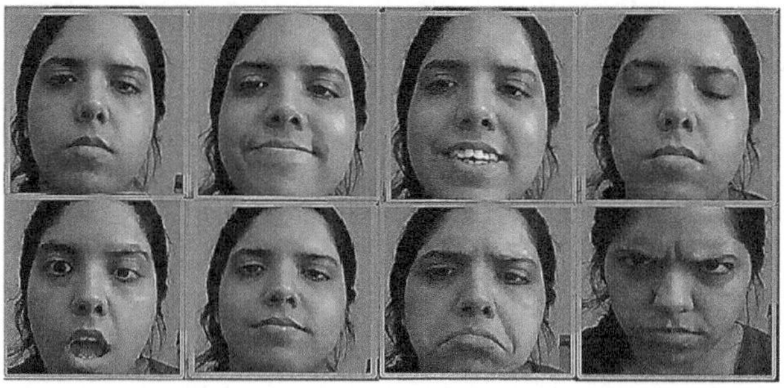

FIGURE 14.19 Facial expressions for training.

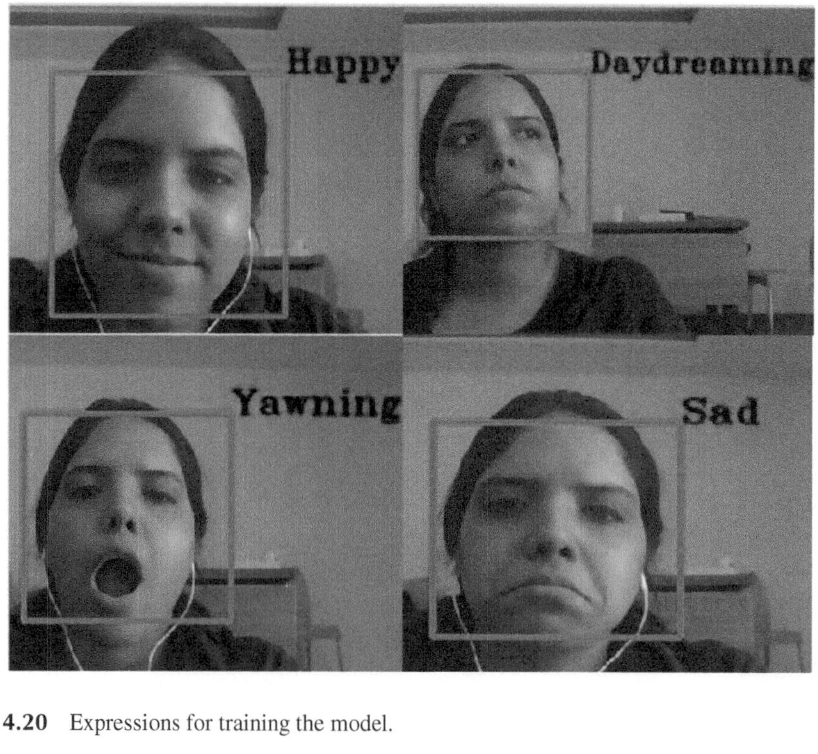

FIGURE 14.20 Expressions for training the model.

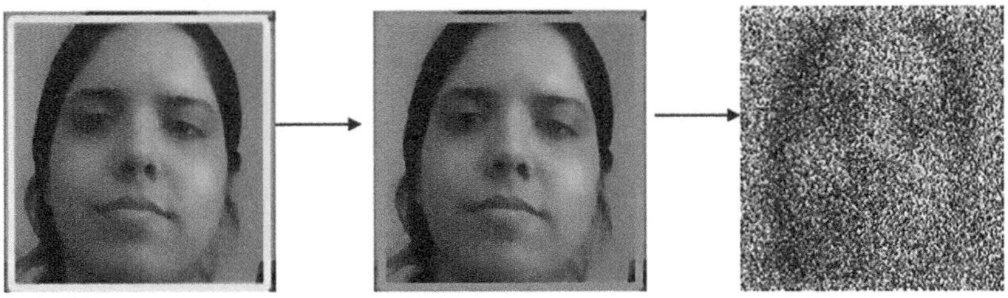

FIGURE 14.21 Triple hybrid crossover.

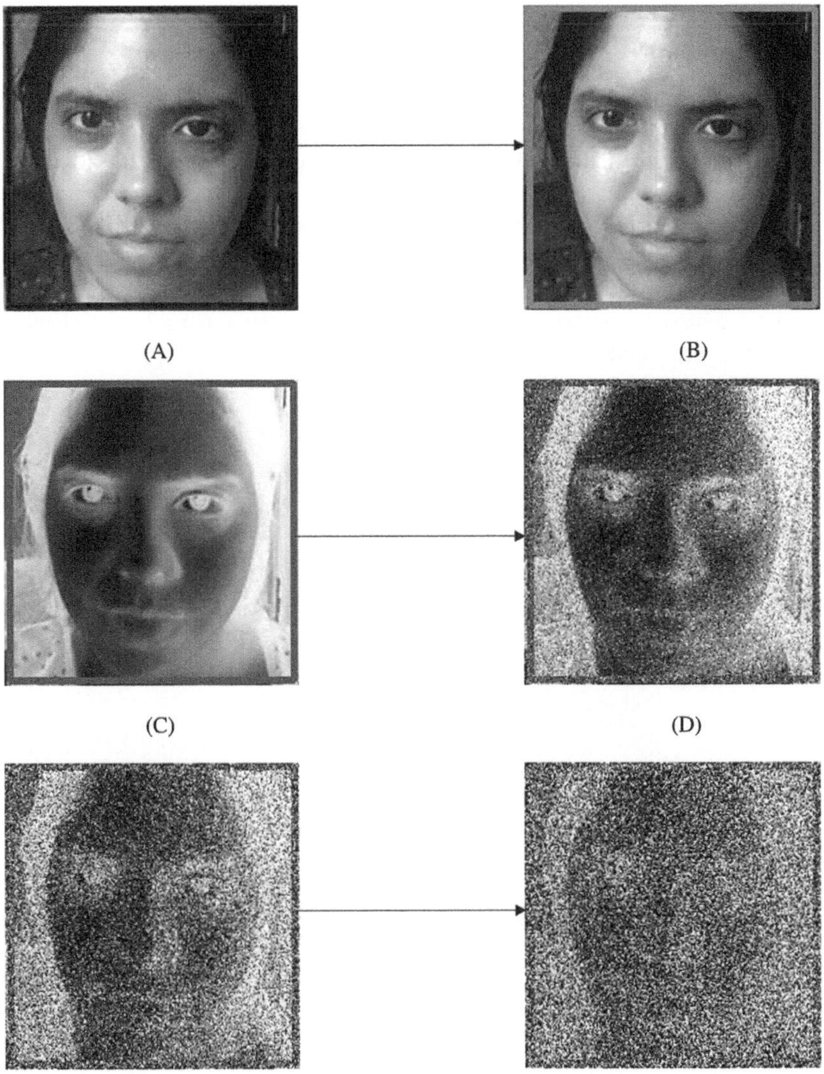

(A) (B)

(C) (D)

(E) (F)

FIGURE 14.22 Step by step mutation and crossover.

TABLE 14.4
Confusion Matrix on User Face

Accuracy		Predicted Expression				
Actual Expression	Expression	Alert	Daydreaming	Drowsy	Yawning	Sleeping
	Alert	99	1	–	–	–
	Daydreaming	10	90	–	–	–
	Drowsy	–	9	91	–	–
	Yawning	–	–	–	100	–
	Sleeping	–	–	–	–	100

14.8.2 IoT Simulation

After extraction and identification of the facial expression, the next task is to securely transfer the data on the network.

OMNET ++ is a component-based C++ simulator library and is generally used for academic learning and understanding.

The simulation of IoT devices connected together over a network is done using OMNET++ (Figures 14.23, 14.24).

Finally, a network is formed and the images are transferred to this network (Figure 14.25).

Using genetic approach, the extracted image pixels are mutated using 1s complement over odd pixel. Crossover is performed using Table 14.1 (Figures 14.26–14.29).

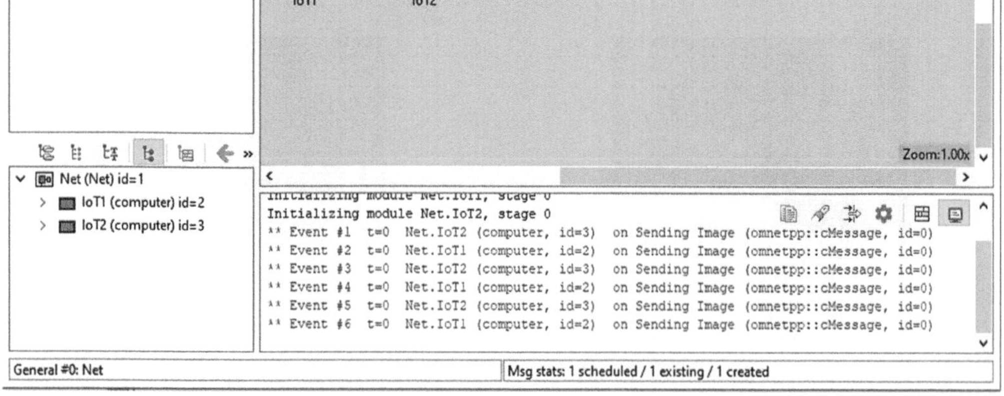

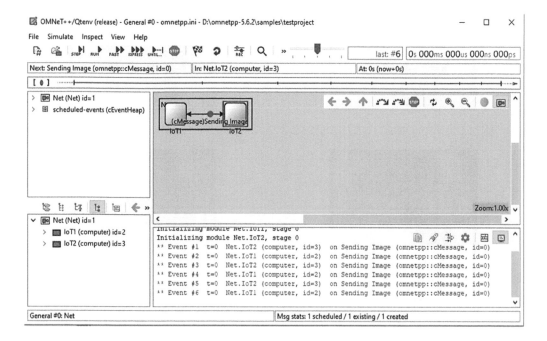

FIGURE 14.23 Step by step implementation of network units.

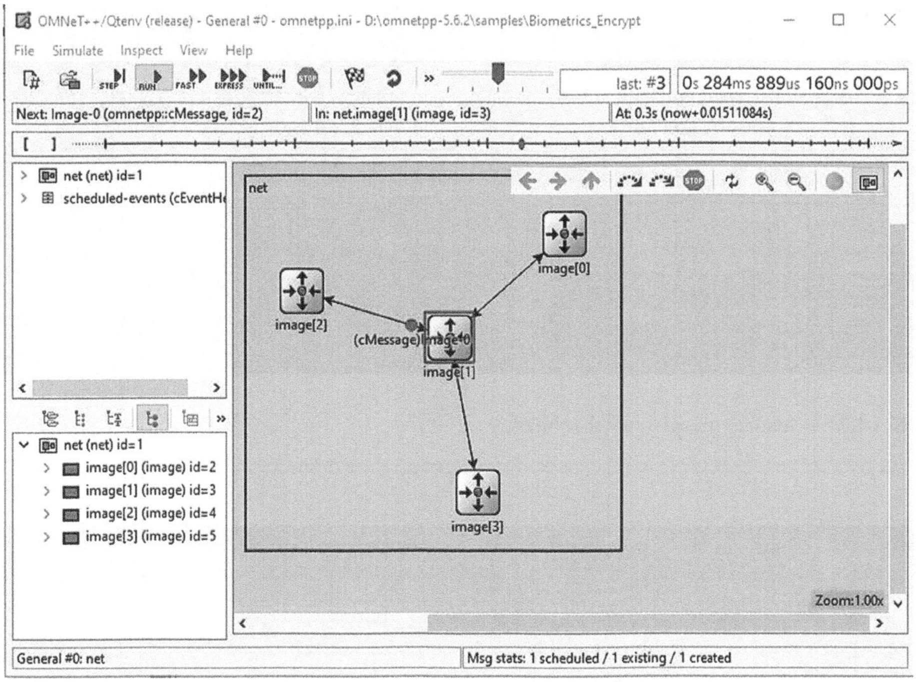

FIGURE 14.24 More number of network units getting added to the system.

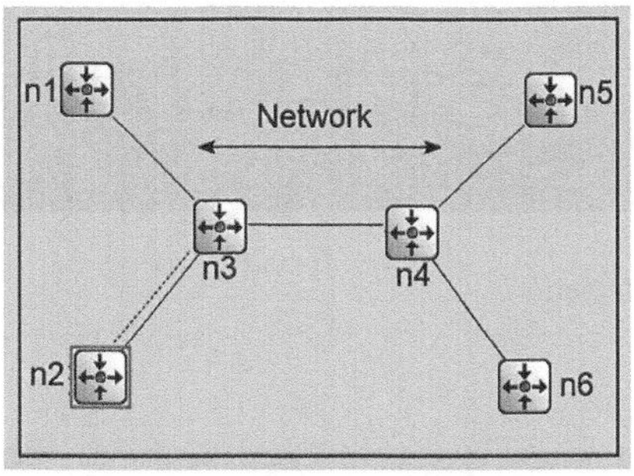

FIGURE 14.25 The resultant network.

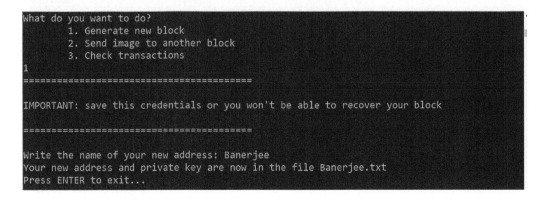

```
What do you want to do?
        1. Generate new block
        2. Send image to another block
        3. Check transactions
1
========================================

IMPORTANT: save this credentials or you won't be able to recover your block

========================================

Write the name of your new address: Banerjee
Your new address and private key are now in the file Banerjee.txt
Press ENTER to exit...
```

FIGURE 14.26 Generating new block.

```
What do you want to do?
        1. Generate new block
        2. Send image to another block
        3. Check transactions
2
From: introduce your block address (public key)
FfeUPqVGtSwENQplPcA2daVIPG3XeQ/VA3/yWIdVHkz3wqpB5NwBGp75ps+uJ+JDaJ2wzReECk+BSHWy8wg6og==
Introduce your private key
072d21a4e452e10012560a1da1cbd793b1ecc4c91e8819a4df9a76c83e2b47ce
To: introduce destination block address
30LQ1tgUG98dO5d6ZpdFokMKkGTo0hELjcPTGVd8LCQ5bI3qbSDb5cvZ//qktl+xRx+GD0E4C+Y9N7+jnr0eqg==
Image: number stating which image you want to send
101587
========================================
```

FIGURE 14.27 Sending image to another block.

```
Is everything correct?

From: FfeUPqVGtSwENQplPcA2daVIPG3XeQ/VA3/yWIdVHkz3wqpB5NwBGp75ps+uJ+JDaJ2wzReECk+BSHWy8wg
6og==
Private Key: 072d21a4e452e10012560a1da1cbd793b1ecc4c91e8819a4df9a76c83e2b47ce
To: 30LQ1tgUG98dO5d6ZpdFokMKkGTo0hELjcPTGVd8LCQ5bI3qbSDb5cvZ//qktl+xRx+GD0E4C+Y9N7+jnr0eq
g==
Image ID: 101587

y/n
y
Transaction submission successful

Press ENTER to exit...
```

FIGURE 14.28 Transaction completion.

```
dress-34nf3i4nflkn3oi', 'image': 1}]}", "hash": "6e8710a9920b8afb5c85f2cce15d49292946123f
1de8ec5e512c1970007b3abc"}, {"index": "6", "timestamp": "1601613926.7166326", "data": "{'
proof-of-work': 2280672, 'transactions': [{'from': 'network', 'to': 'q3nf394hjg-random-mi
ner-address-34nf3i4nflkn3oi', 'image': 1}]}", "hash": "7ae8f65cfd26d19bb593929cdf4677ff4b
fbadc5b030b0cb0b86df4f47950373"}, {"index": "7", "timestamp": "1601613933.6120903", "data
": "{'proof-of-work': 4561344, 'transactions': [{'from': 'network', 'to': 'q3nf394hjg-ran
dom-miner-address-34nf3i4nflkn3oi', 'image': 1}]}", "hash": "863e25349e1ee3dd74d12684960e
8af6bb5658fcae1605d71a26e02a12f7830f"}, {"index": "8", "timestamp": "1601613941.6101308",
 "data": "{'proof-of-work': 9122688, 'transactions': [{'from': 'network', 'to': 'q3nf394h
jg-random-miner-address-34nf3i4nflkn3oi', 'image': 1}]}", "hash": "57aa8b581618aee295ca83
283522f6ab293bf9b202eb4df9e83d42bfa983bc31"}, {"index": "9", "timestamp": "1601613952.534
1434", "data": "{'proof-of-work': 18245376, 'transactions': [{'from': 'FfeUPqVGtSwENQplPc
A2daVIPG3XeQ/VA3/yWIdVHkz3wqpB5NwBGp75ps+uJ+JDaJ2wzReECk+BSHWy8wg6og==', 'to': '30LQ1tgUG
98dO5d6ZpdFokMKkGTo0hELjcPTGVd8LCQ5bI3qbSDb5cvZ//qktl+xRx+GD0E4C+Y9N7+jnr0eqg==', 'image'
: '101587', 'signature': 'XlwhXIGmsK6doMfftvGnEFW/1+Y24fpfiVkaC7DaEaVI0zGqBPEFHeQPAkFaPnH
ndAx5HX5Y8isYpvvQUrgVIw==', 'message': '1601613950'}, {'from': 'network', 'to': 'q3nf394h
jg-random-miner-address-34nf3i4nflkn3oi', 'image': 1}]}", "hash": "175cff72b1637c2a0b00d9
4475cdfc1f9158e3846e58c5bb487cb829b9f6566d"}]
Press ENTER to exit...
```

FIGURE 14.29 Transaction status.

14.9 OUTCOME

The genetic-based approach to deal with variation and hybridization is utilized on the picture information to give better execution. There exist extraordinary public-private key sets, more than hundreds for information encryption and unscrambling. The butterfly impact is utilized to decide the exhibition of the proposed uneven code. Results show that our code is furnishing the butterfly impact with above half affectability of key and plaintext when single hybrid is performed. Moreover, triple hybrid prompts 75% affectability. Expanding the quantity of hybrids more than three prompts expanded affectability however makes it difficult to unscramble the ciphertext, consequently prompting information misfortune. Thus, it is inferred that triple hybrid is the 'Goldie Locks zone' for this code.

REFERENCES

[1] www.robots.net, last assessed on the 15th of Nov, 2020.

[2] Diligentias.com, last assessed on the 15th of Nov, 2020.

[3] Chellappa, R., Wilson, C., & Sirohey, S. (1995). Human and machine recognition of faces: A survey. *Proceedings of the IEEE*, 83(5), 705–741. doi:10.1109/5.381842

[4] Wechsler, H., Phillips, P., Bruce, V., Soulie, F., & Huang, T. (1996). *Face Recognition: From Theory to Applications*, Springer-Verlag.

[5] Shan, C., Gong, S., & McOwan, P. W. (2009). Facial expression recognition based on Local Binary Patterns: A comprehensive study. *Image and Vision Computing*, 27(6), 803–816. doi:10.1016/j.imavis.2008.08.005

[6] Aravinda, C. V., Meng, Lin, & Uday Kumar Reddy, K. R. (2019). An approach for signature recognition using contours based technique. *International Conference on Advanced Mechatronic Systems (ICAMechS)*, Japan.

[7] Aravinda, C. V., Meng, Lin, Uday Kumar Reddy, K. R. & Prabhu, Amar. (2019). Signature recognition and verification using multiple classifiers combination of Hu's and HOG features. *2019 International Conference on Advanced Mechatronic Systems (ICAMechS)*, Japan.

[8] Hietmeyer, R. (2010). Biometric identification promises fast and secure processing of airline passengers. *The Int'l Civil Aviation Organization Journal*, 55(9), 10–11.

[9] Meng, D., Peng, X., Wang, K., & Qiao, Y. (2019). Frame attention networks for facial expression recognition in videos. *2019 IEEE International Conference on Image Processing (ICIP)*. doi:10.1109/icip.2019.8803603

[10] Littlewort, G., Bartlett, M. S., Fasel, I., Susskind, J., & Movellan, J. (2006). Dynamics of facial expression extracted automatically from video. *Image and Vision Computing*, 24(6), 615–625. doi:10.1016/j.imavis.2005.09.011

[11] Yichuan, T. (2013). Deep learning using linear support vector machines. CS, 2013.

[12] Bargal, S. A., Barsoum, E., Ferrer, C. C., & Zhang, C. (2016). Emotion recognition in the wild from videos using images. *Proceedings of the ACM International Conference on Multimodal Interaction - ICMI 2016*. doi:10.1145/2993148.2997627

[13] Knyazev, B., Shvetsov, R., Efremova, N., & Kuharenko, A. (2017). Convolutional neural networks pretrained on large face recognition datasets for emotion classification from video. *Proceedings of the ACM International Conference on Multimodal Interaction – ICMI 2017*.

[14] Hochreiter, S., & Schmidhuber, J. (1997). *Long short-term memory, Neural Computation. Neural computation*, 9(8), 1735–1780.

[15] Tran, D., Bourdev, L., Fergus, R., Torresani, L., & Paluri, M. (2015). Learning spatiotemporal features with 3D convolutional networks. *2015 IEEE International Conference on Computer Vision (ICCV)*. doi:10.1109/iccv.2015.510

[16] Ouyang, X., Kawaai, S., Goh, E., Shen, S., Ding, W., Ming, H., & Huang, D. (2017). Audio-visual emotion recognition using deep transfer learning and multiple temporal models. *Proceedings of the ACM International Conference on Multimodal Interaction – ICMI 2017*.

[17] Vielzeuf, V., Pateux, S., & Jurie, F. (2017). Temporal multimodal fusion for video emotion classification in the wild. *Proceedings of the 19th ACM International Conference on Multimodal Interaction - ICMI 2017*. doi:10.1145/3136755.3143011

[18] Yan, J., Zheng, W., Cui, Z., Tang, C., Zhang, T., & Zong, Y. (2018). Multi-cue fusion for emotion recognition in the wild. *Neurocomputing*, 309, 27–35. doi:10.1016/j.neucom.2018.03.068

[19] Jung, H., Lee, J., Yim, J., Park, S., & Kim, J. (2015). Joint fine-tuning in deep neural networks for facial expression recognition. *ICCV 2015*.

[20] Kahou, S., Pal, C., Bouthillier, X., Froumenty, P., Memisevic, R., Vincent, P., Courville, A., Bengio, Y., & Ferrari, R. (2013). Combining modality specific deep neural networks for emotion recognition in video. *Proceedings of the ACM International Conference on Multimodal Interaction – ICMI 2013*.

[21] Mliki, H., Fourati, N., Hammami, M., & BenAbdallah, H. (2013). Data mining-based facial expressions recognition system. In *SCAI*, 185–194

[22] Cotret, P., Chevobbe, S., & Darouich, M. (2015). Embedded wavelet-based face recognition under variable position. *Real-Time Image and Video Processing 2015*. doi:10.1117/12.2083046

[23] Wang, W., Chang, F., Liu, Y., & Wu, X. (2016). Expression recognition method based on evidence theory and local texture. *Multimedia Tools and Applications*, 76(5), 7365–7379. doi:10.1007/s11042-016-3419-x

[24] Liu, P., Han, S., Meng, Z., & Tong, Y. (2014). Facial expression recognition via a boosted deep belief network. *2014 IEEE Conference on Computer Vision and Pattern Recognition*. doi:10.1109/cvpr.2014.233

[25] Burkert, P., Trier, F., Afzal, M., Dengel, A., & Liwicki, M. (2015). Dexpression: Deep convolutional neural network for expression recognition. *arXiv preprint arXiv:1509.05371*.

[26] Mollahosseini, A., Chan, D., & Mahoor, M. H. (2016). Going deeper in facial expression recognition using deep neural networks. *2016 IEEE Winter Conference on Applications of Computer Vision (WACV)*. doi:10.1109/wacv.2016.7477450

[27] Vaswani, A., Shazeer, N., Parmar, N., Uszkoreit, J., Jones, L., Gomez, A., Kaiser, L., & Polosukhin, I. (2017). Attention is all you need. *Advances in Neural Information Processing Systems*, 30.

[28] Yang, J., Ren, P., Zhang, D., Chen, D., Wen, F., Li, H., & Hua, G. (2017). Neural aggregation network for video face recognition. *2017 IEEE Conference on Computer Vision and Pattern Recognition (CVPR)*. doi:10.1109/cvpr.2017.554

[29] Zhang, T., Zheng, W., Cui, Z., Zong, Y., Yan, J., & Yan, K. (2016). A deep neural network-driven feature learning method for multi-view facial expression recognition, *IEEE Transactions on Multimedia*, 18(12), 2528–2536.

[30] Sun, B., Li, L., Zhou, G., & He, J. (2016). Facial expression recognition in the wild based on multimodal texture features. *Journal of Electronic Imaging*, 25(6), 061407. doi:10.1117/1.jei.25.6.061407

[31] Eng, S. K., Ali, H., Cheah, A. Y., & Chong, Y. F. (2019). Facial expression recognition in JAFFE and KDEF Datasets using histogram of oriented gradients and support vector machine. *5th International Conference on Man Machine Systems, IOP Conf. Series: Materials Science and Engineering 705*.

[32] Jung, H., Lee, S., Yim, J., Park, S., & Kim J. (2015). Joint fine-tuning in deep neural networks for facial expression recognition. *Proceedings of the IEEE International Conference on Computer Vision*, 2015, 2983–2991.

[33] Islam, R., Ahuja, K., Karmakar, S., & Barbhuiya, F. (2016). Sention: A framework for sensing facial expressions. *arXiv preprint arXiv:1608.04489*.

[34] Xie, S., & Hu, H. (2017). Facial expression recognition with FRR-CNN. *Electronics Letters*, 53(4), 235–237. doi:10.1049/el.2016.4328

[35] Thirumalai, C., & Kar, H. (2017). Memory Efficient Multi Key (MEMK) generation scheme for secure transportation of sensitive data over cloud and IoT devices. *International Conference on Innovations in Power and Advanced Computing Technologies [i-PACT2017], 978-1-5090-5682-8 /17/$31.00 ©2017 IEEE.*

[36] He, C., Fan, X., & Li, Y. (2013). Toward ubiquitous healthcare services with a novel efficient cloud platform. *IEEE Transactions on Biomedical Engineering*, 60(1), 230–234. doi:10.1109/tbme.2012.2222404

[37] Chen, B., & Chandran, V. (2007). Biometric based cryptographic key generation from faces. *9th Biennial Conference of the Australian Pattern Recognition Society on Digital Image Computing Techniques and Applications (DICTA 2007)*. doi:10.1109/dicta.2007.4426824

[38] Docs, OpenCV. Face detection using haar cascades. OpenCV: Face Detection Using Haar Cascades (2017). docs.opencv.org/3.3.0/d7/d8b/tutorial_py_face_detection.html

[39] Banerjee, B., & Patel, J. (2016). A symmetric key block cipher to provide confidentiality in wireless sensor networks. *INFOCOMP Journal of Computer Science*, 15(1), 12–18.

15 Blockchain-Based Web 4.0
Decentralized Web for Decentralized Cloud Computing

Arvind Panwar
Universal School of Information Communication and Technology, Guru Gobind Singh Indraprastha University, Delhi, India

Shyla
Research scholar Guru Gobind Singh Indraprastha University, Delhi, India

Vishal Bhatnagar
Netaji Subhas University of Technology (East Campus), Delhi, India

CONTENTS

15.1 INTRODUCTION

The Web is a collection of information systems identified by a uniform resource locator linked by hypertext and is accessible over the internet. The Web is a communication channel that has been used by several generations in a short span. The continuous growth of technology leads to the Web's evolution that offers [1] a piece of rapid information and knowledge diffusion channel by allowing companies to improve their performance and deliver new services assistance to their users. Web technological growth will enable consumers to have an excellent medium to commune with organizations and manifest their outlook about services and products.

DOI: 10.1201/9781003155577-19

The first phase of the Web is defined as Web 1.0 and was extended during the 1990s. Anwar [2] found that Web 1.0 was a read-only Web system where users are allowed to act as a viewer and can only read without having access to edit or deploy any modifications.

The other part of the Web is currently introduced as Web 4.0, which is early. Web 4.0 is a symbiotic, ubiquitous Web and ultra-intelligent electronic agent. [3, 4] found that the symbiotic Web's motive is to create an interaction between machines and humans. Web 4.0 is as robust as humans and leads the headway in evolving telecommunications and controlled interfaces expansion on nanotechnology. Web 4.0 makes machines more capable of allowing systems to read content from the Web and respond by executing and deciding how to manage first for faster access of websites to obtain superior quality performance by building more user-friendly interfaces.

This study represents a comprehensive structure of the World Wide Web that means clarifying and analyzing the concept of Web 4.0. Authors followed a literature review approach to indulge the various ideas and lead toward Web 4.0. The paper is divided into different sections: Section 15.1 is the Introduction; Section 15.2 is History Web; Section 15.3, What Is blockchain; Section 15.4, Working of Blockchain; Section 15.5, Centralized to Decentralized Internetwork; Section 15.6, Features of 4.0; Section 15.7, Comparison of Different Web Generations; Section 15.8, Benefits of Web 4.0; Section 15.9, Example of Web 4.0; Section 15.10, Decentralized Storage and Web 4.0: Future of Cloud Computing; and Section 15.11 concludes the overall paper.

15.2 HISTORY OF WEB

In late 1989, Tim Burners-Lee introduced the term "Web." The tendency of the World Wide Web was determined by three deviations that are correlated with three models: the World Wide Web (Web 1.0), the social Web (Web 2.0), the semantic Web (Web 3.0), and the WebOS that is (Web 4.0). Newman et al. and Nath et al. [5, 6] found that the World Wide Web goes over innumerable stages of change throughot its life. The Web is now inclined toward more data-centric phases in the context of Web 4.0 by going through the end of constant evolution.

Figure 15.1 shows the emergence of technological trends going through several generations ranging from Web 1.0 to Web 4.0.

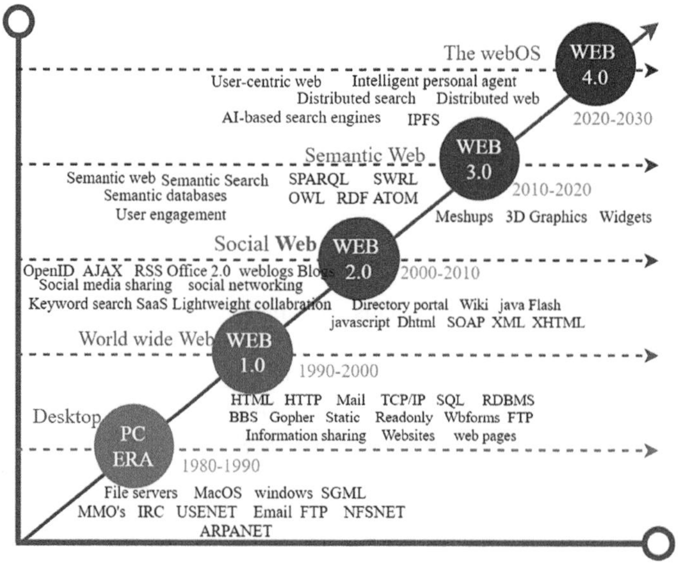

FIGURE 15.1 History of the Web.

- **PC era –** This era is known as the desktop age when the desktop was connected to the internet and transferred files over the internet. [7] found that there was no World Wide Web to share the information. This period refers to the file server age before the year 1990 when data was stored in files.
- **Web 1.0 –** Web 1.0 was defined as Web of information connections that lasted from 1989 to 2000 and is considered the Web's first generation. Tim Berners-Lee, World Wide Web pioneer, acknowledges Web 1.0 as a "read-only." Web that provides a communication between user and website for information exchange but cannot make any modification or fully interact with the website. Web 1.0 includes HTTP, HTML, and URI as core web protocols.
- **Web 2.0 –** Web 2.0 was introduced in 2000 as a second-generation Web by Dale Dougherty. It was considered as a read-write web that allows social interaction among large global crowds with common interests. Davis (2010) found that Web 2.0 brings more interaction, and users can leave many of the controls they have used with less supervision. Web 2.0 is also known as the social Web. Social networking website is getting the attention of internet users, where users make friends on the internet and share life moments, chat, and send pictures with friends. Chat room on Yahoo Messenger and Orkut was very popular at the starting of the 2000s. At the end of 2008–2009, Facebook started getting user attention as the first social media networking choice.
- **Web 3.0 –** Web 3.0 is the contemporary and progressive model correlated with Web 2.0. Web 3.0 was introduced as a third-generation Web, which was first coined by John Markoff in 2006. (Henke et al., 2016) found that Web 3.0 is used to define structured data and link them to provide automation, integration, more effective discovery, and reuse across various applications. Web 3.0 can boost the receptiveness of internetwork, data management, innovation, and creativity simulation.
- **Web 4.0 –** Web 4.0 is a linked, intelligent, and open Web. It will load the page quicker as compared to another web. With the help of IPFS (Interplanetary File System), Web 4.0 can download files with light speed and play online video without buffering compared to Web 3.0. IPFS makes the Web decentralized, and it is a protocol for peer-to-peer networking to store data using the distributed file system. Web 4.0 is like a human brain with the help of AI and Machine learning. Web 4.0 is branded as the WebOS sometimes because the whole Web work as an operating system to share data very securely from one system to another.

15.3 BLOCKCHAIN

Blockchain is a distributed ledger technology (DLT) based on a peer-to-peer (P2P) topology that allows all the users globally to store data on thousands of servers by letting anyone on the network to see every entry in near real-time, which makes it difficult for the user to gain control of the network. Blockchain will take a few more years to become more efficient for sharing information between open and private networks. Biswas et al. and Cyran [8, 9] found that the first blockchain is built around a P2P system, which is a public electronic ledger that is openly shared between different users and is each time-stamped and linked to the previous one to create an unchangeable record of transactions, that data becomes another block in the chain, and these blocks of data forms blockchain. The blockchain can be updated by using different consensus algorithms between participants in the system, and once data is stored, it can never be removed. It is a write-once technology and appends many times, making blockchain a verifiable and auditable record for each transaction.

15.4 WORKING OF BLOCKCHAIN

A transaction is initiated in a blockchain by signing its private key by a user or a node. The unique digital signature is generated by a private key to ensure that it is not amendable. Dai et al. and T. H. E. G. Decentralization et al. [10, 11] found that the digital signature will abate and change awfully

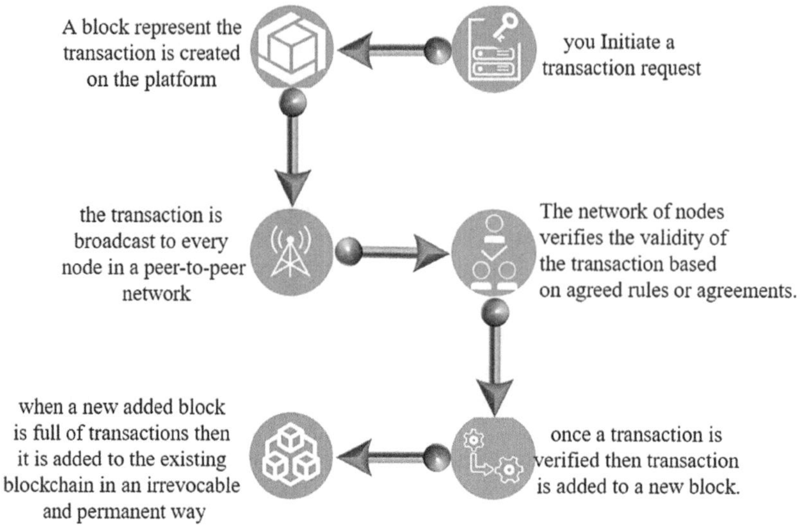

FIGURE 15.2 Working of blockchain.

if an intruder tries to alter information and is unable to authenticate. The data is then transmitted to the systems where the valid and invalid information is authenticated by blockchain methods or algorithms called consensus algorithms. The verified information is placed in a ledger to secure data from any alteration with the accompanied time-stamp value and unique ID that creates a chain of blocks.

Figure 15.2 shows the working of the blockchain, and Figure 15.3 shows blockchain authentication. In the blockchain, there are validated authentication and verifiers to check the requested connection's validity to join any network.

The requester retrieves the RSA public key of the verifier, and then the requester encrypts its blockchain address with the RSA public key and sends it to the uses the blockchain address to retrieve the requester's RSA public key [12]. Verifier then generates a random string. Hash and time-stamp and encrypt it with requesters RSA public key; the verifier then sends the encrypted hash to the requester. The requester uses its own RSA private key to decrypt the hash and signs it with the private key. Then the requester encrypts an envelope containing the digital signatures, the signed hash, and their blockchain address and sends it to the verifier; the verifier then decrypts it with its private key and verifies whether the signature is valid or not, and once the signature is verified, the requester is permitted to enter the network.

A blockchain project can't be complete without digital signature and Hashing, and even we can't think about blockchain without these two [13, 14]. Hashing offers a technique for each node in the blockchain to approve the present state, whereas digital signatures deliver a method to guarantee those entire transactions are only made by the authentic proprietors. Figure 15.3 shows an example of blockchain authentication with the help of the RSA cryptosystem. The majority of blockchain platforms use the ECC (elliptic curve cryptography) algorithm to make digital signatures known as ECDSA (elliptic curve digital signature algorithm). Even though RSA is a very secure asymmetric key cryptography, it has a huge critical problem, so researchers find an alternative to RSA is ECC. RSA and ECC are both asymmetric key cryptography.

15.4.1 Elliptic Curve Cryptography

Elliptic curves are not directly related to ellipses, but they are used to calculate the length of a curve. Elliptic curves are a cubic equation with two variables. The general equation is:

$$Y2 + Q1XY + Q2Y = X3 + P1X2 + P2X + P3$$

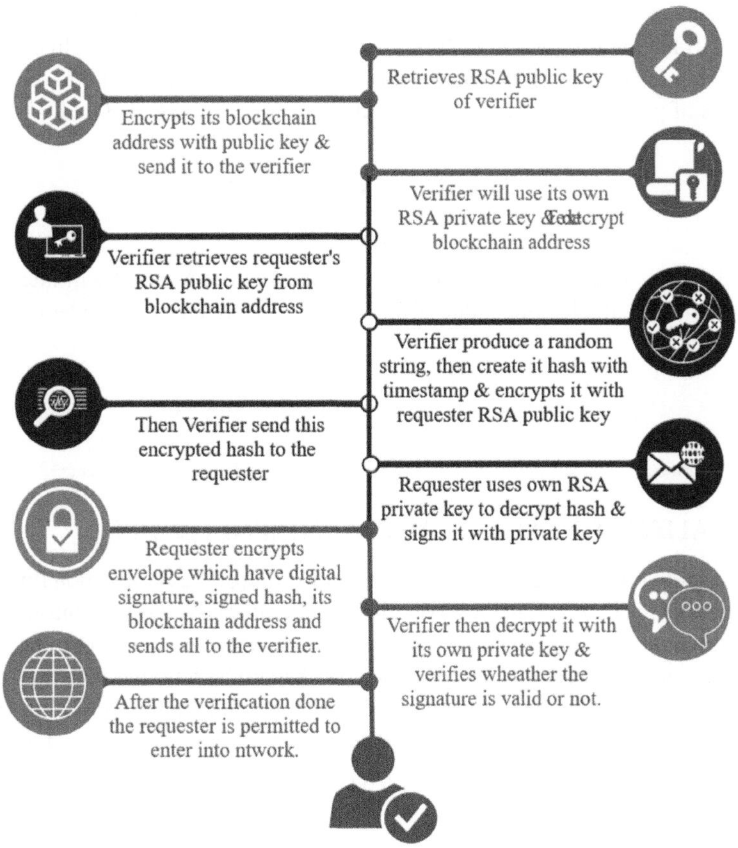

FIGURE 15.3 Blockchain authentication.

With the real number, the elliptic curve uses a special class equation

$$Y2 = X3 + PX + Q$$

The above equation will denote a non-singular elliptic curve equation if $4P3 + 27Q2 \neq 0$; otherwise equation will denote a singular elliptic curve equation. The elliptic curve has two properties that are used in ECDSA; one is point addition, and the second is point doubling.

- **First case:** If there are two points A = (X1, Y1) and B = (X2, Y2) having different coordinates on X-axis and Y-axis, then a line connecting A and B intercepts the curve on a point -C. C is the replication of c to the X-axis. The coordinates of point C can be found by the slope of the line.

$$\text{Slope}(\delta) = (Y2 - Y1)/(X2 - X1) \text{ if } X2 \neq X1$$

If $X2 = X1$ and $Y2 \neq Y1$ then $A + B = \infty$. It means lines that connect A and B will intercept at infinity. After finding the slope, calculate the value of X3 and Y3 coordinate with the help of the following equation:

$$X3 = \delta 2 - X1 - X2 \quad Y3 = \delta(X1 - X3) - Y1$$

- **Second case:** In the second case, point doubling, there are two points A= (X1, Y1) and B= (X2, Y2) having different coordinates on X-axis and Y-axis, then a line that connecting A and B intercepts the curve on a point -C. C is the replication of c to the X-axis. The coordinates of point C can be found by the slope of the line. If A ≠ B and Y1 ≠ 0, then

$$\text{Slope}(\delta) = (3\text{X}1 + \text{a}) / (2\text{Y}1)$$

If A = B and Y1 = 0, then A + B = ∞. It means lines that connect A and B will intercept at infinity. After finding the slope, calculate the value of X3 and Y3 coordinate with the help of the following equation:

$$\text{X}3 = \delta 2 - \text{X}1 - \text{X}2 \ \text{Y}3 = \delta(\text{X}1 - \text{X}3) - \text{Y}1$$

15.5 CENTRALIZED TO DECENTRALIZED INTERNETWORK

In the centralized network, there exists a central server to control the information flow. In the decentralized network, there is no centralized server and authorization overflowing information. The data is broadcasted throughout the network and can be stored anywhere in any equipment with internet access as a toaster and a refrigerator. The Web 4.0 blockchain technology includes properties such as a decentralized network and private network [15]. Figure 15.4 shows the centralized and decentralized internetwork system where the decentralized network is not accompanied by data breaching threats.

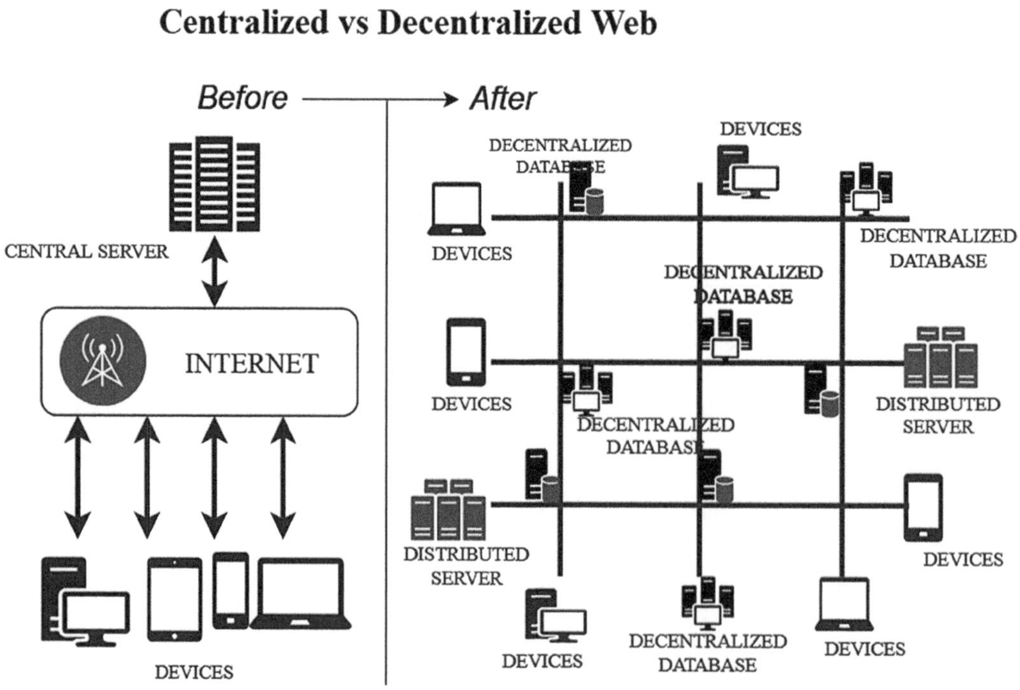

FIGURE 15.4 Centralized to decentralized system.

15.6 FEATURES OF 4.0

Web 4.0 provides different features to its users. The additional features of Web 4.0 include semantic Web, Artificial Intelligence, ubiquity, 3D graphics, peer-to-peer network, and enhanced connectivity [16]. The authors define the features of Web 4.0.

Figure 15.5 shows the features of Web 4.0 such as semantic Web, Artificial Intelligence, ubiquity, enhanced connectivity, peer-to-peer network, and 3D graphics.

- **Enhanced connectivity or internet of everything:** An internet of everything is used to define devices for connecting and using the internet smartly and efficiently. Smart devices such as home assistants, Alexa, and google assistant are interconnected within the network like the Internet of Things (IoT) [17]. The distinctive phenomena of Web 4.0 are IoT. The purpose of IoT is to connect each and every device to the internet.
- **User-centric and peer to peer:** The Web 4.0 blockchain is more inclined toward a user-centric approach that focuses on being a P2P network where users are free to spread information and knowledge that is not controlled by any entity within several devices. There will be no centralized servers in a user-centric system, and users can access the shared information without any supervision. In Web 4.0, the semantic Web allows users to connect easily through semantic metadata [18]. The Web 4.0 stack is all about the users through which users are becoming more interactive by creating blogs and vlogs. Users are not relying upon media content makers and can now freely follow others for information flow.
- **Artificial Intelligence:** Artificial Intelligence (AI) focuses on providing better analysis and results for users. AI is used to find the products that the user is looking for by sorting the internet. Tech giants and researchers are already working on AI to identify the choices and generate results similar to the mentioned choices. Online e-marts, YouTube, Facebook, and e-commerce sites are using AI-based websites for understanding users' preferences and developing options based on those choices [19]. The future is inclining toward person-based marketing strategies instead of using mass-marketing techniques.
- **Semantic Web:** Web 2.0 confides to domain content, information authority, and keywords to estimate the web content. Web 4.0 is based on semantic Web, where blockchain technology understands web content based on human behavior. The semantic Web is connected with machine learning and Artificial Intelligence, and machine learning.

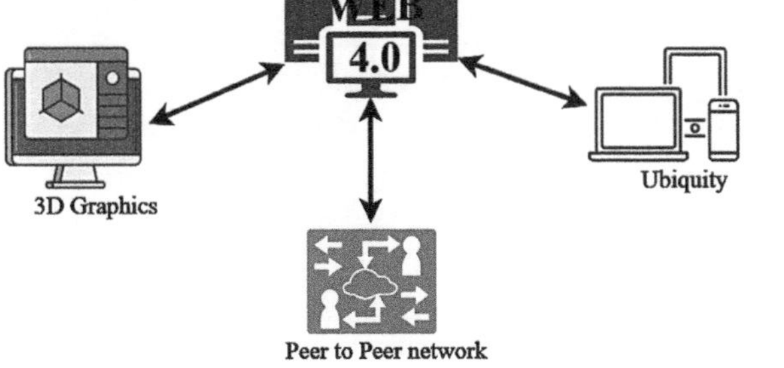

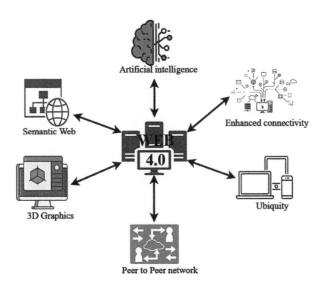

FIGURE 15.5 Features of Web 4.0.

- **Ubiquity:** The extension of ubiquity is interoperability. Web 4.0 allows users to access information crosswise multiple operations beyond the system requirements. If the device is connected by internet components, then it can access Web 4.0 [20]. Ubiquity will allow us to communicate across different technologies like IoT, Artificial Intelligence, and blockchain.
- **3D Graphics with Future of Contents:** Web 4.0 supports 3D graphics Undoubtedly, the Web contents are now becoming more graphical by using Web 4.0 that supports 3D graphics. Web users share videos and images more than plaintexts over the network, which makes data more vulnerable. 3D graphics, augmented reality and virtual reality, is the future of web content where 3D printing is not restricted to labs. Web users will move toward the usage of 3D printing, making it user friendly.

Figure 15.6 shows the layered architecture of Web 4.0, where information flows through different layers in different forms.

- **Application layer –** The application layer acts as the user interface that combines business logic and customer interactions using DApp Browsers, decentralized applications, application hosting, and programming language.

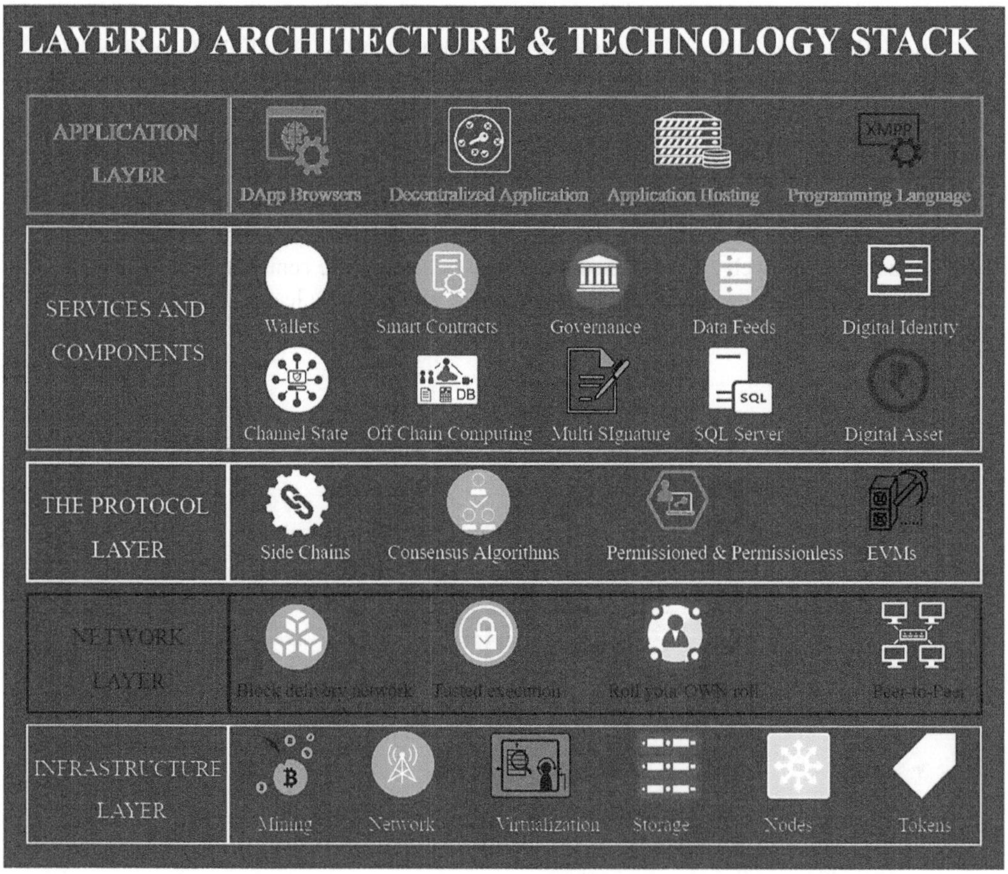

FIGURE 15.6 Layered architecture.

- **Services and optional components –** The technology layers constitute the services and optional components. The DApps tools are executed and modeled by using this layer. The technology layer covers state channels, sidechains, data feeds, and off-chain computing.
- **Protocol layer –** The protocol layer constitutes the virtual machines, participation requirements, and consensus algorithms.
- **Network layer and transport layer –** The trusted execution environment (TEE) and RLPx mainly constitute the network layer.
- **Infrastructure layer –** In-house architecture or blockchain as a service to control the nodes.

15.7 COMPARISON OF DIFFERENT WEB GENERATIONS

Table 15.1 shows the comparison between the various generations of Web on the basis of multiple factors. The time frame of Web 1.0 is ranging from 1990 to 2000, Web 2.0 is 2000–2015, and Web 3.0 is from 2015 onwards.

The different generations will support additional user capacity, for example, Web 1.0 serves millions of users, Web 2.0 helps billions of users, while Web 3.0 gives access to trillions of users. The different generations move from read-only restricted network to read and write accessible network.

TABLE 15.1

S.NO.	WEB 1.0	WEB 2.0	WEB 3.0	WEB 4.0
1	Simple banners and ads were seen	Automatic text graphics and interactive ads replace simple banners.	Artificial Intelligence (AI) will personalize the ads	Decentralization will personalize the ads
2	Essential content delivery networks (CDN) were introduced	B2B and P2P file-sharing protocols were invented	The cloud-based file-sharing system will prevail	A decentralized cloud-based file-sharing system will prevail
3	Personal websites were rare	Blogging became very popular	Semantic Web will take the place of information sharing web pages	Semantic Web with distributed will take the place of information sharing web pages
4	Page Views and screen scrapping were introduced	Cost per click (CPC) and web services replace the older methods	User-centric live streams will replace blogs	User-centric live streams will replace blogs
5	Contents had dictionaries or taxonomy system	Website, image, and video tagging replaced taxonomy system	P2P user engagement replaces them with ancestors	P2P user engagement replaces them ancestors
6	It is the beginning of everything	It is the social revolution	It is the internet of future	It is the decentralized internet of future
7	The file interaction is read-only	The file interaction is read and write	The file interaction is read-write and share	The file interaction is read, write, and execute
8	The Web type is simple	The Web type is social	The web type is semantic	The web type is distributed
9	The purpose is to connect information	The objective is to connect people	The purpose is to connect knowledge	The purpose is to secure the knowledge
10	The network type is centralized	The network type is centralized	The network type is centralized	The network type is decentralized

15.8 BENEFITS OF WEB 4.0

Web 4.0 is a technological revolution that can change the performance of the Web entirely. Web1.0 builds models with the capability to access the internet network. Web 3.0 overcomes the ability of Web 2.0, and Web 3.0 was usually controlled by organizations and corporations. Web 4.0 focuses on maintaining the system's privacy and security instead of making its network more effective. The aspects of Web 4.0 are changed completely. Initially, the Web was simple with reading and writing ability, but now, with Web 4.0 and blockchain, the security features are changed completely.

- **Secure network:** Web 4.0 is protected comparative to other Web generations. This can be achieved by introducing two significant factors that include decentralization and distributed nature. The intruders cannot penetrate into the internetwork, and if they peep into them, their actions can be easily tracked across the internet. It makes it difficult for intruders to overtake the control of an organization without centralization. Most of the blockchain applications and platforms will protect these types of threats.
- **Data ownership:** Web 4.0 provides the feature of data authority to various users. The data is entirely encrypted before broadcasting over the network and provides a command to users to limit the network's information access. The scenario is different among several companies such as Facebook, Amazon, or Google, where users' data is stored in a centralized network and their income, interests, and food habits. In Web 4.0, the users can sell their data confidentially to the corporations and earn from it.
- **Interoperability:** The interoperability with decentralization constitutes the significant features of Web 4.0, where interoperability made it easier for various equipment to work for distinct networks, and appliances as, refrigerator, smartphones, and all electronic equipment.
- **Permission-less blockchain:** The Web 4.0 permission-less blockchains are used to power blockchains that are based on decentralized networks where the address is created by users to participate and join the blockchain network. The authorization of new users irrespective of gender and religion creates a new area of possibility for permission-less blockchains.
- **Semantic Web:** The properties of Web 4.0 is hosted by semantic Web. The improvement of existing Web 3.0 technologies is semantic Web, which validates information to broadcast within various platforms, internetwork, and multiple systems.
- **Ubiquity:** The extension of ubiquity is interoperability. Web 4.0 allows users to access information crosswise multiple operations beyond the system requirements. If the device is connected by internet components, then it can access Web 4.0. Ubiquity will allow us to communicate across different technologies like IoT, Artificial Intelligence, and blockchain [21].

15.9 EXAMPLE OF WEB 4.0

In this section, we discuss a different real-life example of web 4.0. Figure 15.7 shows eight areas where Web 4.0 is working effectively. Let's examine each area in detail.

- **Social networks:** Social media networking has a very vital part of human life. Nowadays, nobody can assume their life without a social media network. It renovates human life and changes the way of communication and interaction. Although the current form of social media network is full of problems. Today's social media is under the control of somebody and work under a plan; Facebook, Twitter, and WeChat are some examples of them. These social media platforms hold complete authorization of the user information, which is transmitted over their platform and stored in their data center. Recently Facebook was caught in a scandal where Cambridge Analytica company accessed user data [22]. Web 4.0 social

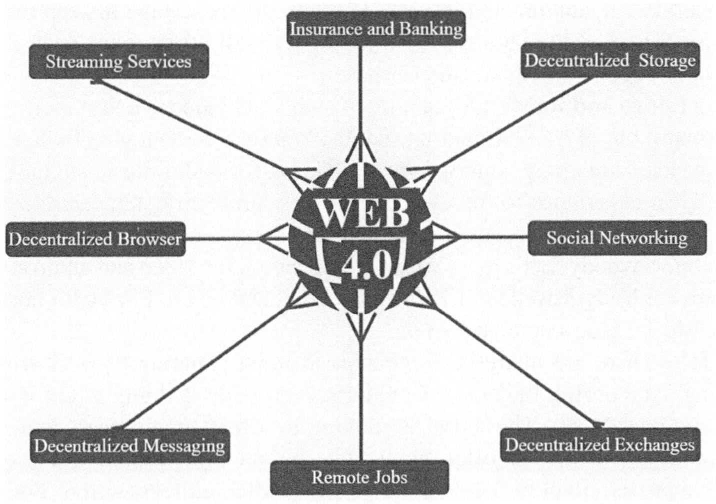

FIGURE 15.7 Example of Web 4.0 in a different area.

media network changes the whole scenario because it uses blockchain technology where users own its data, and nobody can access the permission of data owners. An example of a Web 4.0 social media platform is Sapien, onG.Social, Sola, Steemit, etc.

- **Exchange services:** For applications like exchange services, centralization is never the right choice. In the year of 2014 exchange of Mt. Gox was hacked, which was the biggest failure to date, worth cost $460 million. There are so many examples where a centralized server is compromised at exchange service. The only solution is decentralization. Decentralized trading and exchanges are getting popular day by day as they offer better trading experience without any tension about transparency and hacks. Some exchange service examples are IDEX, EOSFinex, etc., which run on Web 4.0.
- **Messaging:** Chatting and messaging have been an integral part of our lives from the start of the internet. There are many APP for messaging such as WhatsApp, Telegram, and Facebook Messenger; although there are no many drawbacks of the current messaging app, they still carry some issues like social media networking discussed above. To overcome those problems, the Web 4.0-based messaging app is the only solution. Web 4.0-powered apps are ySign, e-chat, Riot, and many more. They offer privacy and fast transaction; owners own the data and can't use them for advertising.
- **Storage:** Data storage is always a problem for everyone because of privacy issues, unwanted uses of data, and sale of data for advertising. There are many innovations done from time to time for data storage, but every design depends on the centralized storage of data. There are many examples of data breaches in centralizing data storage; one of them is the LinkedIn data breach, where hackers stole passwords and usernames of 117 million users of the platform. Another example of centralized data storage failure is faced by Uber when data of 56 million of users were stolen by some hackers. The only solution to the above problem is decentralized data storage. Web 4.0 offers decentralized data storage with Filecoin, MaidSAFE, Storj, and many others.
- **Banking:** Banking and insurance is the most significantly corrupt sectors of civilization. The insurance sector runs with the viewpoint of getting revenues. On the other side, banking is not free from negativity. The current system of insurance and banking is broken and needs to change with more security and transparency. There are many examples of famous bailouts related to the banking and insurance sector; one of them is Yes Bank banking fraud in 2019 when govt found some irregularities during the audit process. The only solution

is blockchain-based banking and insurance system. Block storage to keep the records and smart contract is used to make task automated. Web 4.0 offers many such examples like AiGang, Everledger, Safe Share, and Cashaa.

- **Streaming (video and music):** Streaming of audio and video is a vast industry. As a user, there are many big players around us such as YouTube by Google, Twitch by Amazon, Netflix for video streaming, and Spotify and Gaana for audio music streaming. All these provide a great experience to the user, but the only problem is the centralized storage of data and monopoly on user data by one company. They can use user data for advertising and can sell to anybody. Let's meet Web 4.0 application for video and audio streaming. For video, there are Viuly, Livepeer, LBRY, Videocoin, and so on. For audio music, there are Voise, UjoMusic, Moosecoin, and so on.
- **Remote Job:** There are many IT companies in India planning to work from home for cost-cutting. And during the era of Covid-19, everybody is doing a remote job because of lockdown worldwide. The world is moving to a freelance careers and remote jobs. There are many websites that offer remote jobs, but the first problem is a new application not to get approved quickly. The second problem is linked fees with it. For one website Upwork, it takes 20% of the project cost, which is vast. A decentralized platform can solve these problems link with the remote and freelancing job. Some of the popular websites are CryptoTask, Atlas. Work, Blocklancer, and so on. CryptoTask is no censorship and no-fee platform.
- **Browser:** Browsers are the internet gateways. Firefox and Google Chrome are the two major browsers used worldwide. They both capture most of the market. The current version of web browsers is not secure for the user. Whenever any user of these browsers visits any infected website, user also got infected. All recent browsers offer add-ons programs, which are very vulnerable. The solution is to use a decentralized browser that offers better security to sing blockchain technology. Brave and Breaker Browsers are examples of Web 4.0 that use blockchain technology.

15.10 DECENTRALIZED STORAGE AND WEB 4.0: FUTURE OF CLOUD COMPUTING

Organizations across the globe understood that a decentralized style of computing is the need to hour to fulfill the infrastructure required for the business. Blockchain is the only solution for decentralized computing without compromising the security and privacy of data. Decentralized cloud computing oversimplifies the cloud model to process, position, and assist application and data from geologically scattered positions to encounter requirements for redundancy, performance, and regulations [23, 24]. The old-style cloud computing prototype delivers metered access, on-demand, to computing resources like servers, storage, applications, and databases, to cloud operators who do not need to buy, run, or build their individual IT set-up. Distributed cloud computing divide workload of computation over several, connected, and interrelated distributed server; this concept is known as distributed cloud infrastructure [25, 26]. Figure 15.8 shows the centralized and decentralized app.

15.10.1 Blockchain and Cloud

When we start to look at blockchain quite a system for cryptocurrency transaction, you furthermore may begin to ascertain how using this set of tools can provide accompaniment and improve cloud computing. To add extra security and supplementary resourceful storage, web networks are starting to evolve to decentralized agendas. By operating many sites to accumulate data, supplementary encryption and security measures are involved. Decentralized frameworks using blockchain similarly permit corporate owners to use only the storage they required [27, 28]. Through centralized

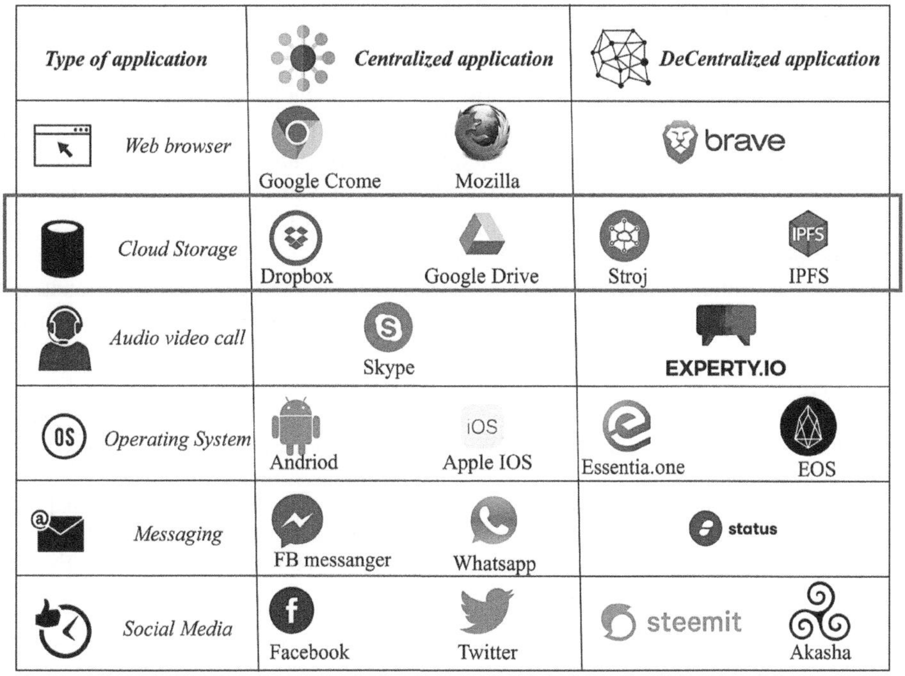
Type of application
Centralized application
DeCentralized application
Web browser
Google Crome
Mozilla
brave
Cloud Storage
Dropbox
Google Drive
Stroj
IPFS
Audio video call
Skype
EXPERTY.IO
Operating System
iOS
Andriod
Apple IOS
Essentia.one
EOS
Messaging
FB messanger
Whatsapp
status
Social Media
Facebook
Twitter
steemit
Akasha

FIGURE 15.8 Transition of apps from centralized to decentralized.

cloud storage, this isn't the case. By using the decentralized method in networks, it is straightforward to make sure that only authorized entity uses and access the data. Security using blockchain is extra extensive because it is distributed among various different storage [29, 30].

15.10.2 Decentralized Cloud Computing

With the help of decentralized cloud computing, the information stored on the cloud is fragmented into more modest lumps, which are put away on various machines far and wide. While this may seem like a muddled and unrealistic idea, a decentralized organization really offers an organization several advantages. At the point when you use a framework with decentralized cloud computing that is like blockchain frameworks, it permits your business:

- **Admittance to top-notch infrastructural provision:** Decentralized cloud computing frameworks are typically connected to a foundation or programming application that makes them simple to work. When there's an excellent foundation set up, approved clients can get to their information whenever on the Web.
- **Extra data security:** Since information is scrambled and put away on various stages, it's more secure from penetrates and hackers. The decentralized idea of distributed computing engineering makes it almost outlandish for an unapproved client to recover information without being caught by the framework first.
- **Adaptability in information stockpiling costs:** With decentralized distributed computing, organizations aren't managing cloud suppliers who lease them space in one area. Blockchain-based distributed computing suppliers don't have one enormous office where they keep their information, so their overhead expenses are by and large lower. This permits distributed computing specialist co-ops to charge lower expenses and give individualized plans that empower entrepreneurs to compensate for the space they require.

15.11 CONCLUSION

World Wide Web, after introduced in 1990. Nowadays in the 21st century, nobody can live without the World Wide Web and the internet. The World Wide Web is the largest universal info media used by the users to read, write, share, and react to data via any electronic device like computer or mobile, linked to the internet. The Web is rising and intensifying with unanticipated speed since the past decade. The fourth industrial revolution is possible because of web advancement with the support of new technologies like big data, the Internet of Things, Artificial Intelligence, cognitive computing, cloud computing, and Industrial IoT. Web 4.0 revolution is depending upon blockchain technology, which provides immutability, transparency, and enhanced security to the system and makes it decentralized. In the upcoming articles, the author will provide the use of IPFS protocol in Web 4.0.

REFERENCES

[1] F. L. Almeida, "Concept and Dimensions of Web 4.0," *Int. J. Comput. Technol.*, vol. 16, no. 7, pp. 7040–7046, 2017.

[2] H. Anwar, "Web 3.0 Will Be Powered by Blockchain Technology Stack," 2018. [Online]. Available: https://101blockchains.com/web-3-0-blockchain-technology-stack/#prettyPhoto. [Accessed: 07-Aug-2018].

[3] Flat World Business, "Web 1.0 vs Web 2.0 vs Web 3.0 vs Web 4.0 – A bird's Eye On the Evolution and Definition," *Flat World Bus.*, pp. 1–18, 2013.

[4] M. Latorre, "Historia De Las Web 1.0, 2.0, 3.0 y 4.0," *Univ. Marcelino Champagnat*, pp. 1–8, 2018.

[5] R. Newman, V. Chang, R. J. Walters, and G. B. Wills, "Web 2. 0 – The Past and the Future 2. The Social Web 3. Cloud Computing Services," *Int. J. Inf. Manage.*, vol. 36, pp. 591–598, 2016.

[6] K. Nath, S. Dhar, and S. Basishtha, "Web 1.0 to Web 3.0 - Evolution of the Web and its various challenges," *ICROIT 2014 - Proc. 2014 Int. Conf. Reliab. Optim. Inf. Technol.*, no. October 2015, pp. 86–89, 2014.

[7] R. Singh, A. Donegan, and H. Tewari, "Web 4.0: An Intelligent Tool from Web-of-thing to Web-of-thought," *J. Xidian Univ.*, vol. 14, no. 5, pp. 5498–5505, 2020.

[8] S. Biswas, K. Sharif, F. Li, B. Nour, and Y. Wang, "A Scalable Blockchain Framework for Secure Transactions in IoT," *IEEE Internet Things J.*, vol. 6, no. 3, pp. 4650–4659, 2019.

[9] M. A. Cyran, "Blockchain as a Foundation for Sharing Healthcare Data," *Blockchain Healthc. Today*, 2018.

[10] H. N. Dai, Z. Zheng, and Y. Zhang, "Blockchain for Internet of Things: A Survey," *IEEE Internet Things J.*, vol. 6, no. 5, pp. 8076–8094, 2019.

[11] T. H. E. G. Decentralization, H. O. W. Web, and M. Rev, "Copyright © 2015 Nick Vogel," pp. 1–13, 2016.

[12] M. Han, D. Wu, Z. Li, Y. Xie, J. S. He, and A. Baba, "A Novel Blockchain-based Education Records Verification Solution," *SIGITE 2018 - Proc. 19th Annu. SIG Conf. Inf. Technol. Educ.*, pp. 178–183, 2018.

[13] B. Liu, X. L. Yu, S. Chen, X. Xu, and L. Zhu, "Blockchain Based Data Integrity Service Framework for IoT Data," *Proc. - 2017 IEEE 24th Int. Conf. Web Serv. ICWS 2017*, pp. 468–475, 2017.

[14] B. Liu, X. L. Yu, S. Chen, X. Xu, and L. Zhu, "Blockchain Based Data Integrity Service Framework for IoT Data," *Proc. - 2017 IEEE 24th Int. Conf. Web Serv. ICWS 2017*, no. November, pp. 468–475, 2017.

[15] G. Zyskind, O. Nathan, and A. S. Pentland, "Decentralizing Privacy: Using Blockchain to Protect Personal Data," *Proc. - 2015 IEEE Secur. Priv. Work. SPW 2015*, pp. 180–184, 2015.

[16] N. Surname, "Altynbek Orumbayev Decentralized Web-based Data Storage for LinkedPipes Applications using Solid," 2020.

[17] I. Makhdoom, M. Abolhasan, and W. Ni, "Blockchain for IoT: The Challenges and a Way Forward," *ICETE 2018 - Proceedings of the 15th International Joint Conference on e-Business and Telecommunications*, 2018, vol. 2, no. July, pp. 428–439.

[18] L. Luu, V. Narayanan, C. Zheng, K. Baweja, S. Gilbert, and P. Saxena, "A Secure Sharding Protocol for Open Blockchains," *Proc. ACM Conf. Comput. Commun. Secur.*, vol. 24–28-October, pp. 17–30, 2016.

[19] H. Natarajan, S. Krause, and H. Gradstein, *Distributed Ledger Technology and Blockchain*, no. 1. 2017.

[20] K. Nath and R. Iswary, "What Comes After Web 3.0? Web 4.0 and the Future," *Int. Conf. Comput. Commun. Syst.*, no. September, pp. 3–5, 2006.

[21] B. Podgorelec, M. Herieko, and M. Turkanovic, "State Channel as a Service Based on a Distributed and Decentralized Web," *IEEE Access*, vol. 8, pp. 64678–64691, 2020.
[22] G. Rathee, A. Sharma, H. Saini, R. Kumar, and R. Iqbal, "A Hybrid Framework for Multimedia Data Processing in IoT-Healthcare Using Blockchain Technology," *Multimed. Tools Appl.*, vol. 79, no. 15–16, pp. 9711–9733, 2020.
[23] R. Singh, A. Donegan, and H. Tewari, "Framework for a Decentralized Web," *arXiv*, 2020.
[24] A. Sharma, F. M. Schuhknecht, D. Agrawal, and J. Dittrich, "How to Databasify a Blockchain: the Case of Hyperledger Fabric," 2018.
[25] R. Singh, A. Donegan, and H. Tewari, "Framework for a Decentralized Web," *arXiv*. 2020.
[26] A. Skarzauskiene, M. Maciuliene, and D. Bar, "Developing Blockchain Supported Collective Intelligence in Decentralized Autonomous Organizations," in *Springer*, 2021, pp. 1018–1031.
[27] A. D. Dwivedi, G. Srivastava, S. Dhar, and R. Singh, "A Decentralized Privacy-Preserving Healthcare Blockchain for IoT," *Sensors (Switzerland)*, vol. 19, no. 2, pp. 1–17, 2019.
[28] S. Figueroa, J. Añorga, and S. Arrizabalaga, "An Attribute-based Access Control Model in RFID Systems Based On Blockchain Decentralized Applications for Healthcare Environments," *Computers*, vol. 8, no. 3, pp. 1–19, 2019.
[29] T. T. Huynh, C. N. Huynh, and T. D. Nguyen, "A Novel Security Solution for Decentralized Web Systems with Real Time Hot-IPs Detection," in *Springer*, 2021, pp. 39–48.
[30] A. G. Khan, A. H. Zahid, M. Hussain, M. Farooq, U. Riaz, and T. M. Alam, "A journey of WEB and Blockchain towards the Industry 4.0: An Overview," *3rd Int. Conf. Innov. Comput. ICIC 2019*, no. November, 2019.

16 Significance of Elliptic Curve Cryptography in Blockchain IoT

Ashok Kumar Yadav and Karan Singh
School of Computer and Systems Sciences, Jawaharlal Nehru University, New Delhi, India

CONTENTS

16.1 INTRODUCTION

Nowadays, we live in the information highway era, which is open and can be accessed from anywhere, anytime where our information or data are traded among various parties or frameworks promptly through correspondence channels. Information highways provide the best opportunity to share our data instantly but with the vulnerability of attacks on eavesdropping or ambidextrous users' information. Over the internet with unreliable channels, storing, accessing, and sharing crucial data and information still have security and privacy challenges open to researchers and scientists. 5G is an emerging wireless communication technology that promises vast coverage, capacity, gigabit-speed, and significantly improved performance with reliability, enabling the vision of Industry 4.0 at the cost of the high density of picocells and femtocells. The primary feature of 5G technology is to facilitate ubiquitous high-bandwidth wireless connectivity to end-users without disrupting their course of duration. The feature of such advanced wired and wireless technology causes the evolution of IoT. It is a new worldview that assesses actual world items by empowering them to employ targeted addressing plans. IoT is a massive worldwide network of connected gadgets uniquely addressable as a usual communication protocol. IoT permits excellent verbal trade designs but the decentralized nature of IoT has challenges in security, privacy, authentication, and identity management. Blockchain emerged as peer-to-peer distributed ledger technology for recording transactions, maintained by many peers without any central regulatory authority through distributed public-key cryptography and consensus mechanism. It has not only given the birth of cryptocurrencies, but it also resolved various security, privacy, and transparency issues of decentralized systems. Blockchain technology is a platform where peers who may not trust each other share their data. It was first referenced in the white paper of Satoshi Nakamoto in 2008 [1]. Blockchain is characterized as a chain of blocks with open and immutable records. Its innovation appeared from the possibility of timestamping given by Stuart Haber and W. Scott Stornetta [2].

DOI: 10.1201/9781003155577-20

IoT has security, privacy, and scalability challenges. Blockchain ensures decentralization, immutability, identity, and access management. Decentralization, immutability, and identity management may address issues of IoT. Blockchain plays an important role to push centralized IoT to decentralized IoT with the support of distributed ledger. It chiefly can handle IoT security and privacy issues. Blockchain innovation can be incorporated with IoT to affirm secure sharing of information and central point failure.

IoT and blockchain may be integrated as IoT-IoT, IoT-blockchain, and a hybrid of both. In IoT-IoT model, information is taken care of in blockchain while in IoT interactions take place without using blockchain. This model is a valuable situation for dependable IoT cooperation with low latency needed. In IoT-blockchain model, interactions go through blockchain. It is useful in situations like an exchange and leases to acquire unwavering security and quality. In hybrid model, some interaction and data are taken care of in blockchain, and the rest shared among IoT. This methodology is an ideal and profitable for both blockchain and ongoing IoT communication. Association technique can be picked based on a throughput agreement system, security, and asset utilization. Blockchain combination with IoT can beat the difficulties in the control of IoT framework. It may enhance IoT's ability by offering trust, sharing assistance for dependability, reasonability, and manageability of data from cloud to distributed framework for QoS enhancement. It likewise scarcely keeps any incredible organizations from controlling the handling and capacity of many individuals' data and improves adaptation to non-critical failure and scalability [3–6].

So, we have observed that to provide proper security, cryptography plays a significant role in blockchain. Art and science of secret writing are known as cryptography, which is of symmetric key and asymmetric key. DES, ADES, and IDEA are a few mainstream instances of secrete key cryptography, while RSA and ECC are famous instances of shared key cryptography. In this work, security diagnosis of two well-known reasonable shared key cryptography has performed. RSA is an underlying viable shared key cryptography, amazingly notable from its beginning, while ECC is getting distinction starting late. Integer factorization problem (IFP) and elliptic curve discrete logarithm problem (ECDLP) are the base behind RSA and ECC cryptosystem, respectively. The critical thought of ECC's fascination over RSA is that ECDLP takes full exponential time complexity and IFP of RSA takes subexponential time complexity. It implies that more modest attribute can be utilized in ECC than RSA, however, with identical security degrees. Figure 16.1 shows the cause of the use of ECC in blockchain IoT.

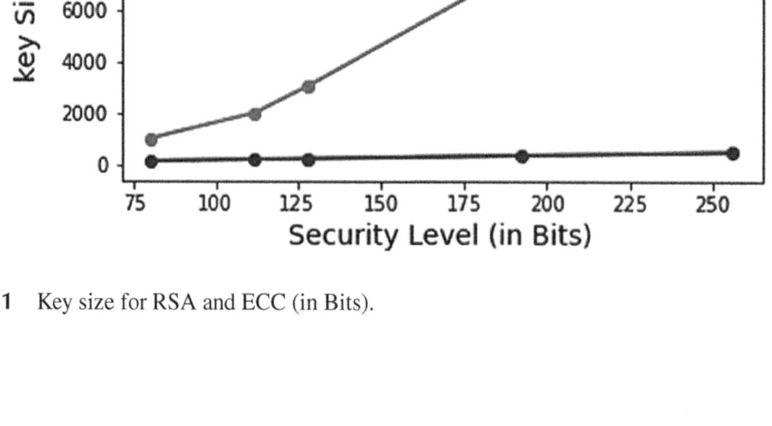

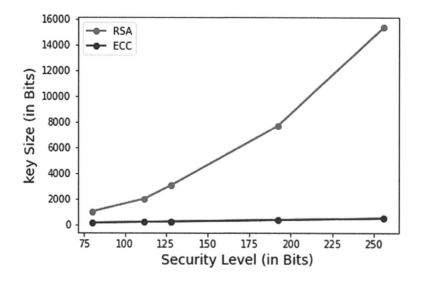

FIGURE 16.1 Key size for RSA and ECC (in Bits).

16.2 LITERATURE REVIEW

Researchers have worked on investigations of ECC and RSA security considering various metrics. Gaur [7] implemented EC point doubling for 160, 192, 224 bit and RSA 1024, 2048 bit on two 8 bit microcontrollers and has given a novel technique to decrease the number of memory references. They have observed that public-key cryptography is practicable on resource constraint devices without increasing the hardware's computing power. Bos [8] evaluates the danger of key use on the premise key length of ECC and RSA. Kute [9] suggested that RSA is quicker; however, security-astute ECC beats RSA. Jansma [10] observed uses of digital signatures in ECC and RSA and proposed that RSA may be the right decision for applications, where checking messages is needed more than signing. Alese [11] proposed that RSA is more grounded than ECC even though they recommended ECC beats than RSA in future. Mahto [12–14] suggested upgrading the security of 64-bits and 256 OTP data communication utilizing ECC over open, unsafe channels.

16.3 RSA

RSA stands for Rivest, Shamir, and Adelman and was proposed by these three scientists. In Linux-based systems, it is used to generate shared and secrete keys. Generally, it is used for keyless login. It is the most popular algorithm used in cryptography even today. It generates shared keys and announces to secretly network their secret key.

16.4 STEPS FOR RSA ALGO FOR KEY GENERATION

1. Let 'p' and 'q' two different large prime numbers
   (generally, p and q are chosen randomly & test primality).
2. Compute n = p*q
   (We cannot directly take a large number 'n' because if we take p & q prime, then it is challenging to identify p & q from n, prime factorization is very difficult.)
3. Ø(n) = Ø(p) * Ø(q) = (p-1) *(q-1)
4. Choose an integer 'e' such that 1< e < Ø(n) & 'e' should be relatively prime to Ø(n).
   i.e. gcd (e, Ø(n)) = 1 then (e, n) will be *Public key*.
5. Determine 'd' such that
   $d \cong e^{(-1)}$ (mod Ø(n)) or e*d = 1(mod Ø(n))
   then (d, n) will be *Private key*.

Implementation of RSA Algorithm to Compute Encryption and Dec

```
import time
import hashlib
import sympy
import math
import random
import crypto_commons as commons
from Crypto.Cipher import AES
starttime = time.time()
from Crypto.PublicKey import RSA
RSAkey = RSA.generate(1024)
p = getattr(RSAkey.key, 'p')
q = getattr(RSAkey.key, 'q')
n = p*q
```

```
t = (p-1)*(q-1)
print("mod: ",n)
print("totient function",t)
e = random.randint(1, t)
while math.gcd(t, e) != 1:
  e = random.randint(1, t)
d=sympy.mod_inverse(e, t)
print(time.time() - starttime," seconds\n")
publickey = e
privatekey = d
m = input("type your message")
ciphertext = pow(m, e, n)
ciphertext = pow(m, e, n)
print("ciphertext: ",ciphertext)
print(time.time() - starttime," seconds\n")
restored = pow(ciphertext, d, n)
print(time.time() - starttime," seconds")
message= input("type your message")
hashHex = hashlib.sha256(message).hexdigest()
hash = int(hashHex, 16)
signature = pow(hash, privatekey, n)
decryptedSignature = pow(signature, publickey, n)
bobHashHex = hashlib.sha256(message).hexdigest()
bobHash = int(bobHashHex, 16)
if bobHash == decryptedSignature:
  print("signature is valid")
else:
  print("signature is not valid!!!")
print(time.time() - starttime," seconds")
key = 1234567891234567 #16 byte
encryptedkey = pow(key, publickey, n)
message =input("type your message")
obj = AES.new(str(key))
ciphertext = obj.encrypt(message)
restoredkey = pow(encryptedkey, privatekey, n)
obj2 = AES.new(str(restoredkey))
restoredtext = obj2.decrypt(ciphertext)
```

16.5 ELLIPTIC CURVE CRYPTOGRAPHY

ECC uses blockchain implementations such as Bitcoin or Ethereum to generate public and private key pairs. "Neal Koblitz and Victor Miller in 1985, invented it. A 256-bit ECC public key gives similar security to 3072-bit RSA public key" [15]. The essential advantage of using cryptography is decreased key size, which improves both speed and memory. Bitcoin and Ethereum both use secp256k1. ECC uses a generator point which can generate all points present in a finite cycle group (1……, p-1). Whenever we want to generate any public key, we use a generator. It provides a trap door function that means reverse computation is not possible. Let K, k, G be public key, private key, and generator, respectively. Public key computed by

$$K = k^{*}G$$

To find discrete k if K and G are given is very difficult. Calculation of the discrete value of k is well known as a discrete logarithm problem.

16.6 IMPLEMENTATION OF ECC ALGORITHM TO COMPUTE ENCRYPTION AND DECRYPTION TIME

```
from tinyec import registry
import time, hashlib, secrets, binascii
starttime = time.time()
C = registry.get_curve ('specP256k1')
def encrypt_ECC(M, puKey):
    CT_PrKey = secrets.randbelow(C.field.n)
    SH_ECCKey = CT_PrKey * puKey
    sec_Key = ecc_point_to_256_bit_key(SH_ECCKey)
    CT, N, AT = encrypt_AES_GCM(M, sec_Key)
    CT_PuKey = CT_PrKey * C.g
    return (CT, N, AT, CT_PuKey)
print(time.time() - starttime," seconds\n")
def decrypt_ECC(encryptedMsg, prKey):
    (CT, N, AT, CT_PuKey) = EMsg
    SH_ECCKey = prKey *  CT_PuKey
    sec_Key = ecc_point_to_256_bit_key(SH_ECCKey)
    PT = decrypt_AES_GCM(CT, N, AT, sec_Key)
    return PT
print(time.time() - starttime," seconds\n")
M = input("enter message")'
prKey = secrets.randbelow(C.field.n)
puKey = privKey * C.g
EMsg = encrypt_ECC(M, puKey)
EMsgObj = {
    'CT': binascii.hexlify(EMsg[0]),
    'N': binascii.hexlify(EMsg[1]),
    'AT': binascii.hexlify(EMsg[2]),
    'CTPuKey': hex(EMsg[3].x) + hex(EMsg [3].y % 2)[2:]
}
DMsg = decrypt_ECC(EMsg, prKey)
```

16.7 SECURITY ANALYSIS OF ECC AND RSA ALGORITHM

This paper implements ECC and RSA in python with 8, 64, and 256 bits using random secrete keys. ECC's efficiency over RSA in terms of encryption and decryption is demonstrated in Figures 16.2–16.4. We have discovered that RSA is proficient in encryption yet delayed in decryption; however, ECC is delayed in encryption yet extremely productive in decryption. Generally, ECC is proficient and more secure than RSA.

In the above analysis, we have found that RSA is not suitable for blockchain IoT. It has more time and space, but unfortunately, IoT devices have very low computing and storage capacity. Elliptic curve cryptography enabled blockchain technology can be used over RSA to make IoT system decentralized and secure. Elliptic curve cryptography enables blockchain to provide security and privacy and ensure high speed and storage and battery issues of IoT devices.

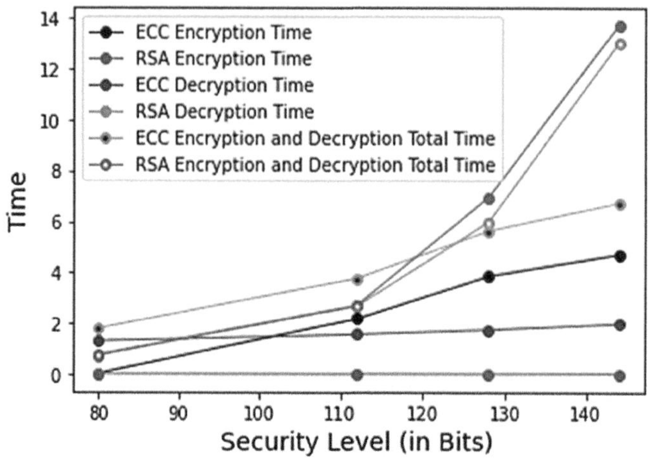

FIGURE 16.2 8 Bit encryption and decryption time.

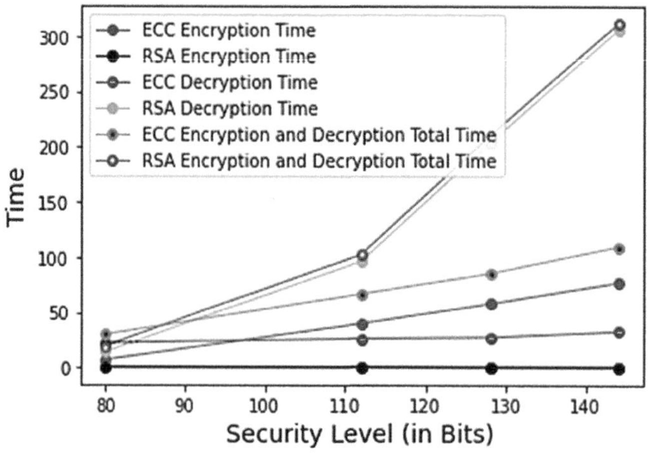

FIGURE 16.3 64 Bit encryption and decryption time.

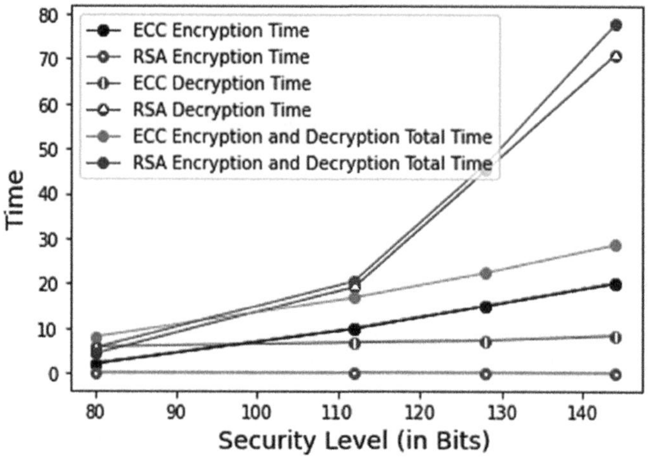

FIGURE 16.4 256 bit encryption and decryption time.

16.8 CONCLUSION

This paper has discussed the blockchain basics overview and blockchain security components ECC. In addition to the core idea of RSA, we focus on the significance of ECC in the incorporation of blockchain with IoT. We also discussed why RSA and key generation, encryption and decryption mechanisms with python implementation are not suitable for IoT-based applications. We analysed the various possible IoT-based applications where the ECC algorithm is better than other algorithms in latency and memory. Security and privacy assurance. At the end of the paper, we have explained comparative analysis of RSA and ECC implementation in python.

REFERENCE

[1] Nakamoto, Satoshi. "Bitcoin: A peer-to-peer electronic cash system (2008)." 2008.

[2] Haber, Stuart, and W. Scott Stornetta. "How to timestamp a digital document." In *Conference on the Theory and Application of Cryptography*, pp. 437–455. Springer, Berlin, Heidelberg, 1990.

[3] Yadav, Ashok Kumar, and Karan Singh. "Comparative analysis of consensus algorithms and issues in integration of blockchain with IoT." In *Smart Innovations in Communication and Computational Sciences*, pp. 25–46. Springer, Singapore, 2020.

[4] Yadav, Ashok Kumar, and Karan Singh. "Comparative analysis of consensus algorithms of blockchain technology." In: Hu, Y.C., Tiwari, S., Trivedi, M., and Mishra, K. (eds.) *Ambient Communications and Computer Systems*, pp. 205–218. Springer, Singapore, 2020.

[5] Yadav, Ashok Kumar. "Comprehensive study on incorporation of blockchain technology with IoT enterprises." In: *Opportunities and Challenges for Blockchain Technology in Autonomous Vehicles*, pp. 22–33. IGI Global.

[6] Cachin, Christian, Marko Vukolic Sorniotti, and Thomas Weigold. "Blockchain, cryptography, and consensus." *IBM Res., Zürich, Switzerland, Tech. Rep* 2016, 2016.

[7] Puthal, Deepak, Nisha Malik, Saraju P. Mohanty, Elias Kougianos, and Gautam Das. "Everything you wanted to know about the blockchain: Its promise, components, processes, and problems." *IEEE Consumer Electronics Magazine* 7, no. 4 (2018): 6–14.

[8] Saxena, Deepak, and Jitendra Kumar Verma. "Blockchain for public health: Technology, applications, and a case study." In: Verma, J. K., Paul, S., and Johri, P. (eds.) *Computational Intelligence and Its Applications in Healthcare*, pp. 53–61. Academic Press, 2020.

[9] Gura, Nils, Arun Patel, Arvinderpal Wander, Hans Eberle, and Sheueling Chang Shantz. "Comparing elliptic curve cryptography and RSA on 8-bit CPUs." In *International Workshop on Cryptographic Hardware and Embedded Systems*, pp. 119–132. Springer, Berlin, Heidelberg, 2004.

[10] Bos, Joppe W., J. Alex Halderman, Nadia Heninger, Jonathan Moore, Michael Naehrig, and Eric Wustrow. "Elliptic curve cryptography in practice." In *International Conference on Financial Cryptography and Data Security*, pp. 157–175. Springer, Berlin, Heidelberg, 2014.

[11] Bos, Joppe, Marcelo Kaihara, Thorsten Kleinjung, Arjen K. Lenstra, and Peter L. Montgomery. "On the security of 1024-bit RSA and 160-bit elliptic curve cryptography. No. REP_WORK." 2009.

[12] Mahto, Dindayal, and Dilip Kumar Yadav. "RSA and ECC: A comparative analysis." *International Journal of Applied Engineering Research* 12, no. 19 (2017): 9053–9061.

[13] Saho, Nelson Josias Gbètoho, and Eugène C. Ezin. "Comparative study on the performance of elliptic curve cryptography algorithms with cryptography through RSA algorithm." In *CARI 2020-Colloque Africain sur la Recherche en Informatique et en Mathématiques Apliquées*, 2020.

[14] Alese, Boniface K., E. D. Philemon, and Samuel O. Falaki. "Comparative analysis of public-key encryption schemes." *International Journal of Engineering and Technology* 2, no. 9 (2012): 1552–1568.

[15] Tsai, Jia-Lun. "An improved cross-layer privacy-preserving authentication in WAVE-enabled VANETs." *IEEE Communications Letters* 18, no. 11 (2014): 1931–1934.

17 Lightweight Trust Evaluation in IoT

Bio-Inspired Metaheuristic Approach

Indu Dohare and Karan Singh
Jawaharlal Nehru University, New Delhi, India

CONTENTS

17.1 INTRODUCTION

Sensor-enabled IoT comprises several sensor devices that are deployed in a very unfriendly and unattended environment [1, 2]. The sensors are basically deployed to gather the data from such an environment. IoT devices simplify and make day-to-day life convenient through their various applications. With the help of numerous work and research, IoT is applicable in many areas such as agriculture and medical care [3]. Although IoT has become advanced nowadays, a lot of issues are still challenging. Among various challenges, energy and security came across as a prime challenge in various applications of wireless networked IoT. Figure 17.1 illustrates the security in IoT applications. In Figure 17.1, the security in the healthcare system needs the identification of ambulance and its authentication while the authorization of patient's data is also required. This data breach may affect the overall functioning of the hospital. Similarly, in other applications, the attacker may attack the platform, and functioning may be affected. So the technique is required for the safety and security of various IoT applications.

DOI: 10.1201/9781003155577-21

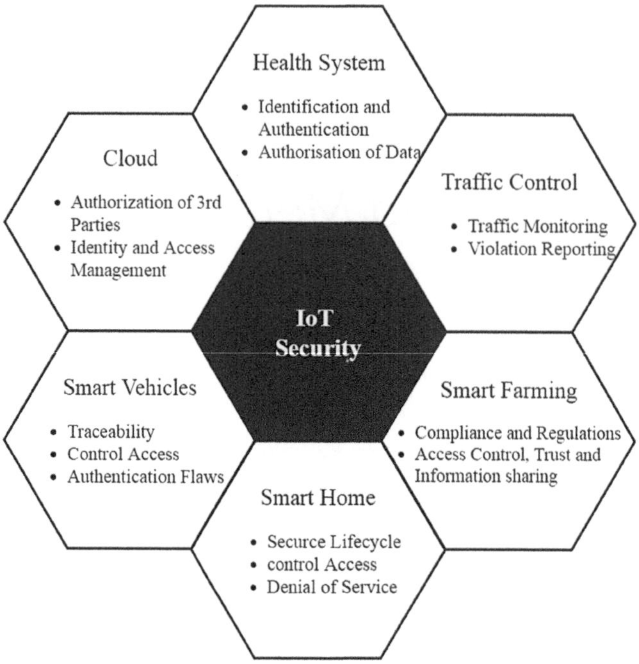

FIGURE 17.1 Security in IoT applications.

The existing security techniques have various limitations so they cannot be utilized in WSN-based IoT. Thus, cryptographic techniques are prone to high computational complexity. The energy and security problem of WSN-based IoT is the major issue because (1) sensors are organized in distant areas that are liable to numerous attacks. (2) The energy of the sensor's devices is also constrained in the proper functioning of sensors. Among various security techniques for wireless network IoT, trust is accountable to provide lesser memory and communication overhead. Furthermore, trust also provides better security from internal attacks in sensor enable IoT [4].

Clustering in sensor-enabled IoT provides one of the solutions for lightweight communication among sensors. In the clustering process, the network area is divided into partitions, and nodes in that area form the set of nodes called clusters [5]. In each cluster, there are some of the cluster members (CM) and a cluster head (CH). The CH is liable to collect the data of their CMs and transfer this data to the base station (BS). For this complete scenario, the CH should be resourceful and trustworthy. Metaheuristic techniques proved to solve various NP-hard problems that cannot be resolved by the rational model. Swarm-based metaheuristic algorithms are constructed on the various facts and mathematical functions that are related to the behaviors of the swarms [6].

17.1.1 Our Contribution

Cluster head selection in sensor-enabled IoT is a prominent task. The suitable selection of cluster head diminishes the energy depletion and enhanced the lifespan of the network. To remove the limitations of existing schemes, we suggest an energy-efficient trust-aware CH election mechanism (EETCH). The prime contributions are discussed following:

(1) A system model for the energy-efficient trust evaluation is specified, which is primarily focused on the RE and direct-indirect trust computation of the sensor nodes.
(2) A fitness function is derived depending on the affecting parameters of power and trust.

(3) An energy-efficient trust-aware CH selection algorithm is proposed, which depends on the swarm-based algorithm chaotic salp optimization algorithm.
(4) Finally, the result has been compared with analogous methods.

The effectiveness of the EETCH is calculated by the mathematical parameters and performance analysis. The rest of the paper is partitioned into five divisions. Section 17.2 discusses the related work that is useful to understand the model. Section 17.3 of the paper labels the proposed model. Section 17.4 demonstrates the evaluated results and finally, the conclusion is presented in the last section, Section 17.5.

17.2 RELATED WORK

The related work based on energy-efficient trust assessment toward lightweight security concerns in the wireless network of IoT has been surveyed.

ETARP [7], energy-efficient trust-aware routing protocol for WSN, is a model designed for the reduction of power depletion and enhances the security in data transmission between sensors. This protocol selects the route based on utility theory. DC-KHO [8], Dual CH selection technique, depends on the Krill Herd Optimization algorithm, used for routing of data in the network. This protocol evaluates the trust value of the route considering power depletion. BTWSN [9] is the cluster head selection algorithm that uses the honey bee mating algorithm. This model prevents the mischievous nodes to be the CH.

BIOSARP [10] is the bio-inspired self-organized secure autonomous routing protocol, which is the enhanced version of SRTLD. BIOSARP uses an improved ACO algorithm for energy-efficient data forwarding route selection. LDTS [11], a lightweight and dependable trust system, this protocol is designed for the clustered WSN. This approach aggregated the trust at the CH level, so it is self-adaptive. This approach reduces the malicious nodes to become the cluster head.

ELACCA [12] is the efficient learning automata-based cell clustering protocol. In this model, the cluster head is selected on a different level by the use of the partition ratio of the nodes. The network area is taken in the shape of a rhombus shape. EAUCF [13] is the fuzzy-based energy ware imbalanced clustering method that solves the hot spots problem. This protocol aims to lessen the intra-cluster communications to those nodes that are near to the BS or the nodes having low RE. LFTM [14] is the linguistic fuzzy trust model that also evaluates the reputation in WSN. This model focused on energy depletion and source utilization during the computation of reputation and trust of the networks.

NBBTE [15] is the trust calculation scheme for WSN, which applies the behavioral Strategies Banding Belief Theory for trust assessment among nodes. This method evaluates the direct and indirect trust values by understanding the behavior of nodes and calculating the weighted average of trust values. The evaluated input vector of evidence by the fuzzy set theory is used by the D-S evidence theory to synthesize the combined indirect and direct trust value of nodes. EDTM [16] is the trust management model for WSN. It is focused on some main parameters like packet received by nodes, recommendation trust, and data trust. Direct trust involves energy, data, and communication trust. The recommendation trust is required to evaluate when it is noticed that the nodes are not gaining communication with the object nodes. MTES [17] is the trust assessment model for sensor cloud-assisted industrial IoT. This approach introduces mobile edge nodes, has strong calculation and storage capability, and is reliable for trust computation. This scheme evaluates the reliability of nodes by using a probabilistic graphical scheme. The analysis of the probability of direct trust is improved by scheduling the moving path of edge nodes. This method also decreases the energy consumption with trustworthiness of the nodes.

17.3 SYSTEM MODEL

This section presents the architecture of the network, which is the basic structure of network design.

17.3.1 Network Model and Energy Model

We consider BS located in the mid of the network area of size 100*100m^2 and n n number of nodes randomly organized. These nodes are resource constrained and use equal battery power. The radio range of all these sensor devices is the same. These sensor nodes form a cluster. Each cluster consists of CMs and a CH. This model uses the energy dissipation model used the same as in LEACH [18].

In data communication, the cluster head takes the responsibility of data gathering and transmission. To transmit the *b-bit* data, let the d distance be covered with the data packets. So the total transmission energy consumption in traveling the *b-bit* data to the d distance can be expressed by Equation (17.1).

$$E_{TX}(b,d) = \begin{cases} b \times E_{ele} + b \times \varepsilon_{FS} \times d^2, & if d < d_0 \\ b \times E_{ele} + b \times \varepsilon_{MP} \times d^4, & if d \geq d_0 \end{cases} \tag{17.1}$$

The energy depletion of a sensor node in receiving the b-bit data can be expressed as:

$$E_{RX} = b \times E_{ele} \tag{17.2}$$

Here, E_{ele} is the energy depletion of a node per bit in the transmission of *b-bit* data packets. The coefficient of free space and transmission amplifier are ε_{FS} and ε_{MP}, respectively. d_0 is the threshold distance. The value of the d_0 can be evaluated as $\sqrt{\varepsilon_{FS}/\varepsilon_{MP}}$.

17.4 PROPOSED MODEL

This section presents the chaotic salp swarm optimization-based energy-efficient trust-aware CH has been elected algorithm (EETCH). In this section, first, we derive the parameters that affect the energy consumption in the network, which are RE and degree of the nodes. After this, we drive the trust-evaluating parameters. The linear programming-based fitness function is also present that uses parameters of energy and trust. And finally, the chaotic salp-based CH election algorithm has been designed. Phases of the complete EETCH are shown in Figure 17.2.

17.4.1 Energy Metrics

Sensors in IoT work on battery, which is non-rechargeable. Furthermore, sensors are deployed in very unfriendly locations; sometimes it becomes very hard to repair them. So balanced energy consumption becomes a very important and challenging task in sensor-enabled IoT. In this article, we have taken two parameters, which are (RE) of a node and degree of the node.

a. **Residual energy of node:** The CH is accountable for data collection and forwarding of those data to the BS. So the cluster head should be energy-rich. The RE of a node can be defined as the energy consumption of a node per round. Mathematically it can be defined as:

$$E_{res} = \sum_{i=1}^{N_{CH}} \frac{1}{RE_{n_i}} \tag{17.3}$$

Here, RE_{ni} is the RE of the ith node. N_{CH} is the total number of cluster heads in the system.

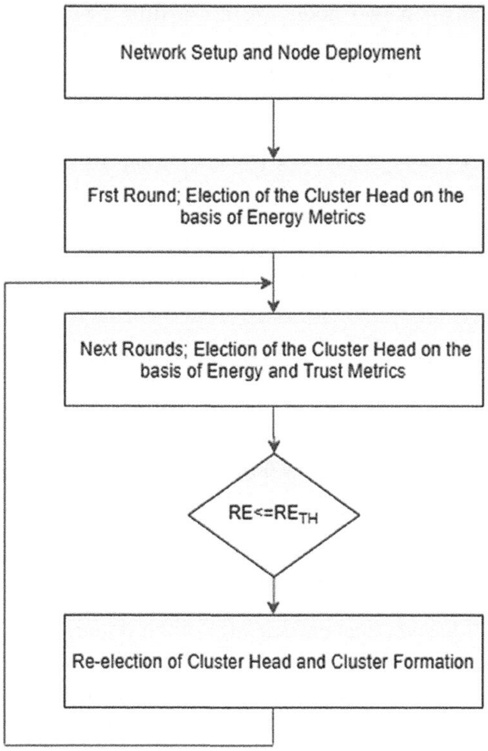

FIGURE 17.2 Phases of EETCH.

b. **Degree of the node:** The degree of a node is the number of nodes associated with the CH. The cluster member node will be associated with that node that has a lower degree. This can be formulated as:

$$Node_{degree} = \sum_{i=1}^{N_{CH}} |CM_i| \tag{17.4}$$

$|CM_i|$ is the cluster members for *i*th cluster head.

17.4.2 Trust Metrics

Sensor-enabled IoT is prone to numerous attacks since the sensors are arranged in a remote and hostile area. The malicious nodes may introduce two types of attacks: internal and external attacks. Internal attacks are tremendously challenging to conquer in comparison to external attacks. Trust models in a network learn from the past behavior of the nodes and apply on future actions. The BS is a highly trusted and resourceful party. The trust is computed in two terms, direct and indirect trust.

In this model we find out the optimal cluster head; for this, we evaluated the intra-cluster trust and this is further direct intra-cluster and indirect intra-cluster trust.

a. **Direct Trust Evaluation:** In intra-cluster trust evaluation, every node keeps the trust value of its adjacent nodes. In this model, we consider that the trust value varies from [0, 1]. Here, 0 means the node is malicious, 0.5 shows the suspicious node and 1 represents that the node is entirely reliable.

The direct trust between two nodes (n, n_i) at time t is the difference between positive response (P_r) of a node to that node and negative response (N_r) of that node at time t−1. Direct trust (DT_{rust}) can be mathematically formulated as

$$DT_{rust}\left(n,n_i\right)=P_r\left(i\right).DT\left(n,n_i\right)^{t-1}-N_r\left(i\right).DT\left(n,n_i\right)^{t-1} \tag{17.5}$$

b. **Indirect Trust Evaluation:** Indirect trust is a belief system that one node utilizes from its neighbor nodes based on past experiences. Indirect trust can be formulated as

$$IT_{rust}\left(n_j,n_i\right)^t=P_r\left(i\right)\sum_{j\in nbr_i,j\neq i}DT_{rust}\left(n_j,n_i\right)^{t-1}-P_r\left(i\right)\sum_{j\in nbr_i,j\neq i}DT_{rust}\left(n_j,n_i\right)^{t-1} \tag{17.6}$$

Here, positive and negative response is the level of energy, if $E_{res} > E_{TH}$ then it is a positive response from a node, and if it's no then it is a negative response.

17.4.3 Chaotic Salp Swarm Algorithm Procedure

Salp algorithm is the swarm-based metaheuristic algorithm; it learns from the behavior of salp [19]. Salps have a transparent body which is similar to jellyfish. They walk in groups and in each group there is a leader and followers. Let suppose *dim dim* is the dimension of the problem, x is the location of the salp and *FD* is the food of salp. Food is assumed as the search space for them. The leader salps updates by the following equation:

$$x_i^1=\begin{cases}FD_i+r_1\left(\left(ub_i-lb_i\right)r_2+lb_i\right), & r_3\geq 0\\ FD_i-r_1\left(\left(ub_i-lb_i\right)r_2+lb_i\right), & r_3<0\end{cases} \tag{17.7}$$

Where x_i^1, the location of the first salp at i^{th} dimension is, acts as leader. Upper bound and lower bound are represented as ub_i and lb_i at i^{th} dimension, respectively. r_1 is the balancing factor between exploration and exploitation. This can be formulated as:

$$r_1=2e^{-\left(\frac{4t}{T}\right)^2} \tag{17.8}$$

Where t is the present iteration and T is the highest number of iteration. r_2 and r_3 are random numbers ranges [0, 1]. The follower salp updates their position by the following equation:

$$x_i^j=\frac{1}{2}\alpha l^2+\beta_0 l \tag{17.9}$$

Where x_i^j is the position of jth follower at i^{th} dimension. β_0 is the initial speed, $\alpha=\frac{\beta_{final}}{\beta_0}$ and l denotes time. At $\beta_0=0$, i^{th} dimension the followers update their position by the following equation:

$$x_i^j=\frac{1}{2}\left(x_i^j+x_i^{j-1}\right) \tag{17.10}$$

The chaotic map is employed only at parameter r_2. O_s denotes the chaotic sequence at S^{th} number. O^t is the evaluated chaotic map value at iteration t^{th}, following are the updated equations:

$$r_2 = o_S \tag{17.11}$$

$$x_i^t = \begin{cases} FD_i + r_1\left(\left(ub_i - lb_i\right)o^t + lb_i\right), & r_3 \geq 0 \\ FD_i - r_1\left(\left(ub_i - lb_i\right)o^t + lb_i\right), & r_3 < 0 \end{cases} \tag{17.12}$$

The agents are transferred from binary to continuous to binary space by Equation (17.11), where B is the random number that ranges from [0, 1].

$$x_i^t = \begin{cases} 1 & \text{if}\left(S\left(x_i^t\right)\right) \geq B \\ 0 & \text{otherwise} \end{cases} \tag{17.13}$$

a. **Linear programming-based fitness function for cluster head selection**

$$\text{fit} = w1 \times E_{\text{res}} + w2 \times \text{Node}_{\text{degree}} + w3 \times DT_{rust} + w4 \times IT_{rust} \tag{17.14}$$

$$w_1 + w_2 + w_3 + w_4 = 1, w_1, w_2, w_3 \text{ and } w_4 \in (0,1)$$

Hence, the fitness function is the weighted sum of RE, degree of nodes, direct trust, and indirect trust. The algorithm for energy-efficient secure CH election algorithm is given below.

b. **Chaotic salp algorithm-based cluster head election algorithm**

ALGORITHM 1: CHAOTIC SALP BASED CLUSTER HEAD SELECTION ALGORITHM

Input:

1. Initialize M as the maximum number of iteration, ub and lb are upper and lower bounds, respectively, number of dimension is dim and fit is the fitness function.
2. Randomly initialize number of sensor nodes $S_n = \{S_1, S_2, \ldots, S_n\}$ and n is the total number of sensor nodes as position of the salp x_i^t here, $i = 1, 2, \ldots n$ and $t = 1, 2, .. M$.
3. Set $t = 1$.

Output: cluster heads x_{best}.

Initialization:

1. **while** (t<M)
2. Evaluate the fitness fit_i for each sensor node S_n by Equation (17.15) i.e., $fit\left(x_j^t\right)$.
3. Set the best salp position to x_{best}
4. Update r_1 by Equation (17.8)
5. Get the value of chaotic map o_t.
6. Update r_2 according to Equation (17.11).

7. **for** (i=1:i≤n) **do**
8. **if** (i == 1) **then**
9. update the location of the leader salp by Equation (17.12)
10. **else**
11. update the location of the following salp by Equation (17.10)
12. **end if**
13. update the salp position by Equation (17.13)
14. **end for**
15. check the viability of x_i^t
16. evaluate the new location of salp x_i^t
17. if fit $\left(x_i^t\right)$ is better than fit (x_{best}) then
18. update the position of best salp
19. **endif**
20. **set** $t = t + 1$
21. **end while**
22. produce best salp position x_{best} as cluster head position

Algorithm 1 is the energy-efficient trust evaluation cluster head election algorithm centered on the salp swarm optimization algorithm. In this algorithm, all the parameters have been initialized based on the problem. The algorithm is started by evaluating the linear programming problem-based fitness function. The best salp position has been assigned and parameters updated according to Equation (17.8). Chaotic map has been assigned to the algorithm and according to the base salp algorithm all the steps start updating. The loop stops where the algorithm matches the condition. The best salp position is considered as the best position of the cluster head.

17.5 SIMULATION RESULTS

In this section, we consider the network area of 100*100m^2, and 100 numbers of nodes are arbitrarily organized in this area. The attacker nodes are taken in the percentage of 10–30%. The initial power of the nodes is taken as *1J*. The radio range of each node is 30m. The network is assumed to be a homogeneous network so that the initial energy of every node is equal. Table 17.1 shows the description of parameters taken for the simulation. The complete simulation has been performed on the MATLAB 2017a. The proposed model has been compared with two swarm-based techniques for trust evaluation in WSN, BTWSN [9], and IASR [15].

TABLE 17.1
Parameter Description

Parameter	Value
Network area	*100*100 m*
Number of nodes	*100 nodes*
Initial energy	*1J*
Number of attacker nodes	*10–30%*
Packet size	*4000bits*
Communication range	*30m*

17.5.1 Simulation Matrices

a) **Detection Rate:** It is demarcated as the number of attacker nodes captured correctly out of complete attacker nodes per round.
b) **Packet Loss:** The term "packet loss" is demarcated as the number of packets that are not transmitted to the BS out of the total number of packets sent.
c) **Residual Energy:** This is described as the amount of power remaining per number of rounds after data transmission in every round.
d) **Alive node per round:** This is determined as the number of nodes with energy till the maximum number of rounds.

17.5.2 Performance Analysis in Terms of Attacker Detection Per Round

Figure 17.3 shows the result examination in terms of attacker node detection per number of rounds. From the figure, the number of attacker nodes detected in our proposed algorithms is high in comparison to other baseline algorithms. At round 20, the numbers of attacker nodes are 24 approximately in our proposed model EETCH, while it is 18 and 11 in BTWSN and IASR, respectively; this is because our proposed algorithm uses a fitness function that uses the trust evaluation method that detects the malicious nodes. Similarly, at round 30 the number of attacker nodes are 17 in EETCH, 30 in BTWSN while these vary in the case of IASR. The reason behind this is that in the proposed we used direct and indirect trust that optimizes the chances of increment of attackers, hence our model displayed improvement over other baseline algorithms.

17.5.3 Performance Analysis in Terms of Packet Loss Per Malicious Nodes

Figure 17.4 shows the result examination in terms of packet loss per malicious node. The figure illustrates that our proposed algorithm dropped fewer packets in comparison to other methods. For example, when the number of malicious nodes is 6, the number of packets that have been lost in EETCH is 7%, while in BTWSN and IASR those are 12% and 13%, respectively. Similarly, when

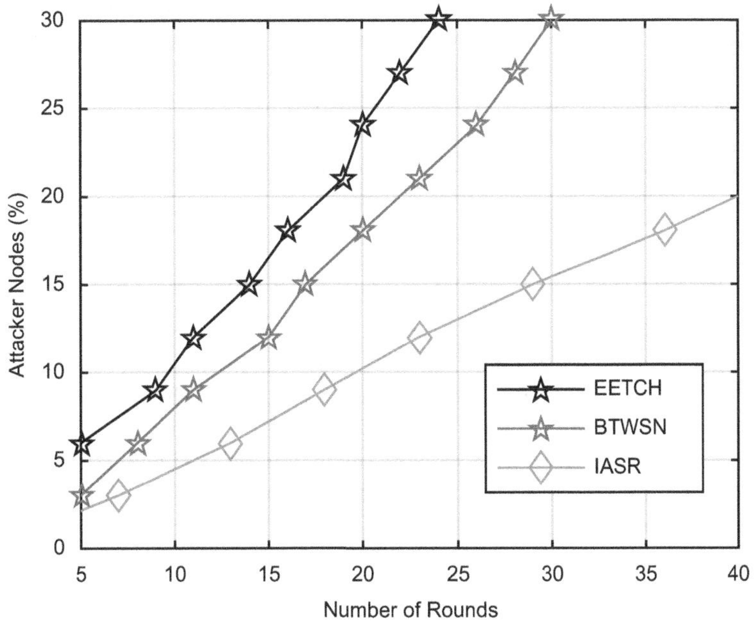

FIGURE 17.3 Performance analysis in terms of attacker nodes per round.

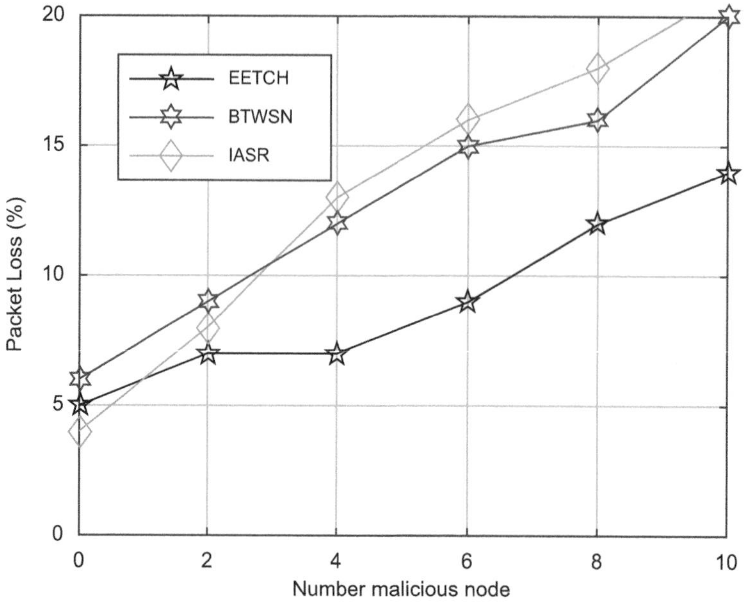

FIGURE 17.4 Performance analysis in terms of packet loss per malicious nodes.

the number of mischievous nodes is 9 the packet loss is 18% in IASR, 16% in BTWSN while it is 12% in EETCH. The reason behind this is that the proposed model uses a salp chaotic algorithm for CH. The performance of chaotic salp is better than other swarm algorithms used in baseline methods.

17.5.4 Performance Analysis in Terms of Residual Energy Per Number of Rounds

Figure 17.5 shows the result examination in terms of RE per number of rounds. The figure demonstrates that EETCH performs better than other schemes in terms of RE per number of the round. For example, at around 150 the RE is 0.8 in our model while is it 0.74 and 0.65 of BTWSN and IASR, respectively. Similarly, 250 the RE is 0.6 in EETCH, while it is 0.56 and 0.45 in the case of BTWSN and IASR, respectively. This is because the selections of cluster heads have been done based on fitness function, which uses node degree and RE of nodes. This enhances the overall lifespan of the network; hence, the average RE of the network increases.

17.5.5 Performance Analysis in Terms of Number of Alive Nodes Per Number of Rounds

Figure 17.6 demonstrates the results between alive nodes per rounds achieved from the simulation accompanied by the proposed EETCH and the state-of-art schemes. It is observed that as the number of rounds increases the number of alive nodes reduces. For example, for rounds 50 and 150, the number of sensor nodes alive are 75 and 36 approximately in EETCH while in the case of BTWSN and IASR for round 50 it is 69 and 58 approximately and for round 150 it is approximately 28 and 19, respectively. The reason behind this is that our proposed model uses the node degree and remaining energy in the fitness function that reduces the power depletion and increases the lifespan of the nodes.

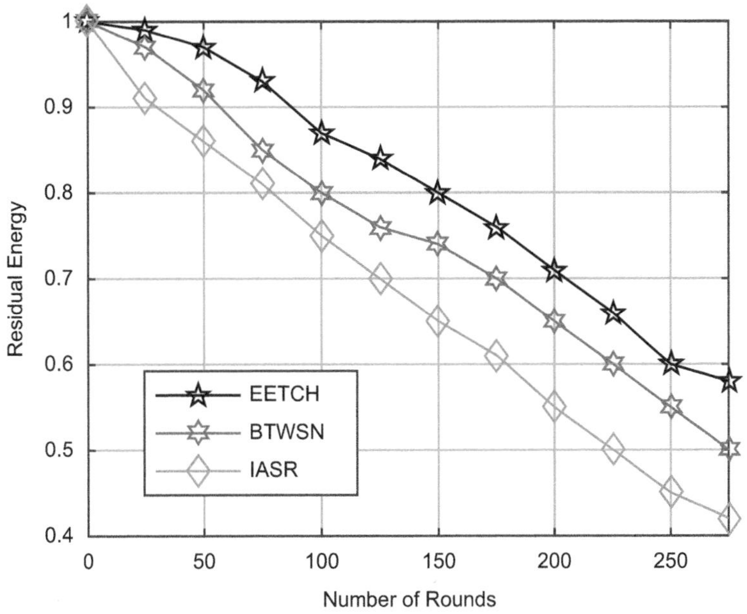

FIGURE 17.5 Performance analysis in terms of residual energy per number of rounds.

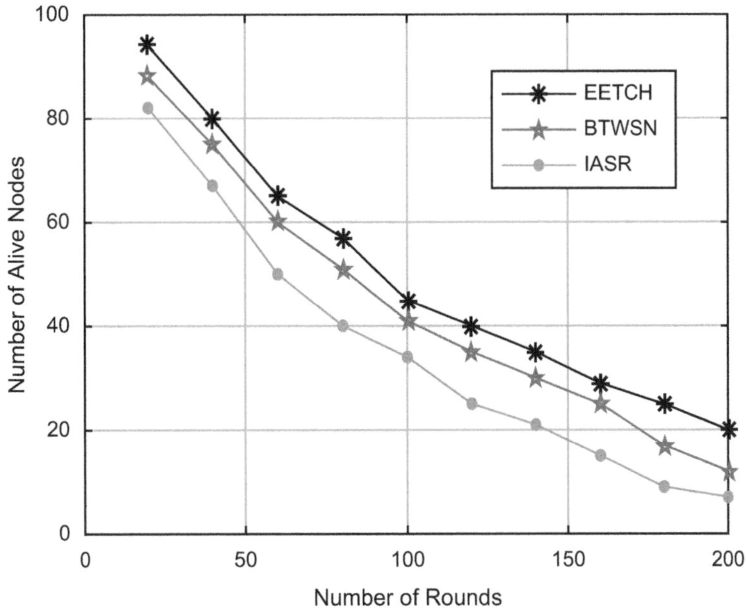

FIGURE 17.6 Performance analysis in terms of alive nodes per number of rounds.

17.6 CONCLUSION AND FUTURE PERSPECTIVE

In this paper, we suggest a chaotic salp algorithm-based energy-efficient trust-aware CH election protocol (EETCH) for sensor-enabled IoT. Our method uses an enhanced version of the salp swarm algorithm, which is the hybridization of chaos theory and salp swarm algorithm. EETCH uses a linear equation-based fitness function that consists of numerous parameters, such as direct trust, indirect trust, remaining energy, and degree of nodes. The proposed model not only secures the network but also minimizes the power consumption for data communication. Detection rate, packet loss, and remaining energy of the nodes are some of the matrices used for result analysis of EETCH. The chaotic salp bio swarm-based cluster head election scheme proved to be better in comparison to the baseline algorithms.

For future perspective, the proposed model can be practiced in real-time applications. Apart from the chaotic salp swarm optimization algorithm, other swarm-based state-of-the-art algorithms can be applied to the same problem of sensor-aided IoT.

ACKNOWLEDGMENT

This work was carried out in a secure and computing laboratory, SC&SS, JNU, New Delhi, India, and was sponsored by the project UPE-II, JNU, New Delhi, PID 115, 2014–2019.

REFERENCES

[1] L. Farhan, R. Kharel, O. Kaiwartya, et al., "Towards green computing for Internet of Things: Energy oriented path and message scheduling approach," *Sustainable Cities and Society*, vol. 38, pp. 195–204, Apr. 2018.

[2] R. Arshad, S. Zahoor, M.A. Shah, et al., "Green IoT: An investigation on energy saving practices for 2020 and beyond," *IEEE Access*, vol. 5, pp. 15667–15681, 2017.

[3] K. Kumar, S. Kumar, O. Kaiwartya, et al., "Cross-layer energy optimization for IoT environments: Technical advances and opportunities," *Energies*, vol. 10, no. 12, p. 2073, 2017.

[4] H. Jiang, F. Shen, S. Chen, et al., "A secure and scalable storage system for aggregate data in IoT," *Future Generation Computer Systems*, vol. 49, pp. 133–141, Aug. 2015.

[5] M. Azharuddin, P. Kuila, and P.K. Jana, "Energy efficient fault tolerant clustering and routing algorithms for wireless sensor networks," *Computers & Electrical Engineering*, vol. 41, pp. 177–190, 2015.

[6] A. M. Zungeru, L. M. Ang, and K. P. Seng, "Classical and swarm intelligence based routing protocols for wireless sensor networks: A survey and comparison," *Journal of Network and Computer Applications*, vol. 35, no. 5, pp. 1508–1536, 2012.

[7] Pu Gong, Thomas M. Chen, and Xu Quan, "ETARP: An energy efficient trust-aware routing protocol for wireless sensor networks," *Journal of Sensors*, vol. 2015, 2015.

[8] P. Visu, T.S. Praba, N. Sivakumar, et al., "Bio-inspired dual cluster heads optimized routing algorithm for wireless sensor networks," *Journal of Ambient Intelligence and Humanized Computing*, pp. 1–9, 2020.

[9] Rashmi Ranjan Sahoo, A. R. Sardar, M. Singh, et al., "A bio inspired and trust based approach for clustering in WSN," *Natural Computing*, vol. 15, no. 3, pp. 423–434, 2016.

[10] K. Saleem, N. Fisal, and J. Al-Muhtadi, "Empirical studies of bio-inspired self-organized secure autonomous routing protocol," *IEEE Sensors Journal*, vol. 14, no, 7, pp. 2232–2239, 2014.

[11] Xiaoyong Li, Feng Zhou, and Junping Du, "LDTS: A lightweight and dependable trust system for clustered wireless sensor networks," *IEEE Transactions On Information Forensics and Security*, vol. 8, no. 6, pp. 924–935, 2013.

[12] Neeraj Kumar, and Jongsung Kim. "ELACCA: Efficient learning automata based cell clustering algorithm for wireless sensor networks," *Wireless Personal Communications*, vol. 73, no. 4, pp. 1495–1512, 2013.

[13] H. Bagci, and A. Yazici, "An energy aware fuzzy approach to unequal clustering in wireless sensor networks," *Applied Soft Computing*, vol. 13, no. 4, pp. 1741–1749, 2013.

[14] Surinder Singh, Vinod Kumar, and Nagendra Prasad Pathak, "Sensors augmentation influence over trust and reputation models realization for dense wireless sensor networks," *IEEE Sensors Journal*, vol. 15, no. 11, pp. 6248–6254, 2015.
[15] X. Feng, X. Xu, X. Zhou et al., "A trust evaluation algorithm for wireless sensor networks based on node behaviors and d-s evidence theory," *Sensors*, vol. 11, pp. 1345–1360, 2011.
[16] J. Jiang, G. Han, F. Wang et al., "An efficient distributed trust model for wireless sensor networks," *IEEE Transactions on Parallel and Distributed Systems*, vol. 26, no. 5, pp. 1228–1237, May 2015.
[17] Tian Wang, Hao Luo, Weijia Jia, et al. "MTES: An intelligent trust evaluation scheme in sensor-cloud enabled industrial Internet of Things," *IEEE Transactions on Industrial Informatics*, 2019.
[18] Zhong Luo, Runze Wan, and Xiaoping Si, "An improved ACO-based security routing protocol for wireless sensor networks," *2013 International Conference on Computer Sciences and Applications*. IEEE, 2013.
[19] Gehad Ismail Sayed, Ghada Khoriba, and Mohamed H. Haggag, "A novel chaotic salp swarm algorithm for global optimization and feature selection," *Applied Intelligence*, vol. 48, no. 10, 3462–3481, 2018.

18 Smart Card Based Privacy-Preserving Lightweight Authentication Protocol

SIGNAL for E-Payment Systems

N. Sasikaladevi, K. Geetha, and S. Aarthi
CSED, SASTRA Deemed University, Thanjavur, India

C. Mala
CSED, National Institute of Technology, Trichy, India

CONTENTS

18.1 INTRODUCTION

As the world moves towards technological development, the use of electronic payment systems and payment processing devices has also been increasing. As the usage of online shopping increases, payment systems also provide a secure means of transactions and allow reduced cash transactions. Credit and debit cards are the most significant forms of electronic remittance methods. There are some surrogate payment methods such as net banking, electronic wallet, smart card and bitcoin wallet. According to the 2018 statistics provided by Avoine et al. in [9], e-payment services have grown rapidly from the year 2016 to 2018 by more than 50%. But security is an indispensable candidate for any transactions that take place over a public network. The following are some of the essential

DOI: 10.1201/9781003155577-22

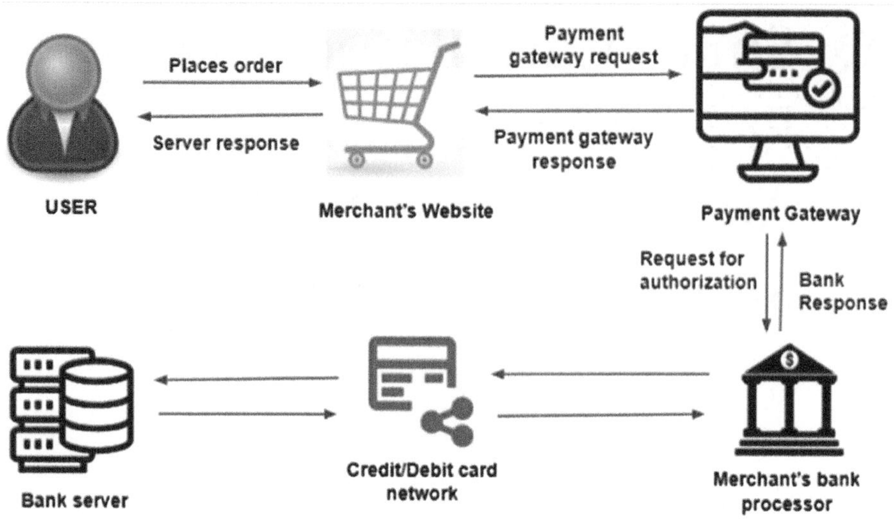

FIGURE 18.1 Architecture of payment system.

requirements of any e-payment transactions: confidentiality, integrity, availability, authenticity, non-reputability and encryption. To enhance security, encryption can be done in a very efficient and realistic way to preserve the information being communicated over the public network, that is, sender encrypts the information with a secret code, so that only the corresponding receiver can decrypt it using the same code. Likewise, to make any purchase on the internet, online users need to share some secret information through public links. If these details are transferred as a plain text, then there is a chance of eavesdropping. This is because any person listening to the network can gain access to sensitive data such as card number and type and also the complete details of cardholders. There are also some other risks like denial of service attack, fabrication attack, modification attack and spoofing attack. The customer may lose faith if the system compromises on his privacy issues. To improve the security of e-payment systems and to resist these types of attacks, a secured authentication protocol for payment systems should be designed.

Figure 18.1 illustrates the architecture of the payment system. In this diagram, it clearly depicts the request-response model. First, the user/client needs to send the request to the bank server by requesting all the intermediate nodes. After getting the appropriate response from all intermediates and a particular bank server, the payment services will enable or abort the connection.

18.2 RELATED WORKS

Lightweight authentication scheme is used in many applications, because simple symmetric cryptography primitives are used, which require fewer computations but produce improved results than others. In RFID (radio frequency identification) systems, RFID tags are used for automatic identification. But it gives space for some security issues like easy access of RFID tags by an adversary, which leads to privacy and forgery problems. In addition, the computational capacity of RFID tags is also limited. In order to overcome such problems, Gope and Hwang [1] proposed a new pragmatic lightweight mutual authentication strategy for RFID systems. This scheme preserves security features such as untraceability, forward security and anonymity in RFID tags. To handle large databases present inside the environment of the Internet of Things (IoT), the key technology to resolve the problem is cloud computing. Legitimate user identification and authentication in wireless sensor network (WSN) is a high-level security issue. Since the sensor node has limited storage and computing capabilities, designing a lightweight authentication protocol is very difficult. Gope et al. [3] depicted a lightweight authentication protocol for a resource-constrained environment that provides

TABLE 18.1
Comparative Study of Various Authentication Protocols

Literature	Types of Authentication	Methods	Potential Requirements
Gope and Hwang [1]	Legitimate user authentication and identification	Xor operation, 1-way hash function, symmetric key encryption and decryption	Untraceability, forward security and anonymity
Luo et al. [4]	Ultra-lightweight authentication	Xor operation, rotation and conversion	Anonymity and untraceability with low computation cost
Li et al. [5], Godar. G et al. [10]	Smart card-based authentication	Elliptic curve Diffie Hellman key exchange	Perfect forward and backward security
Kumari et al. [6]	Biometric-based authentication	Bio hashing and ECC	Anonymity, perfect forward and backward secrecy
Jiang et al. [7], Cheng et al. [14]	Multifactor authentication	Rabin cryptosystem, timestamp and fuzzy verifier	Anonymity, untraceability and smart card revocation
Xuan Hung et al. [11]	Lightweight mutual authentication	Elliptic curve cryptography	Anonymity, untraceability, perfect security
Xudong et al. [15]	Blockchain-based authentication	Identity-based cryptosystem	Perfect forward secrecy, anonymity and untraceability

the following properties such as user anonymity, perfect forward secrecy, backward secrecy and untraceability. Ruhul et al. [2] suggested a new method for improving lightweight user authentication and key agreement scheme for WSN, which implements session key agreement and mutual authentication property (Table 18.1).

Due to the insecurity of data in RFID systems, an ultra-lightweight authentication protocol called Succinct and Lightweight Authentication Protocol (SLAP) has been developed by Luo et al. in [4]. This protocol only consists of operations like componentwise modulo 2 addition operation, clockwise rotation, conversion where these are easily adaptable in tags. Li et al. [5] constructed an authentication scheme based on smart cards. Kumari et al. [6] presented a biometric-based authentication system. Jiang et al. [7] designed a multi-factor authentication protocol specially based on three factors. Roman. R. et al. [8] analyses the various authentication mechanisms such as public-key cryptography, pre-shared key and KMS mathematical model for authentication. Here, the author perfectly illustrates the results of the KMS mathematical model with PKC and pre-shared keys. Avione. G. et al. [9] examined the various ultra-lightweight authentication protocols and recorded the pitfalls that arose during the implementation of these protocols in real-time applications. Wang et al. [12] describe the security imperfections that arose in the two-factor authentication mechanism. Le et al. mathematically differentiate the performance of elliptic curve and discrete log problem and analyses computation costs for each mechanism. Although the security architecture provided by blockchain [15] is highly effective, we have to authenticate the user with high confidential data, leading to a high communication cost and computation cost. In addition, the authentication process is very slow and leads to a low throughput and high latency.

So we need some other effective authentication mechanism for e-payment services with low computation and communication cost, and in addition it must satisfy user anonymity, untraceability and perfect full backward and forward secrecy properties with resistance to attacks described in Section 18.4.

18.3 PROPOSED SCHEME

Our proposed authentication scheme SIGNAL that can be applied for electronic payment system consists of three phases, namely, user registration phase, payment-gateway registration phase and mutual authentication (two-way key authentication) and fresh session key distribution phase.

18.3.1 User Registration Phase

To make use of the banking services, the user needs to register his details such as his user id, password and biometrics with the bank server. The bank server encrypts the user credentials and stores it in the cash plus card and then sends it back to the end users who registered.

Figure 18.2 illustrates the registration of the users (U_i) is based on their identity, password credentials and biometrics for e-payment services with the bank server (BS). First, the user has to send their identity and M1 value to the bank server as a request. M1 value is computed using component-wise modulo 2 addition and cryptographic hash function. Then, the bank server has to create a one-way hash value (TC_i) based on the identity of the user, bank server and M1 value and send again to the user as a response.

18.3.2 Payment-Gateway Registration Phase

Then the payment gateway should be registered with the bank to make the payment securely via the payment gateway. In this phase, initially the payment gateway registers its id with the bank server. The bank server encrypts it and keeps it secret between bank server and payment gateway.

Figure 18.3 describes the payment-gateway registration phase in which the gateway/intermediate node has to be registered for payment services between user and bank server (BS). Here, after requesting the gateway, it has to generate the cryptographic hash value to the user as a response and the value must be stored in the user's memory secretly.

18.3.3 Mutual Authentication and Fresh Session Key Distribution Phase

Inside this mechanism, the user/customer encrypts his credentials and sends them to the payment gateway for signing into the bank server. Then, payment gateway encrypts its credentials and sends

User(U_i)		***Bank Server***(BS)
Select ID_i, PW_i, BIO_i		
$Gen(BIO_i) = (F_i, FP_i)$		
$M1 = FP_i \oplus H(ID_i \| \| PW_i \| \| F_i)$		
	$\{ID_i, M1\}$ → *Via a secure channel*	
		$TC_i = h(ID_i \| \| M1 \| \| S)$
		Store $\{TC_i, h(.)\}$ *into Smart Card* SM_i
	$SM_i = \{TC_i, h(.)\}$ ← *Via a secure channel*	
$O_i = TC_i \oplus M1$		
$RPB_i = M1 \oplus h(TC_i \| \| PW_i \| \| F_i)$		
Embeds $FP_i, O_i, RPB_i, H(.)$ *and* $Gen(.)$		
into smartcard i.e., $\{RPB_i, h(.), H(.)\}$		

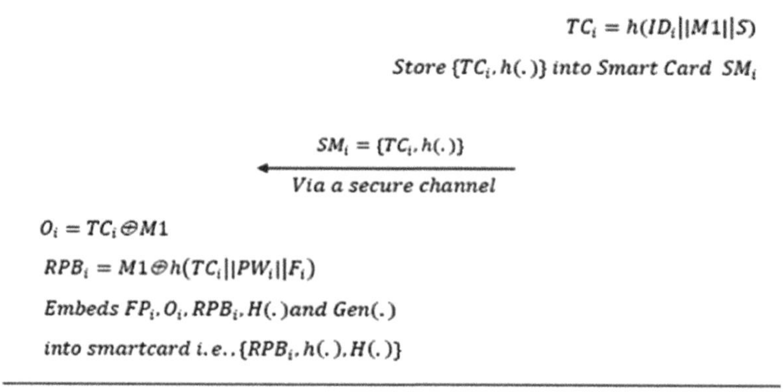

FIGURE 18.2 User registration phase.

Payment Gateway(PG)	Bank Server(BS)
Select ID_j	

$$\{ID_j\}$$
$$\xrightarrow{\hspace{3cm}}$$
via a secure channel

$$Z_j = h(ID_j\|S)$$

$$\{Z_j\}$$
$$\xleftarrow{\hspace{3cm}}$$
via a secure channel

Keep Z_j as secret

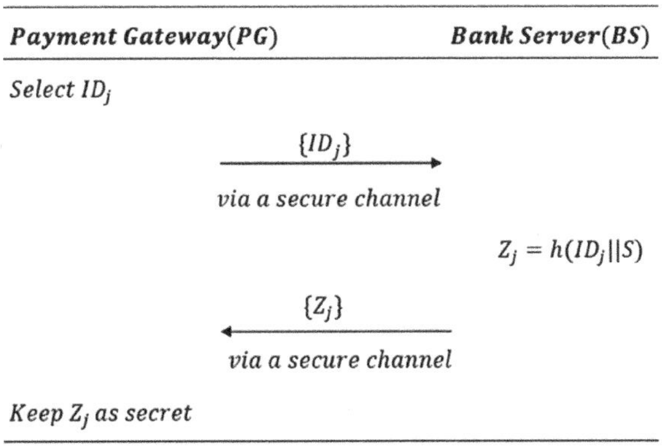

FIGURE 18.3 Payment-gateway registration phase.

User(U_i)	Payment gateway(PG)

U: Input ID_i', PW_i', BIO_i'

computes $F_i' = Rep(BIO_i', FP_i)$

$M1' = TC_i \oplus O_i$

$RPB_i' = M1' \oplus H(TC_i\|PW_i'\|F_i')$

Check if $RPB_i' = RPB_i$

Generate $Ee \in Z_n$

$Eia = Ee.P$

$DID_i = ID_i \oplus h(E_{ia})$

$Qq = h(ID_i\|E_{ia}\|O_i)$

$$Msg1 = \{DID_i, E_{ia}, Qq, M1\}$$
$$\xrightarrow{\hspace{4cm}}$$
(Public channel)

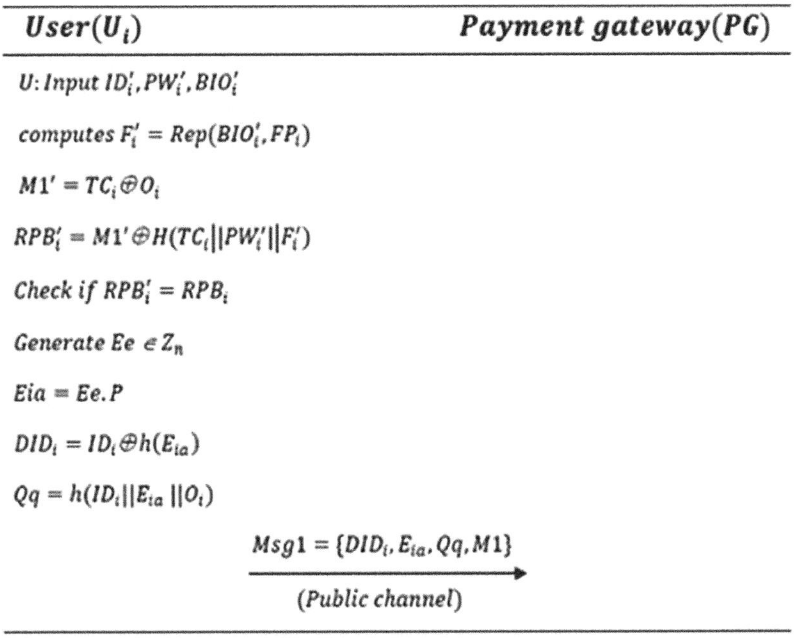

FIGURE 18.4 Login phase.

both user credentials and its credentials to the bank server. Finally, the bank server verifies both the credentials and then forwards the message for authentication to the payment gateway (intermediate) and user.

Figure 18.4 illustrates the user logging process. In which the credentials of the user has to be encrypted using component-wise modulo 2 addition and cryptographic hash function. These details are sent to the bank server (BS) via payment gateway.

Figure 18.5 demonstrates the mutual authentication phase; user (U_i) must be authenticated to the bank server (BS), which in turn must be authenticated to user (U_i). This will be ensured by the above diagram with simple XoR and cryptographic hash functions.

User(U_i)	Payment gateway(PG)	Bank server(BS)

Generate $Ff \in Z_n$
$F_{ja} = Ff.P$
$DID_j = ID_j \oplus h(F_{ja})$
$Xx = h(DID_i||E_{ia}||Qq||F_{ja}||ID_j||Z_j)$

$$\xrightarrow{\quad Msg2 = \{DID_i, E_{ia}, Qq, DID_j, F_{ja}, Xx\} \quad}$$
(Public channel)

$ID_j = DID_j \oplus h(F_{ja})$
$Z_j = h(ID_j||S)$
Check $X_x = h(DID_i||E_{ia}||Qq||F_{ja}||ID_j||Z_j)$
$ID_j = DID_i \oplus h(E_{ia})$
$TC_i = h(ID_i||M1||S)$
$O_i = TC_i \oplus M1$
Check $Qq = h(ID_i||E_{ia}||O_i)$
$AID_i = ID_i \oplus h(F_{ja})$
$BID_j = ID_j \oplus h(E_{ia})$
$Yy = h\left(AID_i||ID_i||ID_j||F_{ja}||Z_i\right)$
$Ww = h(BID_j||ID_i||ID_j||E_{ia}||O_i)$

$$\xleftarrow{\quad Msg3 = \{AID_i, Yy, BID_j, Ww\} \quad}$$
(Public channel)

$ID_i = AID_i \oplus h(F_{ja})$ and Check ID_i?
Check $Yy = h\left(AID_i||ID_i||ID_j||F_{ja}||Z_j\right)$
$KA_{ji} = h\left(ID_i||ID_j||Ff.E_{ia}\right)$
$Tt = h(BID_j||Ww||F_{ja}||ID_i||ID_j||KA_{ji})$

$$\xleftarrow{\quad Msg4 = \{BID_j, Ww, F_{ja}, Tt\} \quad}$$
(Public channel)

$ID_j = BID_j \oplus h(E_{ia})$
Check $= h(BID_j||ID_i||ID_j||E_{ia}||O_i)$
$KA_{ij} = h\left(ID_i||ID_j||Ee.F_{ja}\right)$
Check $Tt = h(BID_j||Ww||F_{ja}||ID_i||ID_j||KA_{ij})$
$Zz = h(BID_j||Ww||F_{ja}||Tt||ID_i||ID_j||KA_{ij})$

$$\xrightarrow{\quad Msg5 = \{Zz\} \quad}$$
(public channel)
Check $Zz = hh(BID_j||Ww||F_{ja}||Tt||ID_i||ID_j||KA_{ij})$

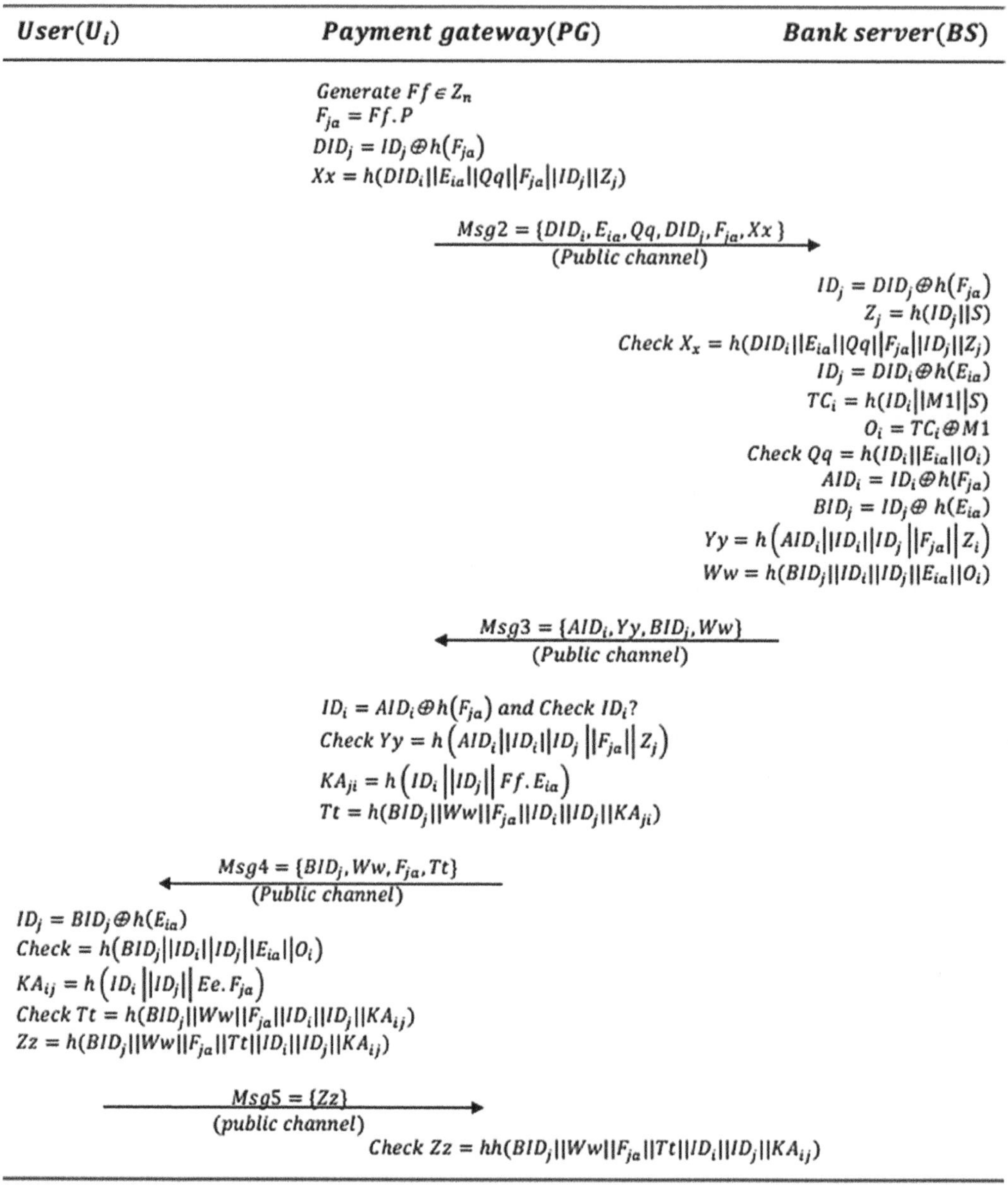

FIGURE 18.5 Mutual authentication and fresh session key distribution.

18.4 INFORMAL SECURITY ANALYSIS

18.4.1 ANONYMITY

U_i's identity is included in $DID_i = ID_ih(E_{ia})$ and $AID_i = ID_ih(F_{ja})$, where $E_{ia} = Ee. P$, $F_{ja} = F_f. P$ in our proposed method. If an adversary wants to access the identity of user, he needs to compute E_{ia} from (Ee, P) and F_{ja} from (F_f, P), which means he needs to compute ECDH problem, else it is impossible to get U_i's identity. Likewise, PG's identity is included in $DID_j = ID_jh(F_{ja})$ and $BID_j = ID_jh(E_{ia})$, where $E_{ia} = Ee. P$, $F_{ja} = F_f. P$ in our scheme. If adversary wants payment gateway's real identity, he needs to compute F_{ja} from (Ff, P) and E_{ia} from (Ee, P), which results in the computation of the ECDH problem, else it is impractical to attain PG's identity.

18.4.2 Mutual Authentication

Bank server (*BS*) can authenticate U_i and *PG* by verifying (*Qq*, *Xx*), respectively. If both of them are correct then bank server (*BS*) generates the authentication code (*Yy*, *Ww*) respectively and transfers it to the U_i and *PG* for future verification. With the help of bank server (*BS*)*PG* could authenticate the *BS* and U_i by checking the validity of *Yy*. And U_i will be able to authenticate *BS* and *PG* by checking the validity of *Ww*.

18.4.3 Full Forward Secrecy

In authentication phase, both U_i and *PG* should agree with shared session key $KA_{ij} = h(ID_i||ID_j||Ee.F_{ja}) = h(ID_i||ID_j||Ee.\ Ff.\ P) = h(ID_i||ID_j||Ff.\ E_{ia}) = KA_{ji}$. Even if adversary intends to compute session key, he requires real identities of U_i and *PG*. He also has to compute *Ee*, *Ff*, *P* from $E_{ia} = Ee.\ P$ and $F_{ja} = Ff.\ P$. As we understood earlier that he needs to solve the ECDH problem to get those parameters. Otherwise, he will not be able to compute a session key properly even though he knows other persistent security parameters.

18.4.4 Resistance to Privilege Escalation Attack

In the registration phase of the user, U_i presents *M*1 to *BS* instead of PW_i. Then, the privileged user of *BS* cannot compute PW_i from $M1 = FP_iH(ID_i||PW_i||F_i)$ because of the uniqueness of F_i and secure one-way bio-hashing. By the way, our scheme resists privileged user attack.

18.4.5 Resistance to Masquerade Attack

During mutual authentication, user initially generates a legal request $Msg1 = \{DID_i, E_{ia}, Qq, M1\}$. In order to masquerade user, an adversary needs to compute $Qq = h(ID_i||E_{ia}||O_i)$. We have already shown that an adversary cannot get correct *Oi* and *Qq* even if the adversary has any two of three factors such as smart card, password or biometric information.

18.4.6 Resistance to Message Replay Attack

Let us consider that an adversary/intruder intercepts the message $Msg1 = \{DID_i, E_{ia}, Qq, M1\}$ in an attempt to impersonate U_i and reply back to *PG*. *PG* will be aware of this replay attack while verifying $Zz = h(BID_j||Ww||F_{ja}||Tt||ID_i||ID_j|KA_{ij})$. So given that adversary has no idea about the nonce $\{Ee, Ff\}$, the adversary will not be able to generate the valid session key $KA_{ij} = h(ID_i||ID_j||EeFfP)$.

18.4.7 Resistance to Payment-Gateway Spoofing Attack

To impersonate *PG*, an adversary needs $Z_j = h(ID_j||S)$ to generate verification challenge $Xx = h(DID_i||E_{ia}||Qq||F_{ja}||ID_j||Z_j)$. Being that $h(\cdot)$ is a one-way hash function which provides semantic security and *BS* holds the value of S with secrecy, it is difficult to spoof payment gateway.

18.4.8 Resistance Against DOS Attack

In DoS attack, the attacker may prevent the secure communication in between user and payment gateway, and payment gateway and bank server. Our proposed protocol resists against DoS attack, since we are using an EAP-IKEv2 (which is Extensible Authentication Protocol – Internet Key Exchange Version 2), which provides mutual authentication and establishes session keys.

```
% OFMC
% Version of 2006/02/13
SUMMARY
  SAFE
DETAILS
  BOUNDED_NUMBER_OF_SESSIONS
PROTOCOL
  /home/span/span/testsuite/results/fully.if
GOAL
  as_specified
BACKEND
  OFMC
COMMENTS
STATISTICS
  parseTime: 0.00s
```

FIGURE 18.6 Output verification using AVISPA.

18.4.9 Simulation Results using AVISPA

Based upon the simulation results of the proposed scheme executed in AVISPA are presented. AVISPA is one of the powerful security verification tools used to verify and confirm the security of an authentication protocol.

In Figure 18.6, the output is verified using the fly mode checker of AVISPA. Here, the protocol produces a safe state for key establishment and authentication for smart card-based e-payment systems.

18.5 CONCLUSION

Our proposed SIGNAL protocol is a three-factor lightweight authentication scheme, designed using ECC, which gives low computation and communication costs. Furthermore, a simulation result of AVISPA makes sure that the proposed multi-factor authentication scheme holds out against both passive and active attacks. Moreover, informal security analyses were performed to prove that our scheme endures various malicious attacks like masquerade attack, privilege escalation attack and interception attack. It also ensures user anonymity, user authenticity and complete secrecy. From now on, we will narrow down the computational complexities of our protocol without negotiating the security properties.

ACKNOWLEDGEMENTS

This part of this research work is supported by the Department of Science and Technology (DST), Science and Engineering Board (SERB), Government of India under the TARE grant (TAR/2020/000259)

REFERENCES

[1] Gope, P. and Hwang, T., 2015. A realistic lightweight authentication protocol preserving strong anonymity for securing RFID systems. *Computers & Security*, *55*, pp. 271–280.

[2] Amin, R. and Biswas, G.P., 2016. A secure lightweight scheme for user authentication and key agreement in multi-gateway based wireless sensor networks. *Ad Hoc Networks*, *36*, pp. 58–80.

[3] Gope, P. and Hwang, T., 2016. A realistic lightweight anonymous authentication protocol for securing real-time application data access in wireless sensor networks. *IEEE Transactions on Industrial Electronics*, *63*(11), pp. 7124–7132.

[4] Luo, H., Wen, G., Su, J. and Huang, Z., 2018. SLAP: Succinct and lightweight authentication protocol for low-cost RFID system. *Wireless Networks*, *24*(1), pp. 69–78.

[5] Li, H., Li, F., Song, C. and Yan, Y., 2015. Towards smart card based mutual authentication schemes in cloud computing. *KSII Transactions on Internet and Information Systems (TIIS)*, *9*(7), pp. 2719–2735.

[6] Kumari, S., Li, X., Wu, F., Das, A.K., Choo, K.K.R. and Shen, J., 2017. Design of a provably secure biometrics-based multi-cloud-server authentication scheme. *Future Generation Computer Systems*, *68*, pp. 320–330.

[7] Jiang, Q., Zeadally, S., Ma, J. and He, D., 2017. Lightweight three-factor authentication and key agreement protocol for internet-integrated wireless sensor networks. *IEEE Access*, *5*, pp. 3376–3392.

[8] R. Roman, Alcaraz, C., Lopez, J. and Sklavos, N., 2011. Key management systems for sensor networks in the context of the Internet of Things. *Computers & Electrical Engineering*, *37*(2), pp. 147–159, Mar.

[9] Avoine, G., Carpent, X. and Hernandez-Castro, J., 2015. Pitfalls in ultra lightweight authentication protocol designs. *IEEE Transactions on Mobile Computing*, *15*(9), pp. 2317–2332.

[10] Godor, G. and Imre, S., 2011. Elliptic curve cryptography based authentication protocol for low-cost RFID tags. In *RFID-Technologies and Applications (RFID_TA), 2011 IEEE International Conference on, vol. 14, IEEE, 2011.*

[11] Le, X.H., Khalid, M. and Sankar, R., 2011. An efficient mutual authentication and access control scheme for wireless sensor networks in healthcare. *Journal of Networks*, *6*(3), pp. 355–364.

[12] Ma, C.-G., Wang, D. and Zhao, S.-D., 2012. Security flaws in two improved remote user authentication schemes using smart cards. *International Journal of Communication Systems*, *27*(10), pp. 2215–2227.

[13] Li, Z., Higgins, J. and Clement, M., 2001. Performance of finite field arithmetic in an elliptic curve cryptosystem. In *The 9th IEEE International Symposium on Modeling, Analysis, and Simulation of Computer and Telecommunications Systems*, pp. 249–256, 2001.

[14] Cheng, Z.-Y., Liu, Y., Chang, C.-C. and Chang, S.-C. 2012. A smart card based authentication scheme for remote user login and verification. *International Journal of Innovative Computing, Information and Control*, *8*(8), pp. 5499–5511.

[15] Jia, Xudong, Hu, Ning, Yin, Shi, Zhao, Yan, Zhang, Chi and Cheng, Xinda. 2020. A2 chain: A2 blockchain-based decentralized authentication scheme for 5G-enabled IoT in mobile information systems. https://doi.org/10.1155/2020/8889192

Index

Q

R

S

T

V

W

Y